Best Wishes,

Steve Roman

# DOSAGE

## PEDIGREE & PERFORMANCE

by Steven A. Roman, Ph.D.

ISBN 0-929346-73-4

**Library of Congress Cataloging-in-Publication Data**

Roman, Steven A., 1943-
    Dosage pedigree and performance / by Steven A. Roman.
        p. cm.
    ISBN 0-929346-73-4
    1. Thoroughbred horse--Pedigrees. 2. Race horses--Breeding--Selection indexes--Statistical methods. I. Title.

    SF293.T5 R66 2002
    636.1'3222--dc21

                                                                2002030499


Cover photo © Katey Barrett, 2002; used with permission.




Published by

**The Russell Meerdink Company, Ltd.**
1555 South Park Ave.
Neenah, WI 54956
(920) 725-0955 Worldwide • (800) 635-6499 U.S. & Canada
www.horseinfo.com

Printed in the United States of America

# TABLE OF CONTENTS

# Foreword

*"We look for the athlete, never mind the bloodlines."*
Trainer D. Wayne Lukas,
Los Angeles Times, 1984

In 1982, after having watched the Kentucky Derby for a dozen years, and pressed by a lady accomplice to render a judgment on that season's classic, finally I wagered.

Aware of the unreliability of the conventional methods of handicapping when doping the Derby—speed figures, class evaluation, pace analysis, form cycles—which, after all, were tethered to performances at middle distances only, and in fact had persistently fallen flat on their Derby predictions, I had not even bothered to scour the past performances of the runners. I had been provoked, however, by a 1981 *Bloodlines* column of *Daily Racing Form*, written by pedigree authority Leon Rasmussen, in which Thoroughbred handicappers and students of pedigree alike had been introduced to the charms of Steven A. Roman's Dosage Index and to Roman's "Dual-Qualifier" methodology for handicapping the Derby and the Belmont Stakes.

As Rasmussen told, Roman's research had demonstrated rather unequivocally that Derby prospects should possess a certain desirable blend of speed and stamina in the recent four-generation pedigree, and that indeed since 1940 no Derby winner had possessed such a blend of speed and stamina greater than Roman's statistical guideline figure, his Dosage Index (DI), of 4.00. As a DI of 1.00 would indicate a perfectly balanced blend of speed and stamina, a DI greater than 4.00 would mean a Derby prospect had inherited too much speed in relation to endurance, and would be highly unlikely to win America's race.

Roman's Dual-Qualifiers combined an acceptable DI with early maturity, defined as a ranking within 10 pounds of the leader on the industry's Experimental Free Handicap, a scale of weights dedicated solely to two-year-old performance.

"It's hardly a strong opinion," I advised my 1982 accomplice, "but I've chanced upon an innovative and sensible approach for evaluating the Derby colts that combines pedigree and performance. It's been referred to as 'Dual-Qualifiers' and only three horses in the bulky field qualify: Gato Del Sol, Laser Light, and Cassaleria. All three should be longshots. One is a colt of southern California, Gato Del Sol. Suppose we back him." I bet $40.00.

Gato Del Sol, a nondescript undistinguished closer at middle distances, won the 1982 Derby from far back, and paid $44.40. Laser Light finished second, and paid $17.00 to place. The life and times of numerous handicappers and horsemen at the Kentucky Derby have not been the same ever since. Roman's Dual-Qualifiers, few in number at the time, dominated the classic during the 1980's, even as they had in the 1970's, continued to prosper during the 1990's, and by the new millennium few handicappers or other interested observers would deny that pedigree plus performance gets the roses. Trainer D. Wayne Lukas had changed his mind as early as 1986.

Much else has changed as a result of Roman's research, including the matings of Thoroughbreds on farms, and the purchases of yearlings at sales, such that a book by the originator of the Dosage Index that explains it all in historical and contemporary detail has been long and seriously overdue. Beyond the relatively narrow but important applications of Dosage to the three-year-old classics, it's been Roman's broader treatment of pedigree evaluation that has marked him as the nation's most influential authority on the relations between the Thoroughbred's inherited aptitudes and its racetrack performances.

That position of authority does not permit the assertions of conclusions unsupported by facts. Happily, the nation's leading researcher on pedigree evaluation for years directed exploratory research on chemical products and processes for Shell Chemical, in Houston, Texas. Roman has been the author of more than 60 patents and publications in chemistry. An author dedicated to the requirements of scientific inquiry, Roman has steadfastly reminded followers and critics alike that his research is strictly empirical. That is, Roman's findings and conclusions have been hinged directly to the Thoroughbred's performances on the racetrack.

In that respect, as opposed to the largely descriptive and normative nature of most statistical studies of pedigree evaluation, Roman has fretted that this text may be perceived as excessively "technical." The scientist need not worry, as Roman qualifies as well as a highly literate and graceful writer. His text is a pleasure to read. Roman should be recognized here as especially adept with multiple regression techniques, which can delineate a line of "best fit" between related variables, such as Dosage and distance. Stallion owners, breeders, buyers, and even handicappers should be provoked by several of the statistical charts, as when Roman shows that studies of open stakes winners from 1983 to 2001 reveal the recommended Dosage Indices for sprinters at six furlongs will be 4.00 to 4.75, but for middle distance runners from eight furlongs to nine furlongs the recommended Dosage will be 2.97 to 3.74, and for the classic prospects from 10 furlongs to 12 furlongs the recommended Dosage will be 2.00 to 2.60.

Whether mating, buying, or betting, that's nice to know.

Horsemen and breeders dare not miss this book, but an audience having a greater incentive to pay attention than many of them might appreciate is the beleaguered array of handicappers toiling for profits at the nation's racetracks and betting parlors. Handicappers generally have known for a couple of decades that horses bred for grass should go well on grass at the first and second attempts, but other applications of pedigree to performance have remained murky and elusive. Roman presents copious performance data on two-year-olds, distance changes, and stakes races that handicappers can scarcely afford to ignore.

Perhaps Roman's signature, most meaningful contribution to the fields of Thoroughbred racing and breeding will be as arbiter and caretaker of the *chef-de-race* roster, that selective membership of prestigious sires that have been deemed "prepotent" and that contribute through the variations in aptitudes they pass to their progeny to the improvement of the breed. No role is more important and no task is more challenging. The great myth is that the sport's most dominant sires should transmit to progeny the attributes they have exhibited as runners on the track.

Roman's extensive, continuous, meticulous research on these matters supplies the evidence that not only documents the unreliability of numerous high-class runners as sires that can make a difference, but also assures the level of quality control over the roster of *chefs* the evaluative objectives demand. The author as scientist and the scientist as author is probably at his best when debating the proper and improper designations of popular sires as *chefs*.

As his book demonstrates in a strict but delightful way, on matters of pedigree evaluation great and small, Roman is not likely to be misled, and neither therefore is the Thoroughbred sport and industry.

James Quinn
Los Angeles, CA
August 2002

# Introduction

Contemporary Dosage methodology was introduced to Thoroughbred racing and breeding in Leon Rasmussen's "Bloodlines" column in *Daily Racing Form* during the spring of 1981. It is a continuation and refinement of research initiated by Lt. Col. J.J. Vuillier in France a century ago and modified by the Italian Dr. Franco Varola in the 1960s. Unlike traditional pedigree analysis, Dosage attempts to identify key ancestors in a Thoroughbred pedigree and ascribe qualities to those ancestors that together describe the horse's character or type. Despite fundamental philosophical differences among the various approaches to Dosage, they all agree on one thing — that the development of the Thoroughbred can be described through the influence of very few ancestors in any era.

Unlike the earlier forms of Dosage, the current technique involves extensive use of statistical analysis to test its premises. As a result, the reader will see numerous tables of data and charts within the text. Many of the charts display statistically generated trend lines that present relationships in a visual form for easier comprehension, the premise being that "a picture is worth a thousand words." Although somewhat technical, the subject matter is not academic. The concepts are accessible to everyone with an interest in how pedigree-performance relationships express themselves in the real world. On the other hand, the information is not merely anecdotal. This is not light storytelling. To fully understand the essence and utility of Dosage, readers will have to absorb the information presented and then draw conclusions for themselves. In addition, the author hopes that much of the data found in the tables and appendixes, while providing evidence in support of the ideas and concepts presented, will be used as basic reference material for owners, breeders, handicappers and general racing fans.

Although the author has written and lectured widely about contemporary Dosage for over 20 years, this is the first comprehensive and complete text on the subject by its creator.

*Steve Roman*
*Houston, TX*
*June 24, 2002*

To my familly - Julie, Abi, Rachael, Michelle and Zorro -
and to the memory of my late mentor, the brilliant Abram S. Hewitt.

# CHAPTER I

# Dosage and Speed

Dosage is a non-traditional method of Thoroughbred pedigree analysis and, as a result, a focus of controversy. Originated as a breeding theory, in its latest form it may be described more accurately as a pedigree classification technique. Dosage largely ignores the typical historical interpretation of pedigrees in which one emphasizes the accomplishments or achievements of individuals from the horse's past. These accomplishments quite often highlight major wins at the track or superior production in the breeding shed.

Rather, Dosage characterizes pedigrees solely through the evaluation and cataloguing of explicit qualities of prepotent or predictable speed and stamina inherited from selected key ancestors. The unique interplay of speed and stamina results in what we call aptitudinal type, those attributes that in combination most likely define the natural talents and abilities of the individual. In reality, speed and stamina are variations of the same phenomenon, much like opposite sides of the same coin. In the racing world, the better horses may be thought of as analogous to higher valued coins, blessed not only with superior speed, but with the ability to sustain it for a longer time. Speed is the defining trait, and stamina is the ability to carry that speed over a given distance. For any individual horse, speed and stamina are inversely related; one is always sacrificed in favor of the other. Whether cheap or high-class, all horses are limited in type by their inherited speed/stamina balance.

Evidence that speed and stamina are part of the same continuum may be found from the data presented below showing North American record times on dirt through the year 2000 in both tabular (Table 1) and graphical (Chart 1) form. The graph displays the correlation between distance in furlongs and average speed of the record holder in feet per second.

## TABLE 1. NORTH AMERICAN RECORD TIMES THROUGH 2000

| Distance | Horse | Track | Year | Time | Avg. Feet/Sec | Avg. Sec/Furlong |
|----------|-------|-------|------|------|---------------|------------------|
| 5.00f | Chinook Pass | Longacres | 1982 | :55 1/5 | 59.78 | 11.04 |
| 6.00f | G Malleah | Turf Paradise | 1995 | 1:06 3/5 | 59.46 | 11.10 |
| 7.00f | Rich Cream | Hollywood Park | 1980 | | | |
| | Time to Explode | Hollywood Park | 1982 | 1:19 2/5 | 58.19 | 11.34 |
| 8.00f | Dr. Fager | Arlington Park | 1968 | 1:32 1/5 | 57.27 | 11.52 |
| 8.50f | Hoedown's Day | Bay Meadows | 1983 | 1:38 2/5 | 57.13 | 11.58 |
| 9.00f | Simply Majestic | Golden Gate Fields | 1988 | 1:45 | 56.57 | 11.67 |
| 10.00f | Spectacular Bid | Santa Anita Park | 1980 | 1:57 4/5 | 56.03 | 11.78 |
| 12.00f | Secretariat | Belmont Park | 1973 | 2:24 | 55.00 | 12.00 |

CHART I. DISTANCE VS. AVERAGE SPEED FOR NORTH AMERICAN RECORD HOLDERS

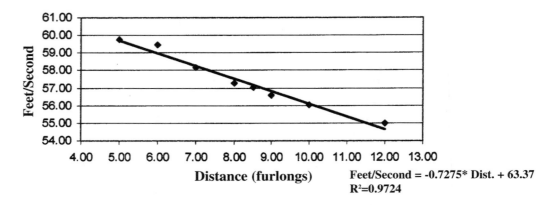

**Average Speed for North American Dirt Records**

Feet/Second = -0.7275* Dist. + 63.37
$R^2$=0.9724

When the individual data points are subjected to a mathematical process called linear regression we create the best straight line that can be derived from them, as shown on the graph. Sometimes the data points can actually be far away from the newly created line. In such a case the fit of the data is not very good and the relationship, here between average speed and distance, would be poor. But, in fact, when we plot the average speed for record times against distance, the correlation is outstanding, as shown by the R-squared value of 0.9724. A perfect or ideal fit would have a maximum R-squared value of 1.0000. In this case, the data points do indeed fall close to the regression line. The significance of the average speed for record times falling close to the straight line lies in specific, definable relationships between the average speed at one distance and the average speed at any other distance. These relationships are fixed relative to one another and, in a sense, describe the current state of physiological and evolutionary development of the breed. The line represents a "frontier of speed" in the Thoroughbred, the ultimate expression of directed breeding for over 200 years.

In the future, records will be broken, one by one, and a new line (or frontier) will be established as the breed evolves toward more speed. This linear relationship between average speed and distance is a permanent phenomenon and can be demonstrated at any point in the past. Any shift in position of the straight line on the graph is merely a visualization of the movement of the frontier of speed.

Consequently, it is fair to say, because of the linearity of the speed-distance relationship, that all of the record holders were equally fast in the context of the distance at which they set their record. That no single horse is likely to ever hold the record for both five and twelve furlongs is simply the result of variation in type, although obviously the record holders at both ends of the spectrum are ultimately part of the same gene pool. They differ by some degree in such things as biomechanical efficiency, cardiovascular characteristics, musculature, and so on. These factors then position their optimum performance traits at different regions of the speed frontier. What they all share in common is they have run as fast as a Thoroughbred can run up to this point in time at a given distance. The decrease in absolute speed with increasing distance is the tradeoff we must always make.

Since Dosage is about speed and its influence on performance, it is worth spending time to discuss speed in greater detail. The concept of speed may be the most mysterious in all of Thoroughbred racing. Ask a few friends which racehorse was the fastest in history and you're likely to get more answers than you bargained for. Was it Secretariat, Citation, Dr. Fager, Ruffian, Man o' War? A potential problem is that unless we all use the same definition of speed there is no real basis for discussion, although virtually everyone will agree that speed is very important.

The gradual decrease in average speed at each succeeding longer distance is clear. In no case has a record holder at a given distance maintained the same average speed as was achieved by a record holder at the next shorter distance. On this basis, the fastest horse on dirt may have been Chinook Pass. Tell that to your friends and they will begin to question your sanity. But in fact, in an absolute sense, and ignoring the notion of fractional speeds which we will address a bit later, Chinook Pass ran faster than any horse we have seen over the course of an entire race run between five and twelve furlongs. If he were able to sustain that rate of speed over a mile and a half he would have beaten Secretariat in the Belmont Stakes by 58 lengths.

Here again we observe the essence of the speed/stamina balance in the racehorse. Speed is not merely the rate at which the horse moves from point to point around the track; it is related to how long he can sustain that rate. As implied earlier, the concept of speed in racehorses has meaning only in the context of the distance involved because the breed is constrained by the present state of evolution and the resulting limits of physiology. It is not physically possible to run the same all-out speed at every distance. If all races were contested at five furlongs, Secretariat and Spectacular Bid would be considered slow because their expression of speed would not be apparent in a short sprint. On the other hand, if all races were run at twelve furlongs, then Chinook Pass and G Malleah would trail the field under the wire because they would not be able to sustain their best pace over the entire mile and a half.

This bears on the high esteem accorded brilliant milers, particularly as breeding animals. Whether we recognize it or not, highlighting the exploits of milers ascribes some notional versatility to a runner which can show near sprint-like speed beyond a pure sprint distance. In fact, milers are no different than any other runners in terms of physiological suitability. They also fit the continuum of the speed-distance relationship described earlier. Rather, we place a value on ability at a distance that essentially represents the average, neither sprint nor route. Actually, there is no special virtue in that view.

Great sires can and do come from all distance categories whether it be sprint (e.g., Mr. Prospector), mile (e.g., Fappiano), or route (e.g., Nijinsky II). Most likely, our affection for brilliance is a consequence of our perception of racing opportunity for the foals. As races become shorter and the pressure for early maturity increases, there will be a "natural selection" for sires thought to be capable of transmitting desired traits of speed and precocity. This trend is, of course, the subject of intense debate throughout the Thoroughbred racing industry.

A different kind of speed is that of instantaneous speed or, more realistically, fractional speed and pace. If one wishes to consider the truly fastest horses, then there are a host of runners capable of getting the first quarter mile in 21 seconds plus or minus a fraction. Most often they show their speed for only a brief time in the early stages of a race, usually tiring dramatically well before the finish. Often we call this "cheap speed." It is called cheap because it is not expressed over the full distance of a race. Actually it is not cheap at all. It is as valid a physiological expression as any other kind of speed. It just so happens that it occurs at one extreme of the speed frontier and well outside our normal frame of reference for meaningful racing. We view these runners in the same way we view runners that hold records at the other end of the continuum, say three miles. In the end, we are drawn to speed displayed at distances that we, as a society, prefer to race. Within those bounds, all record holders are essentially equally fast in terms of genetic expression.

11

To further illustrate the concept of aptitudinal type, in human sports we often describe athletes according to their body structure. In the world of track and field we may refer to a sprinter's physique or a marathoner's physique. Even before the competitor sets foot on the track, we have projected a perceived suitability to the event at hand based on our understanding of how body type affects athletic skills. In this example, the athlete's physique determines his or her "aptitudinal type." In the world of Thoroughbred racing, the essence of Dosage is its ability to relate aptitudinal type to performance on the racetrack, although here the aptitudinal type is not physical type but pedigree type.

# CHAPTER 2

# The Value of Pedigree Classification

Classification, best expressed as the arrangement of something according to a systematic division into classes or groups, is a useful exercise when dealing with complex information requiring substantial and extensive interpretation. It helps structure the information and provides a framework within which the various elements can be examined and compared. Ideally, classification can help create order out of chaos and simplicity out of confusion. Certainly, many would argue that the subject of Thoroughbred pedigrees is both chaotic and confusing. To the extent that it is chaotic and confusing, a practical classification methodology that makes the study of Thoroughbred pedigrees less intimidating and more accessible is a desirable thing.

The concept of classification is not new to Thoroughbred pedigrees. Perhaps the first to apply it was the brilliant though often maligned Bruce Lowe, an Australian living in the last half of the 19th century. Lowe's name survives to this day primarily through his monumental text *Breeding Racehorses by the Figure System*, first published after his death in 1895. Lowe observed that every horse listed in the General Stud Book traced to one of 50 mares. Based on a detailed statistical evaluation of the winners of the English classics, he categorized the tail-female lines from which they descended and assigned a ranking that reflected the number of winners within each family.

The family with the most winners was family No. 1. The family with the second most winners was No. 2, and so on. In all, 43 families had produced an English classic winner. Lowe ranked the others according to his personal opinion of quality. Lowe then attempted to base a breeding theory on his figures, suggesting that the first five "running" families (those with the most classic winners) and the first five "sire" families (those from which the most successful sires were derived) would continue to express their superiority.

This, however, has not been the case, as many female lines have since emerged that have produced a large number of top-class winners. As a result, the Bruce Lowe Figure System has been discredited by many mainstream pedigree pundits. For most people that is the complete story. Lowe is often casually dismissed as the originator of a breeding theory that failed and there are those who resent the influence his work had on the breeding establishment early on. Much of the criticism leveled at Lowe has been bitter and sarcastic, especially by those who would deny the value of any attempt to organize the science of breeding racehorses. To them, "breeding the best to the best" is about as well as one can do, which is fine.

On the other hand, this conventional approach, although perhaps necessary to achieve the highest goals, may not always be sufficient. In fact, Lowe's contributions are fundamental and profound, extending far beyond the failure of the Figure System. His success in organizing and structuring the information presented in *Breeding Racehorses by the Figure System* resulted in one of the most detailed and thorough histories of the Thoroughbred, tracing the breed back through the female lines to the most important mares of the 17th century.

The sense of order that Lowe applied to his work subsequently became the model for the approaches taken by Vuillier and Varola in their development of Dosage. The lasting value of his contribution lies in the integrity of his research, his precise methodology and the philosophical framework he created for other investigators. For the benefit of the reader, the Bruce Lowe families of many classic winners since 1940 are tallied in Appendix V.

Conventional pedigree analysis often lacks a scientific or technical foundation and can take a variety of forms. It may emphasize perceived patterns of inbreeding or linebreeding to notable ancestors to explain a contemporary horse's abilities. In these cases, multiple presences of names in the pedigree and where these names appear are deemed critical. A profound influence is accorded such duplications even when found in far remote generations. Specific patterns of inbreeding or linebreeding may become fashionable from time to time when high-profile individuals representing those patterns become successful. Depending on what transpires on the racetrack, specific patterns can become unfashionable as well.

An issue remaining unresolved is a universal understanding of what inbreeding and linebreeding actually mean. There is no standard definition that is accepted by all students of pedigree. Much of the debate centers on the remoteness of the duplications and what they represent. From the standpoint of rigorous research methodology, it is clearly beneficial to have a definition that all pedigree researchers can agree to. In its absence, data will be interpreted without scientific guidelines. Acceptable science-based definitions are available, and those proposed by Jones and Bogart in *Genetics of the Horse* (Edwards Brothers, Inc., Ann Arbor, Michigan, 1971) seem reasonable:

"Inbreeding is the mating of animals more closely related than the average of the breed. Linebreeding is a form of inbreeding in which the blood of particular individuals is concentrated . . . without an attempt to rapidly inbreed."

By this definition the difference is one of degree rather than kind, and although the distinction may seem trivial, it becomes very important when trying to appreciate the significance of a pedigree interpretation. For example, is a five by six duplication of names truly an expression of inbreeding? Some might say yes while others might say no. Whether it is or isn't affects how one interprets the relevance of the pattern. If the average for the breed is a duplication of four by five, then it could be argued that a five by six duplication should have a marginal effect. Yet duplications in a pedigree far removed from four by five or five by six are invoked routinely to explain some aspect of quality or ability. Even more common is the invocation of multiple duplications that are often credited with an additive effect. Are such claims of a cause and effect relationship justified? Without a standard of measurement it is difficult to say. For the most part, the evidence of an impact on quality from remote duplications in a pedigree is anecdotal at best.

Unfortunately, anecdotal evidence doesn't lend much scientific credibility to one's conclusions. The problem here is that inbreeding or linebreeding patterns have not been catalogued nor their effects measured on a scale such that cause-effect relationships are even recognizable. Inbreeding and linebreeding assuredly have an important role to play in Thoroughbred breeding. There is no intent here to downplay their genetic consequences. However, until a classification system is developed on a population-wide basis that correlates inbreeding and linebreeding patterns with measurable effects, the accuracy and predictive ability of inbreeding- and linebreeding-based pedigree interpretation will always be less than optimal. Conclusions will be vague and obscure. In essence, they are more opinion than fact.

Jones and Bogart praise the theory of linebreeding because linebreeding concentrates the blood of superior individuals without risking the loss in vigor often seen when inbreeding becomes too intense. Nevertheless, they point out that linebreeding is limited by how well we judge the superiority of the individual whose blood is being concentrated. As with duplication patterns, this would be an area of study amenable to classification. Conceivably, one could address the details of what it means to linebreed to Buckpasser versus Mahmoud or Princequillo, for example. For many it is the inbreeding or linebreeding itself that is the driver, not the absolute quality or specific influence of the individuals being concentrated. Here again, predictability is compromised and sub-optimal.

Conventional analysis may also emphasize interactions between bloodlines, a pattern commonly called "nicking." These interactions may have an historical record of success or failure involving specific sires in combination with broodmare sires and broodmare sire lines. Conversely, one may consider how individual broodmare sires have performed when paired with certain sires or sire lines. The concept of two bloodlines or individuals having a unique compatibility is quite appealing because the decision-making process is that much easier.

The fundamental problem with individual nicking patterns, however, is that only rarely are there enough examples to provide a statistically significant sample size. By statistically significant we are referring to the established statistical criteria affording a meaningful confidence level where the observed pattern has only a small probability of being a random event. For example, suppose sire A is bred to mares by sire B and 10 foals are produced. If two of these, or 20 percent, become listed stakes winners and sire A gets 10 percent overall stakes winners, i.e., regardless of his mares' bloodlines, then this A/B cross surpasses sire A's overall stakes winner production by two to one, which some would consider evidence of a positive nick.

On the other hand, suppose that none of the 10 foals (0 percent) won any stakes but three placed in Grade I events. To some, zero stakes winners from 10 foals is a red flag. But here the truth may be that the Grade I stakes-placed runners are far superior to the two listed stakes winners in the first case. Do 20 percent stakes winners represent a positive nick while 0 percent stakes winners represent a negative nick? Probably not. Actually, depending on how you measure the quality of runners (and we all do it differently), you might conclude that the second case indicates a greater affinity between sires A and B than does the first. In extreme cases such as five Grade I stakes winners from five foals produced by the A/B cross or, at the other end, five maiden claimers, the conclusions may be more obvious. But these circumstances are so rare that to generalize about the validity of individual nicking patterns on this basis stretches credibility. Ten or even 20 or 30 specific examples of a cross between A and B may still not be sufficient to establish statistical significance simply because there is no objective universal measure of the success of that cross.

An example of the danger inherent in the use of small sample sizes for defining nicks is the breeding of Baldski to Diplomat Way mares. In 1989, *The Blood-Horse* published tables of nicking patterns for many North American sires. Included were the records of sires which had gotten at least five foals from daughters of a particular broodmare sire. At that time the Baldski/Diplomat Way pattern had resulted in no stakes winners from 19 foals, seemingly supporting the notion of an inferior cross. However, the AEI (Average Earnings Index) for these foals was 1.84 while the CI (Comparable Index) was 1.64. So although there were no stakes winners, Baldski did upgrade the Diplomat Way mares to which he was bred. Perhaps the situation wasn't so bad after all. Subsequently, there appeared a Baldski/Diplomat Way stakes winner named Express Star, which ultimately won seven stakes races with lifetime earnings of more than $450,000. One out of 20, or five percent, stakes winners is not statistically different from Baldski's seven percent lifetime stakes winner production rate at the time. Suddenly the prospect of Baldski being bred to Diplomat Way mares wasn't so terrifying. As of October 2001 there were 28 foals representing the Baldski/Diplomat Way cross. Of these, three (11 percent) are stakes winners, exceeding Baldski's nine percent lifetime percentage of stakes winners. The combined AEI of the 28 foals is 2.03 (which exceeds Baldski's lifetime AEI of 1.75 through 2001), with a CI of 1.59.

The issue raised here relates more to timing than it does to any genetic compatibility. Does a nick change if the one stakes winner from 20 foals is the first foal or the last one? Obviously not. The total record after 20 foals is the same. Bloodline compatibilities can change over long periods of time as new breeding stock from those bloodlines emerge. But the idea that the compatibility between a specific sire and a specific broodmare sire can change over time is suspect.

Another problem with the small sample sizes used in defining individual nicking patterns is the tendency to revert to close up ancestors if there are no specific examples involving the particular sire and broodmare sire. This is more often the case than not. For example, millionaire Dispersal was one of the very best colts in America several years ago and presumably evidence of a superior nick. Dispersal was by Sunny's Halo and out of a Johnny Appleseed mare, certainly not a well-established breeding pattern and for which there is no basis to draw meaningful conclusions about the viability of the cross. Even today there are only three examples, and Dispersal remains the one stakes winner.

If we now look at the record of Sunny's Halo's sire, the deceased Halo, who was a superior stallion of long-standing, we find that he has sired as many as five foals from mares representing only one branch of the Prince Rose broodmare sire line (of which Johnny Appleseed is a representative). From six Prince John mares he has gotten one minor stakes winner, but overall he has seriously downgraded these mares with AEI 0.93 compared to CI 1.97.

This is not the stuff of great nicks. Apparently, using any other representative of a bloodline as a basis for the compatibility of another member of that bloodline is a dangerous practice because with each succeeding generation there is a significant dilution of the genetic relationship between the two.

One can look at nicking patterns more globally by focusing only on bloodlines rather than individuals. For example, it can easily be determined what percentage of Northern Dancer line sires and Raise a Native line broodmare sires are present in a population of stakes winners. For argument's sake let's say that 30 percent of all stakes winners are by Northern Dancer line sires and that of all stakes winners, 10 percent are out of Raise a Native line mares. In a random world, then, we could expect that one in 10 stakes winners

Northern Dancer          Photo Courtesy of the Keeneland Library

sired by a Northern Dancer line stallion would be produced from a Raise a Native line mare. Conversely, three in 10 stakes winners produced from Raise a Native line mares would be sired by Northern Dancer line stallions.

To avoid confusion, we'll use real numbers to illustrate. In a population of 100 stakes winners, a total of 30 would represent the Northern Dancer sire line. If, randomly, 10 percent of all stakes winners are from Raise a Native line mares, then three of the 30 Northern Dancer sire line stakes winners would be expected to represent the Northern Dancer/Raise a Native cross. Similarly, since 30 percent of all stakes winners are by Northern Dancer line sires then three of the 10 stakes winners from Raise a Native line mares would be by those sires. Thus, from either direction, we expect three out of 100 stakes winners in the population to represent the Northern Dancer/Raise a Native cross. If, however, we find that there are actually six or nine of the hundred that are bred Northern Dancer/Raise a Native, we have a situation in which two or three times as many representatives of that cross have been produced than had been anticipated from the total population statistics. This might be construed as a positive nick. But here, too, there are problems associated with interpreting the data.

First, the derived statistics and nicking patterns, as we will see with Dosage, would apply only to large populations and not necessarily to individuals. In fact, we breed individuals, not bloodlines.

Second, do the statistics really reflect general compatibility of bloodlines or the quality of individuals that make up the population? Bloodlines rise and fall for many reasons. But a characteristic of ascending bloodlines is that the individuals representing those bloodline are superior breeding animals relative to the remainder of the population. Declining bloodlines are similarly characterized by inferior breeding animals. Therefore, dominating the situation is the fact that breeding superior sires to mares by superior broodmare sires increases the probability of producing superior foals. This returns us to the concept of individual nicking patterns and the problems associated with statistical significance.

Bloodline compatibilities are statistically meaningful only in terms of large populations and in that context are useful in assessing general trends within bloodlines. On the other hand, individual nicking patterns almost never meet the criteria for statistical significance.

In the context of the two common approaches to pedigree interpretation just discussed, we have highlighted issues of categorization or classification, cause and effect, and statistical significance. These issues will be addressed at length in the following discussion of Dosage.

# CHAPTER 3

# The Origins of Dosage: Vuillier

Dosage was created in the early part of the 20th century by Lt. Col. Jean Joseph Vuillier, a retired French military officer and pedigree authority who was an active and vocal participant in the pedigree debates of his day. One of the more contested issues at the time among racing devotees focused on the relative merits of two of the three stallions from which all of today's Thoroughbreds descend, Eclipse and Herod. Vuillier contributed to a resolution through an in-depth analysis of the pedigrees of major European winners, classic and otherwise. To the delight of one side and to the dismay of the other, he found that Herod was the dominant influence of the two. More importantly, he determined that the proportion of Herod's influence in extended pedigrees through twelve generations was essentially the same in all of the horses analyzed. This was indeed a remarkable discovery, laying the groundwork for further research and development of the Dosage System, eventually published in *Les Croisements Rationnels (Rational Crossbreeding)*.

Vuillier noted that very few ancestors among the thousands present in the extended pedigree of the good horses he studied appeared with great frequency. Furthermore, as with Herod, the influence of these special ancestors through 12 generations also became constant, each with a unique contribution (or "dosage"). This critical observation led to Vuillier's identification of three series of key Thoroughbred ancestors separated by discrete timeframes. He called these ancestors *chefs-de-race*, a term he used to distinguish those rare individuals he believed had a unique, profound and long-term effect on the breed.

Vuillier's first series, from the early 19th century, includes the stallions Pantaloon, ch., 1824 (Castrel-Idalia, by Peruvian); Voltaire, br., 1826 (Blacklock-Phantom Mare, by Phantom); Touchstone, br., 1831 (Camel-Banter, by Master Henry); Bay Middleton, b., 1833 (Sultan-Cobweb, by Phantom); Birdcatcher, ch., 1833 (Sir Hercules-Guiccioli, by Bob Booty); Gladiator, ch., 1833 (Partisan-Pauline, by Moses); and Melbourne, br., 1834 (Humphrey Clinker-Cervantes Mare, by Cervantes). The series also includes one mare, Pocahontas, b., 1837 (Glencoe-Marpessa, by Muley), the only mare Vuillier ever included among his *chefs-de-race*.

The second series, from the middle of the 19th century, includes just two *chefs-de-race*, Newminster, b., 1848 (Touchstone-Beeswing, by Dr. Syntax) and Stockwell, ch., 1849 (The Baron-Pocahontas, by Glencoe).

The third and final series of Vuillier's *chefs-de-race*, now from the late 19th century, includes Hermit, ch., 1864 (Newminster-Seclusion, by Tadmor); Hampton, b., 1872 (Lord Clifden-Lady Langden, by Kettledrum); Galopin, b., 1872 (Vedette-Flying Duchess, by The Flying Dutchman); Isonomy, b., 1875 (Sterling-Isola Bella, by Stockwell); Bend Or, ch., 1877 (Doncaster-Rouge Rose, by Thormanby) and St. Simon, br., 1881 (Galopin-St. Angela, by King Tom).

This process, in which new series of *chefs-de-race* periodically emerge, achieve dominance and establish a constant influence in pedigrees over time, is a rational model for the evolution of the

Thoroughbred. Vuillier's method for measuring the influence of each *chef-de-race* depends on the fact that 4,096 ancestors populate the 12th generation in a pedigree. Using that number as a point total, he allowed that each generation should tally that same figure of 4,096. This leads to the obvious conclusion that every occurrence of a 12th generation ancestor is worth 1 point since that ancestor occupies 1 of 4,096 positions. A parent occupies 1 of 2 positions, equivalent to 2,048 of 4,096. The respective figures assigned for each occurrence in the 1st through the 12th generation are 2,048; 1,024; 512; 256; 128; 64; 32; 16; 8; 4; 2; and 1.

A result of Vuillier's counting technique was the observation that by 1900 the actual percentage of blood of some of the most significant foundation animals in the breed (e.g., Eclipse, Herod and Highflyer) was close to the same in all pedigrees, generally varying by no more than three-quarters of one percent. The same was true for the *chefs-de-race* assigned to Vuillier's three series, although each *chef-de-race* had a different "Dosage" number that could vary greatly from one *chef-de-race* to another. The well-known pedigree authority, Abram S. Hewitt, noted in *The Great Breeders and Their Methods* (Thoroughbred Publishers, Inc., Lexington, Kentucky, 1982) that St. Simon's Dosage figure was more than twice as high as that of Bend Or even though the latter's sire line was far more prevalent in England in the 1920s.

Vuillier believed in designing a mating to align the Dosage figures in the foal with those established for the breed. If, for example, the sire's Dosage figure for St. Simon was too high, then the mare's figure should be lower in order to compensate it. Vuillier applied his skills in the employ of H. H. The Aga Khan who, following World War I, decided to greatly expand his interests in racing. Utilizing Lord Derby's trainer, the Hon. George Lambton, to select individuals, and Lt. Col. Vuillier to evaluate pedigrees, the Aga Khan established one of the most successful buying, racing and breeding operations in history.

Among the yearlings purchased were Teresina, by Tracery (dam of Irish Oaks winner Theresina and of the high-class American sire Alibhai); Mumtaz Mahal, by The Tetrarch (tail-female ancestress of Nasrullah and Mahmoud); Friar's Daughter, by Friar Marcus (dam of English Triple Crown winner Bahram and of Irish Derby winner Dastur); Diophon, by Grand Parade (winner of the 2000 Guineas); Salmon Trout, by The Tetrarch (winner of the St. Leger); Blenheim II, by Blandford (winner of the English Derby and a top-class sire); and Qurrat-al-Ain, by Buchan (dam of 1000 Guineas winner Majideh, she the dam of Belmont Stakes winner Gallant Man and of English and Irish Oaks winner Masaka).

For more than 30 years the Aga Khan also bred an impressive number of superior horses including a host of champions and classic winners. Some of the more prominent include the aforementioned Bahram, Dastur, Majideh, Gallant Man, Nasrullah and Mahmoud, as well as Firdaussi, Turkhan, Khaled, Migoli, Tulyar, Saint Crespin III, Sheshoon, Charlottesville and others.

Although the direct impact of Lt. Col. Vuillier on the Aga Khan's success cannot be quantified, it is true that the Aga Khan's breeding program seriously declined after Vuillier's death. Neither can the actual role of Dosage methodology be accurately measured. However, we can be certain that Lt. Col. Vuillier's creation was instrumental in shaping his pedigree insights and preferences. There is an undeniable link between Vuillier's philosophy and the Aga Khan's achievements.

Vuillier's work leaves many questions unanswered. Will his data and conclusions hold up in the light of today's more sophisticated analytical techniques? Can Dosages be shown truly to differentiate the quality of a pedigree? Do the principles that he developed still apply to contemporary Thoroughbreds? There are students of pedigree who continue to seek answers to these questions. Regardless of the outcome, and regardless of one's acceptance of Vuillier's ideas, it is clear that he made a revolutionary contribution to pedigree evaluation. By creating a methodology that classifies the configuration of an individual pedigree in quantitative terms, he changed forever the philosophical basis of pedigree analysis.

# CHAPTER 4

# The Origins of Dosage: Varola

The next major step in the evolution of Dosage is attributed to Dr. Franco Varola. An Italian lawyer, Varola introduced his approach to pedigree interpretation in a series of articles published in The British Racehorse between 1959 and 1972 and in two books, *Stalloni Capirazza dal 1900 ad oggi* published in 1960, and *Nuovi Dosaggi del Purosangue* published in 1967. These were followed by two more comprehensive volumes, *Typology of the Racehorse* (J. A. Allen, London, 1974), and *The Functional Development of the Thoroughbred* (J. A. Allen, London & New York, 1980).

Varola accepted Vuillier's premise that the evolution of the Thoroughbred takes place through a tiny fraction of the stallions standing at stud in any era. Over time, only a few names will survive in pedigrees while the rest will pass into obscurity. A consequence of this convergence of thought was that Varola also limited his selection of *chefs-de-race* to a relatively small number, although larger than Vuillier's.

The fundamental difference between Vuillier and Varola is the difference between quantitative analysis and qualitative analysis. Whereas Vuillier concerned himself only with the frequency (a quantity) with which his *chefs-de-race* appeared in a pedigree, Varola shifted the emphasis to the aptitudinal type (a quality) contributed to a pedigree by his *chefs-de-race*. Like Vuillier, Varola applied his technique to extended pedigrees. Unlike Vuillier, Varola did not differentiate the contributions of his *chefs-de-race* by generation. In other words, Varola allowed that an aptitudinal contribution in one generation would have the same significance as an aptitudinal contribution in another.

Although his arbitrary dismissal of Galton's Law may disturb purists who believe in a diminishing influence with increasingly remote generations, and despite questions about the scientific accuracy of his approach, Varola offered a new perspective on pedigree interpretation. Instead of simply considering the historical exploits of the various ancestors in a pedigree, he emphasized the dynamic interplay of aptitudinal type that defined the character of the horse being analyzed. He concentrated on the aptitudinal influences passed along at stud rather than highlighting accomplishments on the track, a profound and significant change in direction. The importance of this shift in philosophy cannot be overstated because all too often our assumptions about ancestral influences are based on questionable information.

It is common practice to cite a horse's racing attributes in order to rationalize the potential performance of his progeny. A classic winner is expected to get classic distance runners. A sprint champion is expected to get sprinters or sprinter-miler types. Many times reality does match expectation. English Triple Crown winner Nijinsky II was one of the world's great sires of stayers on both dirt and grass. On the other end of the scale, two-time Eclipse champion sprinter Housebuster gets about 75 percent of his stakes winners at less than a mile. Yet it isn't always that straightforward. There are numerous examples that contradict our expectations. Take, for example, the emerging international sire, Kingmambo.

# Mr. Prospector

DP 23-12-13-4-0, DI 3.95, CD 1.04

Mr. Prospector       Photo Courtesy of Z

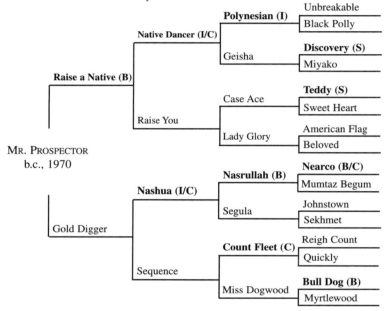

**MR. PROSPECTOR**
b.c., 1970

- Raise a Native (B)
  - Native Dancer (I/C)
    - Polynesian (I)
      - Unbreakable
      - Black Polly
    - Geisha
      - Discovery (S)
      - Miyako
  - Raise You
    - Case Ace
      - Teddy (S)
      - Sweet Heart
    - Lady Glory
      - American Flag
      - Beloved
- Gold Digger
  - Nashua (I/C)
    - Nasrullah (B)
      - Nearco (B/C)
      - Mumtaz Begum
    - Segula
      - Johnstown
      - Sekhmet
  - Sequence
    - Count Fleet (C)
      - Reigh Count
      - Quickly
    - Miss Dogwood
      - Bull Dog (B)
      - Myrtlewood

|  | DP Contribution | Equivalent to: |  |  |  |
|---|---|---|---|---|---|
| Sire | 16 - 8 - 4 - 4 - 0 | DI | 4.43 | CD | 1.13 |
| Dam | 7 - 4 - 9 - 0 - 0 | DI | 3.44 | CD | 0.90 |

Along with Brilliant/Classic *chef-de-race* Northern Dancer, Brilliant/Classic *chef-de-race* Mr. Prospector, b.c., 1970 (Raise a Native-Gold Digger, by Nashua) is arguably one of the two most important North American sires of the last quarter century. His accomplishments as a sire of runners, a sire of sires and a sire of producing mares are legendary. As a performer he was a very fast sprinter, capable of getting six furlongs in under 1:08. His Gulfstream Park six-furlong track record remained unequaled for 26 years. Mr. Prospector derives his speed from both his sire and his dam, with an emphasis on his sire, Brilliant *chef-de-race* Raise a Native. The result is DP 23-12-13-4-0, DI 3.95 and CD 1.04. This is very close to a sprinting "down-the-ladder" pattern and is dominated by the very large number of Brilliant points. Although finishing second in the one-mile 1973 Derby Trial, Mr. Prospector was not truly competitive beyond sprint distances.

Kingmambo, a foal of 1990, is a son of the immortal Mr. Prospector and out of Miesque by Nureyev. Mr. Prospector is arguably the most important Thoroughbred stallion of the last 20 years, with a host of successful sons and producing daughters. He was a brilliantly fast sprinter, able to run six furlongs in under 1:08. As a direct sire of runners, he is generally recognized as a source of speed, getting many early-maturing sprinters and sprinter-milers.

Miesque, considered by many as among the greatest race mares in history, twice won the Grade 1 Breeders' Cup Mile on the turf. Kingmambo himself was a multiple Group 1 winner at a flat mile in France and England, never winning beyond that distance. He has a full brother that was a Group winner in France at six furlongs. Traditionally, a miler out of a miler and by a sprinter and sire of sprinter-milers would be expected to reproduce those qualities in his offspring.

Yet Kingmambo has become a major source of great stamina in a Thoroughbred world ever evolving toward more and more speed. Through mid-2002, the average winning distance of his progeny in North American open stakes races was a very long 9.04 furlongs. Only 2.9 percent of his progeny stakes wins were at less than eight furlongs. His best runners are Belmont Stakes winner Lemon Drop Kid and Japan Cup winner El Condor Pasa, both victorious at 12 furlongs, the former on dirt and the latter on grass.

In contrast to Kingmambo we have the example of Slewpy, a foal of 1980. Slewpy is a son of Triple Crown winner Seattle Slew and out of Rare Bouquet by Prince John. Seattle Slew, in addition to winning the Kentucky Derby, Preakness Stakes and Belmont Stakes, is also the sire of classic winners A.P. Indy and Swale in addition to the champion stayer Slew o' Gold. Rare Bouquet produced two other stakes winners in addition to Slewpy, both winners at middle distances. Slewpy stayed as well, annexing the Grade 1 mile and a sixteenth Young America Stakes as a two-year-old and the mile and a quarter Grade 1 Meadowlands Cup at three.

Thus we have a Grade 1 winner at a classic distance by a Triple Crown winner and sire of classic winners and out of a middle distance to classic distance producer. Conventional wisdom suggests that Slewpy should be a sire of at least middle distance types if not classic performers. The reality is that Slewpy became one of North America's top sprint sires. The average winning distance of his progeny in North American open stakes races is a short 7.07 furlongs and 66 percent of his progeny open stakes wins are at seven furlongs or shorter. His leading earner, Thirty Slews, won the Grade 1 Breeders' Cup Sprint in 1992.

The differences between Kingmambo and Slewpy are dramatic and revealing. In a "logical" world their records at stud would be reversed, with Kingmambo getting the sprinters and Slewpy getting the stayers. The fact that the opposite is true reinforces Varola's insistence that qualities passed along in the breeding shed dominate qualities displayed on the racetrack. For some, it is a difficult notion to accept, but one that separates Dosage from traditional pedigree analysis.

Returning to the concept of ancestral influence, Varola explains his resistance to applying Galton's Law to his being a "humanist" and "not a geneticist nor a scientist." By this exercise in logic, Varola rationalizes the position that he "can afford to take an independent view of the influence of early progenitors" and that he "is concerned with typology in a functional sense, and not with percentage of influence in a genetic sense." Choosing to ignore scientific principles simply because one is not a scientist may be construed by some as a peculiar and self-serving thing to do, but it is consistent with Varola's excitement over his "sociological" rather than genetic interpretation of the Thoroughbred. On the other hand, if one chooses to overlook certain rules of logic, then observing pedigrees in terms of the distribution of aptitudinal qualities is refreshing and often quite revealing.

Varola's initial selection of 20 *chefs-de-race* was based largely on his perception of those sires that had the greatest overall impact on the breed in the 20th century. To ensure adequate typological variation among his *chefs-de-race*, he had to lower his standards somewhat in making later assignments, focusing primarily on their functional contribution. The final list included 120 stallions. The *chefs-de-race* were then separated into five aptitudinal groups he called Brilliant, Intermediate, Classic, Stout and Professional. These groups differ in their "essence or character," not necessarily in their inclination to pass along distance capability. That having been said, Brilliant *chefs-de-race* tend to transmit quickness, speed and early maturity.

Intermediate *chefs-de-race* are so-called "mixers," necessary for a satisfactory balance of class and finesse. They are a connecting link between the aptitudinal extremes. Classic *chefs-de-race* are most often associated with the three-year-old classic races. Stout *chefs-de-race* produce runners of diminished brilliance, but with soundness, a good constitution and a steady temperament. The Professional *chefs-de-race* generally get pure plodders.

More broadly, Varola likened the five aptitudinal groups to positions along the political spectrum ranging from Left (Brilliant), Left of Center (Intermediate), Center (Classic), Right of Center (Stout) and Right (Professional). He believed the political analogy would avoid any misconceptions that the range of aptitudinal groups paralleled distance capability.

The mechanics of Varola's analysis are fairly straightforward and involve the creation of a Dosage Diagram. *Chefs-de-race* in a pedigree are placed one by one into a table according to their designated aptitudinal group. When all of the *chefs-de-race* are accounted for, the presences in each aptitudinal group are added. The sums of the presences within each group constitute the Dosage Diagram. For illustration, we will use Varola's Dosage Diagram of English Derby winner St. Paddy, b., 1957 (Aureole-Edie Kelly, by Bois Roussel):

| Brilliant | Intermediate | Classic | Stout | Professional |
|---|---|---|---|---|
| Hyperion | | Aureole | (3)Chaucer | Bayardo |
| Cicero | | Gainsborough | Bois Roussel | Son-In-Law |
| Phalaris | | Blenheim II | Vatout II | Dark Ronald |
| | | Blandford | Spearmint | |
| | | Clarissimus | | |
| | | (2)Swynford | | |
| | | Tracery | | |
| | | Rock Sand | | |
| 3 | 0 | 9 | 6 | 3 |

The parentheses before a sire's name indicates the total number of presences for that sire found in the pedigree.

The Dosage Diagram of St. Paddy does not necessarily correlate with any specific performance attributes. In fact, Varola insists that Dosage Diagrams have no relation to racing ability.

Rather, the Dosage Diagram of St. Paddy fits within the larger framework of what Varola described in 1980 as "a behavioral perspective of the development of the breed in the course of this century." Each Dosage Diagram stands alone, symbolizing the type of horse one may expect by revealing the "proportional representation of the five aptitudinal groups." Varola does remind us that a balance of aptitudinal factors is desirable in a racehorse. The ability to observe that balance was a primary driving force in the development of his methodology.

Varola distinguishes among several types of Dosage Diagrams based on the aforementioned proportional representation. The Balanced Pattern displays a comparable number of influences in each group. Foals by stallions with a Balanced Pattern will largely retain the Dosage Diagram characteristics of their dam. The Classical Pattern has the highest representation in the Classic group and allows for a variety of mating possibilities. The Wing Pattern has its greatest representation in the Brilliant and Professional groups to the detriment of the Intermediate, Classic and Stout groups. Presumably this pattern is created by breeding at the extremes in the hope of producing an average. Varola notes that this effect is not often achieved, a fact that he offers as evidence of the virtue of a balanced distribution. The Brilliant Pattern is dominated by presences in the Brilliant group. Unlike the Wing Pattern, which may require several generations to restore balance, the Brilliant Pattern is easily "redeemed" according to Varola. The Stout Pattern occurs when the number of Stout *chefs-de-race* is the highest. This particular pattern was noted as typical of French- and Italian-bred horses.

Finally, the Void Pattern describes a situation in which multiple or contiguous groups have no representation at all. Here again, Varola suggests that the existence of top-class sires and runners that display this pattern is further evidence that Dosage Diagrams have no relation to racing ability. They simply establish "type," thereby reinforcing Varola's main point that "Dosages are the study of the differentiation of functions within the Thoroughbred, and not magic formulae."

Varola's complete works are far more intricate than can be fully covered here. His introduction of split aptitudinal groups, half-point sires and split personality sires, intended to enhance "differentiation," either enrich his theories or make them overly complex depending on one's point of view. Nevertheless, students of pedigree would be well-served by reading Varola's publications on their own because, despite any reservations one may have about the specifics of his methodology, the approach offers a novel perspective on the meaning of a Thoroughbred pedigree.

# CHAPTER 5

# Modern Dosage Methodology

Vuillier and Varola had established the foundations of Dosage using distinct quantitative and qualitative approaches. In some ways their philosophies overlapped. In other ways they were quite different. Both employed extended pedigrees and both believed that evolutionary or developmental influences within the Thoroughbred could be defined by a relatively small number of key ancestors. On the one hand, Vuillier applied Galton's Law, assuming a diminishing influence of *chefs-de-race* as generations became more remote. On the other, Varola rejected Galton's Law and gave every *chef-de-race* the same weight regardless of which generation he populated. Vuillier attempted to identify the actual genetic influence of a *chef-de-race* through a quantitative measurement of its presences in a pedigree. Varola tried to assign an aptitudinal type through the qualitative assessment of characteristics prepotently handed down from generation to generation. Neither method relies entirely on conventional pedigree analysis where the emphasis is on the ancestors' achievements on the track or in the breeding shed.

Despite the new directions offered by Vuillier and Varola, some practical problems remained. Not the least of these is the access to extended pedigrees for the vast majority of horsemen. Thanks to computers and both offline and online databases, such pedigrees now may be conveniently generated. Software can be written to calculate the Vuillier Dosage numbers and create the Varola Dosage Diagrams. However, the availability of technology does not guarantee its widespread use, particularly when it is likely to be expensive. Under any circumstances, an analysis technique involving extended pedigrees will always have marginal utility for a general racing audience.

A second limitation of the Vuillier and Varola methodologies is the lack of a statistical framework. Without a statistical base it is difficult to put one's analytical results in the proper context. In other words, if one fails to define control groups or measurable variables that compare the results of one analysis to another, the significance of the results may not be clear. This is particularly true in the case of Varola who specifically dissociated his Dosage Diagrams from any aspect of racing performance. Under those circumstances it is especially difficult to appreciate the real-world significance of pedigree type. Varola opted for "art" over science, and he succeeded. However, his disregard for scientific method clearly puts the user of his technique at a disadvantage, particularly if he or she is looking for a practical application that generates a set of probabilities applicable to real situations.

With these limitations in mind, we sought a next-generation approach to Dosage that retained the best elements of the earlier versions while significantly expanding its utility. To that end, we abandoned the extended pedigree in favor of the readily accessible four-generation pedigree. We also rejected Varola's dismissal of Galton's Law, preferring instead to use a counting method similar to that employed by Vuillier. Finally, we felt that Varola's dissociation of his aptitudinal groups from distance capability was arbitrary and not supported by evidence. The hypothesis we proposed was that the aptitudinal groups cover the entire spectrum of speed to stamina and that the relationship between speed and stamina in the individual will affect every aspect of his racing character, including distance ability. Rather than being contradictory qualities, speed and stamina are inextricably linked. As discussed at the outset, one is always sacrificed in favor of the other. Individual horses, because of the unique traits they have inherited, are positioned at discrete points along the speed-stamina continuum. These points determine their type and affect the full range of performance capabilities.

The *chef-de-race* list used in our original study is displayed in Table 2. The selections are, with minor adjustments, those of Varola as modified by Hewitt in his article on Dosage that appeared in *The Blood-Horse* issue of May 2, 1977. Hewitt modified the Varola list of largely European *chefs-de-race* in order to make Dosage more applicable to American pedigrees. In several cases the two authors disagreed as to aptitudinal placement. In those instances we accepted the assignments at face value, placing the *chef-de-race* in both categories. These *chefs-de-race* are shown in Table 2 with an asterisk (*) next to their name.

We used a counting system based on 16 points for each of the four generations, analogous to Vuillier's 4,096 points for each of his 12 generations. Like Vuillier, we halved the influence of *chefs-de-race* found in each receding generation. In this way, a first generation *chef-de-race* receives 16 points, each second-generation *chef-de-race* receives 8 points, each third-generation *chef-de-race* receives 4 points and each fourth-generation *chef-de-race* receives 2 points. We opted for the 16-8-4-2 pattern over the more obvious 8-4-2-1 pattern to accommodate *chefs-de-race* split between two groups. In this manner, a fourth generation split *chef-de-race* receives a full point in each aptitudinal category rather than a more cumbersome half point.

Finally, for simplicity we stayed with five aptitudinal groups instead of the 10 ultimately proposed by Varola through the splitting of aptitudes. This required the combining of some categories and the repositioning of some *chefs-de-race*. We also used the nomenclature adopted by Hewitt for defining the aptitudinal groups; i.e., Brilliant-Intermediate-Classic-Solid-Professional.

With the key elements in place, the analysis proceeds in a manner similar to Varola's creation of a Dosage Diagram, the main difference being that the points tallied in each aptitudinal group depend on the generational position of the *chef-de-race*. Finally, the initial output of the analysis is called a Dosage Profile (DP) to differentiate it from the Varola Dosage Diagram.

The best way to illustrate the procedure is by example. For this purpose we will use the current *chef-de-race* list as of November 2002 displayed in Tables 3 and 4. Table 3 is an alphabetical listing while Table 4 is a listing by aptitudinal group and includes the year of birth for each *chef-de-race*. Again, sires split between two aptitudinal groups are displayed with an asterisk after their name in Table 4.

**TABLE 2. *Chefs-de-Race* USED IN THE INITIAL CONTEMPORARY DOSAGE STUDIES**

**BRILLIANT**

| | | |
|---|---|---|
| Abernant | Heliopolis | Pharis |
| Black Toney* | Hyperion* | Pompey |
| Bold Ruler | My Babu | Raise a Native |
| British Empire | Nasrullah* | Reviewer |
| Bull Dog | Nearco* | Roman* |
| Cicero | Never Bend* | Royal Charger |
| Court Martial | Olympia | Sir Cosmo |
| Double Jay | Orby | Tudor Minstrel |
| Fair Trial | Panorama | Turn-to* |
| Fairway | Peter Pan | Ultimus |
| Grey Sovereign | Phalaris | What a Pleasure |

## INTERMEDIATE

Ben Brush
Big Game
Black Toney*
Broomstick
Colorado
Congreve
Djebel
Eight Thirty
Equipoise*
Full Sail
Havresac II
Khaled

King Salmon
Mahmoud*
Nashua
Nasrullah*
Native Dancer*
Never Bend*
Northern Dancer
Petition
Pharos
Polynesian
Princequillo*
Roman*

Sir Ivor
Star Kingdom
Star Shoot
Sweep
T.V. Lark
The Tetrarch
Ticino
Tom Fool*
Traghetto
Turn-to*

## CLASSIC

Alibhai
Aureole
Bahram
Blandford
Blenheim II*
Blue Larkspur
Brantome
Buckpasser
Bull Lea
Clarissimus
Count Fleet
Equipoise*
Gainsborough
Graustark*

Gundomar
Hail to Reason
Herbager*
Hyperion*
Mahmoud*
Midstream
Mossborough
Native Dancer*
Navarro
Nearco*
Never Say Die
Persian Gulf
Pilate
Prince Bio

Prince Chevalier
Prince Rose
Ribot*
Rock Sand*
Sicambre
Sideral
Sir Gallahad III
Swynford
Tom Fool*
Tom Rolfe*
Tourbillon*
Tracery
Vieux Manoir
War Admiral

## SOLID

Asterus
Bachelor's Double
Ballymoss
Blenheim II*
Bois Roussel
Chaucer
Discovery
Fair Play*
Gallant Man

Graustark*
Herbager*
Man 'o War
Oleander
Princequillo*
Right Royal
Rock Sand*
Round Table
Sea-Bird

Sunstar
Tantieme
Teddy
Vatout
Worden

## PROFESSIONAL

Admiral Drake
Alcantara II
Alizier
Alycidon
Bayardo
Bruleur
Chateau Bouscaut
Crepello
Dark Ronald
Donatello II
Fair Play*

Foxbridge
Hurry On
La Farina
Le Fabuleux
Massine
Mieuxce
Ortello
Precipitation
Rabelais
Ribot*
Sardanaple

Solario
Son-in-Law
Spearmint
Sunny Boy
Tom Rolfe*
Tourbillon*
Vaguely Noble
Vandale
Vatellor
Wild Risk

## TABLE 3. *Chefs-de-Race* (199) AS OF NOVEMBER 2002 LISTED ALPHABETICALLY

Abernant (B)
Ack Ack (I/C)
Admiral Drake (P)
Alcantara II (P)
Alibhai (C)
Alizier (P)
Alycidon (P)
Alydar (C)
Apalachee (B)
Asterus (S)
Aureole (C)
Bachelor's Double (S)
Bahram (C)
Baldski (B/I)
Ballymoss (S)
Bayardo (P)
Ben Brush (I)
Best Turn (C)
Big Game (I)
Black Toney (B/I)
Blandford (C)
Blenheim II (C/S)
Blue Larkspur (C)
Blushing Groom (B/C)
Bois Roussel (S)
Bold Bidder (I/C)
Bold Ruler (B/I)
Brantome (C)
British Empire (B)
Broad Brush (I/C)
Broomstick (I)
Bruleur (P)
Buckpasser (C)
Bull Dog (B)
Bull Lea (C)
Busted (S)
Caro (I/C)
Chateau Bouscaut (P)
Chaucer (S)
Cicero (B)
Clarissimus (C)
Colorado (I)
Congreve (I)
Count Fleet (C)
Court Martial (B)
Creme dela Creme (C/S)
Crepello (P)
Damascus (I/C)
Danzig (I/C)
Dark Ronald (P)
Discovery (S)

Djebel (I)
Donatello II (P)
Double Jay (B)
Dr. Fager (I)
Eight Thirty (I)
Ela-Mana-Mou (P)
Equipoise (I/C)
Exclusive Native (C)
Fair Play (S/P)
Fair Trial (B)
Fairway (B)
Fappiano (I/C)
Forli (C)
Foxbridge (P)
Full Sail (I)
Gainsborough (C)
Gallant Man (B/I)
Graustark (C/S)
Grey Dawn II (B/I)
Grey Sovereign (B)
Gundomar (C)
Habitat (B)
Hail to Reason (C)
Halo (B/C)
Havresac II (I)
Heliopolis (B)
Herbager (C/S)
High Top (C)
His Majesty (C)
Hoist the Flag (B/I)
Hurry On (P)
Hyperion (B/C)
Icecapade (B/C)
In Reality (B/C)
Intentionally (B/I)
Key To The Mint (B/C)
Khaled (I)
King Salmon (I)
King's Bishop (B/I)
La Farina (P)
Le Fabuleux (P)
Luthier (C)
Lyphard (C)
Mahmoud (I/C)
Man 'o War (S)
Massine (P)
Midstream (C)
Mieuxce (P)
Mill Reef (C/S)
Mossborough (C)
Mr. Prospector (B/C)

My Babu (B)
Nashua (I/C)
Nasrullah (B)
Native Dancer (I/C)
Navarro (C)
Nearco (B/C)
Never Bend (B/I)
Never Say Die (C)
Nijinsky II (C/S)
Niniski (C/P)
Noholme II (B/C)
Northern Dancer (B/C)
Nureyev (C)
Oleander (S)
Olympia (B)
Orby (B)
Ortello (P)
Panorama (B)
Persian Gulf (C)
Peter Pan (B)
Petition (I)
Phalaris (B)
Pharis II (B)
Pharos (I)
Pia Star (S)
Pilate (C)
Polynesian (I)
Pompey (B)
Precipitation (P)
Pretense (C)
Prince Bio (C)
Prince Chevalier (C)
Prince John (C)
Princequillo (I/S)
Prince Rose (C)
Promised Land (C)
Rabelais (P)
Raise a Native (B)
Relko (S)
Reviewer (B/C)
Ribot (C/P)
Right Royal (S)
Riverman (I/C)
Roberto (C)
Rock Sand (C/S)
Roman (B/I)
Rough'n Tumble (B/C)
Round Table (S)
Royal Charger (B)
Run the Gantlet (P)
Sadler's Wells (C/S)

Sardanaple (P)
Sea-Bird (S)
Seattle Slew (B/C)
Secretariat (I/C)
Sharpen Up (B/C)
Shirley Heights (C/P)
Sicambre (C)
Sideral (C)
Sir Cosmo (B)
Sir Gallahad III (C)
Sir Gaylord (I/C)
Sir Ivor (I/C)
Solario (P)
Son-in-Law (P)
Speak John (B/I)
Spearmint (P)
Spy Song (B)
Stage Door Johnny (S/P)
Star Kingdom (I/C)
Star Shoot (I)
Sunny Boy (P)
Sunstar (S)
Sweep (I)
Swynford (C)
T.V. Lark (I)
Tantieme (S)
Teddy (S)
The Tetrarch (I)
Ticino (C/S)
Tom Fool (I/C)
Tom Rolfe (C/P)
Tourbillon (C/P)
Tracery (C)
Traghetto (I)
Tudor Minstrel (B)
Turn-to (B/I)
Ultimus (B)
Vaguely Noble (C/P)
Vandale (P)
Vatellor (P)
Vatout (S)
Vieux Manoir (C)
War Admiral (C)
What A Pleasure (B)
Wild Risk (P)
Worden (S)

**TABLE 4.** *Chefs-de-Race* (199) AS OF NOVEMBER 2002 LISTED BY APTITUDINAL GROUP

## BRILLIANT

Abernant 1946
Apalachee 1971
Baldski* 1974
Black Toney* 1911
Blushing Groom* 1974
Bold Ruler* 1954
British Empire 1937
Bull Dog 1927
Cicero 1902
Court Martial 1942
Double Jay 1944
Fair Trial 1932
Fairway 1925
Gallant Man* 1954
Grey Dawn II* 1962
Grey Sovereign 1948
Habitat 1966
Halo* 1969

Heliopolis 1936
Hoist the Flag* 1968
Hyperion* 1930
Icecapade* 1969
In Reality* 1964
Intentionally* 1956
Key to the Mint* 1969
King's Bishop* 1969
Mr. Prospector* 1970
My Babu 1945
Nasrullah 1940
Nearco* 1935
Never Bend* 1960
Noholme II* 1956
Northern Dancer* 1961
Olympia 1946
Orby 1904
Panorama 1936

Peter Pan 1904
Phalaris 1913
Pharis II 1936
Pompey 1923
Raise a Native 1961
Reviewer* 1966
Roman* 1937
Rough'n Tumble* 1948
Royal Charger 1942
Seattle Slew* 1974
Sharpen Up* 1969
Sir Cosmo 1926
Speak John* 1958
Spy Song 1943
Tudor Minstrel 1944
Turn-to* 1951
Ultimus 1906
What A Pleasure 1965

## INTERMEDIATE

Ack Ack* 1966
Baldski* 1974
Ben Brush 1893
Big Game 1939
Black Toney* 1911
Bold Bidder* 1962
Bold Ruler* 1954
Broad Brush* 1983
Broomstick 1901
Caro* 1967
Colorado 1923
Congreve 1924
Damascus* 1964
Danzig* 1977
Djebel 1937
Dr. Fager 1964
Eight Thirty 1936
Equipoise* 1928

Fappiano* 1977
Full Sail 1934
Gallant Man* 1954
Grey Dawn II* 1962
Havresac II 1915
Hoist the Flag* 1968
Intentionally* 1956
Khaled 1943
King Salmon 1930
King's Bishop* 1969
Mahmoud* 1933
Nashua* 1952
Native Dancer* 1950
Never Bend* 1960
Petition 1944
Pharos 1920
Polynesian 1942
Princequillo* 1940

Riverman* 1969
Roman* 1937
Secretariat* 1970
Sir Gaylord* 1959
Sir Ivor* 1965
Speak John* 1958
Star Kingdom* 1946
Star Shoot 1898
Sweep 1907
T.V. Lark 1957
The Tetrarch 1911
Tom Fool* 1949
Traghetto 1942
Turn-to* 1951

## CLASSIC

Ack Ack* 1966
Alibhai 1938
Alydar 1975
Aureole 1950
Bahram 1932
Best Turn 1966
Blandford 1919
Blenheim II* 1927
Blue Larkspur 1926
Blushing Groom* 1974
Bold Bidder* 1962
Brantome 1931
Broad Brush* 1983
Buckpasser 1963
Bull Lea 1935
Caro* 1967
Clarissimus 1913
Count Fleet 1940
Creme dela Creme* 1963
Damascus* 1964
Danzig* 1977
Equipoise* 1928
Exclusive Native 1965
Fappiano* 1977
Forli 1963
Gainsborough 1915
Graustark* 1963
Gundomar 1942
Hail To Reason 1958
Halo* 1969

Herbager* 1956
High Top 1969
His Majesty 1968
Hyperion* 1930
Icecapade* 1969
In Reality* 1964
Key To The Mint* 1969
Luthier 1965
Lyphard 1969
Mahmoud* 1933
Midstream 1933
Mill Reef* 1968
Mossborough 1947
Mr. Prospector* 1970
Nashua* 1952
Native Dancer* 1950
Navarro 1931
Nearco* 1935
Never Say Die 1951
Nijinsky II* 1967
Niniski* 1976
Noholme II* 1956
Northern Dancer* 1961
Nureyev 1977
Persian Gulf 1940
Pilate 1928
Pretense 1963
Prince Bio 1941
Prince Chevalier 1943
Prince John 1953

Prince Rose 1928
Promised Land 1954
Reviewer* 1966
Ribot* 1952
Riverman* 1969
Roberto 1969
Rock Sand* 1900
Rough'n Tumble* 1948
Sadler's Wells* 1981
Seattle Slew* 1974
Secretariat* 1970
Sharpen Up* 1969
Shirley Heights* 1975
Sicambre 1948
Sideral 1948
Sir Gallahad III 1920
Sir Gaylord* 1959
Sir Ivor* 1965
Star Kingdom* 1946
Swynford 1907
Ticino* 1939
Tom Fool* 1949
Tom Rolfe* 1962
Tourbillon* 1928
Tracery 1909
Vaguely Noble* 1965
Vieux Manoir 1947
War Admiral 1934

## SOLID

Asterus 1923
Bachelor's Double 1906
Ballymoss 1954
Blenheim II* 1927
Bois Roussel 1935
Busted 1963
Chaucer 1900
Creme dela Creme* 1963
Discovery 1931
Fair Play* 1905
Graustark* 1963
Herbager* 1956
Man 'o War 1917

Mill Reef* 1968
Nijinsky II* 1967
Oleander 1924
Pia Star 1961
Princequillo* 1940
Relko 1960
Right Royal 1958
Rock Sand* 1900
Round Table 1954
Sadler's Wells* 1981
Sea-Bird 1962
Stage Door Johnny* 1965
Sunstar 1908

Tantieme 1947
Teddy 1913
Ticino* 1939
Vatout 1926
Worden 1949

## PROFESSIONAL

Admiral Drake 1931
Alcantara II 1908
Alizier 1947
Alycidon 1945
Bayardo 1906
Bruleur 1910
Chateau Bouscaut 1927
Crepello 1954
Dark Ronald 1905
Donatello II 1934
Ela-Mana-Mou 1976
Fair Play* 1905
Foxbridge 1930
Hurry On 1913
La Farina 1911

Le Fabuleux 1961
Massine 1920
Mieuxce 1933
Niniski* 1976
Ortello 1926
Precipitation 1933
Rabelais 1900
Ribot* 1952
Run The Gantlet 1968
Sardanaple 1911
Shirley Heights* 1975
Solario 1922
Son-In-Law 1911
Spearmint 1903
Stage Door Johnny* 1965

Sunny Boy 1944
Tom Rolfe* 1962
Tourbillon* 1928
Vaguely Noble* 1965
Vandale 1943
Vatellor 1933
Wild Risk 1940

# Round Table

## DP 12-8-10-8-2, DI 1.67, CD 0.50

Round Table    Photo Courtesy of the Thoroughbred Times

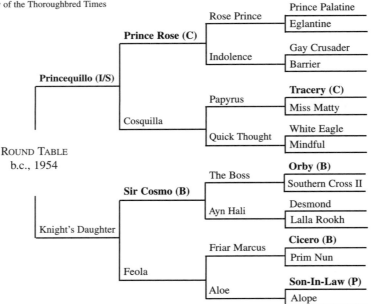

ROUND TABLE
b.c., 1954

| | | | |
|---|---|---|---|
| | | Rose Prince | Prince Palatine |
| | Prince Rose (C) | | Eglantine |
| | | Indolence | Gay Crusader |
| Princequillo (I/S) | | | Barrier |
| | | Papyrus | Tracery (C) |
| | Cosquilla | | Miss Matty |
| | | Quick Thought | White Eagle |
| | | | Mindful |
| | | The Boss | Orby (B) |
| | Sir Cosmo (B) | | Southern Cross II |
| | | Ayn Hali | Desmond |
| Knight's Daughter | | | Lalla Rookh |
| | | Friar Marcus | Cicero (B) |
| | Feola | | Prim Nun |
| | | Aloe | Son-In-Law (P) |
| | | | Alope |

| DP Contribution | | Equivalent to: | |
|---|---|---|---|
| Sire | 0 - 8 - 10 - 8 - 0 | DI 1.00 | CD 0.00 |
| Dam | 12 - 0 - 0 - 0 - 2 | DI 3.44 | CD 0.90 |

Solid *chef-de-race* Round Table, b.c., 1954 (Princequillo-Knight's Daughter, by Sir Cosmo) is an excellent example of breeding classicity to pure speed. His sire, Intermediate/Solid *chef-de-race* Princequillo, contributes a perfectly balanced pattern of aptitudinal influences while his dam contributes sheer brilliance. The result is DP 12-8-10-8-2, DI 1.67 and CD 0.50, with representation in all five aptitudinal groups and significant representation in four. Thus, there are strong elements of both speed and endurance. He had the speed to win stakes as a juvenile, ranking eight pounds below Experimental Free Handicap topweight, Barbizon. He also had the speed to win the Hollywood Gold Cup the next year in 1:58:3, the fastest time for 10 furlongs ever achieved by a three-year-old to that point in racing history. Round Table's ability to carry speed over a range of distances is exemplified by a mile in 1:33.2 under 130 pounds, nine furlongs in world record time of 1:46.4 also under 130 pounds, nine and a half furlongs in American record time of 1:53.2, and ten furlongs on the turf in world record time of 1:58.2 while toting 132 pounds.

# CHAPTER 6

# Dosage Calculations

In order to better understand Dosage figures, it is useful to go through the actual mechanics of doing the calculations. Even though there are computer software programs, computerized databases and even online databases for accessing Dosage figures, seeing how the numbers are generated provides a deeper insight into the interplay of those elements comprising the Dosage Profile and related figures for a particular Thoroughbred. The analogy would be knowing how to do addition, subtraction, multiplication and division even though calculators are universally available to perform those functions. There is always value in understanding the fundamentals.

The subject of the analysis is Hero's Honor, b.c., 1980 (Northern Dancer-Glowing Tribute, by Graustark). His four-generation pedigree follows, with *chefs-de-race* highlighted in bold type.

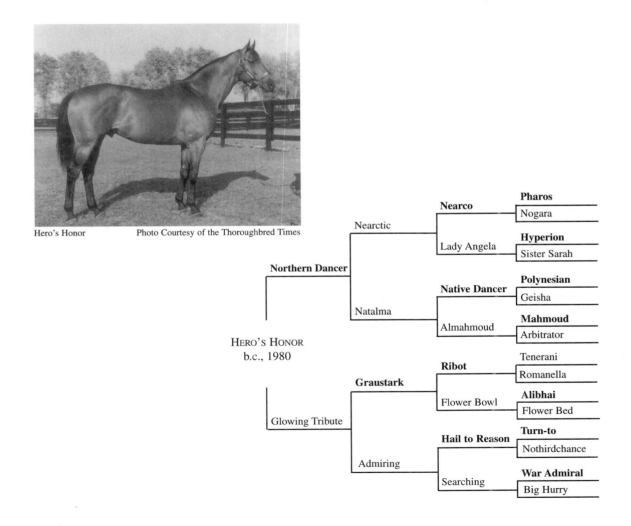

Hero's Honor                Photo Courtesy of the Thoroughbred Times

The first-generation sire, Northern Dancer, is a *chef-de-race* split between the Brilliant and Classic categories (see Table 3 for this and the remaining *chef-de-race* assignments). With 16 points reserved for a *chef-de-race* in generation one, he is assigned 8 points in Brilliant and 8 points in Classic. In the second generation, worth 8 points for each *chef-de-race*, Nearctic is not a *chef-de-race* while Graustark is a *chef-de-race* split between Classic and Solid. No points are added for Nearctic while Graustark is assigned 4 points each in Classic and Solid. We use the same procedure for generations three and four, leading to the distribution of points found in Table 5. All four third generation sires are *chefs-de-race*. These receive a total of four points each: 2 Brilliant and 2 Classic for Nearco; 2 Intermediate and 2 Classic for Native Dancer; 2 Classic and 2 Professional for Ribot; and 4 Classic for Hail to Reason. In the fourth generation, where each *chef-de-race* is assigned two points, there are seven *chefs-de-race* out of the eight sires. There are 2 Intermediate points assigned to Pharos; 1 Brilliant and 1 Classic to Hyperion; 2 Intermediate to Polynesian; 1 Intermediate and 1 Classic to Mahmoud; 2 Classic to Alibhai; 1 Brilliant and 1 Intermediate to Turn-to; and 2 Classic to War Admiral. Tenerani is the only fourth generation sire that is not a *chef-de-race*.

## TABLE 5. CALCULATION OF THE DOSAGE PROFILE (DP) FOR HERO'S HONOR

| Generation (Pts) | Sires (Aptitudinal Group(s)) | B | I | C | S | P |
|---|---|---|---|---|---|---|
| 1st Generation (16) | Northern Dancer (Brilliant/Classic) | 8 | | 8 | | |
| 2nd Generation (8) | Nearctic (N/A) | | | | | |
| | Graustark (Classic/Solid) | | | 4 | 4 | |
| 3rd Generation (4) | Nearco (Brilliant/Classic) | 2 | | 2 | | |
| | Native Dancer (Intermediate/Classic) | | 2 | 2 | | |
| | Ribot (Classic/Professional) | | | 2 | | 2 |
| | Hail to Reason (Classic) | | | 4 | | |
| 4th Generation (2) | Pharos (Intermediate) | | 2 | | | |
| | Hyperion (Brilliant/Classic) | 1 | | 1 | | |
| | Polynesian (Intermediate) | | 2 | | | |
| | Mahmoud (Intermediate/Classic) | | 1 | 1 | | |
| | Tenerani (N/A) | | | | | |
| | Alibhai (Classic) | | | 2 | | |
| | Turn-to (Brilliant/Intermediate) | 1 | 1 | | | |
| | War Admiral (Classic) | | | 2 | | |
| | **Dosage Profile:** | 12 | 8 | 28 | 4 | 2 |

After accounting for all 15 sires within four generations, we add the points in each column: Brilliant, Intermediate, Classic, Solid and Professional. In the example, we are left with a Dosage Profile having 12 points under Brilliant, 8 points under Intermediate, 28 points under Classic, 4 points under Solid and 2 points under Professional. The distribution is normally displayed as DP 12-8-28-4-2.

Hero's Honor's DP has representation in each of the five aptitudinal groups. This is not always the case. Quite often horses will lack representation in one or more categories and their point totals can vary widely. The 54 points out of a possible 64 assigned to Hero's Honor indicate the presence of numerous *chefs-de-race* among the 15 four-generation sires. Within the Thoroughbred population we find considerable variation in DP point totals as well as in the distribution of points in the DP. The many possible configurations lend themselves to other calculations based on the DP that capture the differences in a readily visible form. These are alternative expressions of the aptitudinal characteristics in a pedigree. In combination with the DP they provide a more complete picture of aptitudinal type.

The first of these expressions is the Dosage Index (DI). The DI is a ratio of inherited prepotent speed to stamina. It is derived first by dividing the DP into separate speed and stamina components. The speed component is defined as the Brilliant points plus the Intermediate points plus one-half the Classic points found in the DP. Similarly, the stamina component is defined as one-half the Classic points plus the Solid points plus the Professional points. In effect, we've split the DP down the middle. For Hero's Honor, the speed component is 12 plus 8 plus one-half of 28, or 34. The stamina component is one-half of 28 plus 4 plus 2, or 20. The DI is simply the ratio of the speed component over the stamina component. In this case it is 34 over 20, or 1.70.

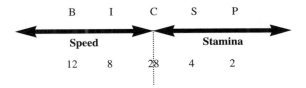

If we imagine the five aptitude groups as points spaced equally along a linear scale where Brilliant is assigned a value of +2.00, Intermediate is assigned a value +1.00, Classic is assigned a value 0.00, Solid is assigned a value of -1.00, and Professional is assigned a value of -2.00, the DP allows for the calculation of the second expression, the Center of Distribution (CD). Think of the scale as you would a seesaw where the aptitudinal groups are evenly spaced and the assigned values represent distances to the left and right of center. Now consider that the seesaw is pivoted in the middle and that the points in the DP are weights placed on the seesaw at the location corresponding to their aptitudinal group. Depending on the "weights," the seesaw will tip to the left or to the right. The CD is that position along the seesaw where the pivot must be moved to bring the system back into balance. In a sense, it is a similar to a center of gravity where all of the weighted aptitudes supplied by *chefs-de-race* in the four generations merge into a single point. A graphical representation of the concept is shown below.

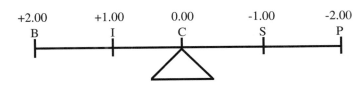

The CD is calculated by adding twice the Brilliant points plus the Intermediate points minus the Solid points minus twice the Professional points and dividing that number by the total points in the DP. For Hero's Honor, the numerator is 24 plus 8 minus 4 minus 4, or 24. The denominator is 12 plus 8 plus 28 plus 4 plus 2, or 54. The CD is then 24 divided by 54, or +0.44. In the following graphic we can see that the pivot point has moved 0.44 units to the left to rebalance the "weights."

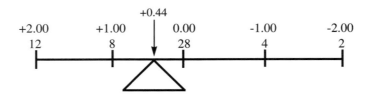

Summarizing Hero's Honor's Dosage figures, he has DP 12-8-28-4-2, DI 1.70 and CD 0.44. By themselves, these numbers mean very little. As we will see, their significance becomes clear when we compare them with the Dosage figures of other Thoroughbreds. With these calculations now available, we can evaluate runners with similar performance characteristics in an attempt to identify patterns linking aptitudinal type to track performance. For the record, Hero's Honor was a Grade 1 winner at up to 11 furlongs on the grass.

As another example of Dosage calculations we will use a horse with distinctly different aptitudinal characteristics, Mr. Greeley, whose four-generation pedigree follows. Again, *chefs-de-race* are highlighted in bold type.

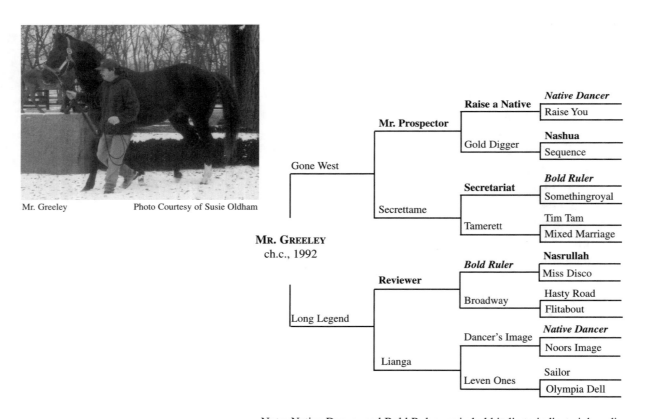

Mr. Greeley          Photo Courtesy of Susie Oldham

Note: Native Dancer and Bold Ruler are in bold italic to indicate inbreeding.

Table 6 displays the contributions of the *chefs-de-race* within four generations and the distribution of points for Mr. Greeley. In this case, the first generation sire, Gone West, is not a *chef-de-race*. There are two second-generation *chefs-de-race* (Mr. Prospector (B/C) and Reviewer (B/C)), three third-generation *chefs-de-race* (Raise a Native (B), Secretariat (I/C) and Bold Ruler (B/I)) and five fourth-generation *chefs-de-race* (Native Dancer (I/C, twice), Nashua (I), Bold Ruler (B/I) again and Nasrullah (B)).

### TABLE 6. CALCULATION OF THE DOSAGE PROFILE (DP) FOR MR. GREELEY

| Generation (Pts) | Sires (Aptitudinal Group(s)) | B | I | C | S | P |
|---|---|---|---|---|---|---|
| 1st Generation (16): | Gone West (N/A) | | | | | |
| 2nd Generation (8): | Mr. Prospector (Brilliant/Classic) | 4 | | 4 | | |
| | Reviewer (Brilliant/Classic) | 4 | | 4 | | |
| 3rd Generation (4): | Raise a Native (Brilliant) | 4 | | | | |
| | Secretariat (Intermediate/Classic) | | 2 | 2 | | |
| | Bold Ruler (Brilliant/Intermediate) | 2 | 2 | | | |
| | Dancer's Image (N/A) | | | | | |
| 4th Generation (2): | Native Dancer (Intermediate/Classic) | | 1 | 1 | | |
| | Nashua (Intermediate/Classic) | | 1 | 1 | | |
| | Bold Ruler (Brilliant/Intermediate) | 1 | 1 | | | |
| | Tim Tam (N/A) | | | | | |
| | Nasrullah (Brilliant) | 2 | | | | |
| | Hasty Road (N/A) | | | | | |
| | Native Dancer (Intermediate/Classic) | | 1 | 1 | | |
| | Sailor (N/A) | | | | | |
| | **DOSAGE PROFILE:** | 17 | 8 | 13 | 0 | 0 |

Mr. Greeley's DP 17-8-13-0-0 obviously is arranged quite differently from that of Hero's Honor. Rather than exhibiting points in all five aptitudinal groups, Mr. Greeley's DP is void of any contributions from the extremes of the stamina wing in the Solid and Professional groups. His highest representation is in the very speedy Brilliant group. Mr. Greeley's DP translates to DI 4.85 (($17 + 8 + 6.5$) / $6.5 = 31.5$ / $6.5$) and CD 1.11 (($2$ x $17$) + $8$)/($17 + 8 + 13$) = $42$ / $38$). These figures vividly contrast with those of Hero's Honor and suggest an individual of substantially different type. In fact, Mr. Greeley was a multiple graded stakes winner at six and seven furlongs, finishing second by a neck in the 1995 Breeders' Cup Sprint (Gr. 1).

| | Hero's Honor | Mr. Greeley |
|---|---|---|
| DI: | 1.70 | 4.85 |
| CD: | 0.44 | 1.11 |
| Type: | Classic distances, grass | Sprinter, dirt |

The observed contrast in type between Hero's Honor and Mr. Greeley is a dramatic example of how classification using Dosage figures can differentiate pedigrees and capture the expression of real-world performance.

A useful consequence of Dosage calculations is the ability to separate the contribution of the sire from the contribution of the dam. With a maximum of 64 possible Dosage points in a DP, 40 can come from the sire's side of the pedigree and 24 from the dam's side, the difference of 16 attributed to the fact that the direct sire himself can be a *chef-de-race*. In the case of Hero's Honor, the sire, Northern Dancer, contributes 11 Brilliant points, 7 Intermediate points, 14 Classic points, 0 Solid points and 0 Professional points, better expressed as 11-7-14-0-0. This is equivalent to DI 3.57. The dam, Glowing Tribute, contributes 1-1-14-4-2, equivalent to DI 0.69. When combined, we have Hero's Honor's previously derived DP 12-8-28-4-2 and DI 1.70. What we see from this perspective, however, is the result of breeding modest speed (DI 3.57) to strong stamina (0.69), thereby offering a deeper insight into the nature of the mating that produced Hero's Honor.

A couple of other examples show the result of breeding speed to speed and stamina to stamina. The former is represented by Gene's Lady, 1981, a high-class sprinting mare by Brilliant *chef-de-race* What a Pleasure and out of Lady T. V., by Intermediate *chef-de-race* T. V. Lark. Gene's Lady earned almost $950,000, winning stakes from ages three to six. Her Dosage figures are DP 27-15-5-3-0 and DI 8.09, obviously shifted toward great speed. She receives 25-6-4-3-0 (equivalent to DI 6.60) from What a Pleasure and 2-9-1-0-0 (equivalent to DI 21.00) from Lady T. V. In this example, breeding speed to speed produced primarily a sprinter, although on occasion Gene's Lady's class enabled her to stretch out as far as a mile and a sixteenth.

The stamina to stamina example is Bien Bien, 1989, a multiple Grade 1-winning turf performer up to a mile and three-quarters. Bien Bien is by champion Manila who contributes 5-1-10-0-6 (equivalent to DI 1.00) to Bien Bien's DP 5-3-22-6-8 and DI 0.76. He is out of Stark Winter, by Classic/Solid *chef-de-race* Graustark. Stark Winter contributes 0-2-12-6-2 (equivalent to DI 0.57). Bien Bien is clearly the product of endurance on top and endurance on the bottom and the outcome is what we would expect from a mating of this type.

For the convenience of the reader, we have provided in Appendix II the contributions of the 150 leading North American sires of 2001 to the DP of their progeny. In some cases we see a disparity between the contribution of a sire and what we know about the performance traits of his runners. This can be especially instructive when considering relatively young stallions since large differences between the Dosage figures and the real-world performance of their progeny could be a signal that we are dealing with an unacknowledged source of aptitudinal prepotence.

Take, for example, Thunder Gulch, winner of the Kentucky Derby and Belmont Stakes and champion three-year-old colt of 1995. His Dosage contribution is a modest 5-0-3-0-0, equivalent to DI 4.33. This suggests a speed orientation that contradicts reality. From just his first three crops he has sired three classic winners in North America and Australia, as well as a Breeders' Cup Distaff-G1 winner. The average winning distance of his progeny in open stakes is a long 8.76 furlongs though mid-2002. This is a longer average winning distance than found for well-known "staying" sires such as Caro, Private Account, Grey Dawn II, Unbridled or Kris S. Only time will reveal whether Thunder Gulch is a source of prepotent type, but it is certain that his progeny are outrunning his present aptitudinal contribution. Similar arguments could be made for A.P. Indy and Kingmambo, young stallions that infuse distance capability in excess of what we would expect from their Dosage contributions.

Thunder Gulch          Photo Courtesy of Martin King Sportpix

# Thunder Gulch

## DP 10-2-8-0-0, DI 4.00, CD 1.10

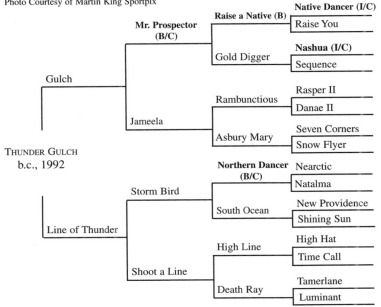

| | | | Raise a Native (B) | Native Dancer (I/C) |
| | Mr. Prospector (B/C) | | | Raise You |
| | | Gold Digger | Nashua (I/C) |
| Gulch | | | Sequence |
| | | Rambunctious | Rasper II |
| | Jameela | | Danae II |
| | | Asbury Mary | Seven Corners |
| | | | Snow Flyer |
| THUNDER GULCH b.c., 1992 | | Northern Dancer (B/C) | Nearctic |
| | Storm Bird | | Natalma |
| | | South Ocean | New Providence |
| | | | Shining Sun |
| Line of Thunder | | High Line | High Hat |
| | | | Time Call |
| | Shoot a Line | Death Ray | Tamerlane |
| | | | Luminant |

| DP Contribution | Equivalent to: | |
|---|---|---|
| Sire  8 - 2 - 6 - 0 - 0 | DI  4.33 | CD  1.13 |
| Dam  2 - 0 - 2 - 0 - 0 | DI  3.00 | CD  1.00 |

Thunder Gulch, b.c., 1992 (Gulch-Line of Thunder, by Storm Bird) annexed two-thirds of the Triple Crown despite Dosage figures suggesting better suitability as a sprinter-miler. His sire was a Breeder's Cup Sprint (G1) winner and an Eclipse champion sprinter who, not surprisingly, transmits significant speed to Thunder Gulch's DP. His dam's contribution to his DP is marginal and with a slight shift toward speed as well. However, Thunder Gulch is a good example of a horse with possible unacknowledged aptitudinal influences that contribute to his performance. The sire of his second dam is the Hyperion-line, English stallion High Line, foaled in 1972. High Line was successful on the track at up to two miles and at stud consistently sired runners capable of staying classic distances and well beyond. Among them is Shoot a Line, a dual Oaks winner and second dam of Thunder Gulch. By the late 1980's, the average winning distance of High Line's progeny was listed as 13.0 furlongs, which is long even by European standards. One could easily make a case for High Line as a source of stamina. As a third-generation sire in Thunder Gulch's pedigree, High Line would make a four point contribution to Thunder Gulch's DP, which would lower his Dosage figures into the more traditional classic range.

In our original research conducted between 1977 and 1980, we examined several categories of performance by distance, surface and age, grouping the average Dosage figures of the winners. The results are summarized in Tables 7, 8 and 9.

**TABLE 7. DOSAGE FIGURES BY DISTANCE AND SURFACE, STAKES WINNERS OF 1980**

| Race Category | Average DI | Average CD |
|---|---|---|
| Sprints on dirt (less than 8f) | 5.52 | 0.91 |
| Middle distances on dirt (8-10f) | 4.05 | 0.71 |
| Routes on dirt (greater than 10f) | 1.74 | 0.29 |
| All races on dirt | 4.62 | 0.79 |
| Sprints on grass (less than 8f) | 5.90 | 0.90 |
| Middle distances on grass (8-10f) | 4.22 | 0.70 |
| Routes on grass (greater than 10f) | 3.48 | 0.39 |
| All races on grass | 4.23 | 0.66 |
| **ALL RACES** | **4.53** | **0.76** |

**TABLE 8. DOSAGE INDEX BY AGE, STAKES WINNERS OF 1980**
**AND GRADED STAKES WINNERS OF 1978-79**

| Age | Average DI, North American SWs,1980 | Average DI, North American Graded SWs,1978-79 |
|---|---|---|
| Two-year-olds | 5.59 | 5.71 |
| Three-year-olds | 4.16 | 4.06 |
| Older horses | 4.41 | 4.07 |
| **ALL HORSES** | **4.53** | **4.30** |

Even in this relatively small study, we see obvious distinctions between juveniles and older runners, between sprinters and stayers, between dirt horse and turf horses, and even by racing era. Two-year-olds, racing primarily at sprint distances, display the higher average Dosage numbers consistent with the greater speed expressed in shorter races. That difference is not observed between three-year-olds and older runners where the average competitive distances are closer. We see similar trends among sprinters, middle-distance types and routers on both dirt and grass. Here the figures reflect the less speed and more stamina required with increasing distance. The uniformly higher figures observed for the various champions of the 1970s compared with those of the 1940s parallel what many believe is an ever-increasing infusion of speed into the Thoroughbred over time. The ability of Dosage to detect these changes makes it a powerful tool for monitoring the evolutionary trends within the breed.

## TABLE 9. DOSAGE FIGURES OF CHAMPIONS BY DECADE

| Race Category | Average DI | Average CD |
|---|---|---|
| Two-year-old colt champions (1941-1980) | 2.20 | |
| Two-year-old colt champions (1941-1950) | 1.63 | 0.15 |
| Two-year-old colt champions (1971-1980) | 2.84 | 0.84 |
| Three-year-old colt champions (1941-1980) | 1.98 | |
| Three-year-old colt champions (1941-1950) | 1.43 | 0.24 |
| Three-year-old colt champions (1971-1980) | 2.46 | 0.70 |
| Handicap champions (1942-1980) | 1.87 | |
| Handicap champions (1942-1950) | 1.52 | 0.27 |
| Handicap champions (1971-1980) | 2.65 | 0.78 |
| Sprint champions (1971-1980) | 3.85 | 0.72 |
| Grass champions (1971-1980) | 2.06 | 0.32 |
| Kentucky Derby winners (1971-1980) | 2.68 | 0.89 |
| Belmont Stakes winners (1971-1980) | 2.37 | 0.60 |

# CHAPTER 7

# Contemporary Dosage Data

Table 10 presents a more complete picture based on Dosage data accumulated between 1983 and 2001 from almost 19,000 open stakes races. We examined races of all types and arranged the data by racing category including distance, surface, age and class of race. The Table shows the number of races in each category, the average distance of the races, the average DP of the winners, the average number of points in the DP, the average Dosage Index (ADI), the average CD (ACD), the composite Dosage Index (CDI) and the composite CD (CCD). Composite figures represent the DI and CD as calculated directly from the average DP rather than the average of all the individual DIs and CDs in the sample. In a sense, the average DP describes the complete distribution of aptitudes within the entire population being examined. The composite figures also attenuate the impact of outliers, as illustrated below.

| | | | |
|---|---|---|---|
| *Horse 1:* | DP 10-7-1-0-0 | DI 35.00 | CD 1.50 |
| *Horse 2:* | DP 6-6-12-2-0 | DI 2.25 | CD 0.62 |
| *Horse 3:* | DP 2-4-12-4-2 | DI 1.00 | CD 0.00 |

*Average DP* 6.00-5.67-8.33-2.00-0.67         *Composite DI* 2.32
*Average DI* 12.75                             *Composite CD* 0.63
*Average CD* 0.71

In this example, the dramatic effect on the averages of Horse 1's DI of 35.00 and CD of 1.50 is attenuated in the composite numbers.

Table 10 clearly reveals dramatic differences among the figures within the various categories. These data provide the strongest evidence of Dosage's ability to correlate pedigree type with racetrack performance.

## Differences by Racing Surface

The average numbers for open stakes winners on dirt (DI 3.74, CD 0.77) are significantly higher than those for open stakes winners on grass (DP 2.67, CD 0.59). These results indicate that the pedigrees of the winners on the respective surfaces are configured differently from one another with regard to the specific *chefs-de-race* influencing each performance category. At the same time, note the significant difference in the average distance of the races on the main track and on turf. The dirt races at an average distance of 7.75 furlongs are over a furlong shorter than the turf races at an average distance of 8.89 furlongs. Considering that the DI and the CD reflect a ratio of inherited speed over stamina, it is entirely consistent that the higher average Dosage figures are associated with the shorter races while the lower average Dosage figures are associated with the longer races. Also note the presence of over twice the number of Dosage points in the Solid and Professional aptitudinal groups for the turf winners compared with the winners on the dirt. This raises the question of whether

47

Solid and Professional *chefs-de-race* contribute not only stamina to a pedigree, but an additional, yet undefined "turf" component as well.

### Differences by Distance Range

We observe a similar pattern here where the races are split between sprints (less than eight furlongs), middle distances (between eight and 10 furlongs) and routes (greater than 10 furlongs). As the average distance of the races in each group increases from 6.29 to 8.69 to 11.78 furlongs, the DI and CD numbers decrease proportionately and as expected. The precision of the analysis is vividly demonstrated by the patterns found within the DP itself. Note that in transitioning from sprints to middle distances to routes, the average number of points decreases in the Brilliant and Intermediate groups and increases in the Classic, Solid and Professional groups. Again, we observe the smooth shift from speed influences to stamina influences as the distances grow longer.

### Differences by Age

In the age category we find a significant difference between the figures for juveniles and those for three-year-olds and for older runners. The two-year-olds compete at an average distance that is a furlong or more shorter than the average for their older counterparts. On the other hand, the difference in average distance between three-year-olds and older runners is quite small. It should come as no surprise, then, that the Dosage figures for the juveniles are higher than those for the three-year-olds and older runners while the figures for the latter two groups are close together. Even here, though, we observe that the differences in the figures are in the right direction with the three-year-old figures being marginally higher than those for the older runners that compete at a slightly longer distance.

### Differences by Class of Race

The data indicate a direct correlation between the class of races and their average distance, with the highest-class races being the longest and the lowest-class races being the shortest. In moving from Grade 1 races through Grade 2 and Grade 3 races to listed events, the average distance declines from 9.22 furlongs to 8.61 furlongs to 8.28 furlongs to 7.64 furlongs. Consistent with this progression is the gradual increase in the Dosage figures with declining class. We also find a drop in the average point contributions in the Brilliant, Classic, Solid and Professional aptitudinal categories, resulting in a modestly lower DP point total with each successive level below Grade 1.

### Differences by Specific Distance

The final set of figures in Table 10 is for races at specific distances between five and 12 furlongs. The trends are similar to those seen in the other performance categories with the Dosage figures inversely correlating with the average distance. We can capture the significance of the differences from one distance to another using simple statistical techniques such as a Student's T-Test. This method can determine the likelihood that the figures for winners at one distance are truly different from those for winners at another distance and not simply the result of random chance. For example, we can compare the Dosage numbers for the six-furlong winners with those for the seven-furlong winners and we can establish a level of confidence that the two groups are not the same. In the analysis, we generate what is known as a P value. If the P value is less than 0.05 we can be confident that the two populations are indeed different from one another. Table 11 displays the P values resulting from a comparison of the average CD of populations at specific distances.

The results are striking. For the distances analyzed, the probability that the respective populations represented by the average CDs are the same is essentially zero, as the P values in all cases are well below 0.05. Said another way, Dosage analysis is precise enough to differentiate the pedigrees of horse populations that win at distances as little as one furlong apart in many cases. In particular, the difference observed between the winners at seven furlongs and a mile is exceptional and represents the logical break between one- and two-turn runners.

### TABLE 10. DOSAGE DATA FOR NORTH AMERICAN OPEN STAKES RACES BETWEEN 1983 AND 2001

| Category | Races | Dist. | DP | PTS | ADI | ACD | CDI | CCD |
|---|---|---|---|---|---|---|---|---|
| All races | 18617 | 8.09 | 7.88 - 4.76 - 9.59 - 1.60 - 0.91 | 24.73 | 3.42 | 0.72 | 2.39 | 0.69 |
| Dirt races | 13046 | 7.75 | 8.15 - 4.91 - 9.11 - 1.39 - 0.78 | 24.35 | 3.74 | 0.77 | 2.62 | 0.75 |
| Turf races | 5571 | 8.89 | 7.24 - 4.39 - 10.71 - 2.07 - 1.21 | 25.63 | 2.67 | 0.59 | 1.97 | 0.56 |
| <8 furlongs | 5913 | 6.29 | 8.55 - 4.90 - 8.29 - 1.18 - 0.57 | 23.48 | 4.34 | 0.86 | 2.99 | 0.84 |
| 8-10 furlongs | 11706 | 8.69 | 7.63 - 4.72 - 10.09 - 1.70 - 1.00 | 25.15 | 3.07 | 0.67 | 2.24 | 0.65 |
| >10 furlongs | 998 | 11.78 | 6.81 - 4.29 - 11.46 - 2.83 - 1.82 | 27.21 | 2.12 | 0.44 | 1.62 | 0.42 |
| 2-year-olds | 2474 | 7.17 | 8.11 - 4.75 - 8.88 - 1.28 - 0.65 | 23.67 | 3.91 | 0.80 | 2.72 | 0.78 |
| 3-year-olds | 5393 | 8.16 | 7.92 - 4.78 - 9.70 - 1.54 - 0.86 | 24.80 | 3.41 | 0.73 | 2.42 | 0.70 |
| Older runners | 10750 | 8.27 | 7.81 - 4.74 - 9.70 - 1.70 - 0.99 | 24.94 | 3.32 | 0.69 | 2.31 | 0.67 |
| G1 races | 2004 | 9.22 | 8.35 - 5.03 - 11.29 - 1.89 - 1.22 | 27.78 | 2.93 | 0.64 | 2.17 | 0.63 |
| G2 races | 2675 | 8.61 | 8.06 - 4.77 - 10.60 - 1.79 - 1.04 | 26.26 | 3.16 | 0.67 | 2.23 | 0.65 |
| G3 races | 4123 | 8.28 | 7.90 - 4.72 - 10.01 - 1.65 - 0.93 | 25.21 | 3.27 | 0.70 | 2.32 | 0.67 |
| Listed races | 9815 | 7.64 | 7.73 - 4.71 - 8.79 - 1.46 - 0.80 | 23.49 | 3.66 | 0.75 | 2.53 | 0.73 |
| 5.50 furlongs | 353 | 5.50 | 8.08 - 4.69 - 7.94 - 1.29 - 0.56 | 22.56 | 4.56 | 0.84 | 2.88 | 0.82 |
| 6.00 furlongs | 2903 | 6.00 | 8.64 - 4.93 - 7.99 - 1.09 - 0.49 | 23.14 | 4.65 | 0.90 | 3.15 | 0.87 |
| 6.50 furlongs | 782 | 6.50 | 8.04 - 4.50 - 7.92 - 1.25 - 0.59 | 22.30 | 4.04 | 0.84 | 2.85 | 0.81 |
| 7.00 furlongs | 1566 | 7.00 | 8.91 - 5.21 - 9.07 - 1.28 - 0.69 | 25.17 | 4.00 | 0.83 | 2.87 | 0.81 |
| 8.00 furlongs | 2091 | 8.00 | 7.92 - 4.73 - 10.07 - 1.69 - 0.87 | 25.28 | 3.21 | 0.70 | 2.33 | 0.68 |
| 8.32 furlongs | 286 | 8.32 | 7.91 - 4.75 - 8.66 - 1.49 - 1.10 | 23.92 | 3.44 | 0.73 | 2.45 | 0.71 |
| 8.50 furlongs | 4491 | 8.50 | 7.63 - 4.72 - 9.84 - 1.61 - 0.94 | 24.75 | 3.18 | 0.69 | 2.31 | 0.67 |
| 9.00 furlongs | 3768 | 9.00 | 7.46 - 4.70 - 10.20 - 1.73 - 1.01 | 25.10 | 2.97 | 0.65 | 2.20 | 0.63 |
| 9.50 furlongs | 253 | 9.50 | 7.28 - 4.54 - 10.52 - 2.30 - 1.28 | 25.92 | 2.58 | 0.56 | 1.93 | 0.55 |
| 10.00 furlongs | 813 | 10.00 | 7.72 - 4.85 - 11.37 - 2.00 - 1.54 | 27.48 | 2.60 | 0.57 | 1.98 | 0.55 |
| 11.00 furlongs | 394 | 11.00 | 6.96 - 4.30 - 11.89 - 2.83 - 1.70 | 27.68 | 2.10 | 0.45 | 1.64 | 0.43 |
| 12.00 furlongs | 503 | 12.00 | 6.68 - 4.25 - 11.24 - 2.87 - 1.84 | 26.88 | 2.06 | 0.42 | 1.60 | 0.41 |

### TABLE 11. STATISTICAL ANALYSIS COMPARING THE AVERAGE CD AT DIFFERENT DISTANCES

| Distances Being Compared | P Value |
|---|---|
| 6f and 7f | 0.000000009 |
| 7f and 8f | 0.0000000000000000000003 |
| 8f and 9f | 0.000008 |
| 9f and 10f | 0.00004 |
| 10f and 12f | 0.00000002 |

# CHAPTER 8

# The Fundamental Relationship Between Dosage Figures and Distance

Plotting the average DIs and average CDs listed in Table 10 against the corresponding average distance for each performance category affords the graphical outputs shown in Charts 2 and 3.

**CHART 2. AVERAGE DI VS. AVERAGE DISTANCE FOR RACING CATEGORIES IN TABLE 10**

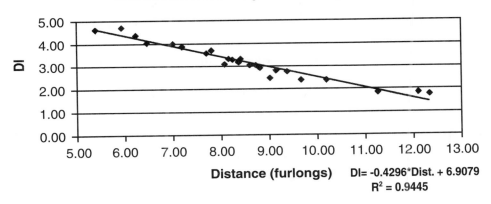

**Average DI vs. Distance**
**North American Open Stakes, 1983-2001**

DI= -0.4296*Dist. + 6.9079
$R^2 = 0.9445$

**CHART 3. AVERAGE CD VS. AVERAGE DISTANCE FOR RACING CATEGORIES IN TABLE 10**

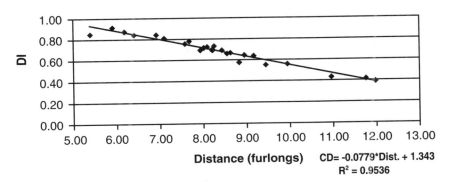

**Average CD vs. Distance**
**North American Open Stakes, 1983-2001**

CD= -0.0779*Dist. + 1.343
$R^2 = 0.9536$

Subjecting the data to the statistical technique called linear regression confirms that both the DI and the CD values are inversely related to the distance over the range from five to twelve furlongs. This relationship is easily visible in the trend lines generated from the data and which run from the upper left to the lower right. In other words, both the DI and the CD decrease as the distances increase. It is also noteworthy that virtually all of the data points fall very close to the straight line created by the regression. This is significant because the closeness of the individual data points to the line is a measure of the strength of the correlation. The R-squared values on the charts quantify the correlations. If every data point fell directly on the linear regression line, R-squared would be exactly 1.0000. The closer R-squared is to 1.0000, the better the fit.

In Chart 2, the R-squared value of 0.9445 indicates that more than 94 percent of the variability in DI (or aptitudinal type) is explained by changes in distance. The result is even better in Chart 3 where more than 95 percent of the variability in CD (an alternative expression of aptitudinal type) is explained by those same distance changes. The remaining variability is attributable to other, undefined factors. It is evident that despite Varola's insistence that no such relationship exists in his methodology, the correlation between modern Dosage methodology and the distance of races is extremely strong. Furthermore, Charts 2 and 3, in their display of the effects of distance on aptitudinal type, provide the most definitive graphical expression of the contemporary Dosage model.

The generality of the model is captured in Chart 4. It breaks down the CD vs. distance relationship even further by displaying the correlations within each separate performance category.

### CHART 4. THE DOSAGE MODEL APPLIED TO EACH RACING CATEGORY

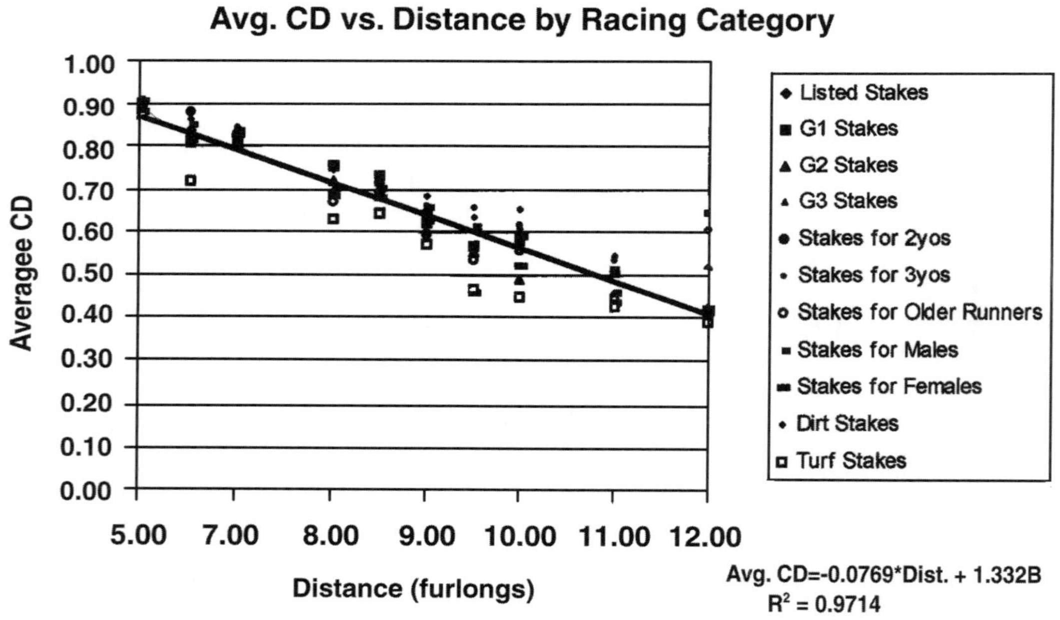

**Avg. CD vs. Distance by Racing Category**

Legend:
- ◆ Listed Stakes
- ■ G1 Stakes
- ▲ G2 Stakes
- ▲ G3 Stakes
- ● Stakes for 2yos
- • Stakes for 3yos
- ○ Stakes for Older Runners
- ▪ Stakes for Males
- ➡ Stakes for Females
- ◆ Dirt Stakes
- ▫ Turf Stakes

X-axis: Distance (furlongs)
Y-axis: Averagee CD

Avg. CD=-0.0769*Dist. + 1.332B
$R^2 = 0.9714$

Every data set follows the same trend of higher CD values at the shorter end of the distance spectrum to lower CD values at the longer end. The consistent patterns confirm a fundamental relationship between the aptitudinal type of a pedigree and its correlation with distance suitability. This is true regardless of age, sex, surface or class of race. The only data point that deviates appreciably is that for three-year-olds at a mile and a half, where the average CD is somewhat higher than the model suggests. The reason for this is unclear, although the number of races at 12 furlongs for three-year-olds is the smallest found in any category in which there are mile and a half races. It could be that the relatively small sample size is having an effect. On the other hand, the deviation may point to an inherent pedigree property of three-year-olds racing the marathon distance. It may well be the result implies that American three-year-olds are not ideally suited as a group to mile and a half racing, although certainly we have seen many individuals that are. If we plot the average CD vs. distance for three-year-old races, the chart (Chart 5) displays a trend line (solid line) that follows the model very well through ten furlongs and than flattens out. Recognizing that the trend line provides a graphical overview of the aptitudinal profile of the population, one could argue that, apart from the performances by exceptions like Secretariat or A.P. Indy or Easy Goer or Point Given, most mile and a half races for three-year-olds are won by horses better suited to shorter distances. On the other hand, the trend line for older runners (dashed line) as seen on Chart 5 fits the general model very well, indicating that older runners successful at 12 furlongs come from a different part of the population in terms of pedigree and may be later maturing.

### CHART 5. THREE-YEAR-OLDS VS. OLDER RUNNERS

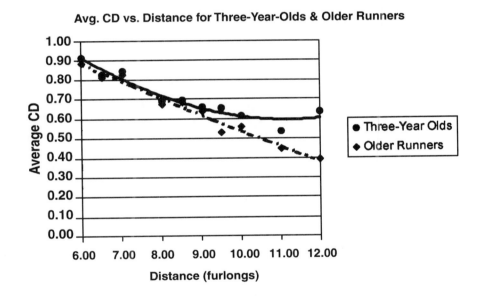

**Avg. CD vs. Distance for Three-Year-Olds & Older Runners**

# CHAPTER 9

# The Relationship Between the Dosage Index (DI) and the Center of Distribution (CD): Dosage Profile Patterns

The core of contemporary Dosage methodology is the Dosage Profile, or DP. It is the series of five numbers that summarize the aptitudinal contributions from *chefs-de-race* in the first four generations of a pedigree. Quite often, much useful information can be derived from the DP alone. For example, and as we will see shortly, regardless of the DI or the CD, a horse with a DP having double-digit representation in the Brilliant group is often a candidate to win sprints. To illustrate the main point, among horses with a DI of exactly 3.00, those with at least 10 points in the Brilliant category of their DP have won 39 percent of their races in sprints. Those with less than 10 points in the Brilliant category have won only 33 percent of their races in sprints.

Not surprisingly, a large component of inherited speed is an asset in shorter races. Although the average DI is the same for both groups, we do see real differences in the average CD. The first group, with at least 10 Brilliant points in their DP, has an average CD of 0.89. The second group, with less than 10 points in their DP, has an average CD of 0.81. The principle here is that the relationship between DI and CD is the direct consequence of how the aptitudinal points are distributed within the DP.

There are numerous examples demonstrating the critical nature of point distribution within the DP. As a basis for analysis we have used our database of open stakes races with an added purse of at least $50,000. Table 12 presents several variations on how DP configuration affects average winning distance (AWD), the percentage of wins in sprints (%SPR) and the percentage of wins on the grass (%TURF) for the population falling within each DP distribution category.

The first column in Table 12 lists the general category of the pattern. For example, "Dominant Aptitude" refers to the situation in which the most points are found in one particular aptitudinal group; Brilliant (B), Intermediate (I), Classic (C), Solid (S) or Professional (P). This category is subsequently divided according to which aptitudinal group dominates and shows how Dosage figures and performance characteristics can vary from pattern to pattern. The next category focuses on the Brilliant group exclusively and shows the effects of total Brilliant points in the DP. The following category does the same for the Classic group and so on.

The second column displays the actual DP patterns themselves and shows the relationships among the various elements within the DP. For example, the first pattern under Dominant Aptitude is designated B>I, C, S or P, indicating a DP in which there are more points found in the Brilliant category than in any other. Similarly, under Wing Breeding, B, P>I, C or S means that more points are found in both the Brilliant and Professional categories than in Intermediate, Classic or Solid.

Next, %SWs indicates what percentage of the general population of open stakes winners since 1983 have that particular DP pattern. This is followed by columns showing the average winning distance (AWD), average points in each of the aptitudinal groups (or average DP), the average DI (ADI), the average CD (ACD), the average total points in the DP, the %SPR and the %TURF for stakes winners representing the pattern.

The bottom row highlights the data for all of the stakes winners in the database and may be considered the average for the breed, suitable as a standard for comparing the various DP patterns.

Within the "Dominant Aptitude" category we observe dramatic and consistent trends in the data. Stakes winners whose DPs have their highest representation in the Brilliant group also have the lowest AWD and %TURF as well as the highest %SPR. As we proceed through the speed/stamina spectrum where the most points in the DP are located, successively, in Intermediate, Classic, Solid and Professional, we find an increasing AWD and %TURF and a decreasing %SPR.

Similarly, the ADI and ACD decrease regularly as the emphasis shifts from speed to endurance in the pedigrees. These observations are expected, as we have shown earlier that lower Dosage figures are consistent with increased stamina resulting in more wins at route distances and greater suitability to turf. In fact, horses with a DP where the most points are in the Professional aptitude group have the longest AWD (9.00f), highest %TURF (52.8 percent) and co-lowest %SPR (14.9 percent) of any in the Table. They constitute a small percentage of the population (0.9 percent), but one can be confident that when they show up they will be ideally suited to long-distance grass races. We may also note that between 80 percent and 85 percent of all the stakes winners are characterized by a DP with the most points in either the Brilliant or Classic category.

Of all the races in the database, 32 percent are sprints, and the highest absolute percentage of sprint winners is found among those runners having a DP with a "down-the-ladder" pattern. This is a term describing a DP distribution with more Brilliant than Intermediate points, more Intermediate than Classic points, more Classic than Solid points, and more Solid than Professional points. DP 8-6-4-2-0 fits the definition.

Horses with a "down-the-ladder" pattern win 46 percent of their races at less than a mile, a significantly higher percentage than for the entire population. They also express their speed orientation with a double-digit average of Brilliant points. At the same time, they are the least successful on grass, winning only 18 percent of their races on that surface, well below the database average of 30 percent.

Similarly, horses with zero points in either the Solid or the Professional category account for just over a third of the population and win 40 percent of their races at sprint distances. This, too, exceeds the percentage found for all stakes winners in the database. However, when these "double zero" horses also show more points in the Classic category than in the Brilliant and Intermediate categories together, their %SPR drops below the average to 24 percent while their %TURF shifts from well below average (23 percent) to substantially above (38 percent).

Thus, the effect of "Dominant Classicity" is profound. The term Dominant Classicity was coined by Leon Rasmussen, former "Bloodlines" columnist for *Daily Racing Form*, to describe a DP in which the Classic points exceed the total number of points in all of the other categories combined. This is a situation found among only 18 percent of the population and its effect on performance can be dramatic, as noted for the "double zero" horses in particular.

The overall impact of high point totals in the Classic category cannot be overstated, especially in the context of distance ability. Runners with at least 20 points in Classic (just 5 percent of the population) have the lowest percentage of wins in sprints (15 percent) and, except for the very small group with the most points in Professional, the highest percentage of wins on grass (48 percent). Their AWD of 8.76 furlongs is exceeded only by the 9.00 furlong AWD of that same group dominated by Professional points.

At the other end of the distance spectrum are horses with double digits in the Brilliant category. These horses run shorter than average with %SPR values in the mid-30 to mid-40 percent range depending on how many points are present. Not surprisingly, their %TURF figures are below average, spanning the mid-20 to high-teen percent range. When double digits in Brilliant are combined with double digits in Classic (17 percent of the population), the effect on distance is dramatically different as the %SPR drops to 22 percent, far below the average. However, the %TURF increases only to a small degree and remains marginally below average at 28 percent. Apparently, the negative effect of a large Brilliant contribution on turf performance is significant and cannot easily be overcome by an equally large Classic influence.

One of the more unusual DP patterns is that in which no points are present in either the Classic, Solid or Professional groups - a "no stamina" pattern. This is a rare situation, occurring in just 1% of stakes winners. However, the pattern is characterized by the shortest AWD and the highest ACD in Table 12, consistent with an absence of stamina contributions. It has associated with it the third highest %SPR behind "down-the-ladder" DP types and runners with 16 to 20 Brilliant points in their DP, as well as a below average %TURF. Most notable is the absence of a DI figure. This results from the fact that division by zero is a forbidden mathematical operation. A DP with no points in Classic, Solid or Professional, must have a denominator of zero in the DI calculation. Since dividing by zero is not allowed, there is no such thing as a DI in those cases. For descriptive purposes only, no DI occasionally has been referred to as a DI of infinity. This is not mathematically correct, although it does convey the image of a DP devoid of aptitudinally prepotent stamina.

TABLE 12. THE EFFECTS OF VARIOUS DP POINT DISTRIBUTIONS ON PERFORMANCE TRAITS

| Category | Pattern | %SWs | AWD | B | I | C | S | P | ADI | ACD | PTS | %SPR | %TURF |
|---|---|---|---|---|---|---|---|---|---|---|---|---|---|
| Dominant Aptitude | B>I, C, S or P | 32.6% | 7.73 | 11.00 | 4.51 | 5.91 | 1.32 | 0.58 | 5.40 | 1.06 | 23.33 | 42.5% | 22.1% |
| | I>B, C, S or P | 6.0% | 7.94 | 5.35 | 9.45 | 5.98 | 1.09 | 0.53 | 4.84 | 0.82 | 22.40 | 35.5% | 23.5% |
| | C>B, I, S or P | 49.2% | 8.32 | 6.51 | 4.42 | 13.22 | 1.61 | 1.02 | 2.13 | 0.52 | 26.78 | 24.8% | 35.7% |
| | S>B, I, C or P | 1.7% | 8.74 | 4.51 | 3.10 | 4.60 | 8.86 | 0.60 | 0.84 | 0.04 | 21.67 | 15.0% | 46.7% |
| | P>B, I, C or S | 0.9% | 9.00 | 4.22 | 2.53 | 5.19 | 1.17 | 11.37 | 0.65 | -0.56 | 24.48 | 14.9% | 52.8% |
| Brilliant Points | B<=5 | 32.1% | 8.27 | 3.41 | 3.88 | 8.70 | 1.59 | 1.10 | 2.39 | 0.45 | 18.68 | 26.9% | 34.7% |
| | B>5, B<=10 | 43.2% | 8.08 | 7.82 | 4.68 | 9.52 | 1.54 | 0.86 | 3.52 | 0.77 | 24.42 | 31.4% | 29.6% |
| | B>10, B<=15 | 19.7% | 7.92 | 12.50 | 5.82 | 10.75 | 1.62 | 0.73 | 4.40 | 0.94 | 31.42 | 37.7% | 25.4% |
| | B>15, B<=20 | 3.7% | 7.71 | 17.39 | 6.82 | 10.93 | 1.48 | 0.68 | 5.51 | 1.08 | 37.30 | 45.9% | 18.3% |
| | B>20 | 1.3% | 7.85 | 23.42 | 6.88 | 12.78 | 3.50 | 1.06 | 4.54 | 1.03 | 47.63 | 36.4% | 19.9% |
| Classic Points | C<=5 | 26.4% | 7.84 | 7.26 | 4.01 | 3.20 | 1.43 | 0.64 | 5.69 | 0.94 | 16.54 | 39.8% | 25.1% |
| | C>5, C<=10 | 35.7% | 8.01 | 7.70 | 4.67 | 7.94 | 1.50 | 0.87 | 3.06 | 0.72 | 22.68 | 33.6% | 26.8% |
| | C>10, C<=15 | 23.1% | 8.22 | 8.09 | 5.08 | 12.78 | 1.58 | 1.03 | 2.39 | 0.60 | 28.56 | 27.5% | 33.5% |
| | C>15, C<=20 | 9.9% | 8.43 | 8.47 | 5.42 | 17.73 | 2.09 | 1.23 | 2.02 | 0.49 | 34.95 | 22.0% | 36.7% |
| | C>20 | 4.9% | 8.76 | 10.29 | 6.44 | 24.67 | 2.27 | 1.48 | 1.95 | 0.47 | 45.15 | 14.9% | 47.6% |
| High Brilliant/Classic Points | B>10, C>10 | 16.5% | 8.10 | 13.01 | 5.94 | 15.37 | 1.63 | 0.92 | 2.89 | 0.79 | 36.87 | 22.2% | 28.1% |
| "Down-the-Ladder" Pattern | B>I>C>S>P | 3.1% | 7.71 | 12.33 | 7.51 | 4.83 | 2.06 | 0.11 | 5.34 | 1.12 | 26.84 | 46.0% | 18.2% |
| "Double Zero" Pattern | S=0, P=0 | 34.4% | 7.77 | 7.78 | 4.57 | 8.59 | 0.00 | 0.00 | 5.33 | 0.99 | 20.93 | 40.3% | 23.1% |
| "No Stamina" Pattern | C=0, S=0, P=0 | 1.0% | 7.67 | 6.42 | 2.97 | 0.00 | 0.00 | 0.00 | | 1.68 | 9.39 | 44.7% | 27.9% |
| Points in All Five Groups | B, I, C, S, P all>0 | 16.5% | 8.47 | 7.75 | 4.95 | 11.51 | 3.29 | 2.61 | 1.79 | 0.38 | 30.10 | 22.0% | 37.0% |
| Dominant Classicity | S=0, P=0, C>(B+I) | 7.0% | 8.25 | 5.57 | 3.60 | 14.47 | 0.00 | 0.00 | 2.27 | 0.61 | 23.63 | 24.4% | 38.4% |
| | C>(B+I+S+P) | 17.8% | 8.41 | 5.45 | 3.42 | 16.05 | 1.14 | 0.75 | 1.82 | 0.43 | 26.81 | 21.6% | 40.1% |
| Total Points | PTS<=10 | 6.7% | 7.95 | 3.04 | 1.75 | 2.70 | 0.44 | 0.35 | 4.14 | 0.82 | 8.28 | 34.7% | 28.8% |
| | PTS>10, <=20 | 31.3% | 7.90 | 5.81 | 3.36 | 5.96 | 0.93 | 0.58 | 4.14 | 0.78 | 16.63 | 36.9% | 25.7% |
| | PTS>20, <=30 | 38.7% | 8.12 | 8.22 | 4.96 | 9.96 | 1.68 | 0.92 | 3.18 | 0.70 | 25.75 | 30.6% | 30.9% |
| | PTS>30, <=40 | 16.5% | 8.31 | 10.45 | 6.43 | 14.19 | 2.45 | 1.37 | 2.69 | 0.64 | 34.89 | 26.7% | 32.7% |
| | PTS>40, <=50 | 4.8% | 8.50 | 13.21 | 8.57 | 18.36 | 3.25 | 1.65 | 2.62 | 0.63 | 45.03 | 23.0% | 38.8% |
| | PTS>50 | 1.9% | 8.37 | 15.83 | 9.59 | 23.77 | 3.18 | 2.27 | 2.47 | 0.61 | 54.64 | 26.4% | 36.1% |
| "Wing" Breeding | B, P>I, C or S | 0.6% | 8.45 | 7.61 | 2.45 | 2.87 | 0.36 | 7.45 | 1.51 | 0.18 | 20.74 | 26.9% | 42.0% |
| | ALL | | 8.09 | 7.88 | 4.75 | 9.59 | 1.59 | 0.91 | 3.42 | 0.72 | 24.72 | 31.8% | 29.9% |

# Kelso

## DP 2-2-27-6-1, CD 0.05

Kelso    Photo Courtesy of the Thoroughbred Times

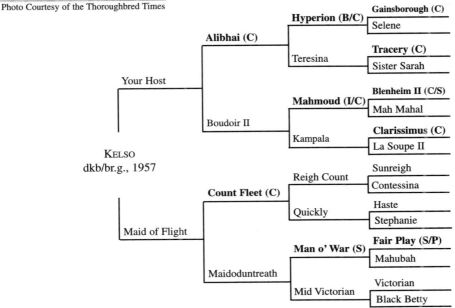

KELSO
dkb/br.g., 1957

- Your Host
  - Alibhai (C)
    - Hyperion (B/C)
      - Gainsborough (C)
      - Selene
    - Teresina
      - Tracery (C)
      - Sister Sarah
  - Boudoir II
    - Mahmoud (I/C)
      - Blenheim II (C/S)
      - Mah Mahal
    - Kampala
      - Clarissimus (C)
      - La Soupe II
- Maid of Flight
  - Count Fleet (C)
    - Reigh Count
      - Sunreigh
      - Contessina
    - Quickly
      - Haste
      - Stephanie
  - Maidoduntreath
    - Man o' War (S)
      - Fair Play (S/P)
      - Mahubah
    - Mid Victorian
      - Victorian
      - Black Betty

### DP Contribution          Equivalent to:
Sire  2 - 2 - 19 - 1 - 0     DI  1.29   CD   0.21
Dam  0 - 0 -  8 - 5 - 1      DI  0.40   CD  -0.50

Five-time Horse of the Year Kelso, dkb/br.g., 1957 (Your Host-Maid of Flight, by Count Fleet) is the product of breeding classic stamina to extreme stamina. The result is a fairly well balanced DP 2-2-27-6-1, DI 0.85 and CD –0.05. This pattern is consistent with five consecutive victories in the two-mile Jockey Club Gold Cup between 1960 and 1964. His American record of 3:19.1 for two miles, set in 1964, still stands. Although superior on dirt, Kelso also won on the grass at distances up to a mile and a half. His performance correlates well with the Dominant Classicity of his DP and the significant representation in its Solid-Professional wing. A winner on class at sprint distances as a two-year-old and early three-year-old, after his initial start at four he never again won a sprint in four tries, even at the allowance level. Showing the versatility often associated with Dominant Classicity, Kelso could win from the front, while pressing the lead, or from far back.

# Ridgewood Pearl

## DP 0-0-0-0-0, DI (none), CD (none)

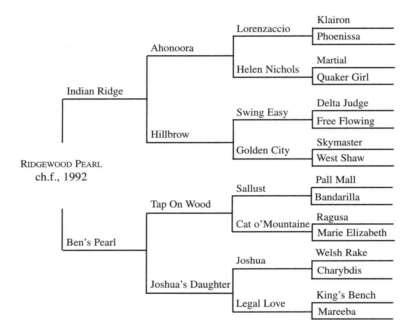

RIDGEWOOD PEARL
ch.f., 1992

| | DP Contribution | Equivalent to: |
|---|---|---|
| Sire | 0 - 0 - 0 - 0 - 0 | DI (none)  CD (none) |
| Dam | 0 - 0 - 0 - 0 - 0 | DI (none)  CD (none) |

Ridgewood Pearl, ch.f., 1992 (Indian Ridge-Ben's Pearl, by Tap On Wood) was a multiple Grade/Group 1-winning turf miler, winning the Breeders' Cup Mile and the Irish 1000 Guineas in 1992. She is unusual in not having any *chefs-de-race* appearing within her first four generations, a pattern found in only one other North American graded stakes winner. Consequently, Ridgewood Pearl has neither a DI nor a CD figure because of the mathematically forbidden operation of dividing by zero during the Dosage calculations. Nevertheless, there is no implication that Ridgewood Pearl lacks prepotent aptitudinal influences. In this case, her pedigree is relatively obscure for a contemporary American stakes winner, with few of her close up ancestors having generated a consistent pattern of data in American racing. This pedigree illustrates the opportunity for internationalizing Dosage research, a process that has begun but still has a long way to go.

The total points in a DP also correlate with performance type. First, by grouping DP point totals according to ranges of 0 to10, 11 to 20, 21 to 30, 31 to 40, 41 to 50, and 51 to a possible maximum of 64, we can observe how the point totals are distributed within the population. We can also identify several major differences and trends.

Relatively few horses (6.7 percent) have 10 or fewer DP points and an equal number have over 40. Most horses fall within the 11 to 40 range with 31.3 percent from 11 to 20, 38.7 percent from 21 to 30 and 16.5 percent from 31 to 40. As the point total increases, the ADI and ACD decrease, suggesting that more DP points enhance the probability of staying a route of ground.

For example, runners with 20 or fewer DP points have an AWD between 7.9 and 8.0 furlongs. Those with greater than 40 points have an AWD from 8.4 to 8.5 furlongs. Not surprisingly, the lower point total runners (with 20 points or less) have a higher than average %SPR (35-37 percent) and a lower than average %TURF (26-29 percent). At the other end of the point spectrum (i.e., runners with more than 40 points) we find the reverse is true. Here the horses have a lower than average %SPR (23-26 percent) and a higher than average %TURF (36-39 percent).

Table 10 showed that DP point totals also vary progressively by grade of race, with Grade 1 winners having the highest average and listed stakes winners having the lowest. This highlights the issue of whether more points in a DP correlate with higher potential class. On the one hand we have a correlation between class and points, and on other, between winning distance and points. Consequently there is a similar correlation between class and winning distance.

These data are reproduced in Table 13. The difficulty arises when trying to isolate the true cause and effect relationship. Is it distance and points or class and points?

**TABLE 13. DP POINT VARIATIONS BY CLASS OF RACE AND DISTANCE OF RACE**

| Class | Distance | Points | Distance | Points |
|-------|----------|--------|----------|--------|
| G1 | 9.22 | 27.78 | 12.00 | 26.88 |
| G2 | 8.61 | 26.26 | 11.00 | 27.68 |
| G3 | 8.28 | 25.21 | 10.00 | 27.48 |
| Ungraded | 7.64 | 23.49 | 9.50 | 25.92 |
| | | | 9.00 | 25.10 |
| | | | 8.50 | 24.75 |
| | | | 8.32 | 23.92 |
| | | | 8.00 | 25.28 |
| | | | 7.00 | 25.17 |
| | | | 6.50 | 22.30 |
| | | | 6.00 | 23.14 |
| | | | 5.50 | 22.56 |

One approach to the problem is to isolate each class of race and observe how point totals are distributed within that class. As we have seen in Table 12, the distributions by point total range have already been determined for the population at large. The analogous distributions by racing class are presented in Table 14.

|  | Class of Race | | | | |
| Points | G1 | G2 | G3 | Listed | All |
| --- | --- | --- | --- | --- | --- |
| 0-10 | 5.1% | 5.6% | 6.2% | 7.6% | 6.7% |
| 11-20 | 22.7% | 27.6% | 29.8% | 34.6% | 31.3% |
| 21-30 | 37.2% | 38.2% | 39.0% | 39.0% | 38.7% |
| 31-40 | 22.9% | 18.6% | 17.5% | 14.2% | 16.5% |
| 41-50 | 8.1% | 7.0% | 5.6% | 3.3% | 4.8% |
| 50-64 | 4.0% | 3.1% | 1.8% | 1.2% | 1.9% |

Decreasing class

On the surface the distributions are similar, having a maximum between 21 and 30 points and falling away as one shifts to lower or higher point totals. However, there are some subtle trends that differentiate the classes of race and that provide useful clues. Note, for example, that the percentages increase smoothly in the 0 to 10 and 11 to 20 point ranges with a decrease in class. By contrast, the percentages decrease just as smoothly in the 41 to 50 and 50 to 64 point ranges with a decrease in class. The result is that we observe more runners with lower point totals in the lower-class races and more runners with higher point totals in the higher-class races. These patterns are displayed in Chart 6.

CHART 6. DP POINT TOTAL RANGES BY RACING CLASS

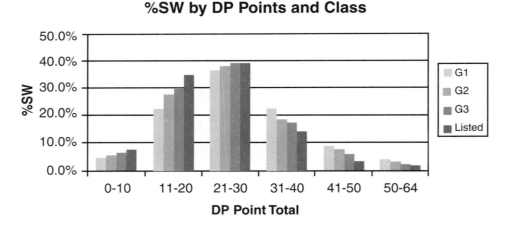

The skewed nature of the distributions is readily apparent when the distribution data are presented as in Chart 7. Here the shift toward higher point totals as the class of race increases is unmistakable. Most important, we do not find the same smooth transitions in point totals at comparable distances between seven furlongs and ten furlongs. The point range distribution data at seven, eight, eight and one half, nine and ten furlongs are displayed in Table 15 followed by a graphical representation of the distributions in Chart 8. Regardless of distance, the distributions tend to overlap more closely. There is no skewing of the distributions with distance as seen with racing class. This difference in behavior suggests the relationship between Dosage points and class is stronger than the relationship between Dosage points and distance. That total points do increase with distance may be more a consequence of the fact that higher-class races tend to be run at longer distances.

**CHART 7. DP POINT TOTAL DISTRIBUTIONS BY RACING CLASS**

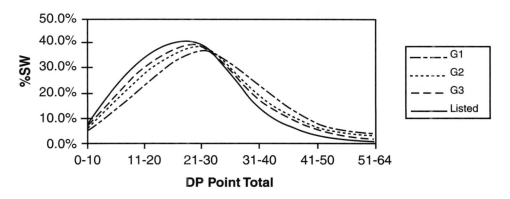

**TABLE 15. PERCENT OF WINNERS WITHIN DP POINT TOTAL RANGES BY DISTANCE**

| Pts | Distance (furlongs) | | | | |
| | 7.00 | 8.00 | 8.50 | 9.00 | 10.00 |
|---|---|---|---|---|---|
| 0-10 | 5.9% | 6.7% | 6.6% | 6.9% | 4.1% |
| 11-20 | 32.6% | 30.2% | 30.0% | 28.8% | 26.0% |
| 21-30 | 37.5% | 38.4% | 40.5% | 39.3% | 37.5% |
| 31-40 | 16.2% | 16.5% | 16.5% | 18.2% | 20.5% |
| 41-50 | 5.2% | 5.5% | 5.0% | 4.7% | 7.9% |
| 51-64 | 2.7% | 2.7% | 1.4% | 2.0% | 4.1% |

**CHART 8. DP POINT TOTAL DISTRIBUTIONS BY DISTANCE**

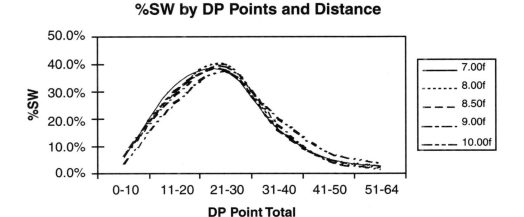

The observed relationship between DP points and racing class is highly linear, with the distance increasing by 21 percent from listed stakes to Grade 1 stakes and the DP point totals increasing by 18 percent. The extraordinary degree of linearity is expressed in the R-squared value approaching 0.999 as shown in Chart 9. We may conclude that more points in a DP imply higher class within the general population. Since the difference between listed stakes winners and Grade 1 stakes winners is on the order of 20 percent, the effect is not a dramatic one, yet appears to be real. We can readily explain the phenomenon by recalling that DP point totals capture both the position and number of *chefs-de-race* in a four-generation pedigree.

**CHART 9. THE LINEAR RELATIONSHIP BETWEEN DP POINT TOTALS AND RACING CLASS**

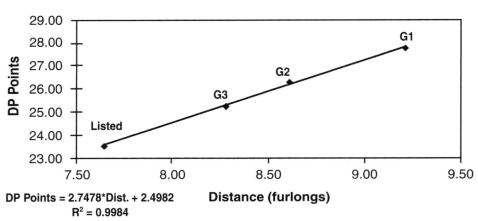

**DP Points vs. Class of Race**

DP Points = 2.7478*Dist. + 2.4982
$R^2 = 0.9984$

Another aspect of point totals directly relates to the accuracy of the resultant Dosage figures. Of particular interest are those cases where the DP point total is 10 or less. Some refer to these small point totals as "trivial" points. It has been suggested that when the point total in a DP is very low, the correlation between the Dosage figures and performance is compromised.

To test this idea, we have determined how well Dosage figures derived from DPs with 10 or less points fit the established Dosage model relating those figures to distance. Chart 10 presents the data for two groups. One is for stakes winners encompassing all DP point totals. The other is for stakes winners with "trivial" point totals as defined earlier. The correlation examined is between the average CD of those stakes winners and their average winning distance. The distance range used is between six and nine furlongs only. The limited distance range is necessary to ensure a large enough sample size for the stakes winners with low DP point totals. Since these horses constitute only 6.7 percent of the population, there are but a few examples of such stakes winners below six furlongs and beyond nine furlongs.

The obvious result is that stakes winners with "trivial" DP point totals do follow the general Dosage model to the extent that decreasing average CD values correlate with increasing distance in linear fashion. However, although the correlation is good, it is not as strong as it is for the general population of stakes winners. This is seen in the lower R-squared value of 0.7278 for the low point total stakes winners compared with the R-squared value of 0.9644 for all stakes winners. There is also a slight shift toward a higher average CD at each distance. Nevertheless, the data show that Dosage figures derived from DPs with low point totals cannot be arbitrarily dismissed even if not quite as accurate as those derived from DPs with more total points.

CHART 10. "TRIVIAL" DP POINTS AND AVERAGE WINNING DISTANCE

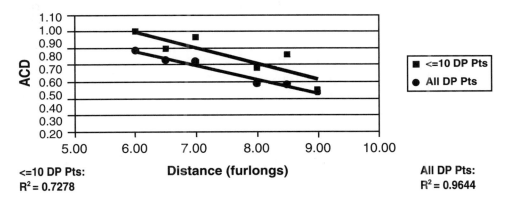

**DP Points and the Relationship Between Average CD and Average Winning Distance**

<=10 DP Pts:
$R^2 = 0.7278$

All DP Pts:
$R^2 = 0.9644$

With regard to the relationship between performance in sprints and on grass, Table 12 suggests that in those cases where DP patterns correlate with high %SPR figures, the associated %TURF figures tend to be low, and vice versa. For example, horses with the most points in the Brilliant category display %SPR and %TURF values of 42.5 percent and 22.1 percent, respectively. Conversely, horses with the most points in the Professional category display an opposite pattern of 14.9 %SPR and 52.8 %TURF. This phenomenon appears to be general and applies across all DP distributions.

Chart 11 shows the relationship in graphical terms for all of the DP configurations listed in Table 12. The associated trend lines are virtually mirror images, indicating that sprinting ability and an affinity for the turf are inversely related. The correlations are also very strong as reflected in high R-squared values. Of course there are turf sprinters as well as dirt stayers, but for the most part, horses bred to sprint are less successful on the grass than are horses bred to stay a route of ground. Similarly, horses bred for the turf are less successful in sprints than are horses bred for dirt.

CHART 11. THE RELATIONSHIP BETWEEN AVERAGE WINNING DISTANCE, TURF RACES AND SPRINTS

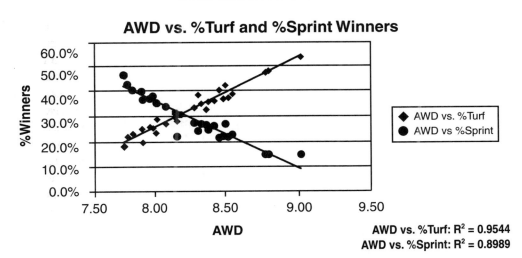

**AWD vs. %Turf and %Sprint Winners**

AWD vs. %Turf: $R^2 = 0.9544$
AWD vs. %Sprint: $R^2 = 0.8989$

We can explore in greater detail how DP distributions can affect overall type by examining several DP configurations for a given DI. The DPs in Table 16 are all equivalent to a DI of 3.00. Note, however, the wide range of possible CD values depending on how the DP is configured.

TABLE 16. VARIATION IN CD FOR DI 3.00 DEPENDING ON THE DP DISTRIBUTION

| DP | CD |
|---|---|
| 0-3-0-0-1 | 0.25 |
| 0-3-0-1-0 | 0.50 |
| 0-2-2-0-0 | 0.50 |
| 2-0-2-0-0 | 1.00 |
| 3-0-0-0-1 | 1.00 |
| 3-0-0-1-0 | 1.25 |

In all cases, the CD range for any DI spans one full CD unit. For DI 3.00, the median CD is 0.75, and the range is from 0.25 to 1.25. It is reasonable to suspect that a horse with DI 3.00 and CD 0.25 may be quite different in type from a horse with DI 3.00 and CD 1.25. In fact, we find real differences between those horses with DI 3.00 and CD greater than and less than 0.75.

In the former case, 36 percent of the races won are sprints and the average distance of their wins is 7.88 furlongs. In the latter case, the percentage falls to 30 percent sprint wins and the average distance rises to 8.24 furlongs. Thus, we confirm that horses with the same DI are not necessarily the same type in terms of performance attributes.

For reference, the general equation to find the median CD for any given DI is:

$$\text{Median CD} = \frac{3 \times (\text{DI} - 1)}{2 \times (\text{DI} + 1)}$$

The median, maximum and minimum CD for some common DI values are displayed in Table 17.

TABLE 17. MEDIAN, MAXIMUM AND MINIMUM CDs FOR A RANGE OF DI VALUES

| DI | Median CD | Maximum CD | Minimum CD |
|---|---|---|---|
| 0.00 | -1.50 | -1.00 | -2.00 |
| 0.50 | -0.50 | 0.00 | -1.00 |
| 1.00 | 0.00 | 0.50 | -0.50 |
| 2.00 | 0.50 | 1.00 | 0.00 |
| 3.00 | 0.75 | 1.25 | 0.25 |
| 4.00 | 0.90 | 1.40 | 0.40 |
| 5.00 | 1.00 | 1.50 | 0.50 |
| 6.00 | 1.07 | 1.57 | 0.57 |
| 7.00 | 1.13 | 1.63 | 0.63 |
| 8.00 | 1.17 | 1.67 | 0.67 |
| 9.00 | 1.20 | 1.70 | 0.70 |
| 10.00 | 1.23 | 1.73 | 0.73 |
| 20.00 | 1.36 | 1.86 | 0.86 |
| 30.00 | 1.40 | 1.90 | 0.90 |

Some important observations emerge from this analysis. First, differences in DI at the lower end of the DI range are more significant than they are at the higher end. For example, the difference in the median CD for DIs 1.00 and 2.00 is 0.50 CD units. In contrast, the difference in the median CDs for DIs 10.00 and 20.00 is only 0.14 CD units. Doubling the DI at the lower end has a far greater effect on the median CD than it does at the higher end. Second, and most important, neither the DI alone nor the CD alone is sufficient for an adequate aptitudinal evaluation of a pedigree. The critical component remains the DP, and its configuration is responsible for the interplay between the DI and the CD. Consequently, all of the Dosage figure components — the DP, the DI and the CD — are complementary and all are necessary for the best and most accurate interpretation.

Citation        Photo Courtesy of the Thoroughbred Times

# Citation

## DP 12-0-24-6-8, DI 0.92, CD 0.04

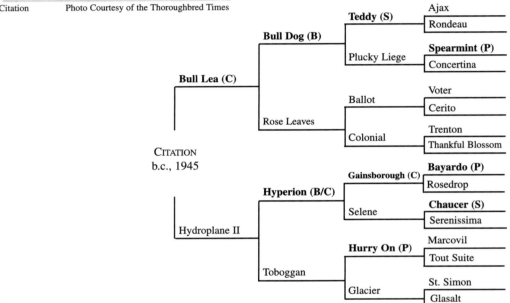

```
                                                              Ajax
                                            Teddy (S)
                                                              Rondeau
                          Bull Dog (B)
                                                              Spearmint (P)
                                            Plucky Liege
                                                              Concertina
          Bull Lea (C)
                                                              Voter
                                            Ballot
                                                              Cerito
                          Rose Leaves
                                                              Trenton
                                            Colonial
                                                              Thankful Blossom
CITATION
b.c., 1945
                                                              Bayardo (P)
                                            Gainsborough (C)
                                                              Rosedrop
                          Hyperion (B/C)
                                                              Chaucer (S)
                                            Selene
                                                              Serenissima
          Hydroplane II
                                                              Marcovil
                                            Hurry On (P)
                                                              Tout Suite
                          Toboggan
                                                              St. Simon
                                            Glacier
                                                              Glasalt
```

| DP Contribution | | Equivalent to: | |
|---|---|---|---|
| Sire | 8 - 0 - 16 - 4 - 2 | DI 1.14 | CD 0.27 |
| Dam | 4 - 0 - 8 - 2 - 6 | DI 0.67 | CD 0.30 |

A son of Classic *chef-de-race* Bull Lea, the premier classic sire of the mid-20th century, Triple Crown winner Citation, b.c., 1945 (Bull Lea-Hydroplane II, by Hyperion) has Dosage figures entirely consistent with his performance characteristics. Bred on the pattern of classic speed from his sire to stamina from his dam, the result is an almost ideally balanced DP 12-0-24-6-8, DI 0.92 and CD 0.04. Citation won at two miles, a mile and five-eighths and five times at a mile and a quarter. He also won eleven sprints, although his overall record below a mile (19-12-4-2), even though outstanding and representative of his exceptional class, was not as strong as his record in routes where he never finished worse than second while accumulating twenty wins and six seconds in twenty-six starts.

Spend a Buck          Photo Courtesy of the Thoroughbred Times

# Spend a Buck

## DP 6-7-18-1-0, DI 2.20, CD 0.56

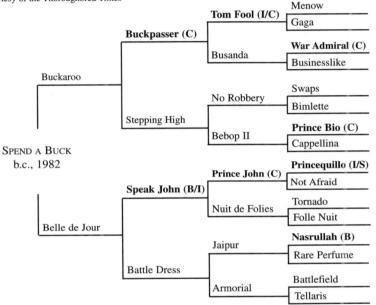

| | | | | Menow |
| --- | --- | --- | --- | --- |
| | | **Tom Fool (I/C)** | |
| | **Buckpasser (C)** | | | Gaga |
| | | | | **War Admiral (C)** |
| | | Busanda | |
| Buckaroo | | | | Businesslike |
| | | | | Swaps |
| | | No Robbery | |
| | Stepping High | | | Bimlette |
| | | | | **Prince Bio (C)** |
| | | Bebop II | |
| **SPEND A BUCK** | | | | Cappellina |
| **b.c., 1982** | | | | **Princequillo (I/S)** |
| | | **Prince John (C)** | |
| | **Speak John (B/I)** | | | Not Afraid |
| | | | | Tornado |
| | | Nuit de Folies | |
| Belle de Jour | | | | Folle Nuit |
| | | | | **Nasrullah (B)** |
| | | Jaipur | |
| | Battle Dress | | | Rare Perfume |
| | | | | Battlefield |
| | | Armorial | |
| | | | | Tellaris |

## DP Contribution

|  | | | | | | Equivalent to: | |
| --- | --- | --- | --- | --- | --- | --- | --- |
| Sire | 0 - 2 - 14 - 0 - 0 | | | | | DI 1.29 | CD 0.13 |
| Dam | 6 - 5 - 4 - 1 - 0 | | | | | DI 4.33 | CD 1.00 |

Horse of the Year Spend a Buck, b.c., 1982 (Buckaroo-Belle de Jour, by Speak John) was a tepid second choice in the 1985 Kentucky Derby because of concerns about his on-the-lead racing style and the tremendous speed he had exhibited in earlier races at two and three. As it turned out, he established himself as a classic horse of the highest order with a facile wire-to-wire romp, winning by 5¼ lengths in 2:00.1, third fastest in Derby history to that time behind only Secretariat and Northern Dancer. His six-furlong fraction of 1:09.3 remains the standard. He did this while defeating one of the strongest Derby fields in history that included two future Breeders' Cup Classic winners, the future Preakness Stakes record setter, and the previous year's two-year-old champion. Prior to the Derby, Spend a Buck won the nine-furlong Garden State Stakes by 9½, again on the front end, in 1:45.4. This is quite possibly the fastest mile and an eighth ever run by a three-year-old around two turns. Following the Kentucky Derby, Spend a Buck went wire-to-wire in the mile and a quarter Jersey Derby, this time challenged head-to-head through six furlongs in 1:09 flat by a rabbit named Huddle Up, and then holding safe through the entire stretch the future Belmont Stakes winner and confirmed closer Crème Fraiche, whose time for the mile and a half classic has been bettered by only seven other Belmont Stakes winners.

Spend a Buck is the result of breeding stamina on top through his sire and speed on the bottom through his dam. Despite his tremendous speed, his Dosage figures (DP 6-7-18-1-0, DI 2.20 and CD 0.56) suggest the ability to stay classic distances, which he did in grand style even when setting blazing fractions.

# CHAPTER 10

# The Relationship Between Pedigree and Performance: Two-Year-Olds

A fascinating and illustrative use of Dosage as a tool for understanding aptitudinal trends is revealed in its application to the analysis of two-year-old racing. Specifically, we can monitor the moving average of the DI for winners of juvenile stakes throughout the year. A moving average is simply a shifting average over a series of successive events. The moving average changes with each additional data point. In our example, we arranged the two-year-old stakes winners in chronological order for each of the years 1983 through 2001. We then determined the average DI for each of the races in sequence through the year. In other words, we calculated the average DI for all of the first juvenile stakes from 1983 through 2001 then did the same for the second, the third and so on. We then plotted the change in the average DI from race 1 through race 120, encompassing over 2200 races in all. The result of the plot is displayed in Chart 12.

### CHART 12. DOSAGE APPLIED TO TWO-YEAR-OLD RACING

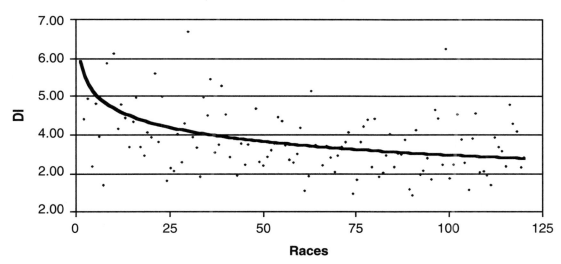

**Moving Average of DI for 2YO Races Through the Season (1983-2001)**

Although there is considerable but not unexpected scatter within the data, the computer-generated trend line is unequivocal and exactly as one would expect. The average DI drops continuously throughout the year as the average distance of the races increases. The analysis graphically captures the progression from the 4½ furlong "baby" races at Keeneland in April through the 8½ to 9 furlong races leading up to and beyond the Breeders' Cup, with speed-bred high DI horses dominating the early season races and more stamina-bred lower DI horses taking over in the fall. Occasionally an April Keeneland juvenile such as Summer Squall will win a classic race, and another, such as Horse of the Year Favorite Trick, may go on to great things. More often than not, however, the fall two-year-old races and the following year's three-year-old route races tend to be dominated by colts and fillies that come out in late spring and into the fall.

# CHAPTER II

# The Relationship Between Pedigree and Performance: "Elite" Thoroughbreds

Table 18 includes Dosage figures for selected groups of "elite" Thoroughbreds since 1983. We define "elite" Thoroughbreds for this exercise as superior performers either on the racetrack or in the breeding shed. They include winners of the Kentucky Derby, Horses of the Year, Annual Leading Earners, Annual Leading Sires by Progeny Earnings, Annual Leading Broodmare Sires by Progeny Earnings, and Kentucky Broodmares of the Year.

The individual and combined figures are compared with those for open stakes winners over the same timeframe. Abbreviations in the table are ADI for average Dosage Index; ACD for Average Center of Distribution; CDI for Composite Dosage Index; and CCD for Composite Center of Distribution. Recall that we derive composite figures by adding the points in each aptitude category for all members of the group and then calculating the DI and CD in the normal way.

### TABLE 18. DOSAGE FIGURES FOR "ELITE" THOROUGHBREDS

| | DP | ADI | ACD | CDI | CCD | PTS |
|---|---|---|---|---|---|---|
| Kentucky Derby Winners, 1983-2002 (20) | 8.30 - 4.60 - 11.65 - 1.65 - 1.50 | 2.87 | 0.64 | 2.09 | 0.60 | 27.70 |
| Horse of the Year, 1983-2001 (19) | 8.53 - 4.16 - 11.21 - 2.11 - 0.00 | 2.85 | 0.77 | 2.37 | 0.73 | 26.00 |
| Leading Earners, 1983-2001 (19) | 7.53 - 5.95 - 14.42 - 1.74 - 0.05 | 2.77 | 0.65 | 2.30 | 0.65 | 29.68 |
| Leading Sires, 1983-2001 (19) | 12.16 - 8.05 - 15.32 - 1.68 - 0.68 | 3.22 | 0.80 | 2.78 | 0.77 | 37.89 |
| Leading Broodmare Sires, 1983-2001 (19) | 10.89 - 9.00 - 16.68 - 5.32 - 2.42 | 2.24 | 0.45 | 1.76 | 0.47 | 44.32 |
| Kentucky Broodmares of the Year, 1983-2001 (19) | 11.26 - 6.74 - 16.21 - 3.11 - 1.63 | 3.78 | 0.61 | 2.03 | 0.59 | 38.95 |
| Total Elite (115) | 9.77 - 6.40 - 14.23 - 2.59 - 1.05 | 2.95 | 0.65 | 2.16 | 0.62 | 34.03 |
| Open Stakes Winners, 1983-2001 (18,617) | 7.88 - 4.76 - 9.59 - 1.60 - 0.91 | 3.42 | 0.72 | 2.39 | 0.69 | 24.73 |

Several differences between the "elite" horses and typical stakes winners are immediately obvious. Although there is some variation from group to group, all of the "elite" groups show double-digit representation in the Classic aptitudinal category. The typical stakes winners do not. All of the "elite" groups have more total Dosage points than the stakes winners, mainly concentrated in the breeding stock (sires, broodmares, and broodmare sires). The "elite" runners have fewer Dosage points than the "elite" breeding animals. The "elite" horses as a group have more representation in the stamina wing of the DP (Solid and Professional aptitudinal categories). The leading sires possess far more Brilliant and Classic points than do the stakes winners, while the broodmares and broodmare sires are most heavily weighted toward stamina, having the largest Solid and Professional representation of any "elite" groups. The Dosage figures are generally lower for the "elite" horses, again with variation from group to group.

Note that the ADI of the Kentucky Broodmare of the Year group is heavily influenced by one representative with very high numbers. This is not as obvious in the CDI.

The conclusion one might draw from these data is that we can differentiate the pedigrees of superior Thoroughbreds from the pedigrees of typical Thoroughbred stakes winners by the magnitude and degree to which they have inherited prepotent elements of speed and endurance.

# CHAPTER 12

# The Relationship Between Pedigree and Performance: The Breeders' Cup

Even though The Breeders' Cup has a relatively short history, a discernable pattern is emerging for the average Dosage figures of the winners in the various divisions. Table 19 displays the average figures along with the average distance of the races in each division from the initial Breeders' Cup in 1984 through 2002. Several divisions show unusual average distances because of occasional past changes in distance from year to year.

## TABLE 19. THE HISTORY OF DOSAGE IN THE BREEDERS' CUP

| Race | Avg. Dist. | DP | | | | | DI | CD | PTS |
|------|-----------|------|------|-------|------|------|------|------|------|
| Classic | 10.00 | 8.89 - | 5.74 - | 13.37 - | 1.68 - | 1.47 | 2.52 | 0.61 | 31.16 |
| Distaff | 9.21 | 9.32 - | 6.63 - | 11.63 - | 1.32 - | 1.00 | 3.45 | 0.77 | 29.89 |
| Filly & Mare Turf | 10.50 | 4.00 - | 6.25 - | 17.75 - | 2.50 - | 0.50 | 1.78 | 0.36 | 31.00 |
| Juvenile | 8.45 | 11.63 - | 7.00 - | 12.89 - | 0.89 - | 1.26 | 3.49 | 0.82 | 33.68 |
| Juvenile Fillies | 8.45 | 8.16 - | 5.11 - | 11.74 - | 1.47 - | 1.11 | 3.07 | 0.68 | 27.58 |
| Mile | 8.00 | 8.95 - | 5.37 - | 16.42 - | 3.00 - | 0.79 | 2.06 | 0.55 | 34.53 |
| Sprint | 6.00 | 11.26 - | 5.32 - | 10.37 - | 1.47 - | 0.63 | 4.66 | 0.87 | 29.05 |
| Turf | 12.00 | 6.47 - | 4.47 - | 14.11 - | 4.63 - | 2.21 | 1.49 | 0.26 | 31.89 |

Most striking are the data for the Sprint and the Turf where the highest and lowest figures correlate with the shortest and longest distance. Also of note are the generally lower figures for the turf races compared to those on dirt. These results parallel those for the Thoroughbred population at large. Finally, the average DP point totals in every division are equal to or greater than those for all Grade 1 winners since 1983 as shown in Table 10. To the extent that high DP point totals result from a combination of more and/or closer up *chefs-de-race* in a pedigree, and that the appearance of these *chefs-de-race* may represent superior breeding, it seems as though the winners of The Breeders' Cup races are "better bred" than even typical Grade 1 winners.

75

# Smile

## DP 18-8-10-2-0, DI 4.43, CD 1.11

Smile      Photo Courtesy of Serita Hult

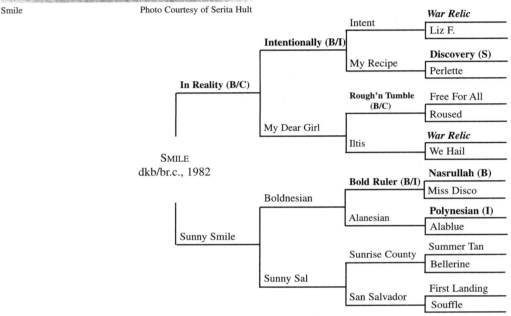

| | | | | | War Relic |
| | | | Intent | | Liz F. |
| | | Intentionally (B/I) | | | |
| | | | My Recipe | | Discovery (S) |
| | In Reality (B/C) | | | | Perlette |
| | | | Rough'n Tumble (B/C) | | Free For All |
| | | My Dear Girl | | | Roused |
| | | | Iltis | | War Relic |
| SMILE | | | | | We Hail |
| dkb/br.c., 1982 | | | | | Nasrullah (B) |
| | | | Bold Ruler (B/I) | | Miss Disco |
| | | Boldnesian | | | |
| | | | Alanesian | | Polynesian (I) |
| | Sunny Smile | | | | Alablue |
| | | | Sunrise County | | Summer Tan |
| | | Sunny Sal | | | Bellerine |
| | | | San Salvador | | First Landing |
| | | | | | Souffle |

## DP Contribution     Equivalent to:

| | | | |
|---|---|---|---|
| Sire | 14 - 4 - 10 - 2 - 0 | DI 3.27 | CD 1.00 |
| Dam | 4 - 4 - 0 - 0 - 0 | | CD 1.50 |

Second in the Breeders' Cup Sprint (G1) at three and the winner of the race at four, champion Smile, dkb/br.c., 1982 (In Reality-Sunny Smile, by Boldnesian) was produced by breeding the intermediate speed of Brilliant/Classic *chef-de-race* In Reality to the pure speed of Sunny Smile. The resultant DP 14-4-10-2-0, DI 4.43 and CD 1.11 suggest a sprint-oriented pedigree supported by the fourteen points in the Brilliant aptitudinal group, yet with a bit of stamina derived from ten points in the Classic aptitudinal group and two points in the Solid aptitudinal group. Smile's greatest success came in the 1986 Breeders' Cup Sprint (G1), although as a three-year-old he won the mile and an eighth Grade 1 Arlington Classic, expressing his speed throughout in a wire-to-wire romp. This is a classic example of a pedigree predisposed toward speed yet with enough residual stamina to rationalize carrying that speed beyond a sprint distance under advantageous conditions of pace and class.

# CHAPTER 13

# The Relationship Between Pedigree and Performance: Steeplechasing

Table 20 displays the Dosage figures for North American steeplechasing champions since 1948.

### TABLE 20. DOSAGE FIGURES FOR STEEPLECHASE CHAMPIONS SINCE 1948

| Year | Champion | DP | DI | CD |
|------|----------|-----|------|------|
| 1948 | American Way | 0 - 4 - 5 - 3 - 2 | 0.87 | -0.21 |
| 1949 | Trough Hill | 0 - 0 - 4 - 0 - 12 | 0.14 | -1.50 |
| 1950 | Oedipus | 12 - 4 - 16 - 6 - 0 | 1.71 | 0.58 |
| 1951 | Oedipus | 12 - 4 - 16 - 6 - 0 | 1.71 | 0.58 |
| 1952 | Jam | 0 - 0 - 0 - 3 - 3 | 0.00 | -1.50 |
| 1953 | The Mast | 4 - 0 - 1 - 11 - 2 | 0.33 | -0.39 |
| 1954 | King Commander | 2 - 2 - 0 - 0 - 0 | 0.00 | 1.50 |
| 1955 | Neji | 2 - 2 - 0 - 6 - 8 | 0.29 | -0.89 |
| 1956 | Shipboard | 2 - 0 - 1 - 16 - 5 | 0.12 | -0.92 |
| 1957 | Neji | 2 - 2 - 0 - 6 - 8 | 0.29 | -0.89 |
| 1958 | Neji | 2 - 2 - 0 - 6 - 8 | 0.29 | -0.89 |
| 1959 | Ancestor | 1 - 1 - 16 - 2 - 0 | 1.00 | 0.05 |
| 1960 | Benguala | 18 - 0 - 7 - 14 - 3 | 1.05 | 0.38 |
| 1961 | Peal | 0 - 2 - 2 - 0 - 6 | 0.43 | -1.00 |
| 1962 | Barnaby's Bluff | 4 - 0 - 8 - 4 - 0 | 1.00 | 0.25 |
| 1963 | Amber Diver | 2 - 4 - 12 - 2 - 6 | 0.86 | -0.23 |
| 1964 | Bon Nouvel | 9 - 3 - 0 - 4 - 0 | 3.00 | 1.06 |
| 1965 | Bon Nouvel | 9 - 3 - 0 - 4 - 0 | 3.00 | 1.06 |
| 1966 | Tuscalee | 4 - 0 - 6 - 0 - 0 | 2.33 | 0.80 |
| 1967 | Quick Pitch | 4 - 4 - 6 - 6 - 0 | 1.22 | 0.30 |
| 1968 | Bon Nouvel | 9 - 3 - 0 - 4 - 0 | 3.00 | 1.06 |
| 1969 | L'Escargot | 0 - 0 - 2 - 0 - 2 | 0.33 | -1.00 |
| 1970 | Top Bid | 28 - 2 - 8 - 2 - 0 | 5.67 | 1.40 |
| 1971 | Shadow Brook | 6 - 4 - 4 - 4 - 6 | 1.00 | 0.00 |
| 1972 | Soothsayer | 1 - 1 - 6 - 6 - 2 | 0.45 | -0.44 |
| 1973 | Athenian Idol | 9 - 0 - 6 - 1 - 14 | 0.67 | -0.37 |
| 1974 | Gran Kan | 0 - 0 - 1 - 5 - 2 | 0.07 | -1.13 |
| 1975 | Life's Illusion | 1 - 3 - 4 - 2 - 2 | 1.00 | -0.08 |

| Year | Champion | DP | | | | | DI | CD |
|------|----------|-----|-----|-----|-----|-----|------|------|
| 1976 | Fire Control | 8 | - 14 | - 10 | - 6 | - 4 | 1.80 | 0.38 |
| 1977 | Café Prince | 20 | - 2 | - 14 | - 10 | - 0 | 1.71 | 0.70 |
| 1978 | Café Prince | 20 | - 2 | - 14 | - 10 | - 0 | 1.71 | 0.70 |
| 1979 | Martie's Anger | 19 | - 3 | - 5 | - 1 | - 0 | 7.00 | 1.43 |
| 1980 | Zaccio | 2 | - 12 | - 2 | - 0 | - 2 | 5.00 | 0.67 |
| 1981 | Zaccio | 2 | - 12 | - 2 | - 0 | - 2 | 5.00 | 0.67 |
| 1982 | Zaccio | 2 | - 12 | - 2 | - 0 | - 2 | 5.00 | 0.67 |
| 1983 | Flatterer | 9 | - 2 | - 3 | - 0 | - 0 | 8.33 | 1.43 |
| 1984 | Flatterer | 9 | - 2 | - 3 | - 0 | - 0 | 8.33 | 1.43 |
| 1985 | Flatterer | 9 | - 2 | - 3 | - 0 | - 0 | 8.33 | 1.43 |
| 1986 | Flatterer | 9 | - 2 | - 3 | - 0 | - 0 | 8.33 | 1.43 |
| 1987 | Inlander | 2 | - 0 | - 6 | - 8 | - 2 | 0.38 | -0.44 |
| 1988 | Jimmy Lorenzo | 5 | - 2 | - 7 | - 0 | - 6 | 1.11 | 0.00 |
| 1989 | Highland Bud | 10 | - 3 | - 16 | - 5 | - 2 | 1.40 | 0.39 |
| 1990 | Morley Street | 8 | - 0 | - 8 | - 0 | - 4 | 1.50 | 0.40 |
| 1991 | Morley Street | 8 | - 0 | - 8 | - 0 | - 4 | 1.50 | 0.40 |
| 1992 | Lonesome Glory | 2 | - 3 | - 21 | - 4 | - 0 | 1.07 | 0.10 |
| 1993 | Lonesome Glory | 2 | - 3 | - 21 | - 4 | - 0 | 1.07 | 0.10 |
| 1994 | Warm Spell | 6 | - 4 | - 7 | - 5 | - 0 | 1.59 | 0.50 |
| 1995 | Lonesome Glory | 2 | - 3 | - 21 | - 4 | - 0 | 1.07 | 0.10 |
| 1996 | Correggio | 9 | - 8 | - 26 | - 9 | - 0 | 1.36 | 0.33 |
| 1997 | Lonesome Glory | 2 | - 3 | - 21 | - 4 | - 0 | 1.07 | 0.10 |
| 1998 | Flat Top | 8 | - 5 | - 13 | - 1 | - 5 | 1.56 | 0.31 |
| 1999 | Lonesome Glory | 2 | - 3 | - 21 | - 4 | - 0 | 1.07 | 0.10 |
| 2000 | All Gong | 5 | - 1 | - 8 | - 4 | - 2 | 1.00 | 0.15 |
| 2001 | Pompeyo | 6 | - 2 | - 12 | - 0 | - 0 | 2.33 | 0.70 |
| **AVERAGE** | | **6.09** | **- 2.87** | **- 7.74** | **- 3.74** | **- 2.33** | **2.06** | **0.22** |

The relatively low DI and CD numbers resulting from large *chef-de-race* contributions to the Solid and Professional aptitude groups are generally consistent with the longer distances of steeple-chase races. However, there are some unusual patterns one may observe.

The DI distribution is somewhat bimodal with the vast majority (74 percent) of the champions having a DI of less than 2.00. Surprisingly, another 17 percent have a DI above 4.00, while only 9 percent have a DI in the typical middle distance range of 2.00 to 4.00. A graphical representation of the bimodal distribution is seen in Chart 13 (solid line) where it is compared with the DI distribution found among open stakes winners (dashed line).

## DI Distributions Since 1983

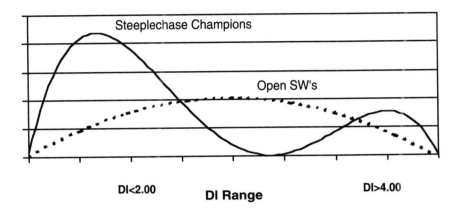

Thus, there appear to be predominantly two types of pedigrees associated with world-class performance in North American steeplechasing. The first is the strongly endurance-oriented pedigree in which stamina influences prevail, enabling the horse to be competitive over marathon distances. The second is the sprint-type pedigree in which speed is dominant. Although the latter initially may seem contradictory, many handicappers have observed the successful transition of sprinters on the flat to races over jumps. The rationale is that the typical pace of steeplechase races is not so demanding that sprinters necessarily will falter. In fact, any fatigue characteristics may be compensated by increased agility and quickness over the jumps. The desired interaction between stamina and jumping ability seems to find its best expression when shifted more to one trait or the other. The paucity of middle-distance pedigrees among these champions is certainly surprising considering that almost 50 percent of open stakes winners on the flat since 1983 have a DI between 2.00 and 4.00. In fact, until 2001 there hadn't been a steeplechase champion since 1968 with a pedigree that had fallen within the DI 2.00 to 4.00 range.

# CHAPTER 14

# The Relationship Between Pedigree and Performance: The Racetrack Surface

The following data in Table 21 present the Dosage figures for stakes winners at various racetracks in North America. The data are for stakes races since 1983 and include tracks with at least 100 total stakes races, and at least 50 stakes races each at sprint (less than one mile) and route (greater than or equal to a mile) distances. The Table displays the average winning distance, average Dosage Profile (DP), average Dosage Index (ADI), and average Center of Distribution (ACD) for the winners of all the races, followed by separate columns for the average winning distance, average DI (ADI) and average CD (ACD) of the winners in both sprints and routes. It is apparent that the tracks vary widely in the aptitudinal types that are successful. It is also apparent that tracks have different profiles in terms of sprint winner aptitudes versus route winner aptitudes.

### TRACK ABBREVIATIONS SHOWN IN TABLES 21 & 22

| | |
|---|---|
| AKS (Ak-Sar-Ben) | KEE (Keeneland) |
| AP (Arlington Park) | KEY (Keystone) |
| AQU (Aqueduct) | LAD (Louisiana Downs) |
| Bel (Belmont Park) | LGA (Longacres) |
| BM (Bay Meadows) | LRL (Laurel) |
| CD (Churchill Downs) | LS (Lone Star) |
| CRC (Calder) | MED (The Meadowlands) |
| DEL (Delaware Park) | MTH (Monmouth Park) |
| DMR (Del Mar) | NP (Northlands Park) |
| ELP (Ellis Park) | OP (Oaklawn Park) |
| FG (Fair Grounds) | PHA (Philadelphia Park) |
| FPX (Fairplex) | PIM (Pimlico) |
| GG (Golden Gate Fields) | RP (Remington Park) |
| GP (Gulfstream Park) | SA (Santa Anita) |
| GS (Garden State Park) | SAR (Saratoga) |
| HAW (Hawthorne) | SPT (Sportsmans Park) |
| HIA (Hialeah) | TP (Turfway) |
| HOL (Hollywood Park) | WO (Woodbine) |

## TABLE 21. DOSAGE FIGURES BY RACETRACK

| Track | Races | Dist. | DP | ADI | ACD | Dist. (Sprints) | ADI (Sprints) | ACD (Sprints) | Dist. (Routes) | ADI (Routes) | ACD (Routes) |
|---|---|---|---|---|---|---|---|---|---|---|---|
| | | | All Races | | | Sprints | | | Routes | | |
| AKS | 131 | 7.99 | 7.57 - 5.27 - 8.52 - 1.43 - 1.02 | 3.76 | 0.77 | 5.94 | 5.11 | 0.93 | 8.76 | 3.24 | 0.71 |
| AP | 478 | 8.50 | 7.59 - 4.48 - 9.65 - 1.65 - 0.97 | 3.42 | 0.70 | 6.37 | 5.01 | 0.94 | 8.99 | 3.05 | 0.64 |
| AQU | 1158 | 8.03 | 8.58 - 5.09 - 9.94 - 1.63 - 0.97 | 3.65 | 0.73 | 6.29 | 4.81 | 0.88 | 9.06 | 2.97 | 0.65 |
| BEL | 1278 | 8.50 | 8.74 - 5.29 - 11.64 - 1.89 - 1.01 | 3.21 | 0.69 | 6.39 | 4.52 | 0.87 | 9.34 | 2.69 | 0.61 |
| BM | 530 | 7.92 | 7.47 - 4.66 - 8.91 - 1.81 - 0.73 | 3.34 | 0.71 | 6.11 | 4.08 | 0.89 | 8.51 | 3.10 | 0.65 |
| CD | 686 | 8.13 | 8.34 - 4.81 - 10.38 - 1.60 - 0.97 | 3.34 | 0.72 | 6.29 | 4.37 | 0.86 | 8.71 | 3.01 | 0.68 |
| CRC | 894 | 8.16 | 7.77 - 4.79 - 8.90 - 1.48 - 0.90 | 3.60 | 0.75 | 6.53 | 4.36 | 0.88 | 9.03 | 3.20 | 0.68 |
| DEL | 283 | 7.88 | 7.20 - 4.05 - 10.12 - 1.29 - 0.89 | 2.83 | 0.67 | 5.86 | 3.68 | 0.83 | 8.85 | 2.41 | 0.59 |
| DMR | 427 | 8.11 | 7.94 - 4.81 - 10.31 - 1.69 - 0.85 | 3.15 | 0.68 | 6.52 | 3.84 | 0.81 | 8.88 | 2.82 | 0.61 |
| ELP | 124 | 7.71 | 7.57 - 4.37 - 8.97 - 1.47 - 0.78 | 3.27 | 0.73 | 6.76 | 3.20 | 0.79 | 8.42 | 3.32 | 0.69 |
| FG | 388 | 7.79 | 7.66 - 4.66 - 10.11 - 1.24 - 1.02 | 3.06 | 0.70 | 6.04 | 3.64 | 0.85 | 8.70 | 2.76 | 0.63 |
| FPX | 126 | 7.77 | 7.17 - 4.50 - 8.48 - 1.29 - 0.67 | 3.38 | 0.74 | 6.42 | 3.81 | 0.83 | 8.69 | 3.09 | 0.68 |
| GG | 446 | 7.95 | 7.52 - 4.44 - 8.70 - 1.54 - 0.85 | 3.56 | 0.73 | 6.05 | 4.70 | 0.90 | 8.83 | 3.05 | 0.65 |
| GP | 774 | 8.27 | 8.10 - 4.96 - 10.08 - 1.69 - 0.94 | 3.27 | 0.71 | 6.53 | 4.04 | 0.85 | 9.05 | 2.93 | 0.65 |
| GS | 140 | 8.30 | 8.30 - 5.19 - 9.39 - 2.24 - 0.91 | 4.11 | 0.73 | 5.89 | 6.66 | 0.95 | 8.90 | 3.46 | 0.68 |
| HAW | 308 | 7.95 | 8.10 - 5.11 - 9.14 - 1.49 - 0.74 | 3.81 | 0.76 | 6.40 | 4.82 | 0.84 | 8.59 | 3.39 | 0.72 |
| HIA | 239 | 8.54 | 7.67 - 5.35 - 9.87 - 1.70 - 0.89 | 2.97 | 0.69 | 6.72 | 3.85 | 0.86 | 9.05 | 2.71 | 0.64 |
| HOL | 1134 | 8.14 | 7.90 - 4.39 - 9.93 - 1.86 - 0.99 | 3.36 | 0.67 | 6.21 | 4.28 | 0.85 | 8.97 | 2.96 | 0.60 |
| KEE | 502 | 8.27 | 7.90 - 4.99 - 10.77 - 1.50 - 0.84 | 3.10 | 0.70 | 6.36 | 3.84 | 0.82 | 8.92 | 2.85 | 0.66 |
| KEY | 102 | 7.31 | 8.47 - 5.32 - 6.63 - 1.36 - 0.78 | 5.06 | 0.90 | 6.38 | 5.15 | 0.92 | 8.53 | 4.94 | 0.89 |
| LAD | 385 | 8.20 | 7.65 - 4.65 - 7.68 - 1.49 - 0.79 | 3.62 | 0.80 | 6.53 | 4.38 | 0.91 | 8.90 | 3.31 | 0.75 |
| LGA | 113 | 8.52 | 6.08 - 4.55 - 6.83 - 2.65 - 0.88 | 3.18 | 0.63 | 6.38 | 4.11 | 0.79 | 8.80 | 3.06 | 0.61 |
| LRL | 719 | 8.01 | 7.68 - 4.90 - 8.71 - 1.39 - 0.90 | 3.72 | 0.76 | 6.38 | 4.47 | 0.86 | 9.03 | 3.25 | 0.70 |
| LS | 104 | 7.43 | 6.58 - 3.80 - 10.18 - 1.08 - 0.67 | 2.75 | 0.66 | 6.18 | 2.97 | 0.70 | 8.46 | 2.56 | 0.64 |
| MED | 359 | 8.43 | 8.23 - 5.21 - 10.36 - 1.58 - 1.01 | 3.61 | 0.71 | 5.97 | 5.85 | 0.99 | 8.99 | 3.09 | 0.65 |
| MTH | 476 | 7.77 | 8.15 - 5.01 - 9.61 - 1.43 - 0.77 | 3.53 | 0.76 | 5.86 | 4.42 | 0.91 | 8.55 | 3.17 | 0.70 |
| NP | 118 | 8.63 | 6.19 - 4.03 - 7.22 - 1.39 - 0.71 | 4.21 | 0.76 | 6.49 | 6.48 | 1.03 | 9.54 | 3.36 | 0.64 |
| OP | 380 | 7.48 | 8.55 - 4.63 - 9.33 - 1.21 - 0.82 | 3.67 | 0.81 | 5.94 | 4.37 | 0.92 | 8.48 | 3.23 | 0.74 |
| PHA | 183 | 7.72 | 7.85 - 4.81 - 8.99 - 1.27 - 0.70 | 3.62 | 0.78 | 6.21 | 4.30 | 0.87 | 8.67 | 3.20 | 0.73 |
| PIM | 524 | 7.93 | 7.92 - 5.11 - 9.02 - 1.47 - 0.82 | 3.81 | 0.78 | 5.79 | 5.05 | 0.92 | 8.95 | 3.24 | 0.71 |
| RP | 144 | 8.03 | 8.22 - 4.92 - 9.56 - 1.31 - 0.99 | 3.44 | 0.74 | 6.81 | 3.89 | 0.84 | 8.79 | 3.16 | 0.68 |
| SA | 1333 | 8.15 | 7.70 - 4.37 - 9.81 - 1.83 - 1.07 | 3.06 | 0.65 | 6.49 | 3.69 | 0.78 | 9.13 | 2.69 | 0.57 |
| SAR | 526 | 8.10 | 8.67 - 5.27 - 11.25 - 1.49 - 0.94 | 3.22 | 0.72 | 6.43 | 4.08 | 0.90 | 9.49 | 2.50 | 0.56 |
| SPT | 202 | 7.71 | 8.00 - 4.73 - 7.96 - 1.33 - 0.84 | 3.81 | 0.80 | 6.18 | 4.32 | 0.85 | 8.54 | 3.54 | 0.77 |
| TP | 246 | 7.66 | 7.93 - 4.68 - 9.48 - 1.12 - 0.73 | 3.82 | 0.77 | 6.24 | 4.36 | 0.86 | 8.58 | 3.48 | 0.72 |
| WO | 879 | 7.98 | 7.39 - 4.17 - 9.26 - 1.40 - 0.89 | 3.29 | 0.71 | 6.19 | 4.12 | 0.84 | 9.12 | 2.77 | 0.62 |

Table 22 examines more closely the relationship between the average CD at sprint and at route distances for each track. The last column shows the percentage decrease in average CD in going from sprints to routes. The tracks are sorted in order of decreasing percent decrease. Those near the bottom, such as Sportsmans Park, Ellis Park and Hawthorne, display small differences, while those near the top, such as Saratoga, the Meadowlands and Arlington Park, display large differences. The reason for the variations in percent decrease is not immediately obvious. However, the individual percent decreases are characteristic of each track. In any case, the data tell us that sprinters at Sportsmans Park, for example, appear to have a much easier time moving up to routes than do sprinters at Saratoga, at least in terms of pedigree type. A relationship between speed and track surface may be implicated.

### Table 22. Differences in Sprint and Route Average CD Values by Racetrack

| Track | Sprint ACD | Route ACD | % Decrease: Sprints To Routes |
|---|---|---|---|
| SAR | 0.90 | 0.56 | 37% |
| MED | 0.99 | 0.65 | 34% |
| AP | 0.94 | 0.64 | 32% |
| HOL | 0.85 | 0.60 | 30% |
| BEL | 0.87 | 0.61 | 30% |
| DEL | 0.83 | 0.59 | 29% |
| GG | 0.90 | 0.65 | 27% |
| BM | 0.89 | 0.65 | 27% |
| WO | 0.84 | 0.62 | 27% |
| AQU | 0.88 | 0.65 | 27% |
| SA | 0.78 | 0.57 | 26% |
| FG | 0.85 | 0.63 | 26% |
| HIA | 0.86 | 0.64 | 25% |
| DMR | 0.81 | 0.61 | 24% |
| GP | 0.85 | 0.65 | 24% |
| CRC | 0.88 | 0.68 | 23% |
| PIM | 0.92 | 0.71 | 23% |
| MTH | 0.91 | 0.70 | 23% |
| CD | 0.86 | 0.68 | 21% |
| OP | 0.92 | 0.74 | 20% |
| KEE | 0.82 | 0.66 | 19% |
| RP | 0.84 | 0.68 | 19% |
| FP | 0.83 | 0.68 | 19% |
| LRL | 0.86 | 0.70 | 18% |
| LAD | 0.91 | 0.75 | 17% |
| TP | 0.86 | 0.72 | 16% |
| PHA | 0.87 | 0.73 | 16% |
| HAW | 0.84 | 0.72 | 14% |
| ELP | 0.79 | 0.69 | 13% |
| SPT | 0.85 | 0.77 | 10% |

# CHAPTER 15

# The Relationship Between Pedigree and Performance: Claiming Horses

All of the data previously presented are derived from North American open stakes winners between 1983 and 2001. The emphasis on stakes winners is intentional, and with good reason. Stakes winners represent the highest level of Thoroughbred performance. Horses competing in stakes races are generally in better physical condition than those competing at lower levels. If physical problems do exist, the problems are likely better managed. Horses competing in stakes races are more consistent. If they stay healthy they can be expected to put in a competitive effort on a continual basis. Horses competing in stakes races will usually be suited to the particular race conditions. With larger purses on the line, and with a limited number of races in a horse's career, the connections of stakes horses tend to make management decisions that optimize opportunity. This isn't always the case at the lower end of the class structure.

Cheaper horses are often raced into shape and their native talents easily can be obscured by chronic injury. Their form cycles are more erratic than those of their more gifted peers. Therefore, the intentions surrounding these runners are not always apparent. With stakes horses, on the other hand, there is an excellent probability that they belong in their race. By the time they are mature they will have found their best distance profile and most competitive racing class. They are in to win, or at least get a part of the purse. The result of superior talent that is well managed and purposefully intended is that the outcome of races involving those animals is a better reflection of their innate qualities.

In other words, it is a reasonable assumption that stakes horses more accurately express their genetic potential than do horses running in claiming races. A secondary result is that the data obtained from their races is more reliable, and reliable data is absolutely critical if the objective is to develop a better appreciation of the relationship between pedigree and track performance. Nevertheless, it is instructive to see how well the Dosage model applies to the lower end of the racing spectrum.

Fortunately, such information is available through the efforts of John Denbleyker and his student research thesis in the Sports Management Program at St. Cloud State University in St. Cloud, Minnesota. Denbleyker investigated more than 1,500 claiming races in the years 2000 and 2001 at fourteen tracks: Arlington Park, Belmont Park, Calder, Churchill Downs, Del Mar, Ellis Park, Gulfstream Park, Hollywood Park, Keeneland, Lone Star Park, Pimlico, Prairie Meadows, Santa Anita, and Saratoga. He calculated the Dosage figures for each of the winners and arranged the data according to racing category. His results, reproduced with his permission, are presented in Table 23. Included are the analogous data for just under 2000 open stakes races over the same time frame, allowing for a direct comparison.

## TABLE 23. A COMPARISON OF CLAIMING HORSE AND STAKES HORSE DOSAGE DATA (2000-2001)

*Claiming Horses (2000-2001)*

| Category | Races | Dist. | DP | Pts. | ADI | ACD | CDI | CCD |
|---|---|---|---|---|---|---|---|---|
| All | 1564 | 7.21 | 6.77 - 3.79 - 9.16 - 1.06 - 0.58 | 21.36 | 3.00 | 0.72 | 2.43 | 0.71 |
| Dirt | 1294 | 7.01 | 6.82 - 3.72 - 8.96 - 0.97 - 0.53 | 21.00 | 3.09 | 0.74 | 2.51 | 0.73 |
| Turf | 270 | 8.12 | 6.52 - 4.12 - 10.15 - 1.50 - 0.81 | 23.10 | 2.56 | 0.63 | 2.13 | 0.61 |
| Sprints | 857 | 6.21 | 6.99 - 3.76 - 8.64 - 0.89 - 0.48 | 20.76 | 3.23 | 0.77 | 2.65 | 0.77 |
| Routes | 707 | 8.42 | 6.51 - 3.83 - 9.79 - 1.27 - 0.71 | 22.11 | 2.73 | 0.66 | 2.22 | 0.64 |
| Two-Year-Olds | 71 | 6.32 | 5.68 - 3.06 - 7.94 - 0.92 - 0.54 | 18.14 | 2.71 | 0.69 | 2.34 | 0.6 |
| Three-Year-Olds | 514 | 7.12 | 6.50 - 3.81 - 9.17 - 0.93 - 0.50 | 20.91 | 2.99 | 0.72 | 2.48 | 0.71 |
| Older Runners | 979 | 7.31 | 6.99 - 3.84 - 9.25 - 1.13 - 0.63 | 21.84 | 3.03 | 0.72 | 2.42 | 0.71 |
| 5.00 Furlongs | 40 | 5.00 | 7.08 - 3.18 - 7.98 - 0.93 - 0.25 | 19.42 | 3.83 | 0.86 | 2.76 | 0.82 |
| 5.50 Furlongs | 50 | 5.50 | 6.80 - 3.24 - 7.94 - 1.00 - 0.72 | 19.70 | 3.06 | 0.76 | 2.46 | 0.73 |
| 6.00 Furlongs | 447 | 6.00 | 7.11 - 3.68 - 8.38 - 0.88 - 0.40 | 20.45 | 3.26 | 0.79 | 2.74 | 0.79 |
| 6.50 Furlongs | 167 | 6.50 | 6.68 - 3.90 - 9.06 - 0.89 - 0.57 | 21.10 | 3.11 | 0.74 | 2.52 | 0.72 |
| 7.00 Furlongs | 141 | 7.00 | 7.21 - 4.13 - 9.42 - 0.86 - 0.61 | 22.23 | 3.18 | 0.75 | 2.60 | 0.74 |
| 8.00 Furlongs | 299 | 8.00 | 6.43 - 3.77 - 9.59 - 1.12 - 0.71 | 21.62 | 2.75 | 0.67 | 2.26 | 0.65 |
| 8.50 Furlongs | 291 | 8.50 | 6.49 - 3.79 - 9.77 - 1.34 - 0.67 | 22.06 | 2.77 | 0.66 | 2.20 | 0.64 |
| 9.00 Furlongs | 98 | 9.00 | 6.41 - 4.08 - 10.36 - 1.22 - 0.85 | 22.92 | 2.55 | 0.62 | 2.16 | 0.61 |

*Stakes Winners (2000-2001)*

| Category | Races | Dist. | DP | Pts. | ADI | ACD | CDI | CCD |
|---|---|---|---|---|---|---|---|---|
| All | 1999 | 8.01 | 6.92 - 3.88 - 10.42 - 1.17 - 0.68 | 23.07 | 2.81 | 0.67 | 2.27 | 0.66 |
| Dirt | 1332 | 7.65 | 7.20 - 3.85 - 9.70 - 0.98 - 0.57 | 22.29 | 3.08 | 0.74 | 2.49 | 0.72 |
| Turf | 667 | 8.75 | 6.37 - 3.93 - 11.85 - 1.56 - 0.91 | 24.62 | 2.26 | 0.54 | 1.93 | 0.54 |
| Sprints | 658 | 6.16 | 7.31 - 3.72 - 8.79 - 0.98 - 0.44 | 21.24 | 3.39 | 0.80 | 2.65 | 0.78 |
| Routes | 1341 | 8.92 | 6.73 - 3.95 - 11.22 - 1.26 - 0.80 | 23.96 | 2.52 | 0.61 | 2.12 | 0.61 |
| Two-Year-Olds | 259 | 7.01 | 6.69 - 3.46 - 8.45 - 0.80 - 0.46 | 19.85 | 3.36 | 0.77 | 2.62 | 0.76 |
| Three-Year-Olds | 590 | 8.14 | 7.07 - 3.99 - 10.82 - 1.14 - 0.59 | 23.61 | 2.79 | 0.69 | 2.31 | 0.67 |
| Older Runners | 1150 | 8.17 | 6.90 - 3.91 - 10.66 - 1.27 - 0.78 | 23.52 | 2.69 | 0.65 | 2.19 | 0.63 |
| 5.50 Furlongs | 54 | 6.00 | 6.52 - 3.89 - 8.09 - 1.22 - 0.50 | 20.22 | 3.56 | 0.72 | 2.51 | 0.73 |
| 6.00 Furlongs | 325 | 6.50 | 7.80 - 3.94 - 9.70 - 0.97 - 0.41 | 22.82 | 3.56 | 0.82 | 2.66 | 0.78 |
| 6.50 Furlongs | 66 | 7.00 | 7.52 - 3.81 - 9.11 - 0.81 - 0.44 | 21.68 | 3.33 | 0.82 | 2.74 | 0.79 |
| 7.00 Furlongs | 140 | 8.00 | 6.50 - 3.84 - 10.64 - 1.19 - 0.66 | 22.83 | 2.57 | 0.63 | 2.19 | 0.63 |
| 8.00 Furlongs | 254 | 8.50 | 6.84 - 3.93 - 10.72 - 1.10 - 0.69 | 23.30 | 2.65 | 0.66 | 2.25 | 0.65 |
| 8.50 Furlongs | 458 | 9.00 | 6.92 - 4.04 - 11.33 - 1.27 - 0.79 | 24.34 | 2.52 | 0.62 | 2.15 | 0.62 |
| 9.00 Furlongs | 391 | 10.00 | 6.96 - 4.00 - 13.77 - 1.41 - 0.95 | 27.09 | 2.16 | 0.52 | 1.93 | 0.54 |
| 10.00 Furlongs | 79 | 11.00 | 6.31 - 3.90 - 13.15 - 2.15 - 1.42 | 26.92 | 2.12 | 0.47 | 1.66 | 0.43 |
| 12.00 Furlongs | 58 | 12.00 | 5.43 - 4.00 - 12.10 - 2.14 - 1.50 | 25.17 | 1.82 | 0.37 | 1.60 | 0.39 |

Data from Table 23 are shown graphically in Charts 14 and 15. Chart 14 plots the average DI for the winning claiming horses and the stakes winners against the average winning distance. Chart 15 does the same for the average CD. Again, the Dosage figure versus distance graph is a visual display of the fundamental Dosage model.

**CHART 14. AVERAGE DI VS. DISTANCE FOR CLAIMERS AND STAKES WINNERS**

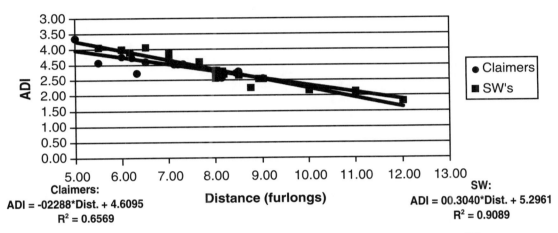

Claimers:
ADI = -02288*Dist. + 4.6095
$R^2$ = 0.6569

SW:
ADI = 00.3040*Dist. + 5.2961
$R^2$ = 0.9089

**CHART 15. AVERAGE CD VS. DISTANCE FOR CLAIMERS AND STAKES WINNERS**

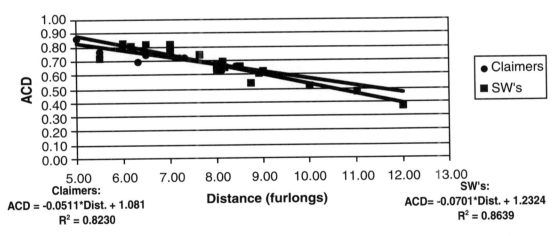

Claimers:
ACD = -0.0511*Dist. + 1.081
$R^2$ = 0.8230

SW's:
ACD= -0.0701*Dist. + 1.2324
$R^2$ = 0.8639

The graphical output of the data is unequivocal. The general Dosage model applies to runners at the lower end of the class ladder as it does to stakes winners. Also as expected, for reasons outlined above, we find a better fit of the data for the stakes winners. This observation is confirmed by their higher R-squared values, both in the DI and the CD plot.

As Denbleyker summarizes in his thesis, "the claiming-level race winners' relationship between DI or CD and average winning distance measures up well to that of open stakes winners. The statistically significant negative linear correlation holds up for the claiming horses . . . as well with respect to pedigree/performance. While expected to have more scatter and less associative strength than open stakes winners, the claiming-level race winners R-squares . . . for the DI and CD establish that such a pedigree/performance relationship holds also for a wider population of racehorses than just a highly selected subset of it."

# CHAPTER 16

# The Universality of Dosage

Contemporary Dosage methodology has its largest following in North America, with the vast majority of data collected in support of Dosage coming from races run in the United States and Canada. The analysis and interpretation of those data built the foundation for most of Dosage's applications. Nevertheless, the general utility of Dosage as a pedigree classification technique requires a broader geographic scope, especially as borders and oceans no longer present barriers to international competition. As it happens, there are Thoroughbred pedigree researchers in other parts of the world who have an intense interest in the subject and whose contributions have increased our understanding of Dosage's universality. Among them is Steve Miller from the UK who has been instrumental in identifying modern-day European-based sires for inclusion on the *chef-de-race* list. John Hutchinson in Australia has gone so far as to create a supplementary *chef-de-race* list specifically for racing in Australia and New Zealand. Similar efforts are under way in other parts of the world as well, including South America.

In order to demonstrate the relevance of Dosage across a range of racing venues, it is necessary to generate data for other locations similar to those generated in North America. This task involves the calculation of Dosage figures for the winners of races over a range of distances in other countries and on other continents, followed by an analysis to determine whether the data fit the model already established for North America.

The results of such a study are presented in Chart 16. The chart graphically displays the relationship between the average CD of major race winners in North America, Europe, Australia, Japan and South Africa and the average distance of the races won. The model holds for every venue with some variation in the slope of the lines. This variation is probably due to differences in the character of the racing surfaces throughout the racing world. Nevertheless, the direct relationship between Dosage and distance is confirmed on a global basis. Undoubtedly the data would improve if regional *chefs-de-race* were identified and included in the calculations. As noted below, this is the case for the Australian racing data. Otherwise, the data were generated using only the current North American list of *chefs-de-race*. We shortly will see the value of applying regional *chefs-de-race* in a more advanced study of South African racing.

The North American data (additionally separated by racing surface) include Grade 1 stakes since 1990. The European data come from 38 annual Group events in England, Ireland and France also since 1990. The Australian data were obtained from John Hutchinson and include data for five Group 1 races, three since 1960 and two since 1980. In this particular case, the CDs were calculated using Mr. Hutchinson's amended *chef-de-race* list. Finally, the Japanese data are for all Group 1 races since 1990 while the South African data include 20 Group 1 races since 1990. The plot shows the relationship between the average CD of the winners and the average distance of the races over the timeframes involved. The straight lines were generated by linear regression performed on each data series.

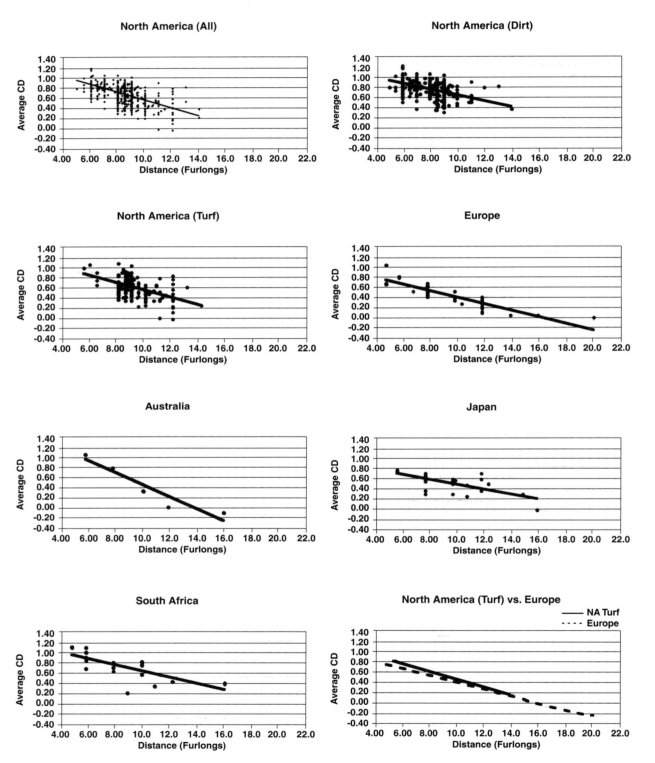

**CHART 16. DOSAGE RELATIONSHIPS IN NORTH AMERICA, EUROPE, AUSTRALIA, JAPAN AND SOUTH AFRICA**

One aspect of the South African study is particularly enlightening because it confirms the principle that Dosage is directly related to the distance influence of individual sires in the pedigree, despite the contrary view espoused by Varola. The data series for South African racing as illustrated in Chart 16 is based on the published current *chef-de-race* list. However, data available from South Africa has allowed us to modify the *chef-de-race* list to include influential sires from that region of the world as provisional *chefs-de-race*.

The South African Thoroughbred journal, *Racing Record*, publishes a document called "Stamina Influence of Sires" in their *Sires Handbook*. This document lists dozens of South African sires along with the winning distance ranges of their successful progeny.

Five distance ranges are defined: 1,000 to 1,300 meters, 1,400 and 1,500 meters, 1,600 to 1,800 meters, 1,900 to 2,200 meters and 2,300 meters or more. For this exercise consider these ranges as areas along the speed/stamina spectrum. Consequently, we associated the 1,000 to 1,300-meter range with the Brilliant aptitudinal group within a DP. In similar fashion, 1,400 to 1,500 meters is associated with Intermediate; 1,600 to 1,800 meters is associated with Classic; 1,900 to 2,200 meters is associated with Solid and 2,300 meters or more is associated with Professional. These assignments do not imply a rigorous correlation; however, they are convenient for our purpose.

The "average" South African sire has 38 percent winners in the 1,000- to 1,300-meter range, 15 percent in the 1,400- to 1,500-meter range, 29 percent in the 1,600- to 1,800-meter range, 13 percent in the 1,900- to 2,200 meter range and 5 percent in the 2,300-meters or more range. If we arrange these percentages as 38-15-29-13-5, they take on the general appearance of a DP with 38 points in B, 15 points in I, 29 points in C, 13 points in S and 5 points in P. This DP format then allows us to calculate the equivalent of a CD using the standard formula. In the example, 38-15-29-13-5 equals a "CD" of 0.68. We can then do the same for each of the South African sires. The two examples shown below are for Harry Hotspur (SAF), 1971 (Mexico (GB)-Saturna (SAF), by Silver Tor (IRE)) and Rakeen, 1987 (Northern Dancer (CAN)-Glorious Song (CAN), by Halo (USA)).

|  | No. of Wins | 1000-1300m | 1400-1500m | 1600-1800m | 1900-2200m | 2300m+ |
|---|---|---|---|---|---|---|
| Average |  | 38% | 15% | 29% | 13% | 5% |
| Harry Hotspur | 724 | 80% | 10% | 8% | 2% | 1% |
| Rakeen | 253 | 8% | 10% | 40% | 28% | 14% |

| | |
|---|---|
| Average"CD" | $((2 \times 38) + 15 - 13 - (2 \times 5))/100 = 68/100 = 0.68$ |
| Harry Hotspur "CD" | $((2 \times 80 + 10 - 2 - (2 \times 1))/101 = 166/101 = 1.64$ |
| Rakeen"CD" | $((2 \times 8) + 10 - 28 - (2 \times 14))/100 = -30/100 = -0.30$ |

We calculated a "CD" for all of the sires on the list, after which we sorted the sires by decreasing "CD" to generate another list with the most speed-oriented at the top and the most stamina-oriented at the bottom. Limiting the number of sires to those with at least 200 progeny wins, we assigned notional *chef-de-race* categories to each sire depending on his position on the list. Table 24 shows the sires in descending order of "CD" along with the notional *chef-de-race* assignment.

## TABLE 24. PROVISIONAL SOUTH AFRICAN *chefs-de-race*

| Sire | B | I | C | S | P | CD | CDR Assignment |
|---|---|---|---|---|---|---|---|
| Song of Songs | 81 | 10 | 8 | 2 | 0 | 1.68 | B |
| Harry Hotspur | 80 | 10 | 8 | 2 | 1 | 1.64 | B |
| Golden Thatch | 76 | 12 | 10 | 2 | 0 | 1.62 | B |
| Mexico II | 73 | 15 | 10 | 1 | 0 | 1.62 | B |
| Argosy | 65 | 18 | 14 | 3 | 0 | 1.45 | B |
| Caerdeon | 68 | 13 | 15 | 3 | 1 | 1.44 | B |
| Rocky Marriage | 68 | 15 | 12 | 3 | 2 | 1.44 | B |
| Waterville Lake | 64 | 16 | 17 | 4 | 0 | 1.39 | B |
| National Assembly | 61 | 16 | 17 | 5 | 0 | 1.34 | B |
| Sunny North | 52 | 19 | 21 | 4 | 3 | 1.14 | B/I |
| Divine King | 57 | 11 | 21 | 11 | 0 | 1.14 | B/I |
| Hard Up | 53 | 15 | 23 | 7 | 1 | 1.13 | B/I |
| Comic Blush | 51 | 19 | 23 | 6 | 1 | 1.13 | B/I |
| Mistral Dancer | 53 | 13 | 23 | 9 | 1 | 1.09 | B/I |
| Peaceable Kingdom | 49 | 17 | 26 | 8 | 0 | 1.07 | B/I |
| Phantom Earl | 45 | 23 | 23 | 7 | 1 | 1.05 | B/I |
| Qui Danzig | 50 | 17 | 24 | 6 | 3 | 1.05 | B/I |
| Proclaim | 48 | 22 | 20 | 6 | 4 | 1.04 | B/I |
| Jallad | 46 | 17 | 29 | 6 | 1 | 1.02 | B/I |
| Folmar | 46 | 21 | 23 | 8 | 2 | 1.01 | B/I |
| Fine Edge | 47 | 17 | 27 | 7 | 2 | 1.00 | B/I |
| All Fired Up | 48 | 18 | 24 | 8 | 3 | 0.99 | I |
| Best By Test | 50 | 16 | 23 | 8 | 4 | 0.99 | I |
| Freedom Land | 45 | 19 | 28 | 6 | 2 | 0.99 | I |
| Really and Truly | 45 | 17 | 25 | 8 | 4 | 0.92 | B/C |
| On Stage | 48 | 12 | 26 | 11 | 3 | 0.91 | B/C |
| Centenary | 38 | 23 | 27 | 11 | 0 | 0.89 | B/C |
| Complete Warrior | 40 | 19 | 31 | 9 | 1 | 0.88 | B/C |
| Piaffer | 39 | 26 | 24 | 6 | 5 | 0.88 | B/C |
| Shoe Danzig | 42 | 17 | 30 | 9 | 2 | 0.88 | B/C |
| Damascus Gate | 44 | 19 | 24 | 9 | 5 | 0.87 | B/C |
| Lords | 44 | 17 | 23 | 10 | 5 | 0.86 | B/C |
| Lost Chord | 42 | 14 | 28 | 12 | 3 | 0.81 | I/C |
| Russian Fox | 39 | 21 | 23 | 15 | 2 | 0.80 | I/C |
| Rainbow Dream | 42 | 15 | 26 | 11 | 5 | 0.79 | I/C |
| Northern Guest | 37 | 19 | 32 | 9 | 4 | 0.75 | I/C |
| Tilden | 45 | 7 | 32 | 10 | 6 | 0.75 | I/C |
| Averof | 37 | 19 | 28 | 12 | 4 | 0.73 | I/C |

TABLE 24. (CONTINUED)

| Sire | B | I | C | S | P | CD | CDR Assignment |
|------|---|---|---|---|---|-----|----------------|
| ALL | 38 | 15 | 29 | 13 | 5 | 0.68 | I/C |
| Al Mufti | 32 | 18 | 38 | 9 | 3 | 0.67 | I/C |
| Volcanic | 31 | 18 | 37 | 12 | 1 | 0.67 | I/C |
| Only a Pound | 32 | 18 | 38 | 11 | 2 | 0.66 | I/C |
| Jungle Cove | 35 | 15 | 34 | 15 | 2 | 0.65 | I/C |
| Elliodor | 32 | 18 | 33 | 14 | 4 | 0.59 | C |
| The Eliminator | 33 | 15 | 32 | 18 | 2 | 0.59 | C |
| Esplendor | 32 | 21 | 26 | 17 | 5 | 0.57 | C |
| Home Guard | 36 | 13 | 33 | 11 | 8 | 0.57 | C |
| Steady Beat | 28 | 18 | 39 | 13 | 2 | 0.57 | C |
| Secret Prospector | 27 | 19 | 38 | 13 | 3 | 0.54 | C |
| Fair Season | 30 | 18 | 31 | 16 | 5 | 0.52 | C |
| Dancing Champ | 29 | 18 | 34 | 16 | 4 | 0.51 | C |
| Model Man | 26 | 20 | 35 | 16 | 3 | 0.50 | C |
| Over the Air | 34 | 12 | 28 | 19 | 7 | 0.47 | C/S |
| Our Casey's Boy | 30 | 15 | 33 | 18 | 5 | 0.47 | C/S |
| Royal Chalice | 24 | 17 | 40 | 12 | 6 | 0.41 | C/S |
| Royal Prerogative | 24 | 17 | 35 | 20 | 4 | 0.37 | C/S |
| Northfields | 26 | 13 | 37 | 19 | 6 | 0.34 | C/S |
| Foveros | 28 | 13 | 32 | 18 | 9 | 0.33 | C/S |
| Truly Nureyev | 28 | 12 | 30 | 25 | 5 | 0.33 | C/S |
| Badger Land | 20 | 16 | 40 | 18 | 5 | 0.28 | C/S |
| Roland Gardens | 22 | 15 | 35 | 21 | 6 | 0.26 | C/S |
| Peacetime | 25 | 13 | 31 | 20 | 9 | 0.26 | C/S |
| Lucy's Axe | 18 | 15 | 41 | 17 | 10 | 0.14 | S |
| Elevation | 19 | 13 | 35 | 25 | 7 | 0.12 | S |
| Condorcet | 15 | 15 | 37 | 26 | 7 | 0.05 | C/P |
| Politician | 22 | 11 | 28 | 26 | 13 | 0.03 | C/P |
| Coastal | 18 | 12 | 33 | 24 | 13 | -0.02 | C/P |
| Dolpour | 9 | 8 | 51 | 25 | 7 | -0.13 | S/P |
| Concertino | 16 | 9 | 34 | 25 | 17 | -0.18 | S/P |
| Rakeen | 8 | 10 | 40 | 28 | 14 | -0.30 | P |
| Del Sarto | 9 | 10 | 37 | 28 | 16 | -0.32 | P |
| Hobnob | 9 | 8 | 34 | 31 | 18 | -0.41 | P |

Finally, we used the current *chef-de-race* list along with the new South African modified *chef-de-race* list to recalculate the Dosage figures for the South African Group 1 races examined in the initial evaluation. Chart 18 presents the results of the "CD" vs. distance study for both the original case and the "improved" case using notional South African *chefs-de-race*. Two things have occurred. First, the slope of the linear regression trend line has increased. The significance of an increased slope is greater separation of Dosage figures by distance. The original case indicates a span of just under

0.6 CD units over a distance range of five to sixteen furlongs. The addition of South African *chefs-de-race* increases the CD span to over 0.9 CD units for the same distance range. Greater separation of populations by Dosage figures implies increased accuracy in aptitudinal pedigree classification. Second, the R-squared value has risen from 0.5555 to 0.7486. The higher the R-squared value, the better the correlation between Dosage figures and distance.

The increase in slope and the improved correlation both confirm that applying a sire's progeny distance profile is a useful and appropriate method of identifying aptitudinal prepotence. It further suggests that similar techniques can be used internationally to enhance the utility of Dosage on a global scale. It also suggests that Varola was wrong when he insisted Dosage and distance potential were unrelated. Recall that the original contemporary Dosage studies utilized Varola's own *chefs-de-race* as modified slightly by Hewitt.

**CHART 17. "IMPROVED" CORRELATION WHEN APPLYING PROVISIONAL SOUTH AFRICAN CHEFS-DE-RACE**

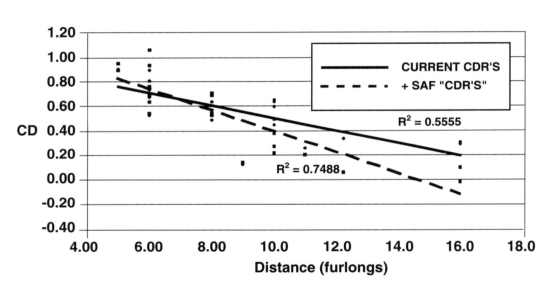

It is immediately obvious that the Dosage model holds not only for North America but for Europe, Japan, Australia and South Africa as well. The inverse relationship between Dosage figures and distance transcends racing surfaces, nations, continents and hemispheres. Of particular interest is the closeness of the trend lines for European races and for North American races on the turf.

**Chapter 17**

# Inbreeding in *Chefs-de-Race*, Their Sires and Their Dams

At this point we will refer again to the Jones and Bogart definition of inbreeding as the mating of two individuals more closely related than the average of the breed. Jones and Bogart highly recommend that serious breeders know the amount of inbreeding in their stock in order to appreciate the rate at which homozygosity is developing, homozygosity being the condition where genes inherited from the sire and the dam are alike. The amount of inbreeding estimates the percentage of genes put in a homozygous condition. This estimate is always less than the actual because historical records will not allow for every relationship that exists. Horses that are highly homozygous tend to stamp their own characteristics on their offspring, a phenomenon often called "prepotency." Prepotency also may be considered a regular or predictable transmission of particular traits.

The amount of inbreeding can be calculated using a formula proposed by Wright in 1923 (*Mendelian Analysis of the Pure Breeds of Livestock*, J. Hered. 14:339-348). Wright's formula generates a fraction (the coefficient of inbreeding) which, when multiplied by 100, affords the amount of inbreeding as a percentage.

The information presented below includes the amount of inbreeding through six generations for all 199 *chefs-de-race*, as well as for their sires and their dams. The raw data are preceded by some general statistics.

Observations:

The percentage of inbreeding among *chefs-de-race* declined steadily throughout the 20th century. The relationship between the percentage of inbreeding and time is expressed by the following formula: % Inbreeding = -0.0109 * Year + 22.328

Therefore, the rate at which inbreeding has declined between 1900 and 2001 is 0.0109 percent per year. Whether this pattern among *chefs-de-race* represents the pattern found among all Thoroughbreds is not known at this time. In any case, *chefs-de-race* foaled in successive 10-year time frames display a diminishing amount of inbreeding.

The amount of inbreeding found among *chefs-de-race* covers the range from more than 13 percent for Ultimus down to 0 percent for Speak John, with some of the most influential stallions being found at both ends of the spectrum. For example, Havresac II (a key link to Ribot) and Bayardo (a key link to Hyperion) are among the most highly inbred, while Native Dancer (the close up ancestor of Raise a Native and Mr. Prospector) and Ribot himself are among the least inbred.

Arguably the best runners among the *chefs-de-race* — Secretariat (0.1953 percent), Man o' War (0.8350 percent), Ribot (0.1465 percent), Nearco (0.9839 percent) and Sea-Bird (0.3906 percent) — were all inbred below the average percentage of inbreeding for the timeframe in which they were foaled.

There is no significant pattern covering the relationship between inbreeding in the *chefs-de-race* and inbreeding in their parents. Most (36.2 percent) are less inbred than either parent, followed by 32.7 percent that are inbred more than one parent but less than the other, and 28.6 percent that are inbred more than either parent. The remaining 2.5 percent are inbred the same as one parent.

Secretariat

Photo Courtesy of Dell Hancock

# Secretariat

## DP 20-4-7-9-0, DI 3.00, CD 0.90

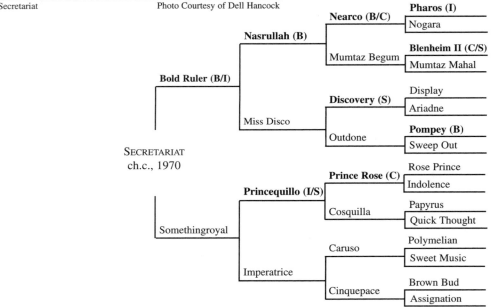

SECRETARIAT
ch.c., 1970

| | | | |
|---|---|---|---|
| | | **Nearco (B/C)** | **Pharos (I)** |
| | **Nasrullah (B)** | | Nogara |
| | | Mumtaz Begum | **Blenheim II (C/S)** |
| **Bold Ruler (B/I)** | | | Mumtaz Mahal |
| | | **Discovery (S)** | Display |
| | Miss Disco | | Ariadne |
| | | Outdone | **Pompey (B)** |
| | | | Sweep Out |
| | | **Prince Rose (C)** | Rose Prince |
| | **Princequillo (I/S)** | | Indolence |
| | | Cosquilla | Papyrus |
| Somethingroyal | | | Quick Thought |
| | | Caruso | Polymelian |
| | Imperatrice | | Sweet Music |
| | | Cinquepace | Brown Bud |
| | | | Assignation |

| DP Contribution | | Equivalent to: | |
|---|---|---|---|
| Sire | 20 - 10 - 3 - 5 - 0 | DI 4.85 | CD 1.18 |
| Dam | 0 - 4 - 4 - 4 - 0 | DI 1.00 | CD 0.00 |

Intermediate/Classic *chef-de-race* Secretariat, ch.c., 1970 (Bold Ruler-Somethingroyal, by Princequillo) is considered by many to be the greatest Thoroughbred racehorse of all time. A Triple Crown winner and Horse-of-the-Year at two and three, his accomplishments are legendary and transcend the achievements of mere mortal horses. He is the product of breeding the brilliant speed of his sire, Brilliant/Intermediate *chef-de-race* Bold Ruler, to the classic stamina of his dam, resulting in DP 20-14-7-9-0, DI 3.00 and CD 0.90. Although it may seem that the figures are high by classic standards, the DI is well within classic guidelines and the CD captures his potential for speed. That speed is vividly expressed in his fractions during the unforgettable 1973 Belmont Stakes, which he won on the front end by an amazing 31 lengths: a half in :46.1; three-quarters in 1:09.4; a mile in 1:34.1; a mile and a quarter in 1:59 flat; and a mile and a half in 2:24 flat. These are previously unheard of fractions in a race of that distance. Later in the year, he clocked a mile in 1:33 flat en route to a world record 1:45.2 against older horses in the nine-furlong Marlboro Cup Handicap. Secretariat won from six furlongs to a mile and five eighths, on dirt and on grass, from dead last and wire-to-wire. Although his style was versatile, he had awesome speed when called upon to use it.

For 55.6 percent of the *chefs-de-race*, their sire is more highly inbred than their dam.   For 43.2 percent of the *chefs-de-race*, the reverse is true.   There are two examples (1.0 percent) where the sire and dam of the *chef-de-race* exhibit the same level of inbreeding.

There are observable differences in inbreeding among *chefs-de-race* sorted by aptitudinal contribution; however, these differences are not statistically significant.

One may conclude from the data that the amount of inbreeding in a *chef-de-race* or his parents is unrelated to his ability to transmit consistent aptitudinal type to his progeny.   Prepotence for aptitudinal type apparently has a different origin.

*General Statistics:*

| | |
|---|---|
| Average % inbreeding of all *chefs-de-race*: | 1.1258 |
| Average % inbreeding of the sires of all *chefs-de-race*: | 1.1655 |
| Average % inbreeding of the dams of all *chefs-de-race*: | 1.1989 |

*% Inbreeding Over Time:*

| | |
|---|---|
| Average % inbreeding of *chefs-de-race* born before 1910: | 1.8091 |
| Average % inbreeding of *chefs-de-race* born 1910-1919: | 1.5773 |
| Average % inbreeding of *chefs-de-race* born 1920-1929: | 1.3128 |
| Average % inbreeding of *chefs-de-race* born 1930-1939: | 1.0025 |
| Average % inbreeding of *chefs-de-race* born 1940-1949: | 0.9687 |
| Average % inbreeding of *chefs-de-race* born 1950-1959: | 0.9521 |
| Average % inbreeding of *chefs-de-race* born 1960-1969: | 0.9310 |
| Average % inbreeding of *chefs-de-race* born after 1969: | 0.9481 |

| Chefs-de-Race *with Highest % Inbreeding* | | Chefs-de-Race *with Lowest % Inbreeding* | |
|---|---|---|---|
| Ultimus: | 13.2935 | Speak John: | 0.0000 |
| Havresac II: | 6.5796 | Native Dancer: | 0.0488 |
| Bayardo: | 4.2163 | Relko: | 0.0488 |
| Gallant Man: | 4.0015 | Stage Door Johnny: | 0.0977 |
| Turn-to: | 3.8940 | Bold Bidder: | 0.0977 |
| Broad Brush: | 3.4644 | Djebel: | 0.0977 |
| In Reality: | 3.2764 | King's Bishop: | 0.0977 |
| Spy Song: | 3.2495 | Ribot: | 0.1465 |
| Sunny Boy: | 3.2227 | Promised Land: | 0.1465 |
| Colorado: | 2.8198 | Secretariat: | 0.1953 |
| Vatout: | 2.6855 | | |

*% Inbreeding in Chefs-de-Race Relative to Their Sire and Dam*

| | |
|---|---|
| % of *chefs-de-race* with % inbreeding < % inbreeding in either sire or dam: | 36.2 |
| % of *chefs-de-race* with % inbreeding > % inbreeding in either sire or dam: | 28.6 |
| % of *chefs-de-race* with % inbreeding > % inbreeding in sire and < % inbreeding in dam: | 13.6 |
| % of *chefs-de-race* with % inbreeding < % inbreeding in sire and > % inbreeding in dam: | 19.1 |
| % of *chefs-de-race* with % inbreeding = % inbreeding in either sire or dam: | 2.5 |

*% Inbreeding in Chefs-de-Race by Aptitudinal Group Representation*

| | |
|---|---|
| Average % inbreeding for *chefs-de-race* in Brilliant: | 1.3653 |
| Average % inbreeding for *chefs-de-race* in Intermediate: | 1.1407 |
| Average % inbreeding for *chefs-de-race* in Classic: | 0.9271 |
| Average % inbreeding for *chefs-de-race* in Solid: | 0.9242 |
| Average % inbreeding for *chefs-de-race* in Professional: | 1.0300 |

Top runners among *chefs-de-race* that were inbred below the average percentage for the timeframe in which they were foaled.

(Photo Courtesy of the Thoroughbred Times)

Nearco 0.9839 %

(Photo Courtesy of the Keeneland Library)

Ribot 0.1465 %

(Photo Courtesy of the Keeneland Library)

Sea Bird 0.3906 %

(Photo Courtesy of the Keeneland Library)

Man o' War 0.8350 %

# CHAPTER 18

# The Selection of *Chefs-de-Race*

No aspect of Dosage is more confusing to the general racing public than the selection of *chefs-de-race*. By contrast, the significance and meaning of the statistical indexes (i.e., DP, DI and CD) derived from Dosage methodology are reasonably well understood, although much of the subtlety associated with interpretation of the figures is often ignored by the turf media. Also lost is the direct link between the figures and the assignment and placement of the *chefs-de-race*. In fact, it is critical that the selection of a *chef-de-race* reflects an undeniable aptitudinal contribution by the stallion proposed for inclusion. The type of contribution he makes not only must be readily identifiable, it must be consistent as well. That is to say, any candidate being considered as a *chef-de-race* must display prepotence, a condition in which an individual consistently transmits a similar quality to his offspring.

Acknowledging a virtually infinite number of possible genetic combinations and permutations, it is truly unusual when a specific trait is passed along almost without exception. The broad scope of biological variation essentially precludes that every immediate descendant displays that trait, but in a statistical sense the trait appears with overwhelming regularity. The requirement that stallions exhibit prepotence is the very essence of Dosage methodology.

Since Dosage is a technique for classifying pedigrees by type, its predictive capability depends on the aptitudinal qualities inherited from particular sires being largely the same from one foal to another. Imagine a situation in which the transmission of characteristics from generation to generation is a totally random affair. There would be no way to predict accurately what the product of a mating would be like. Breeding would be a game of pure chance and luck. Fortunately there is a degree of order and sense to genetics that allows for a reasonable amount of planning in the matching of stallions and mares. Although luck always plays a part, we have learned enough in more than 200 years of selective breeding at least to have an expectation that our choices will result in a foal that reflects the qualities of the sire and the dam.

Most breeding animals, however, are not especially prepotent and we are limited in the accuracy of our predictions. On the other hand, those few breeding animals that are truly prepotent dramatically increase our ability to design a mating with a well-defined objective in mind. Since the goal of Dosage is to provide a method for classifying Thoroughbred pedigrees to better appreciate the relationship between pedigree and performance, it is essential to focus exclusively on those relatively few prepotent animals whose traits are passed on with regularity. The non-prepotent influences will introduce some uncertainty into the interpretation, but the prepotent influences do bring order to a complex process. Because few sires in any era actually are prepotent for type, once they are identified, the task of pedigree interpretation is facilitated when applying the Dosage techniques.

To elaborate, all versions of Dosage accept the principle that relatively few individuals account for most of the evolutionary forces within the breed. A consequence of this principle is the belief that a reasonable aptitudinal interpretation of a pedigree can be achieved by limiting the analysis to include only those select individuals. In reality, every ancestor plays a role although not many will pass along definable traits in a regular manner.

For our purposes we exclude the non-prepotent influences solely because of their unpredictability. Such exclusion can lead to errors if actual prepotence for type hasn't been confirmed. This is something to consider particularly when dealing with newer stallions that haven't yet proven their case for prepotency. For example, young sires like A.P. Indy, Kingmambo and Thunder Gulch are showing signs they may be consistent sources of classic stamina. If future developments confirm these suspicions, they could eventually emerge as *chef-de-race* candidates. In the meantime, it is a good idea to at least consider the possibility of unacknowledged aptitudinal prepotence in a pedigree and to make mental adjustments to the Dosage figures to account for them. This procedure may affect the analysis for an individual horse while having virtually no effect on the figures for the general Thoroughbred population.

There are other considerations when assessing unacknowledged sources of prepotent type. These are implicit in *chef-de-race* selection, a process that is not universally understood. For example, there is the exclusion of dams as *chefs-de-race*. The explanation for this relies on an appreciation of the fundamentals of Dosage methodology.

The latest version of Dosage is based on statistics derived from large populations of Thoroughbreds. Pedigrees are grouped according to categories of performance type such as sprinters, routers, dirt horses, turf horses, juveniles, older runners, graded stakes performers and so on. By grouping the pedigrees, Dosage can identify common pedigree characteristics among the members of those categories. The Dosage figures are unique to the groups and the figures for one group may be readily differentiated from the figures for other groups. In any statistical study there is usually significant variation observed among the individuals, but the statistical results for the entire group are unique to that group. Any one horse will have little effect on the overall statistics for the population under study.

It is for this reason that mares have been excluded. A stallion may have hundreds of foals in a lifetime, but a mare will have only a few. Accordingly, mares have a minor impact on the broader statistical base. There is no suggestion here that mares don't influence their foals profoundly. Obviously they contribute 50 percent of the genetic material plus qualities perhaps less well defined. On the other hand, they contribute little to population-wide Dosage statistics. Furthermore, since most mares are represented by *chefs-de-race* in their own pedigree, their aptitudinal impact is generally accounted for. Separately, many mares appear in the pedigree of *chefs-de-race* that are among their descendants. The aptitudinal prepotence of these *chefs-de-race* certainly reflects the influence of these mares. Including only stallions among the *chefs-de-race* simplifies the analysis while having a marginal effect on the accuracy of the population statistics.

However, making mental adjustments to the figures to account for special mares is justified here as it is for the emerging young sires discussed earlier. A desirable objective of Dosage is the accuracy of individual pedigree interpretation even if the broad conclusions of Dosage apply to the entire population.

In the end, Dosage reserves the term *chef-de-race* for the aptitudinally prepotent and uniquely influential animal. We recall that at the beginning of the 20th century, Vuillier was content to name only 15 *chefs-de-race* in three series covering the early, middle and late 1800s. Varola created an expanded *chef-de-race* list to include 120 stallions foaled mainly after 1900. The current number of *chefs-de-race* (as of November 2002) stands at 199 and includes Varola's 120, plus additions made by Hewitt in the 1970s. Since the introduction of the latest Dosage version in 1981 we have made further additions and refinements.

The method of identifying new *chefs-de-race* is inextricably linked to the philosophy that drives each variation of Dosage. Vuillier had it relatively easy. He observed that a select group of ancestors in the pedigrees of top class horses appeared with a frequency far greater than that of the other horses that were present. His task was to confirm this dominance by tallying those appearances. Among more recent sires, names such as Bold Ruler, Raise a Native, Northern Dancer, Ribot, and perhaps Turn-to come to mind as meeting the Vuillier requirement.

Varola focused on only "those sires who had transmitted such prepotent and unmistakable traits that any study of pedigrees would be meaningless without them." That in itself is a reasonable goal. However, Varola then compared the influence of sires to peaks in a mountain range and he excluded sires that failed to attain a particularly high altitude. As noble as his intentions may have been, his approach denies the existence of prepotence for type in any other than the most highly regarded stallions. Apart from there being no evidence for such a phenomenon, it weakens, through a largely arbitrary exclusion process, any attempt to accurately define a pedigree in terms of inherited aptitudes.

We apply one absolute criterion to *chef-de-race* selection. The *chef-de-race* candidate must be prepotent for aptitudinal type. Furthermore, we must be able to demonstrate his prepotence using statistical analysis. It would be helpful, although not necessary to the analysis if the *chef-de-race* candidate were a sire of sires or a sire of quality broodmares. In this way we would increase the sample size and show that prepotent influences carry through to successive generations. This obviously wouldn't be relevant to young sires that may have only a small number of sons and daughters at stud even though their aptitudinal prepotence is clearly visible in their racing progeny. Finally, a sire's reputation at stud is of minimal concern. The critical factor is enough racing data generated by his runners to allow for a meaningful statistical study.

Keep in mind that we use the data from stakes races to develop our case. Stakes races are the most formful of all races and stakes horses are the most consistent of all runners. Horses entered in stakes generally belong in those races and the outcomes are likely to be the result of a suitable genetic expression of type. A decent stakes sire can often generate more than enough progeny data to make a case for his aptitudinal prepotence.

Nevertheless, there is often pressure to consider for selection as a *chef-de-race* any stallion that establishes a superior record as a sire of runners. Quite often there is a parallel between prepotence and exceptional stud performance, but not always. No one could deny, for example, that Brilliant *chef-de-race* Raise a Native, one of the purest sources of speed in the last 50 years, was also among the leading stallions of his era, getting runners and breeding sons like Alydar, Majestic Prince and Mr. Prospector. Even more important in the context of Thoroughbred evolution is the definitive transmission of his speed through succeeding generations. That speed is so compelling that Raise a Native even has a significant impact on breeding in the American Quarter Horse.

In contrast, many excellent stallions, despite outstanding progeny performance, have failed to display an overpowering aptitudinal influence from one generation to the next. Commonly, the types of foals they produce, regardless of talent, are more a reflection of the mares to which they have been bred. In effect, they are capable of getting world-class athletes but not necessarily of a definable type. Sometimes this is hard to discern because the prepotent effects in the mare will obscure the absolute effect of the sire, but over time certain patterns will develop in a sire's offspring that give clues to his own prepotence. Occasionally it may take one or two generations to become clear. By contrast, some sires with less than world-class credentials have expressed extraordinary prepotence, easily overpowering the aptitudinal contributions of their mates. Their failure to reach the top of the sire lists may result from lack of opportunity more than any other factor. Often the mares to which they are bred are second or third rank as producers.

Such was the case of Apalachee, who was not among the leading sires when named a Brilliant *chef-de-race* in the late 1980s. However, between 1983 and 1991, Apalachee sired the winners of more major six-furlong stakes races than any North American sire other than Mr. Prospector and Fappiano. He also got a series of blazingly fast sprinting fillies such as Clocks Secret, Pine Tree Lane and Lazer Show, each capable of going a half-mile in under 44 seconds. He did this despite being a son of Solid *chef-de-race* Round Table. Undoubtedly the source of his speed is his female family descended from Rough Shod II through the brilliant Moccasin. Rough Shod II, in turn, is a direct male-line descendant of Brilliant *chef-de-race* Orby. Nevertheless, excluding the consistently predictable speed influence associated with Apalachee's name in a four-generation pedigree because he wasn't a "good enough" sire misses the entire point of aptitudinal analysis, not to mention resulting in an incorrect interpretation of the pedigree in which he appears. Regardless of the source, failure to acknowledge the speed influence of Apalachee in a pedigree will certainly result in a misinterpretation of the aptitudinal characteristics of his descendants. For the sake of accuracy, one must take into account his undeniable prepotence.

The most easily identifiable *chef-de-race* candidates are those like Apalachee whose exclusion in aptitudinal pedigree analysis leads to a grossly inaccurate picture of the pedigree type being evaluated. Using the data derived from thousands of pedigrees classified by performance type, we know where the figures lie for populations whose abilities are expressed in particular racing categories. In evaluating a subpopulation of pedigrees that have in common the appearance of a particular sire, we can compare the Dosage figures derived from that subpopulation with the figures established for the breed at large. When there is a significant difference in the figures between the subpopulation and the general population of the same performance type, it is evidence that an aptitudinal influence in the subpopulation is being overlooked. That influence could well be the sire that the subpopulation has in common.

An example is a population of sprinters all with "Sire X" somewhere in their pedigree and with combined Dosage figures more typical of the general population of stayers. In this case it is likely that a prepotent influence from "Sire X" has been ignored. There is no reason to expect any group of sprinters not to conform to population standards established in thousands of races. When, through empirical calculations, a sire is placed in the appropriate aptitudinal group or groups and recalculation of the figures realigns the subpopulation with the general population, we can feel confident that we have identified and correctly assigned a new *chef-de-race*.

We can further illustrate the logic behind *chef-de-race* selection with specific examples, using the previously published assignments for Fappiano and Broad Brush.

Apalachee       Photo Courtesy of the Thoroughbred Times

# Apalachee

## DP 9-4-7-20-0, DI 0.70, CD 0.05

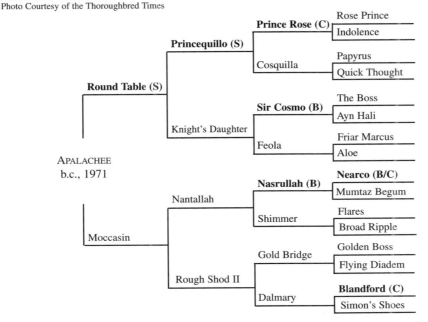

| DP Contribution | Equivalent to: |
|---|---|
| Sire   4 - 4 - 4 - 20 - 0 | DI   0.45    CD   -0.25 |
| Dam   5 - 0 - 3 -  0 - 0 | DI   4.33    CD   1.25 |

The Dosage interpretation of Apalachee's pedigree is included here not because his figures match his performance, but precisely because they do not. The implications of this mismatch between pedigree and performance are fundamental to an understanding of the selection process for *chefs-de-race*.

Brilliant *chef-de-race* Apalachee, b.c., 1971 (Round Table-Moccasin, by Nantallah) is considered one of the great two-year-old runners of the 20th century in Great Britain. His Timeform rating of 137 pounds is surpassed by only twenty-one runners of any age. Undefeated as a juvenile, he won all three of his starts including a smashing win in the Group 1 Observor Gold Cup at a mile. As an early three-year-old he defeated older horses in the Group 3 Gladness Stakes in Ireland, but failed to live up to his promise in the English Two Thousand Guineas by running third to Nonoalco and Giacometti. Nominally bred for tremendous endurance, he was instead a brilliant sprinter-miler. Apalachee is bred on a stamina over speed pattern, with his sire, Solid *chef-de-race* Round Table, contributing a full 20 Solid points to Apalachee's DP. His pedigree is virtually identical to that of Grade 1 winner

King Pellinore whose dam, Thong, is a full sister to Apalachee's dam, Moccasin. In contrast to Apalachee, King Pellinore won the 1976 Oak Tree Invitational Stakes (G1) at a mile and a half on the grass. Round Table sired many other stayers on dirt and grass, even when bred to speed mares. These include such Grade/Group 1 winners as Duel, He's a Smoothie, Dignitas, Drumtop, Tell, Royal Glint and Artaius. It appears as if the speed through Rough Shod II dominates Apalachee's pedigree in this instance and it carries over to Apalachee's descendants which include many spectacularly brilliant sprinters like Clocks Secret, Lazer Show, Pine Tree Lane, Artax and Texas Glitter. The disparity between Apalachee's influence on his descendants' pedigrees and the aptitudinal characteristics he passes along from his ancestors is the key factor in his selection as a *chef-de-race*. As a Brilliant *chef-de-race*, Apalachee contributes 20-2-2-10-0 to the DP of his foals. The very large Brilliant contribution he makes readily accounts for their performance. Denying his speed influence would invariably lead to an aptitudinal misinterpretation.

Fappiano                Photo Courtesy of John Noye

## FAPPIANO, C., 1977 (MR. PROSPECTOR-KILLALOE, BY DR. FAGER), ASSIGNED AUGUST 1998:

To determine the prepotent aptitudinal influences contributed by Fappiano to his descendants, we examined more than 200 open stakes races since 1983 where Fappiano or one of his sons is the sire, or where Fappiano is the broodmare sire of the winner. In other words, Fappiano is the one constant in the pedigree of all the winners of these races. At an average winning distance of 7.84 furlongs, the Dosage figures for these winners are average DP 10.81-3.62-9.34-1.13-1.14, average DI 3.37, and average CD 0.86. The comparative standards for distance established by almost 15,000 stakes winners since 1983 are as follows. At seven furlongs: average DP 9.11-5.19-8.99-1.37-0.73, average DI 4.06, and average CD 0.84. At eight furlongs: average DP 8.28-4.83-9.97-1.81-0.94, average DI 3.30, and average CD 0.71. The predicted numbers for Fappiano's descendants, based on an extrapolation of these figures are average DI 3.42 and average CD 0.76. Although there is good agreement with the average DI value, the average CD of Fappiano's runners is more typical of six-and-a-half to seven furlong performers than of the near milers they actually are as a group. The challenge, then, is to identify aptitudinal placements that best bring the figures for Fappiano's descendants in line with the general population having similar performance characteristics.

It quickly became apparent that no placement of Fappiano alone would adequately satisfy the requirements for bringing this subpopulation of runners in line with the population at large. A balanced relationship between the DI and CD could not be achieved. However, invoking prepotent aptitudinal influences from Fappiano's broodmare sire, Dr. Fager, and from Dr. Fager's sire, Rough'n Tumble, provided an acceptable solution.

An accommodation was achieved between the Dosage figures of the general population of stakes winners and the subpopulation of stakes winners with Fappiano in their pedigree by making the following aptitudinal assignments: Fappiano, Intermediate/Classic; Dr. Fager, Intermediate; Rough'n Tumble, Brilliant/Classic.

Applying these aptitudinal influences, we obtain revised figures for Fappiano's descendants: Average DP 11.32-12.46-15.67-1.13-1.14, average DI 3.43, and average CD 0.77. The numbers are now essentially identical to those predicted on the basis of average winning distance, and suggest an accurate placement of the three sires.

Some have argued that Fappiano in a pedigree represents true classic stamina. This argument is based on his appearance in the pedigree of Derby winners Unbridled, Grindstone, and Real Quiet, and in the pedigree of Belmont Stakes winner Victory Gallop, all in the decade of the 1990s. In fact, the distance capabilities of Unbridled and his son, Grindstone, can be easily explained by the presence of Professional *chef-de-race* Le Fabuleux as the broodmare sire of Unbridled. Their Dosage figures are already well within the classic range without invoking additional stamina from Fappiano. Similarly, Victory Gallop's figures are within classic guidelines, mainly through the influence of Classic-Professional *chef-de-race* Tom Rolfe, sire of Hoist the Flag, he the broodmare sire of Victory Gallop's sire, Cryptoclearance.

Dr. Fager

Photo Courtesy of the Thoroughbred Times

# Dr. Fager

## DP 15-1-10-2-0, DI 3.00, CD 1.04

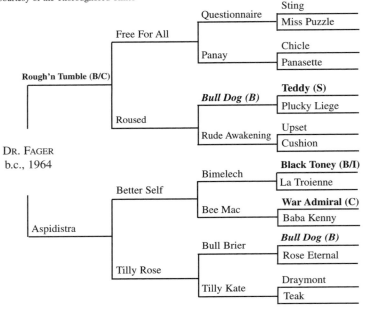

| | | | |
|---|---|---|---|
| | | Questionnaire | Sting |
| | Free For All | | Miss Puzzle |
| | | Panay | Chicle |
| Rough'n Tumble (B/C) | | | Panasette |
| | | Bull Dog (B) | Teddy (S) |
| | Roused | | Plucky Liege |
| | | Rude Awakening | Upset |
| | | | Cushion |
| DR. FAGER b.c., 1964 | | Bimelech | Black Toney (B/I) |
| | Better Self | | La Troienne |
| | | Bee Mac | War Admiral (C) |
| | | | Baba Kenny |
| Aspidistra | | Bull Brier | Bull Dog (B) |
| | Tilly Rose | | Rose Eternal |
| | | Tilly Kate | Draymont |
| | | | Teak |

## DP Contribution    Equivalent to:

| | | |
|---|---|---|
| Sire  12 - 0 - 8 - 2 - 0 | DI  2.6 | CD  1.00 |
| Dam  3 - 1 - 2 - 0 - 0 | DI  5.00 | CD  1.17 |

The extraordinary Intermediate *chef-de-race* Dr. Fager, b.c., 1964 (Rough'n Tumble-Aspidistra, by Better Self), certainly one of the fastest Thoroughbreds in history, displays a pedigree with elements of both brilliance and classicity. His sire, Brilliant/Classic *chef-de-race* Rough'n Tumble, contributes both stamina and speed while his dam contributes a more modest component of sprinting speed. The result is DP 15-1-10-2-0, DI 3.00 and CD 1.04. These figures represent a middle distance-type DI derived from dominant double-digit brilliance, double-digit classicity and a touch of stamina, affording a CD consistent with sprinting speed. During a three-year racing career, Dr. Fager went undefeated in sprints, winning by an average margin of just under six lengths. These included a record-breaking time of 1:20.1 for seven furlongs (with internal fractions of :43.4 and 1:07.4) while toting 139 pounds in the 1968 Vosburgh Handicap. Dr. Fager also won twice at a mile and a quarter in under 2:00 minutes (although the only times he failed to finish first past the age of two were at that distance). He still holds the record for a mile on dirt (1:32.1) after thirty-four years, and won his only start on grass in the United Nations Handicap while giving sixteen pounds to the previous year's turf champion, Fort Marcy. He is inbred 3x4 to Brilliant *chef-de-race* Bull Dog. In terms of style, Dr. Fager invariably raced on the pace or closely pressing it.

Although Fappiano may, in fact, be transmitting some classic strength, his overall effect (which includes the influences of his close up ancestors) is moderately shifted toward speed. This is reflected in his average winning distance of 7.84 furlongs compared with our database average of 8.11 furlongs. Also, an examination of all sires in the database having at least 20 progeny stakes wins shows Fappiano with 60 percent of his open stakes winners at a mile or less. The average for all of the sires is 42 percent. Fappiano's speed influence is even more apparent as a broodmare sire. Here his daughters have produced 83 percent of their open stakes winners at a mile or less.

Inevitably there will be questions about Real Quiet. In 1998 he became the second Derby winner since 1929 to exceed the historical Derby guideline of DI 4.00. Prior to the Derby, Real Quiet's Dosage figures were DP 13-2-7-0-0, DI 5.29, and CD 1.27. The additions of Fappiano, Dr. Fager, and Rough'n Tumble change these figures to DP 14-12-12-0-0, DI 5.33, and CD 1.05, which leave Real Quiet's DI well above the guideline while lowering the CD.

Rough'n Tumble                    Photo Courtesy of the Keeneland Library

How do we rationalize this? Simply by understanding the nature of statistics. The standard deviation of the DI for descendants of Fappiano is 1.08. Statistics tell us that 95 percent of the data points within a normal distribution will fall within two standard deviations. In other words, 19 of 20 descendants of Fappiano should have a DI that falls between 5.59 (or 3.43 + 2.16) and 1.27 (or 3.43 − 2.16). Sixty-eight percent should fall within one standard deviation, or between DI 4.56 and DI 2.35. In fact, Real Quiet's DI is between one and two standard deviations of the average and is part of the general distribution. He is not what could be called an outlier. On the other hand, if one accepts his Derby as meeting the historical standard of classic performance, we should be prepared to look for other sources of stamina.

In that regard, I suggest that Real Quiet's sire, Quiet American, should be watched closely. Although he's had just a few crops to race, and a limited number of open stakes winners, his average winning distance is a relatively long 8.41 furlongs. Additionally, just 38 percent of his progeny open stakes wins are at a mile or less. For young sires whose early runners initially have greater opportunity in shorter races, these statistics are indicative of early stamina. Only time can be the judge.

Consider also that forecasts based on moving averages over the last 60 years predict that the average DI of Derby winners will reach 4.00 by about the year 2020. Unless we see a reversion to increased stamina in Thoroughbred bloodlines, it is inevitable that more Derby winners will exceed the historical DI guideline between now and then.

For the present, we are satisfied that the new assignments accurately represent the prepotent aptitudinal influences derived from Fappiano, Dr. Fager, and Rough'n Tumble.

Broad Brush            Photo Courtesy of the Thoroughbred Times

## BROAD BRUSH, C., 1983 (ACK ACK-HAY PATCHER, BY HOIST THE FLAG), ASSIGNED JULY 2000:

Open stakes winners by Broad Brush have an average winning distance (AWD) of 8.39 furlongs, which is somewhat longer than the general average of 8.10 furlongs. It is worth noting that the standard deviation, which measures how far the numbers in a data set tend to be from the average, is just 11 percent of the AWD. This is the smallest standard deviation next to Nodouble's 10 percent of any sire over the last two decades with at least 50 progeny open stakes wins. The significance of this small standard deviation is that Broad Brush's runners tend to perform within a relatively narrow distance range, suggesting that he prepotently dominates the aptitudinal influences of the mares to which he is bred. Aptitudinal prepotence remains the single most important factor in the identification of a *chef-de-race*.

Further evidence of aptitudinal prepotence is the disparity between the Dosage figures (Dosage Profile (DP), Dosage Index (DI) and Center of Distribution (CD)) of Broad Brush's open stakes winners and those for the breed at large displaying similar distance capability. The current figures for Broad Brush's runners are average DP 7.18-9.73-8.81-0.38-1.32, average DI 3.71 and average CD 0.77 based on 79 races. The predicted figures at an average distance of 8.39 furlongs are DI 3.33 and CD 0.68. It appears as though Broad Brush is contributing a moderate degree of stamina beyond that which is found close up in his own pedigree.

An Intermediate/Classic (I/C) *chef-de-race* designation for Broad Brush modifies his progeny figures to average DP 7.18-17.73-16.81-0.38-1.32, average DI 3.37 and average CD 0.67. These revisions create an almost perfect alignment between the Broad Brush stakes winners and those in the general population displaying similar distance characteristics. A direct result of the assignment is a change in the contribution Broad Brush makes to the DP of his offspring: from DP 4-8-5-0-1 (equivalent to DI 4.14 and CD 0.78) to DP 4-16-13-0-1 (equivalent to DI 3.53 and CD 0.65). The closeness of the overall fit is powerful evidence for both the justification and accuracy of an I/C *chef-de-race* designation for this exceptional stallion.

# CHAPTER 19

# Dosage and the Classics: Dual Qualifiers

One of the most provocative applications of Dosage combines it with an assessment of juvenile form. Together, these factors function as a guide to classic potential and have gone a long way toward defining the unique qualities of the American classic horse.

Each spring, many horsemen and handicappers turn their attention to the so-called Dual Qualifiers, a select group of three-year-old Thoroughbreds sharing similar characteristics. These are characteristics typically found among American classic horses but not among the general Thoroughbred population. For this reason, Dual Qualifiers stand apart from the rest of their generation. In the early 1980s we introduced (in Leon Rasmussen's "Bloodlines" column in *Daily Racing Form*) the idea that American classic performers generally have distinguishing traits in common. Since then, the concept's ability to isolate legitimate classic contenders has increased its visibility greatly, although as we'll see later, subtle variations in breeding patterns over time suggest that the long-standing characteristics of American classic horses may be changing. The ability of Dosage to rapidly identify and highlight these subtle shifts in pedigree and performance relationships is one of its greatest strengths.

The standard definition of a Dual Qualifier is a three-year-old with a Dosage Index (DI) of 4.00 or less and ranked as a two-year-old within 10 pounds of the high-weight on the Experimental Free Handicap (EFH), or designated a champion in another country. The DI is a mathematical expression of the balance between speed and stamina inherited from selected aptitudinally prepotent ancestors. The higher the DI, the greater the influence of speed in a pedigree. Historically, only three Kentucky Derby winners since 1940 had a DI greater than 4.00. The list of Derby winners is presented in Table 25 where the cited Dosage figures are those on the day the Derby was won and may not reflect changes to the *chef-de-race* list since that time. Two others, Tables 26 and 27, displaying similar lists for the Preakness Stakes and the Belmont Stakes, follow Table 25. There have been nine Preakness winners and five Belmont winners with pedigrees exceeding the DI guideline figure of 4.00 since 1940. Among contemporary stakes winners on dirt, between 25 and 30 percent have a DI over 4.00. The percentage rises to 35 percent for stakes winners under a mile, but drops to less than 15 percent for stakes winners at a mile and a quarter. In general, the percentage of stakes winners with a DI over 4.00 on dirt or grass decreases steadily with increasing distance:

| Distance | Dirt (% with DI>4) | Turf (% with DI >4) |
|----------|--------------------|---------------------|
| 6f | 38 | 38 |
| 7f | 21 | 28 |
| 8f | 26 | 15 |
| 8fif | 21 | 14 |
| 9f | 20 | 12 |
| 10f | 15 | 8 |
| 12f | 3 | 6 |

## TABLE 25. DOSAGE HISTORY OF THE KENTUCKY DERBY SINCE 1940

| Year | Derby Winner | DP | | | | | DI | CD | Points |
|------|--------------|----|----|----|----|----|------|------|--------|
| 2002 | War Emblem | 9 - | 4 - | 8 - | 1 - | 0 | 3.40 | 0.95 | 22 |
| 2001 | Monarchos | 2 - | 2 - | 13 - | 1 - | 0 | 1.40 | 0.28 | 18 |
| 2000 | Fusaichi Pegasus | 22 - | 10 - | 24 - | 0 - | 0 | 3.67 | 0.96 | 28 |
| 1999 | Charismatic | 9 - | 10 - | 9 - | 0 - | 0 | 5.22 | 1.00 | 28 |
| 1998 | Real Quiet | 13 - | 2 - | 7 - | 0 - | 0 | 5.29 | 1.27 | 38 |
| 1997 | Silver Charm | 3 - | 5 - | 17 - | 5 - | 0 | 1.22 | 0.20 | 30 |
| 1996 | Grindstone | 6 - | 4 - | 6 - | 0 - | 6 | 1.44 | 0.18 | 22 |
| 1995 | Thunder Gulch | 10 - | 2 - | 8 - | 0 - | 0 | 4.00 | 1.10 | 20 |
| 1994 | Go For Gin | 8 - | 5 - | 16 - | 7 - | 6 | 1.00 | 0.05 | 42 |
| 1993 | Sea Hero | 3 - | 5 - | 22 - | 4 - | 2 | 1.12 | 0.08 | 36 |
| 1992 | Lil E. Tee | 6 - | 2 - | 8 - | 0 - | 0 | 3.00 | 0.88 | 16 |
| 1991 | Strike The Gold | 10 - | 6 - | 4 - | 0 - | 0 | 9.00 | 1.30 | 20 |
| 1990 | Unbridled | 11 - | 3 - | 10 - | 0 - | 12 | 1.12 | 0.03 | 36 |
| 1989 | Sunday Silence | 4 - | 3 - | 9 - | 0 - | 0 | 2.56 | 0.69 | 16 |
| 1988 | Winning Colors | 10 - | 14 - | 8 - | 0 - | 4 | 3.50 | 0.72 | 36 |
| 1987 | Alysheba | 12 - | 4 - | 6 - | 2 - | 0 | 3.80 | 1.08 | 24 |
| 1986 | Ferdinand | 14 - | 2 - | 16 - | 8 - | 0 | 1.50 | 0.55 | 40 |
| 1985 | Spend A Buck | 2 - | 3 - | 18 - | 1 - | 0 | 1.40 | 0.25 | 24 |
| 1984 | Swale | 8 - | 1 - | 11 - | 2 - | 0 | 1.93 | 0.68 | 22 |
| 1983 | Sunny's Halo | 4 - | 5 - | 13 - | 2 - | 0 | 1.82 | 0.46 | 24 |
| 1982 | Gato Del Sol | 6 - | 3 - | 5 - | 2 - | 2 | 1.77 | 0.50 | 18 |
| 1981 | Pleasant Colony | 7 - | 1 - | 9 - | 1 - | 4 | 1.32 | 0.27 | 22 |
| 1980 | Genuine Risk | 14 - | 10 - | 24 - | 2 - | 0 | 2.57 | 0.72 | 50 |
| 1979 | Spectacular Bid | 9 - | 6 - | 2 - | 3 - | 0 | 4.00 | 1.05 | 20 |
| 1978 | Affirmed | 8 - | 6 - | 26 - | 0 - | 0 | 2.08 | 0.55 | 40 |
| 1977 | Seattle Slew | 7 - | 6 - | 4 - | 5 - | 0 | 2.14 | 0.68 | 22 |
| 1976 | Bold Forbes | 11 - | 4 - | 9 - | 4 - | 0 | 2.29 | 0.79 | 28 |
| 1975 | Foolish Pleasure | 27 - | 10 - | 11 - | 4 - | 2 | 3.70 | 1.04 | 54 |
| 1974 | Cannonade | 9 - | 14 - | 14 - | 3 - | 4 | 2.14 | 0.48 | 44 |
| 1973 | Secretariat | 20 - | 14 - | 7 - | 9 - | 0 | 3.00 | 0.90 | 50 |
| 1972 | Riva Ridge | 19 - | 4 - | 7 - | 2 - | 2 | 3.53 | 1.06 | 34 |
| 1971 | Canonero II | 5 - | 0 - | 7 - | 2 - | 2 | 1.13 | 0.25 | 16 |
| 1970 | Dust Commander | 9 - | 4 - | 3 - | 3 - | 1 | 2.64 | 0.85 | 20 |
| 1969 | Majestic Prince | 27 - | 11 - | 12 - | 4 - | 2 | 3.67 | 1.02 | 56 |
| 1968 | Forward Pass | 22 - | 2 - | 17 - | 1 - | 0 | 3.42 | 1.07 | 42 |
| 1967 | Proud Clarion | 11 - | 8 - | 26 - | 4 - | 3 | 1.60 | 0.38 | 52 |
| 1966 | Kauai King | 0 - | 22 - | 18 - | 8 - | 0 | 1.82 | 0.29 | 48 |
| 1965 | Lucky Debonair | 2 - | 0 - | 15 - | 3 - | 0 | 0.90 | 0.05 | 20 |
| 1964 | Northern Dancer | 8 - | 16 - | 15 - | 3 - | 0 | 3.00 | 0.69 | 42 |
| 1963 | Chateaugay | 4 - | 16 - | 6 - | 0 - | 4 | 3.29 | 0.53 | 30 |
| 1962 | Decidedly | 2 - | 2 - | 17 - | 6 - | 3 | 0.71 | -0.20 | 30 |
| 1961 | Carry Back | 4 - | 2 - | 12 - | 6 - | 0 | 1.00 | 0.17 | 24 |
| 1960 | Venetian Way | 5 - | 9 - | 4 - | 2 - | 0 | 4.00 | 0.85 | 20 |
| 1959 | Tomy Lee | 20 - | 2 - | 26 - | 0 - | 4 | 2.06 | 0.65 | 52 |
| 1958 | Tim Tam | 10 - | 11 - | 17 - | 4 - | 0 | 2.36 | 0.64 | 42 |

110

| Year | Winner | DP | DI | CD | Points |
|------|--------|-----|-----|-----|--------|
| 1957 | Iron Liege | 8 - 2 - 28 - 11 - 3 | 0.86 | 0.02 | 52 |
| 1956 | Needles | 4 - 2 - 10 - 2 - 2 | 1.22 | 0.20 | 20 |
| 1955 | Swaps | 4 - 18 - 14 - 4 - 8 | 1.53 | 0.13 | 48 |
| 1954 | Determine | 4 - 4 - 41 - 3 - 2 | 1.12 | 0.09 | 54 |
| 1953 | Dark Star | 8 - 2 - 0 - 4 - 8 | 0.83 | -0.09 | 22 |
| 1952 | Hill Gail | 8 - 0 - 26 - 9 - 3 | 0.84 | 0.02 | 46 |
| 1951 | Count Turf | 8 - 0 - 16 - 0 - 2 | 1.60 | 0.46 | 26 |
| 1950 | Middleground | 6 - 0 - 4 - 0 - 2 | 2.00 | 0.67 | 12 |
| 1949 | Ponder | 4 - 0 - 22 - 10 - 4 | 0.60 | -0.25 | 40 |
| 1948 | Citation | 12 - 0 - 24 - 6 - 8 | 0.92 | 0.04 | 50 |
| 1947 | Jet Pilot | 0 - 0 - 29 - 13 - 2 | 0.49 | -0.39 | 44 |
| 1946 | Assault | 6 - 6 - 8 - 1 - 3 | 2.00 | 0.46 | 24 |
| 1945 | Hoop, Jr. | 0 - 4 - 16 - 8 - 4 | 0.60 | -0.38 | 32 |
| 1944 | Pensive | 8 - 0 - 16 - 8 - 8 | 0.67 | -0.20 | 40 |
| 1943 | Count Fleet | 0 - 2 - 1 - 1 - 0 | 1.67 | 0.25 | 4 |
| 1942 | Shut Out | 4 - 14 - 9 - 3 - 6 | 1.67 | 0.19 | 36 |
| 1941 | Whirlaway | 0 - 12 - 20 - 8 - 0 | 1.22 | 0.10 | 40 |
| 1940 | Gallahadion | 0 - 0 - 16 - 8 - 8 | 0.33 | -0.75 | 32 |
| **AVERAGE** | | **8.19 - 5.41 - 13.43 - 3.38 - 2.16** | **2.19** | **0.45** | **32.38** |

## TABLE 26. DOSAGE HISTORY OF THE PREAKNESS STAKES SINCE 1940

| Year | Winner | DP | DI | CD | Points |
|------|--------|-----|-----|-----|--------|
| 2002 | War Emblem | 9 - 4 - 8 - 1 - 0 | 3.40 | 0.95 | 22 |
| 2001 | Point Given | 8 - 0 - 8 - 0 - 0 | 3.00 | 1.00 | 16 |
| 2000 | Red Bullet | 7 - 10 - 11 - 0 - 6 | 1.96 | 0.35 | 34 |
| 1999 | Charismatic | 9 - 10 - 9 - 0 - 0 | 5.22 | 1.00 | 28 |
| 1998 | Real Quiet | 13 - 2 - 7 - 0 - 0 | 5.29 | 1.27 | 22 |
| 1997 | Silver Charm | 3 - 5 - 17 - 5 - 0 | 1.22 | 0.20 | 30 |
| 1996 | Louis Quatorze | 11 - 7 - 8 - 0 - 0 | 5.50 | 1.12 | 26 |
| 1995 | Timber Country | 11 - 5 - 22 - 0 - 0 | 2.45 | 0.71 | 38 |
| 1994 | Tabasco Cat | 7 - 3 - 5 - 1 - 0 | 3.57 | 1.00 | 16 |
| 1993 | Prairie Bayou | 6 - 4 - 6 - 0 - 0 | 4.33 | 1.00 | 16 |
| 1992 | Pine Bluff | 10 - 12 - 22 - 0 - 0 | 3.00 | 0.73 | 44 |
| 1991 | Hansel | 10 - 3 - 13 - 2 - 0 | 2.29 | 0.75 | 28 |
| 1990 | Summer Squall | 9 - 10 - 16 - 1 - 0 | 3.00 | 0.75 | 36 |
| 1989 | Sunday Silence | 4 - 3 - 9 - 0 - 0 | 2.56 | 0.69 | 16 |
| 1988 | Risen Star | 12 - 7 - 19 - 4 - 2 | 1.84 | 0.52 | 44 |
| 1987 | Alysheba | 12 - 4 - 6 - 2 - 0 | 3.80 | 1.08 | 24 |
| 1986 | Snow Chief | 0 - 4 - 2 - 0 - 0 | 5.00 | 0.67 | 6 |
| 1985 | Tank's Prospect | 14 - 6 - 8 - 0 - 0 | 6.00 | 1.21 | 28 |
| 1984 | Gate Dancer | 13 - 4 - 17 - 2 - 0 | 2.43 | 0.78 | 36 |
| 1983 | Deputed Testamony | 6 - 3 - 9 - 2 - 0 | 2.08 | 0.65 | 20 |
| 1982 | Aloma's Ruler | 13 - 10 - 6 - 1 - 0 | 6.50 | 1.17 | 30 |
| 1981 | Pleasant Colony | 7 - 1 - 9 - 1 - 4 | 1.32 | 0.27 | 22 |
| 1980 | Codex | 5 - 1 - 6 - 0 - 4 | 1.29 | 0.19 | 16 |

| Year | Winner | DP | | | | | DI | CD | Points |
|------|--------|----|----|----|----|----|-----|-----|--------|
| 1979 | Spectacular Bid | 9 | 6 | 2 | 3 | 0 | 4.00 | 1.05 | 20 |
| 1978 | Affirmed | 8 | 6 | 26 | 0 | 0 | 2.08 | 0.55 | 40 |
| 1977 | Seattle Slew | 7 | 6 | 4 | 5 | 0 | 2.14 | 0.68 | 22 |
| 1976 | Elocutionist | 10 | 5 | 13 | 2 | 0 | 2.53 | 0.77 | 30 |
| 1975 | Master Derby | 8 | 6 | 2 | 0 | 0 | 15.00 | 1.38 | 16 |
| 1974 | Little Current | 8 | 12 | 9 | 16 | 1 | 1.14 | 0.22 | 46 |
| 1973 | Secretariat | 20 | 14 | 7 | 9 | 0 | 3.00 | 0.90 | 50 |
| 1972 | Bee Bee Bee | 2 | 2 | 3 | 2 | 1 | 1.22 | 0.20 | 10 |
| 1971 | Canonero II | 5 | 0 | 7 | 2 | 2 | 1.13 | 0.25 | 16 |
| 1970 | Personality | 11 | 9 | 26 | 2 | 2 | 1.94 | 0.50 | 50 |
| 1969 | Majestic Prince | 27 | 11 | 12 | 4 | 2 | 3.67 | 1.02 | 56 |
| 1968 | Forward Pass | 22 | 2 | 17 | 1 | 0 | 3.42 | 1.07 | 42 |
| 1967 | Damascus | 10 | 4 | 3 | 1 | 0 | 6.20 | 1.28 | 18 |
| 1966 | Kauai King | 0 | 22 | 18 | 8 | 0 | 1.82 | 0.29 | 48 |
| 1965 | Tom Rolfe | 4 | 8 | 14 | 4 | 8 | 1.00 | -0.11 | 38 |
| 1964 | Northern Dancer | 8 | 16 | 15 | 3 | 0 | 3.00 | 0.69 | 42 |
| 1963 | Candy Spots | 2 | 12 | 4 | 0 | 2 | 4.00 | 0.60 | 20 |
| 1962 | Greek Money | 12 | 4 | 10 | 0 | 0 | 4.20 | 1.08 | 26 |
| 1961 | Carry Back | 4 | 2 | 12 | 6 | 0 | 1.00 | 0.17 | 24 |
| 1960 | Belly Ache | 16 | 0 | 4 | 2 | 2 | 3.00 | 1.08 | 24 |
| 1959 | Royal Orbit | 22 | 8 | 15 | 6 | 7 | 1.83 | 0.55 | 58 |
| 1958 | Tim Tam | 10 | 11 | 17 | 4 | 0 | 2.36 | 0.64 | 42 |
| 1957 | Bold Ruler | 26 | 8 | 8 | 11 | 1 | 2.38 | 0.87 | 54 |
| 1956 | Fabius | 6 | 4 | 12 | 2 | 2 | 1.60 | 0.38 | 26 |
| 1955 | Nashua | 22 | 8 | 10 | 2 | 4 | 3.18 | 0.91 | 46 |
| 1954 | Hasty Road | 10 | 14 | 10 | 15 | 3 | 1.26 | 0.25 | 52 |
| 1953 | Native Dancer | 4 | 18 | 0 | 9 | 1 | 2.20 | 0.47 | 32 |
| 1952 | Blue Man | 1 | 3 | 8 | 10 | 2 | 0.50 | - 0.38 | 24 |
| 1951 | Bold | 7 | 3 | 4 | 7 | 1 | 1.20 | 0.36 | 22 |
| 1950 | Hill Prince | 2 | 10 | 10 | 10 | 0 | 1.13 | 0.13 | 32 |
| 1949 | Capot | 10 | 0 | 4 | 3 | 1 | 2.00 | 0.83 | 18 |
| 1948 | Citation | 12 | 0 | 24 | 6 | 8 | 0.92 | 0.04 | 50 |
| 1947 | Faultless | 8 | 0 | 21 | 9 | 2 | 0.86 | 0.08 | 40 |
| 1946 | Assault | 6 | 6 | 8 | 1 | 3 | 2.00 | 0.46 | 24 |
| 1945 | Polynesian | 9 | 1 | 1 | 3 | 0 | 3.00 | 1.14 | 14 |
| 1944 | Pensive | 8 | 0 | 16 | 8 | 8 | 0.67 | - 0.20 | 40 |
| 1943 | Count Fleet | 0 | 2 | 1 | 1 | 0 | 1.67 | 0.25 | 4 |
| 1942 | Alsab | 2 | 6 | 0 | 2 | 2 | 2.00 | 0.33 | 12 |
| 1941 | Whirlaway | 0 | 12 | 20 | 8 | 0 | 1.22 | 0.10 | 40 |
| 1940 | Bimelech | 16 | 12 | 0 | 8 | 0 | 3.50 | 1.00 | 36 |
| **AVERAGE** | | **9.10** | **6.21** | **10.16** | **3.44** | **1.29** | **2.83** | **0.63** | **30.19** |

## TABLE 27. DOSAGE HISTORY OF THE BELMONT STAKES SINCE 1940

| Year | Winner | DP | | | | | DI | CD | Points |
|------|--------|----|----|----|----|----|------|------|--------|
| 2002 | Sarava | 8 | 6 | 8 | 0 | 0 | 4.50 | 1.00 | 22 |
| 2001 | Point Given | 8 | 0 | 8 | 0 | 0 | 3.00 | 1.00 | 16 |
| 2000 | Commendable | 17 | 11 | 14 | 0 | 0 | 5.00 | 1.07 | 42 |
| 1999 | Lemon Drop Kid | 13 | 4 | 21 | 0 | 0 | 2.62 | 0.79 | 38 |
| 1998 | Victory Gallop | 10 | 2 | 9 | 0 | 1 | 3.00 | 0.91 | 22 |
| 1997 | Touch Gold | 4 | 3 | 17 | 0 | 0 | 1.82 | 0.46 | 24 |
| 1996 | Editor's Note | 10 | 4 | 11 | 0 | 3 | 2.29 | 0.64 | 28 |
| 1995 | Thunder Gulch | 10 | 2 | 8 | 0 | 0 | 4.00 | 1.10 | 20 |
| 1994 | Tabasco Cat | 7 | 3 | 5 | 1 | 0 | 3.57 | 1.00 | 16 |
| 1993 | Colonial Affair | 8 | 1 | 19 | 4 | 2 | 1.19 | 0.26 | 34 |
| 1992 | A. P. Indy | 13 | 6 | 16 | 3 | 0 | 2.45 | 0.76 | 38 |
| 1991 | Hansel | 10 | 3 | 13 | 2 | 0 | 2.29 | 0.75 | 28 |
| 1990 | Go And Go | 11 | 3 | 10 | 1 | 1 | 2.71 | 0.85 | 26 |
| 1989 | Easy Goer | 10 | 6 | 14 | 0 | 0 | 3.29 | 0.87 | 30 |
| 1988 | Risen Star | 12 | 7 | 19 | 4 | 2 | 1.84 | 0.52 | 44 |
| 1987 | Bet Twice | 10 | 3 | 6 | 9 | 0 | 1.33 | 0.50 | 28 |
| 1986 | Danzig Connection | 6 | 12 | 14 | 2 | 0 | 2.78 | 0.65 | 34 |
| 1985 | Crème Fraiche | 15 | 4 | 1 | 0 | 0 | 39.00 | 1.70 | 20 |
| 1984 | Swale | 8 | 1 | 11 | 2 | 0 | 1.93 | 0.68 | 22 |
| 1983 | Caveat | 8 | 6 | 5 | 1 | 2 | 3.00 | 0.77 | 22 |
| 1982 | Conquistador Cielo | 18 | 10 | 6 | 0 | 0 | 10.33 | 1.35 | 34 |
| 1981 | Summing | 8 | 7 | 10 | 1 | 0 | 3.33 | 0.85 | 26 |
| 1980 | Temperence Hill | 7 | 4 | 13 | 0 | 0 | 2.69 | 0.75 | 24 |
| 1979 | Coastal | 13 | 7 | 17 | 1 | 0 | 3.00 | 0.84 | 38 |
| 1978 | Affirmed | 8 | 6 | 26 | 0 | 0 | 2.08 | 0.55 | 40 |
| 1977 | Seattle Slew | 7 | 6 | 4 | 5 | 0 | 2.14 | 0.68 | 22 |
| 1976 | Bold Forbes | 11 | 4 | 9 | 4 | 0 | 2.29 | 0.79 | 28 |
| 1975 | Avatar | 1 | 2 | 22 | 9 | 4 | 0.58 | 0.34 | 38 |
| 1974 | Little Current | 8 | 12 | 9 | 16 | 1 | 1.14 | 0.22 | 46 |
| 1973 | Secretariat | 20 | 14 | 7 | 9 | 0 | 3.00 | 0.90 | 50 |
| 1972 | Riva Ridge | 19 | 4 | 7 | 2 | 2 | 3.53 | 1.06 | 34 |
| 1971 | Pass Catcher | 9 | 4 | 13 | 2 | 4 | 1.56 | 0.38 | 32 |
| 1970 | High Echelon | 11 | 12 | 9 | 6 | 0 | 2.62 | 0.74 | 38 |
| 1969 | Arts And Letters | 5 | 2 | 11 | 2 | 8 | 0.81 | -0.21 | 28 |
| 1968 | Stage Door Johnny | 1 | 4 | 33 | 12 | 0 | 0.75 | -0.12 | 50 |
| 1967 | Damascus | 10 | 4 | 3 | 1 | 0 | 6.20 | 1.28 | 18 |
| 1966 | Amberoid | 1 | 3 | 6 | 0 | 4 | 1.00 | -0.21 | 14 |
| 1965 | Hail To All | 10 | 5 | 21 | 5 | 3 | 1.38 | 0.32 | 44 |
| 1964 | Quadrangle | 4 | 4 | 22 | 6 | 0 | 1.12 | 0.17 | 36 |
| 1963 | Chateaugay | 4 | 16 | 6 | 0 | 4 | 3.29 | 0.53 | 30 |
| 1962 | Jaipur | 22 | 16 | 16 | 4 | 0 | 3.83 | 0.97 | 58 |
| 1961 | Sherluck | 4 | 10 | 8 | 0 | 4 | 2.25 | 0.38 | 26 |
| 1960 | Celtic Ash | 1 | 0 | 29 | 6 | 4 | 0.63 | -0.30 | 40 |
| 1959 | Sword Dancer | 2 | 0 | 2 | 5 | 1 | 0.43 | -0.30 | 10 |
| 1958 | Cavan | 6 | 6 | 26 | 2 | 12 | 0.93 | -0.15 | 52 |

| Year | Winner | DP | DI | CD | Points |
|------|--------|-----|-----|-----|--------|
| 1957 | Gallant Man | 0 - 4 - 18 - 16 - 2 | 0.48 | -0.40 | 40 |
| 1956 | Needles | 4 - 2 - 10 - 2 - 2 | 1.22 | 0.20 | 20 |
| 1955 | Nashua | 22 - 8 - 10 - 2 - 4 | 3.18 | 0.91 | 46 |
| 1954 | High Gun | 20 - 2 - 12 - 7 - 3 | 1.75 | 0.66 | 44 |
| 1953 | Native Dancer | 4 - 18 - 0 - 9 - 1 | 2.20 | 0.47 | 32 |
| 1952 | One Count | 2 - 0 - 16 - 9 - 1 | 0.56 | -0.25 | 28 |
| 1951 | Counterpoint | 4 - 2 - 16 - 7 - 1 | 0.88 | 0.03 | 30 |
| 1950 | Middleground | 6 - 0 - 4 - 0 - 2 | 2.00 | 0.67 | 12 |
| 1949 | Capot | 10 - 0 - 4 - 3 - 1 | 2.00 | 0.83 | 18 |
| 1948 | Citation | 12 - 0 - 24 - 6 - 8 | 0.92 | 0.04 | 50 |
| 1947 | Phalanx | 0 - 4 - 24 - 4 - 0 | 1.00 | 0.00 | 32 |
| 1946 | Assault | 6 - 6 - 8 - 1 - 3 | 2.00 | 0.46 | 24 |
| 1945 | Pavot | 6 - 2 - 1 - 19 - 2 | 0.40 | -0.30 | 30 |
| 1944 | Bounding Home | 2 - 2 - 0 - 5 - 1 | 0.67 | -0.10 | 10 |
| 1943 | Count Fleet | 0 - 2 - 1 - 1 - 0 | 1.67 | 0.25 | 4 |
| 1942 | Shut Out | 4 - 14 - 9 - 3 - 6 | 1.67 | 0.19 | 36 |
| 1941 | Whirlaway | 0 - 12 - 20 - 8 - 0 | 1.22 | 0.10 | 40 |
| 1940 | Bimelech | 16 - 12 - 0 - 8 - 0 | 3.50 | 1.00 | 36 |
| **AVERAGE** | | **8.35 - 5.38 - 11.76 - 3.76 - 1.57** | **2.85** | **0.51** | **30.73** |

Chart 18 captures in dramatic detail the evolutionary changes that have occurred among Kentucky Derby winners over the last 60 years or so. The graph plots the DI of the Derby winner by year and includes a trend line derived by linear regression and extended forty years ahead. The shift toward more speed in the pedigree is vividly displayed. Should the trend remain the same, with even more speed being infused into pedigrees, there likely will be as many Derby winners around the year 2020 with a DI above 4.00 as there are below. At this stage one can only speculate as to the implications of increasing speed in pedigrees on the whole fabric of future racing. However, it may be relevant that the percentage of ten-furlong open stakes races contested on dirt in the years 1983 through 1989 decreased by 23 percent in the years 1995 through 2001.

### CHART 18. DOSAGE TREND FOR KENTUCKY DERBY WINNERS SINCE 1940

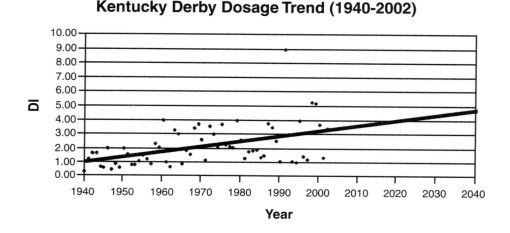

114

Charts 19 and 20 confirm similar trends in both the Preakness and Belmont Stakes since 1940. The shift toward speed among American classic winners is undeniable.

**CHART 19. DOSAGE TREND FOR PREAKNESS STAKES WINNERS SINCE 1940**

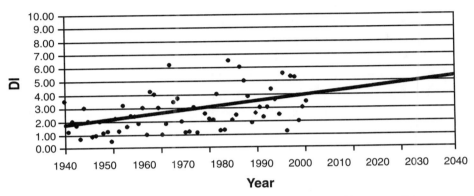

**CHART 20. DOSAGE TREND FOR BELMONT STAKES WINNERS SINCE 1940**

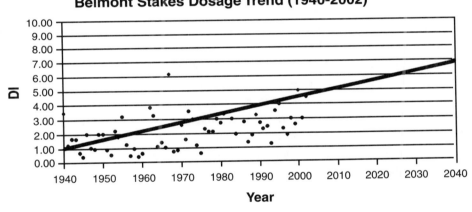

The EFH is a system of rating the performance of two-year-olds. A panel of experts evaluates the year's stakes quality juveniles and assigns them weights relative to one another. Normally, the highest weight for a colt is 126 pounds. Occasionally, a truly exceptional colt will be weighted higher. These include Bimelech (130) in 1939, Alsab (130) in 1941, Count Fleet (132) in 1942, Native Dancer (130) in 1952, Summer Tan (128) in 1954, Bold Lad (130) in 1964, Silent Screen (128) in 1969, Secretariat (129) in 1972, Foolish Pleasure (127) in 1974, Devil's Bag (128) in 1983, Arazi (130) in 1991 and Favorite Trick (128) in 1997. Although there is a degree of subjectivity involved in the EFH selection process, it still remains a reasonable guide to relative two-year-old ability. In the absence of a more objective assessment methodology, the EFH serves its purpose fairly well.

Now the question is: Why should a DI of 4.00 or less coupled with a prominent ranking on the EFH be important to classic potential? In the case of the Kentucky Derby (and perhaps to some degree the other classics as well) the reasons are intimately linked to the unique demands of the race, which is like no other run in North America. The answer to the question becomes clearer when we recall that the DI is a guide to distance ability while the EFH ranking is an approximation of early maturity and outstanding two-year-old form.

A pedigree suited to the distance, along with demonstrated high class early in a racing career are the historical trademarks of the majority of classic winners over the last quarter century and beyond. First and foremost, the distance presents a formidable challenge. None of the contenders, at least none that raced exclusively in North America, have previously been asked to negotiate a mile and a quarter. The suitability of their breeding to the distance is paramount, and the DI suggests that suitability. A horse bred excessively for speed is unlikely to stay the course at this level of competition except when the pace is especially undemanding or the quality of the field is suspect. Those would be unusual circumstances for America's premier classic.

Second, there are several attributes of the Derby that are constant from year to year. The overall quality and depth of the field are normally outstanding, with an abundance of regional superstars converging to meet for the first time. The pace is usually fast, pressure-packed, and stressful. The size of the field often can be very large, resulting in a race that is extremely physical as jockeys maneuver their horses into position. The horses are still young and immature; they are a long way from adulthood. The atmosphere is electric and filled with a spectacle that the horses have never experienced. It is reasonable that contenders with an edge in class as well as an edge in emotional and physical maturity should have an advantage.

The Dual Qualifiers are blessed with staying pedigrees as expressed in their DI, and an advanced degree of class and maturity as reflected by their superior performance at two and acknowledged by their position on the EFH.

The correlation between Dual Qualifier status and success in the Derby is very strong. Between 1972 and 2002 there were 502 starters in the Derby, although in one year, 1998, no Dual Qualifiers were entered. Of these 502, 104 (21 percent) were Dual Qualifiers, representing 102 separate wagering interests. That's an average of less than three and one-half per race in an average-size field of just more than 16 starters. Twice there was just one Dual Qualifier and both won, Cannonade in 1974 in a field of 23 starters, and Foolish Pleasure in 1975 in a field of 15. The largest number of Dual Qualifiers in a single Derby since 1972 is six, three times. A Dual Qualifier has captured 20 of the 30 Derbies (67 percent) in which a Dual Qualifier was entered. Thirteen other Dual Qualifiers (13 percent) finished second while another nine (9 percent) ran third. Overall, 40 percent of all Dual Qualifiers finished in the money. Thirty-three Dual Qualifiers (32 percent) won at least one American classic race but only 4 percent of the non-qualifiers did the same. In the 30 Derbies in which they started, Dual Qualifiers accounted for nine exactas and five trifectas.

A straight two-dollar win bet on each Dual Qualifier wagering interest, independent of all other handicapping considerations, has yielded a 63 percent profit not including exotic payoffs. It should be easy to see why the Dual Qualifier concept has aroused so much interest. These results are strong evidence that a staying pedigree, early maturity, and an early expression of high class have been more critical to a Derby victory than some of the conventional criteria used to predict the winner. The Derby favorite is often the "form" horse, a colt or filly coming off a smashing win in his or her last Derby prep race. As we are all aware, these favorites have failed every year since 1978 except for Fusaichi Pegasus' Derby victory in 2000.

One conclusion that may be drawn from the success of the Dual Qualifiers, often long odds winners, is that form at nine furlongs in the preps is not always a good predictor of form at 10 furlongs in the Derby. The unique circumstances of the Derby provide the environment in which the Dual Qualifier factors, or rather what they represent, become dominant. Other factors are often less significant.

The historical significance of Dual Qualifiers extends even farther back in time, although there is nothing comparable to the 16 straight Dual Qualifier wins in the Derby achieved between 1972 and 1987. Table 28 presents the complete history of Dual Qualifiers in the Derby since 1946 and includes the name of the Dual Qualifier and his finishing position. Winning Dual Qualifiers are highlighted in bold type.

### TABLE 28. THE HISTORY OF DUAL QUALIFIERS IN THE KENTUCKY DERBY (1946-2002)

| Year | Dual Qualifier | Finish | Starters | Win Payoff |
|------|----------------|--------|----------|------------|
| 2002 | Came Home | 6 | 18 | |
| | Johannesburg | 8 | | |
| | Saarland | 10 | | |
| 2001 | Point Given | 5 | 17 | |
| | A P Valentine | 7 | | |
| | Dollar Bill | 15 | | |
| 2000 | More Than Ready | 4 | 19 | |
| | Captain Steve | 8 | | |
| | Exchange Rate | 12 | | |
| | Anees | 13 | | |
| | High Yield | 15 | | |
| 1999 | Cat Thief | 3 | 19 | |
| | Prime Timber | 4 | | |
| | Excellent Meeting | 5 | | |
| | Lemon Drop Kid | 9 | | |
| | Answer Lively | 10 | | |
| | Three Ring | 19 | | |
| 1998 | | | 15 | |
| 1997 | **Silver Charm** | 1 | 13 | $10.00 |
| | Hello | 8 | | |
| 1996 | Cavonnier | 2 | 19 | |
| | Unbridled's Song | 5 | | |
| | Editor's Note | 6 | | |
| | Diligence | 9 | | |
| | Matty G | 18 | | |
| | Honour and Glory | 19 | | |
| 1995 | **Thunder Gulch** | 1 | 19 | $51.00 |
| | Tejano Run | 2 | | |
| | Timber Country | 3 | | |
| | Eltish | 6 | | |
| | Talkin Man | 12 | | |
| | Serena's Song | 16 | | |
| 1994 | **Go for Gin** | 1 | 14 | $20.20 |
| | Blumin Affair | 3 | | |
| | Brocco | 4 | | |
| | Tabasco Cat | 6 | | |
| | Valiant Nature | 13 | | |
| 1993 | **Sea Hero** | 1 | 19 | $27.80 |

| Year | Dual Qualifier | Finish | Starters | Win Payoff |
|---|---|---|---|---|
| 1993 | Silver of Silver | 8 | | |
| | Truth of It All | 10 | | |
| 1992 | Pine Bluff | 5 | 18 | |
| | Arazi | 8 | | |
| 1992 | Pistols and Roses | 16 | | |
| 1991 | Best Pal | 2 | 16 | |
| | Fly So Free | 5 | | |
| | Hansel | 10 | | |
| | Happy Jazz Band | 11 | | |
| 1990 | **Unbridled** | 1 | 15 | $23.60 |
| | Summer Squall | 2 | | |
| | Pleasant Tap | 3 | | |
| | Mister Frisky | 8 | | |
| 1989 | Easy Goer | 2 | 15 | |
| | Hawkster | 5 | | |
| | Irish Actor | 7 | | |
| 1988 | Forty Niner | 2 | 17 | |
| | Regal Classic | 5 | | |
| | Kingpost | 15 | | |
| 1987 | **Alysheba** | 1 | 17 | $18.80 |
| | Bet Twice | 2 | | |
| | Conquistarose | 9 | | |
| | Capote | 16 | | |
| | Demons Begone | 17 | | |
| 1986 | **Ferdinand** | 1 | 16 | $37.40 |
| | Groovy | 16 | | |
| 1985 | **Spend a Buck** | 1 | 13 | $10.20 |
| | Stephan's Odyssey | 2 | | |
| 1984 | **Swale** | 1 | 20 | $8.80 |
| | Fali Time | 4 | | |
| | Life's Magic | 8 | | |
| 1983 | **Sunny's Halo** | 1 | 20 | $7.00 |
| | Caveat | 3 | | |
| | Pax In Bello | 7 | | |
| 1982 | **Gato del Sol** | 1 | 19 | $44.40 |
| | Laser Light | 2 | | |
| | Casseleria | 13 | | |
| 1981 | **Pleasant Colony** | 1 | 21 | $9.00 |
| | Pass the Tab | 6 | | |
| | Noble Nashua | 9 | | |
| | Cure the Blues | 15 | | |
| 1980 | **Genuine Risk** | 1 | 13 | $28.60 |
| | Rumbo | 2 | | |
| | Rockhill Native | 5 | | |

| Year | Dual Qualifier | Finish | Starters | Win Payoff |
|------|----------------|--------|----------|------------|
| 1980 | Plugged Nickle | 7 | | |
| | Execution's Reason | 11 | | |
| 1979 | **Spectacular Bid** | 1 | 10 | $3.20 |
| | General Assembly | 2 | | |
| 1979 | Golden Act | 3 | | |
| 1978 | **Affirmed** | 1 | 11 | $5.60 |
| | Alydar | 2 | | |
| | Believe It | 3 | | |
| 1977 | **Seattle Slew** | 1 | 15 | $3.00 |
| | Get the Axe | 4 | | |
| | For the Moment | 7 | | |
| | Nostalgia | 13 | | |
| 1976 | **Bold Forbes** | 1 | 9 | $8.00 |
| | Honest Pleasure | 2 | | |
| | Elocutionist | 3 | | |
| | Cojak | 6 | | |
| 1975 | **Foolish Pleasure** | 1 | 15 | $5.80 |
| 1974 | **Cannonade** | 1 | 23 | $5.00 |
| 1973 | **Secretariat** | 1 | 13 | $5.00 |
| | Angle Light | 10 | | |
| 1972 | **Riva Ridge** | 1 | 14 | $5.00 |
| | Hold Your Peace | 3 | | |
| | Freetex | 6 | | |
| 1971 | Jim French | 2 | 20 | |
| 1970 | My Dad George | 2 | 17 | |
| | High Echelon | 3 | | |
| | Silent Screen | 5 | | |
| | Terlago | 11 | | |
| 1969 | Dike | 3 | 8 | |
| | Traffic Mark | 4 | | |
| | Top Knight | 5 | | |
| 1968 | T. V. Commercial | 3 | 16 | |
| | Don B. | 7 | | |
| | Captain's Gig | 11 | | |
| | Iron Ruler | 12 | | |
| 1967 | Successor | 6 | 14 | |
| | Ruken | 8 | | |
| | Diplomat Way | 9 | | |
| | Lightning Orphan | 14 | | |
| 1966 | Advocator | 2 | 15 | |
| | Amberoid | 7 | | |
| 1965 | Tom Rolfe | 3 | 11 | |
| | Native Charger | 4 | | |
| | Hail to All | 5 | | |

| Year | Dual Qualifier | Finish | Starters | Win Payoff |
|------|----------------|--------|----------|------------|
| 1965 | Swift Ruler | 7 | | |
| | Bold Lad | 10 | | |
| 1964 | **Northern Dancer** | 1 | 12 | $8.80 |
| | Roman Brother | 4 | | |
| | Quadrangle | 5 | | |
| | Mr. Brick | 6 | | |
| | Ishkoodah | 9 | | |
| | Wil Rad | 10 | | |
| 1963 | Never Bend | 2 | 9 | |
| | Candy Spots | 3 | | |
| | No Robbery | 5 | | |
| 1962 | Ridan | 3 | 15 | |
| | Crimson Satan | 6 | | |
| 1961 | **Carry Back** | 1 | 15 | $7.00 |
| | Globemaster | 6 | | |
| | Ambiopoise | 12 | | |
| 1960 | **Venetian Way** | 1 | 13 | $14.60 |
| | Bally Ache | 2 | | |
| | Victoria Park | 3 | | |
| | Tompion | 4 | | |
| | Bourbon Prince | 5 | | |
| 1959 | **Tomy Lee** | 1 | 17 | $9.40 |
| | Sword Dancer | 2 | | |
| | First Landing | 3 | | |
| | Royal Orbit | 4 | | |
| | Finnegan | 6 | | |
| | Dunce | 7 | | |
| | Atoll | 9 | | |
| | Rico Tesio | 10 | | |
| 1958 | Jewel's Reward | 4 | 14 | |
| 1957 | **Iron Liege** | 1 | 9 | $18.80 |
| | Round Table | 3 | | |
| | Bold Ruler | 4 | | |
| | Federal Hill | 5 | | |
| | Mister Jive | 7 | | |
| 1956 | **Needles** | 1 | 17 | $5.20 |
| | Career Boy | 6 | | |
| | Head Man | 8 | | |
| | Ben A. Jones | 16 | | |
| 1955 | Nashua | 2 | 10 | |
| | Summer Tan | 3 | | |
| 1954 | **Determine** | 1 | 17 | $10.60 |
| | Hasty Road | 2 | | |
| | Goyamo | 4 | | |

| Year | Dual Qualifier | Finish | Starters | Win Payoff |
|------|----------------|--------|----------|------------|
| 1954 | Correlation | 6 | | |
| | Fisherman | 7 | | |
| 1953 | Native Dancer | 2 | 11 | |
| | Invigorator | 3 | | |
| | Straight Face | 6 | | |
| 1952 | **Hill Gail** | 1 | 16 | $4.20 |
| | Sub Fleet | 2 | | |
| 1951 | Battle Morn | 6 | 20 | |
| | Big Stretch | 18 | | |
| 1950 | **Middleground** | 1 | 14 | $17.80 |
| | Hill Prince | 2 | | |
| | Oil Capitol | 5 | | |
| | Your Host | 9 | | |
| 1949 | Capot | 2 | 14 | |
| | Palestinian | 3 | | |
| | Olympia | 6 | | |
| | Johns Joy | 9 | | |
| | Wine List | 13 | | |
| 1948 | **Citation** | 1 | 6 | $2.80 |
| | My Request | 3 | | |
| | Grandpere | 5 | | |
| | Escadru | 6 | | |
| 1947 | **Jet Pilot** | 1 | 13 | $12.80 |
| | Phalanx | 2 | | |
| | Faultless | 3 | | |
| | Cosmic Bomb | 5 | | |
| 1946 | **Assault** | 1 | 17 | $18.40 |
| | Spy Song | 2 | | |
| | Lord Boswell | 4 | | |
| | Knockdown | 5 | | |
| | Marine Victory | 15 | | |

In Table 29 we provide a comparative summary for Dual Qualifiers and non-Dual Qualifiers in the Derby from 1946 through 2002.

**TABLE 29. DUAL QUALIFIERS VS. NON-DUAL QUALIFIERS IN THE KENTUCKY DERBY (1946-2002)**

|  | Dual Qualifiers | Non-Dual Qualifiers (DI>4) | Non-Dual Qualifiers (DI<=4) |
|---|---|---|---|
| Starters | 200 | 137 | 525 |
| % Starters/Race | 23% | 16% | 61% |
| % Derbies Won | 58% | 5% | 37% |
| Avg. Finish Position | 5.7 | 10.0 | 9.2 |
| Impact Value* | 2.5 | 0.3 | 0.6 |
| % ROI** | +17% | -65% | -59% |

*Impact Value (IV) is a ratio of success to opportunity. For example, Dual Qualifiers won 2.5 times the expected number of Derbies between 1946 and 2002 based on the percentage of Dual Qualifier winners vs. percentage of Dual Qualifier starters. Specifically, 23 percent of the starters were Dual Qualifiers and they won 58 percent of the Derbies. The ratio of 58 over 23 is 2.5. ** ROI is the return on investment when a $2.00 wager is placed on every Derby starter between 1946 and 2002 sharing a common characteristic. Two hundred Dual Qualifiers require $400 in wagers. Those bets returned $467.80 for a 17.0 percent ROI.*

Despite its predictive value, the Dual Qualifier concept was never initially intended as a handicapping tool. It was originally offered as a study of the defining qualities of American classic runners, the things that differentiate classic winners from their contemporaries. What may have been lost in its popularization is a full appreciation of the underlying principles. Sometimes a strict application of the "rules" can lead us astray and cause us to miss the point.

Part of the problem lies in the subjectivity that goes into EFH rankings and, for that matter, in the limitations of the DI. The EFH is a product of the collective judgment of experts. Sometimes their judgment is imperfect. The DI is based on data derived from, and applied to, large populations. Occasionally there will be aptitudinally prepotent ancestors in an individual pedigree not accounted for by the current state of knowledge. It was in this framework that we developed the notion of a "conceptual Dual Qualifier;" i.e., a Derby contender that satisfies the criteria of a distance pedigree and superior juvenile form, yet may have been overlooked by the "rules."

The idea first surfaced in the late 1980s with the Derby wins of two non-Dual Qualifiers, Winning Colors and Sunday Silence, both of which had a DI below 4.00. Neither was eligible for EFH ranking because they failed to compete in stakes races. However, Winning Colors won at first asking while defeating eventual juvenile champion filly Epitome by several lengths in a Saratoga Maiden Special Weight event. An injury kept her away until December when she returned to easily win an allowance race. One could argue based on her performance that she would have been near the top of her class had she raced through the fall.

Similarly, Sunday Silence had broken his maiden at Hollywood Park by ten lengths in 1:09.2 in mid-November and returned three weeks later to lose an allowance race by a head to Houston. Houston became one of the winter-book Derby favorites after winning the Bay Shore Stakes (G2) as an early three-year-old. Arguments could be made that both Winning Colors and Sunday Silence were clearly among the best of their respective crops. Both conformed to the principles supporting the Dual Qualifier concept even though neither fit the "rules."

In recent years we have highlighted other conceptual Dual Qualifiers at *The Blood-Horse* Interactive Triple Crown Mania web site. They include Grindstone, Captain Bodgit, and Free House. All performed admirably in the Derby, and all were identified as conceptual Dual Qualifiers prior to the race.

Often the conceptual Dual Qualifier will not be apparent until the classic contender steps forward as a three-year-old. Horses that he or she defeated at two may emerge as major forces in the division. His or her juvenile form may have been obscured by a campaign-stopping injury, yet resurface in spectacular fashion the following spring. Again, one must use judgment. However, a conceptual Dual Qualifier is not a horse that simply faced the battles the previous year. There should be convincing evidence that the horse was among the best. Typically, several potential candidates will likely emerge during the course of a winter/spring pre-Derby campaign, although most probably will not make it to the Derby.

Legitimate Derby contenders always will be relatively few in number. The success of Dual Qualifiers for almost a half century is a testament to that fact. A horse with a pedigree ill-suited to the distance and/or an inexperienced, late-developing type, even though highly talented, will often falter when confronted by a true stayer that matured quickly, and that successfully competed at the highest levels in the early stages of its career. These Dual-Qualifier traits contribute to the definition of American classic horses.

Even though Dosage has come under attack in recent years because its Kentucky Derby success in the 1990s did not match its success in the previous two decades, the actual accomplishments of Dual Qualifiers in Triple Crown races suggest that those who believe "Dosage is dead" are taking a rather narrow view.

The following tables display the record of Dual Qualifiers (Table 30) and non-Dual Qualifiers (Table 31) since 1973 in all Triple Crown races in which both types competed. The races with no starting Dual Qualifiers were excluded for the obvious reason that they had no opportunity to win. The data are presented in terms of overall Impact Value (IV) by decade and by individual Triple Crown race. IV statistics for Dual Qualifiers are calculated by dividing the percentage of classic winners that were Dual Qualifiers by the percentage of Dual Qualifiers that started in the classic races. For example, if 20 percent of the races were won by Dual Qualifiers and 20 percent of the starters were Dual Qualifiers, then the IV is 1.00. However, if 40 percent were won by Dual Qualifiers with the same 20 percent Dual Qualifier starters, then the IV is 2.00 or twice the expectation. The same calculations were made for non-Dual Qualifiers. In a random world where no traits offer an advantage, the IV would approach 1.00 for all contenders. As the reader will observe in Table 30, the IVs for Dual Qualifiers are well over 2.50 for each of the Triple Crown races over the past 30 years. IV is, in effect, a ratio of success associated with a set of characteristics relative to the opportunity available.

By contrast, the results for non-Dual Qualifiers as presented in Table 31 are generally quite poor. Critics may argue the point, but the success of Dual Qualifiers in defining North American classic type is apparent. It should be noted, however, that the IV for the Derby has declined in each successive decade since the 1970s. This could mean that the characteristics of Derby winners are slowly evolving as more speed-bred or late developing types emerge as stronger Derby candidates. On the other hand, the Preakness and Belmont IV numbers have held up strongly for more than 30 years.

It also may be noteworthy that it is only since 1998 that Triple Crown races have been run in the absence of any Dual Qualifiers. Between 1973 and 1997, every Triple Crown race had at least one Dual Qualifier among the starters. Between 1998 and 2002, five of the 15 Triple Crown races lacked a Dual Qualifier, one in the Derby, two in the Preakness and two in the Belmont.

The significance of this dramatic change in the makeup of American classic fields in recent years is unclear. It is possible that the prominent juveniles of today are no longer as well-suited to distance racing as they once were and tend to be more precocious and speed-oriented than in the past. Speed bred to speed may be adequate for success in juvenile races as presently configured, but it fails when challenged by classic distances.

There certainly can be no argument that many prominent North American stallions are speed sires that cater to an early sales market. High-class speed from a sire is still high class, but perhaps not over a classic distance, and especially when coupled with speed from the mare. It is also possible that increased fragility in the Thoroughbred diminishes the probability of early developing types surviving the rigors of a two-year-old campaign and a long three-year-old pre-classic campaign. This could account for their displacement by later-developing runners that have been subjected to less stress.

### TABLE 30. DUAL QUALIFIERS (DQs) IN TRIPLE CROWN RACES SINCE 1973

| Years | Derby | Preakness | Belmont | All |
|---|---|---|---|---|
| 2000-2002 | 3 races | 2 races | 1 race | 6 races |
| | 0 winners (0.0%) | 1 winner (50.0%) | 1 winner (100.0%) | 2 winners (33.3%) |
| | 11 DQs (20.4%) | 5 DQs (26.3%) | 3 DQs (15.0%) | 19 DQs (23.2%) |
| | 54 starters | 19 starters | 9 starters | 82 starters |
| | IV = 0.00 | IV = 1.90 | IV = 6.67 | IV = 1.44 |
| 1990-1999 | 9 races | 9 races | 10 races | 28 races |
| | 5 winners (50.0%) | 6 winners (60.0%) | 6 winners (60.0%) | 17 winners (56.7%) |
| | 39 DQs (25.7%) | 19 DQs (19.2%) | 21 DQs (20.0%) | 79 DQs (22.2%) |
| | 152 starters | 99 starters | 105 starters | 356 starters |
| | IV = 1.95 | IV = 3.13 | IV = 3.00 | IV = 2.55 |
| 1980-1989 | 10 races | 10 races | 10 races | 30 races |
| | 8 winners (80.0%) | 2 winners (20.0%) | 5 winners (50.0%) | 15 winners (50.0%) |
| | 33 DQs (19.3%) | 13 DQs (13.8%) | 14 DQs (13.5%) | 60 DQs (16.3%) |
| | 171 starters | 94 starters | 104 starters | 369 starters |
| | IV = 4.15 | IV = 1.45 | IV = 3.70 | IV = 3.07 |
| 1973-1979 | 7 races | 7 races | 7 races | 21 races |
| | 7 winners (100.0%) | 5 winners (71.4%) | 4 winners (50.0%) | 16 winners (76.2%) |
| | 18 DQs (19.8%) | 15 DQs (26.8%) | 11 DQs (20.4%) | 45 DQs (21.8%) |
| | 96 starters | 56 starters | 54 starters | 206 starters |
| | IV = 5.05 | IV = 2.66 | IV = 2.45 | IV = 3.50 |
| 1973-2002 | 29 races | 28 races | 28 races | 85 races |
| | 20 winners (69.0%) | 14 winners (50.0%) | 16 winners (57.1%) | 50 winners (58.8%) |
| | 102 DQs (21.6%) | 52 DQs (19.4%) | 49 DQs (18.0%) | 200 DQs (20.0%) |
| | 473 starters | 268 starters | 272 starters | 1013 starters |
| | IV = 3.19 | IV = 2.58 | IV = 3.17 | IV = 2.94 |

# TABLE 31. NON-DUAL QUALIFIERS (NON-DQS) IN TRIPLE CROWN RACES SINCE 1973

| Years | Derby | Preakness | Belmont | All |
|---|---|---|---|---|
| 2000-02 | 3 races | 2 races | 1 races | 6 races |
| | 3 winners (100.0%) | 1 winner (50.0%) | 0 winner (0.0%) | 4 winners (66.7%) |
| | 43 non-DQs (79.6%) | 14 non-DQs (73.7%) | 6 non-DQs (66.7%) | 63 non-DQs (76.8%) |
| | 54 starters | 19 starters | 9 starters | 82 starters |
| | IV = 1.26 | IV = 0.68 | IV = 0.00 | IV = 0.86 |
| | | | | |
| 1990-99 | 9 races | 9 races | 10 races | 30 races |
| | 4 winners (44.4%) | 4 winners (44.4%) | 4 winners (40.0%) | 13 winners (43.3%) |
| | 113 DQs (74.3%) | 80 non-DQs (80.8%) | 84 non-DQs (80.0%) | 302 non-DQs (79.3%) |
| | 152 starters | 99 starters | 105 starters | 381 starters |
| | IV = 0.60 | IV = 0.55 | IV = 0.50 | IV = 0.55 |
| | | | | |
| 1980-89 | 10 races | 10 races | 10 races | 30 races |
| | 2 winners (20.0%) | 8 winners (80.0%) | 5 winners (50.0%) | 15 winners (50.0%) |
| | 138 non-DQs (80.7%) | 81 non-DQs (86.2%) | 90 non-DQs (86.5%) | 309 non-DQs (83.7%) |
| | 171 starters | 94 starters | 104 starters | 369 starters |
| | IV = 0.25 | IV = 0.93 | IV = 0.58 | IV = 0.60 |
| | | | | |
| 1973-79 | 7 races | 7 races | 7 races | 21 races |
| | 0 winners (0.0%) | 2 winners (28.6%) | 3 winners (42.9%) | 5 winners (23.8%) |
| | 77 non-DQs (80.2%) | 41 non-DQs (73.2%) | 43 non-DQs (79.6%) | 161 non-DQs (78.2%) |
| | 96 starters | 56 starters | 54 starters | 206 starters |
| | IV = 0.00 | IV = 0.39 | IV = 0.54 | IV = 0.30 |
| | | | | |
| 1973-2002 | 29 races | 28 races | 28 races | 85 races |
| | 9 winners (31.0%) | 15 winners (53.6%) | 12 winners (42.9%) | 36 winners (42.4%) |
| | 371 non-DQs (78.4%) | 216 non-DQs (80.6%) | 223 non-DQs (82.0%) | 810 non-DQs (80.0%) |
| | 473 starters | 268 starters | 272 starters | 1013 starters |
| | IV = 0.40 | IV = 0.67 | IV = 0.52 | IV = 0.53 |

# CHAPTER 20

# The Controversy Surrounding Dosage

Anyone even remotely familiar with modern-day Dosage is aware of the controversy it has spawned. The source of the controversy is problematic at best and often results from a gross misinterpretation of Dosage's purpose and intent. As stated at the outset, contemporary Dosage is simply a pedigree classification technique. It is not, as some have claimed, a breeding theory. It is not, as still others maintain, a handicapping system. However, the information Dosage provides may be used in both breeding and handicapping. The way people use it depends on how it addresses their particular need. Those who apply it to the breeding of racehorses and who feel comfortable with the result are perfectly free to do so. If Dosage affords a better idea of the type of foal a mating might produce, then it has served its purpose. Those who believe it can help identify the potential winners of races are equally free to use it in that manner. If Dosage can increase the horseplayer's chances of cashing a ticket, who is in a position to deny him the opportunity? The only measure of Dosage's validity is if its application enhances one's understanding and whether it provides insights one wouldn't have without it.

The most obvious source of negative reaction to Dosage may be that it challenges conventional thinking. In that regard it represents a threat to those heavily invested in traditional ways of interpreting Thoroughbred pedigrees. A defensive posture in such circumstances is typical of human behavior. The perception of a threat from Dosage may be enhanced by the fact that it is constructed within the context of rigorous statistical analysis. Few if any other approaches to pedigree interpretation are as well-supported by such a statistical framework.

For the most part, traditional pedigree interpretation is anecdotal in character. There are many misconceptions and false principles espoused as truth that are based on subjectivity and intuition rather than real data or solid facts. One such misconception is the notion of a direct correlation between a horse's characteristics as a runner and its ability to transmit those same characteristics to its descendants. Such a correlation can obviously exist in individual cases, but it is not predictable with any degree of certainty. We have alluded to this in our earlier discussions. If it were, then Kingmambo, a miler by a sprinter and sire of sprinter-milers and out of a champion miler, would hardly be a candidate to consistently sire classic distance types. Yet he does.

Similarly, we would not expect Slewpy, a Grade 1 winner at a classic distance by a classic sire and out of a producer of middle-distance horses, to have been predominantly a sire of sprinters. Yet he was.

In fact, Dosage avoids the trap created when the emphasis is on an ancestor's racing performance rather than its actual performance at stud. That doesn't make Dosage a superior method, just an alternative one. The problem is that some people have a difficult time dealing with things that are different from what they know and what they understand. Nevertheless, there are legitimate questions raised about Dosage methodology that should be answered.

Perhaps the most sensitive issue is that of *chef-de-race* selection. Many critics insist that the list of *chefs-de-race* should comprise only those sires "worthy" of inclusion based on their overall excellence at stud or that have achieved a level of recognition within the breed that elevates them far beyond the ordinary. That would be fine if the *chef-de-race* list were a roster of great sires — a Stallion Hall of Fame, so to speak. But it isn't. A requirement for stallion greatness in a *chef-de-race* candidate conforms to Varola's selection philosophy discussed earlier. However, contemporary Dosage methodology seeks the most accurate possible aptitudinal interpretation of a pedigree. If a strong case can be made for a less than stellar sire, yet one that is successful enough to generate sufficient data from his descendants to confirm aptitudinal prepotence, he becomes more important to an interpretation than the leading sire with no evidence of such prepotence. Those who are most concerned with honoring stallions will be served best by other systems of pedigree analysis. Dosage must rely on demonstrated prepotence for type as the driver behind the *chef-de-race* selection process.

One consequence of a *chef-de-race* selection process requiring convincing statistical evidence can be a time lag in updating the aptitudinal interpretation of some pedigrees. This is a legitimate concern and is most apparent with younger, unproven sires that have not had enough time to establish their aptitudinal credentials. It may also be the case with more established sires that haven't met the statistical criteria for *chef-de-race* assignment. The result can be a shortage of first- and second-generation *chefs-de-race* in many pedigrees. Although the impact on population-wide Dosage trends is likely to be minimal, this situation can and does influence the aptitudinal interpretation of individual pedigrees.

To deal with this situation we can catalog recent non-*chef-de-race* sires according to the general performance characteristics of their better runners, using the average winning distance of their progeny in open stakes races as a convenient guide. The same may be done for recent non-*chef-de-race* broodmare sires.

Appendix IV classifies many current and recent prominent sires and broodmare sires according to the apparent qualities of speed they transmit to their progeny. Five categories have been chosen that are analogous to the five aptitudinal groups in a Dosage Profile. They, too, may be thought of as points on a speed-stamina spectrum ranging from Dominant Speed to Intermediate Speed to Balanced Speed to Intermediate Stamina to Dominant Stamina. Individual classifications may change from year to year, especially for the younger sires as the number of their progeny stakes wins increases.

An assignment to a category does not imply aptitudinal prepotence. That is reserved for *chefs-de-race*. Rather, the classification reflects the general character of their runners. In many cases, the speed or stamina seen may derive from prepotent ancestors in their own pedigree. Nevertheless, the classifications are a guide to the typical performance traits of the sire's runners, where speed is associated with shorter races, and stamina with longer races and, quite often, turf. The Tables are a useful guide in cases where *chefs-de-race* are not present close up in a pedigree. In those situations, making a mental adjustment to the Dosage Profile can be helpful in better understanding the aptitudinal makeup of the horse in question.

Still another area of controversy focuses on the influence of mares. Many critics allege that mares are ignored in the Dosage calculations. The role of mares in contemporary Dosage methodology is adequately explained by the European Dosage expert Steve Miller in a recently published response to critics:

"... *it is a common misconception that the system does not take account of the dam's side — it does through qualifying chef-de-race sires that are present in that half of the pedigree. The reasons females are excluded as individuals are: 1) characteristics transmitted by a given individual are not necessarily those they possessed as a racehorse and 2) there is not enough data to make any assumption based of the performance of a mare's progeny — even the most successful mare may have only a small handful of offspring that make it to the racecourse in their lifetime, whereas a stallion may have more than 1,000 individuals racing over less than a decade. It is clearly unsafe to base any claim of aptitudinal prepotence on such a relatively tiny progeny sample as a mare can offer and unwise to base it on an individual's racecourse performances."*

Even for individual mares, however, the argument used for non-*chef-de-race* sires and broodmare sires would apply. If one is convinced of a reliable aptitudinal influence from a mare, then the same process for making a mental adjustment to the Dosage Profile is justified.

The critics of Dosage most often come out in force when an individual horse's performance contradicts its Dosage figures, particularly in high profile races. Rarely do those same critics acknowledge the validity of Dosage when conventional analysis falters and Dosage prevails. Of course, these isolated examples have no bearing on the issue anyway.

As the reader has no doubt noticed, Dosage is presented as a tool for developing statistical studies on large populations of Thoroughbreds in order to facilitate the observation of aptitudinal trends within the breed. Insistence that every individual conform to an arbitrary standard is a pointless exercise. Within large populations, especially those involving biological systems, we will always find a broad distribution range of characteristics. If, however, Dosage can statistically differentiate one subgroup from another even in the face of broad distributions within each group, then it has achieved its purpose. For example, as noted earlier, Dosage can confirm that the pedigrees of seven-furlong stakes winners are configured differently from those of eight-furlong stakes winners. Nevertheless, within each group there will be individuals with Dosage figures more suited to five furlongs or to 12 furlongs. Their presence in the subgroups has already been accounted for in the statistical analysis that showed the seven- and eight-furlong winners were indeed dissimilar in terms of pedigree construction.

Whenever one deals with distributions within large populations, one must always consider the probability that an individual's traits will conform to those of the general population. A reasonable analogy may be the five-pack-a-day smoker who lives to be 100 years old. Most people who smoke five packs a day will expire long before their 100th birthday. But such hardy individuals certainly do exist. Their survival against the odds does not in any way bring into question the validity of the demographic studies done on smoking and life expectancy. The same is true of individual horses with Dosage figures that fail to conform to those of the majority of the group they populate.

In this context, it is noteworthy that the critics of Dosage have never been able to challenge the accuracy of the data. For the most part they ignore it and don't try. They probably don't try because, as the reader has seen, the correlations are so strong and so compelling that it would be fruitless to do so. If one finds Dosage a waste of time, that determination will result not from the data that support it, but from a philosophical barrier that exists between conventional and progressive thought.

In retrospect, much of the controversy could have been avoided had the subject matter been presented not as a continuation of Dosage theory but as a separate study of the effects of inherited speed on performance. The terms Speed Profile and Speed Index seem far less intimidating than Dosage Profile and Dosage Index.

In truth, the current studies have only a marginal association with the historical aspects of Dosage theory. They do borrow the concepts of ancestral prepotence and aptitudinal type, but in a context very different from that proposed by either Vuillier or Varola. Latter day *chefs-de-race* are less icons of racing greatness than they are centers of inherited speed within a pedigree. Vuillier emphasized the class of the pedigrees that were populated with his *chefs-de-race*. Varola also emphasized class, but within a "sociological" framework of aptitudinal type and by taking great pains to dissociate type from specific performance traits.

The latest iteration of Dosage concerns itself only with the relationship between aptitudinal type and racing performance. Sires are considered not for their place in Thoroughbred history but for the characteristics of speed and stamina they may consistently pass along to their descendants. Those who think about modern day Dosage in this way and who appreciate the value of a pedigree classification system as a research tool should find the material not the least bit controversial.

Occasionally the criticism borders on bizarre. A stunning example of the prejudicial criticism often leveled at Dosage theory is a silly outburst in 1985 by a prominent racing newsletter publisher. In the days leading up to the Kentucky Derby, he defiantly proclaimed his intention to double his exacta wager on Chief's Crown and Tank's Prospect solely because they were Dosage non-qualifiers. Chief's Crown, the previous year's two-year-old champion and the 6-5 favorite, was coming off a 5 ½ length win in the Grade 1 Blue Grass Stakes, while Tank's Prospect at 11-1 had just taken the Grade 1 Arkansas Derby by 6 ½ lengths. They finished third, 5 ¾ lengths behind, and seventh, 11 lengths behind. The only two Dual Qualifiers in the 1985 Kentucky Derby, Spend a Buck at 4-1 and Stephan's Odyssey at 13-1, ran first and second.

Similarly, a nationally renowned turf writer falsely declared to his reading audience that Dosage was self-fulfilling because *chefs-de-race* were chosen after the fact on the basis of previous Derby results in order to ensure the winners had a DI of 4.00 or less. This assertion is more a reflection of the columnist's credibility that it is an indictment of Dosage. Had he researched the original *Daily Racing Form* editions that introduced Dosage to the public, he would have known, as readers of the book do, that the original *chefs-de-race* were those of Varola as modified by Hewitt. The Kentucky Derby had no part in their selection. That discovery wasn't made until later during the course of research using the new Dosage methodology.

It is hard to imagine what is gained by this sort of non-constructive criticism and misrepresentation of the facts.

# Gay Hostess

DP 24-8-26-2-4, DI 2.37, CD 0.72

Gay Hostess — Photo Courtesy of the Thoroughbred Times

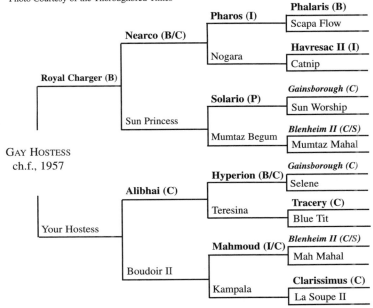

GAY HOSTESS
ch.f., 1957

- Royal Charger (B)
  - Nearco (B/C)
    - Pharos (I)
      - Phalaris (B)
      - Scapa Flow
    - Nogara
      - Havresac II (I)
      - Catnip
  - Sun Princess
    - Solario (P)
      - Gainsborough (C)
      - Sun Worship
    - Mumtaz Begum
      - Blenheim II (C/S)
      - Mumtaz Mahal
- Your Hostess
  - Alibhai (C)
    - Hyperion (B/C)
      - Gainsborough (C)
      - Selene
    - Teresina
      - Tracery (C)
      - Blue Tit
  - Boudoir II
    - Mahmoud (I/C)
      - Blenheim II (C/S)
      - Mah Mahal
    - Kampala
      - Clarissimus (C)
      - La Soupe II

**DP Contribution**     **Equivalent to:**
Sire  22 - 6 - 7 - 1 - 4     DI  3.7     CD  1.03
Dam   2 - 2 - 19 - 1 - 0    DI  1.29    CD  0.21

Gay Hostess, ch.f., 1957 (Royal Charger - Your Hostess, by Alibhai) is the dam of Kentucky Derby winner and leading sire Majestic Prince. She was unraced. Therefore, her Dosage figures would seem to be irrelevant. Obviously, from a performance perspective, they are. However, Gay Hostess is presented here as an example of the rare Thoroughbred with a full complement of 64 Dosage points, 40 from her sire and 24 from her dam.

# CHAPTER 21

# The Future of Dosage

Dosage will survive as it has for more than a century; perhaps not in its current form, but in a form that integrates current knowledge with what we learn in the future. This is the same process that brought us from the original Dosage concept of Vuillier through Varola to today. It is the process by which science builds on the foundation of what came before. Dosage will continue to evolve as long as there is the desire by pedigree aficionados, owners, breeders and handicappers for a better, more accurate model of the Thoroughbred world of breeding and racing.

We will undoubtedly continue to see a growing international interest in the subject. Significant efforts already are under way in Europe and Australia, designed to complement and reinforce the work done in the United States. New *chefs-de-race* will emerge to replace those lost from four-generation pedigrees. Fresh ideas will be introduced that refine the Dosage model and narrow the distributions within populations. This will increase the statistical separation of populations based on performance characteristics and increase the accuracy of the pedigree interpretation. We probably will see advances in *chef-de-race* selection as well, using techniques as yet undefined.

In the background, however, is a fundamental philosophical issue that may ultimately affect the direction of Dosage research. That issue relates to the definition and continuity of classicity through time. It is best captured in the question: Is the classic horse of today the same type as the classic horse of the past?

Current methodology makes no assumption that classicity is a constant. It merely observes the evolutionary development of aptitudinal traits within the Thoroughbred breed. In so doing, it has identified a progression toward ever-increasing speed and there is practical evidence of this shift in aptitudinal character.

Between 1983 and 2001, the percentage of open stakes races in the United States at 10 furlongs or longer on the dirt decreased by 23 percent. The reason for this change is not entirely obvious. On the one hand, there may be fewer horses now that are competitive at classic distances. On the other, the change may be cultural, with races having been shortened in response to fan interest. If the latter is true, then Dosage will have a difficult time identifying traditional stamina influences because sires will have less opportunity to express those attributes. The dilemma, then, is deciding which route to follow over the long term. The present scheme apparently is accurate in highlighting the transition to shorter races and the increased need for speed over shorter distances.

The alternative, proposed by some, is to redefine classicity continually, using as the standard how contemporary classic horses are bred. In that way, classic winners of today are assumed to possess the same aptitudinal qualities as classic winners of long ago. By this approach we assume that the historical standards of stamina continue to exist as they always have, but that their full expression is obscured by the loss of opportunity resulting from fewer distance events. Which direction is the correct one is a matter of judgment. We can define aptitudinal type in two ways. The first is in response to the evolving culture and the changing configuration of racing over time. The second is by continuously re-evaluating classicity in contemporary terms. Either way, the research opportunities are virtually unlimited.

Dosage is an intellectually stimulating area of research with infinite possibilities and a broad range of applications. As long as it remains focused on aptitudinal prepotence and rejects a politically correct but scientifically questionable "honor roll of sires" approach, Dosage will enhance our appreciation of the aptitudinal evolution of the Thoroughbred. At the same time, Dosage requires more than a superficial understanding of its principles and how they are applied. As a result, many within the Thoroughbred industry will continue to consider it an esoteric system of pedigree analysis.

# CHAPTER 22

# A Few Dosage Guidelines for Breeders and Handicappers

## FOR BREEDERS:

• If you are breeding to race, have clear, well-defined objectives concerning the aptitudinal type desired from a mating. For example, are you looking for a classic prospect, a futurity winner, or a marathoner on the turf? Breeding extreme speed to extreme speed will probably not produce a Derby winner. Breeding extreme stamina to extreme stamina will probably not produce a two-year-old champion.

• High Dosage numbers imply speed, shorter distance racing and suitability for the main track. Low Dosage numbers imply stamina, longer distance racing and suitability for turf.

• There are no such things as good or bad Dosage figures. Dosage figures merely describe a pedigree in terms of aptitudinal type. The figures themselves are like classification codes that enable one to compare the performance characteristics of other horses with similar figures.

•Understand the aptitudinal contribution of your mare, in terms of both type and magnitude. She can contribute a maximum of 24 points to the DP of her foals.

• Look for potential "hidden" sources of aptitudinal prepotence in your mare, although do so in a conservative manner. If warranted, make provisional adjustments to her DP contribution.

• Especially consider compatible emerging young sires that appear to be passing along consistent type but have not yet generated enough statistical information to absolutely confirm aptitudinal prepotence. Make provisional adjustments to the DP here as well.

• Emphasize stallion selection from among the best, established sires in your stud fee range. Unproven sires are high-risk propositions when breeding to race because very few stallions ever become successful. When favoring new stallions, recall that the most successful sires usually have high DP point totals.

• If possible, determine the aptitudinal type of the mares most successful with a sire of choice to see if a clear pattern emerges.

• The total number of DP points in your proposed foal's pedigree may correlate marginally with potential class. However, higher point totals are desirable mainly because the aptitudinal interpretation of the pedigree is likely to be more accurate. Don't arbitrarily assume superior class because of high DP point totals.

- Use common sense and appreciate that the breeding quality of the stallion and the mare, as well as their conformational compatibility, are more important than any statistical formula. Dosage can be supportive of your breeding decisions, but it should never be the primary driver.

## FOR HANDICAPPERS:

- Develop an appreciation for the Dosage model correlating Dosage figures with average winning distance and where sprinters tend to have high Dosage numbers while stayers tend to have low Dosage numbers.

- Understand that the interplay of the DP, DI and CD are more meaningful than any of the individual figures alone. The DI by itself is not sufficient for evaluating aptitudinal type. Know when the CD is unusually high or low for a particular DI.

- The following charts show the average winning distance (AWD) in open stakes of horses with Dosage figures (DI and CD) falling within defined ranges. They may be used as a general guide to the typical Dosage figure/distance profile.

### DI RANGE VS. AVERAGE DISTANCE

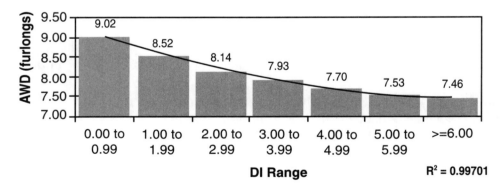

136

## Average Winning Distance (AWD) by CD Range
## (1983-2001)

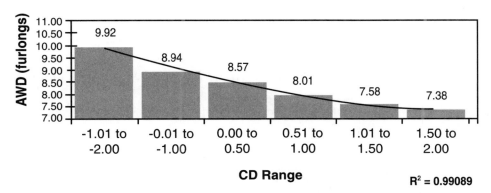

- Runners with double-digit representation in the Brilliant aptitudinal group will often express front-running speed as well as early maturity.

- Do not arbitrarily dismiss low Dosage figure runners in sprints if they also have significant representation in the Brilliant aptitudinal group, particularly double digits.

- Among juveniles, a first-time starter with a speed-oriented DP is often a good play against maidens that have started but have fared poorly in their initial efforts. Since most juvenile maiden wins are accomplished in wire-to-wire fashion, speed types, even though inexperienced, often can get to the front and stay out of trouble.

- Do not ignore first-time steeplechasers coming from the ranks of sprinters on the flat. In races where the pace is likely to be moderate, their quickness and agility can be a benefit in getting cleanly over the hurdles.

- Consider first-time starters on the turf with strong representation in the Solid and/or Professional aptitudinal groups.

- Classic races are won by a disproportionately high percentage of horses with a DI of 4.00 or less.

- Ron J. White, a software design engineer with Microsoft Corporation, has identified the following Dosage trends in the Kentucky Derby that find a high percentage of winners while eliminating other starters:
    - Eighty-seven percent of Derby winners over the last half-century have a *chef-de-race* within two generations.

    - In the last 50 years, every Derby winner had at least 16 Dosage points.

    - Since 1950, 87 percent of Derby winners have had at least four Brilliant points in their DP, 90 percent have had at least three Brilliant points, and 98 percent have had at least two Brilliant points.

- In the last 50 runnings of the Derby, 90 percent of the winners had at least two Intermediate points in their DP.

- Since 1950, 94 percent of all Derby winners had at least four Classic points in their DP.

- Don't necessarily eliminate two-year-old speedsters going a route of ground. Two-year-olds with sprint type Dosage figures can win around two turns on the basis of class. However, these same horses, when mature, often revert back to type and will no longer be competitive in routes.

- Always consider the racing surface in the context of aptitudinal type. Does the track favor speed or stamina? Which horses seem best suited by Dosage to track and race conditions?

- Starters with DI<1.00 or CD<0.00 virtually can be eliminated from contention in sprints unless they hold a significant class edge. Only 12 percent of stakes winners with DI<1.00 and 14 percent of stakes winners with CD<0.00 win their races at less than a mile.

- Horses with more than 20 Classic points in their DP win 85 percent of their races over a route of ground.

- Only 21 percent of stakes winners at a classic distance or beyond have no DP points in either the Solid or Professional group while only 12 percent of sprinters have points in both.

- Always consider Dosage (or pedigree) in the context of class. Higher class runners will often defeat lower class runners even when pedigree suggests an unsuitable distance.

- Most important, as noted by the great breeding authority, Abram S. Hewitt, Dosage is as much art as it is science. There are no shortcuts. Applying Dosage to handicapping requires an understanding of its fundamental principles as well as its myriad subtleties. Usefulness comes with experience.

## Dosage Figures for Winners of Grade I Stakes (1990-2002)

These lists of North American Grade 1 stakes include those approved for the 2001 racing year and run continuously for at least four consecutive years at Grade 1 level. Races included are through October 30, 2002

### ACORN S, THREE-YEAR-OLD FILLIES, 8F, DIRT:

| YEAR | WINNER | SIRE | BROODMARE SIRE | DP | DI | CD | PTS |
|------|--------|------|----------------|-----|-----|-----|-----|
| 1990 | STELLA MADRID | ALYDAR | GALLANT ROMEO | 14 - 6 - 20 - 0 - 0 | 3.00 | 0.85 | 40 |
| 1991 | MEADOW STAR | MEADOWLAKE | IN REALITY | 15 - 11 - 10 - 0 - 0 | 6.20 | 1.14 | 36 |
| 1992 | PROSPECTORS DELITE | MR. PROSPECTOR | HOIST THE FLAG | 24 - 10 - 21 - 2 - 5 | 2.54 | 0.74 | 62 |
| 1993 | SKY BEAUTY | BLUSHING GROOM | NIJINSKY II | 21 - 0 - 17 - 4 - 4 | 1.79 | 0.65 | 46 |
| 1994 | INSIDE INFORMATION | PRIVATE ACCOUNT | KEY TO THE MINT | 10 - 9 - 17 - 3 - 1 | 2.20 | 0.60 | 40 |
| 1995 | CAT'S CRADLE | FLYING PASTER | LINKAGE | 7 - 2 - 2 - 2 - 1 | 2.50 | 0.86 | 14 |
| 1996 | STAR DE LADY ANN | STAR DE NASKRA | SIR IVOR | 7 - 11 - 6 - 0 - 0 | 7.00 | 1.04 | 24 |
| 1997 | SHARP CAT | STORM CATACK | ACK ACK | 5 - 9 - 8 - 0 - 0 | 4.50 | 0.86 | 22 |
| 1998 | JERSEY GIRL | BELONG TO ME | VALID APPEAL | 8 - 8 - 16 - 0 - 0 | 3.00 | 0.75 | 32 |
| 1999 | THREE RING | NOTEBOOK | CUTLASS | 1 - 4 - 6 - 0 - 3 | 1.33 | 0.00 | 14 |
| 2000 | FINDER'S FEE | STORM CAT | MR. PROSPECTOR | 11 - 5 - 10 - 0 - 0 | 4.20 | 1.04 | 26 |
| 2001 | FOREST SECRETS | FOREST WILDCAT | TIME FOR A CHANGE | 4 - 3 - 8 - 0 - 3 | 1.57 | 0.28 | 18 |
| 2002 | YOU | YOU AND I | HOMEBUILDER | 5 - 2 - 9 - 1 - 1 | 1.77 | 0.50 | 18 |
| | | | MEDIAN= | | 2.54 | 0.75 | 26.0 |

### ALABAMA S, THREE-YEAR-OLD FILLIES, 10F, DIRT:

| YEAR | WINNER | SIRE | BROODMARE SIRE | DP | DI | CD | PTS |
|------|--------|------|----------------|-----|-----|-----|-----|
| 1990 | GO FOR WAND | DEPUTY MINISTER | CYANE | 6 - 2 - 4 - 0 - 0 | 5.00 | 1.17 | 12 |
| 1991 | VERSAILLES TREATY | DANZIG | BUCKPASSER | 5 - 17 - 28 - 0 - 0 | 2.57 | 0.54 | 50 |
| 1992 | NOVEMBER SNOW | STORM CAT | ALYDAR | 7 - 4 - 13 - 0 - 0 | 2.69 | 0.75 | 24 |
| 1993 | SKY BEAUTY | BLUSHING GROOM | NIJINSKY II | 21 - 0 - 17 - 4 - 4 | 1.79 | 0.65 | 46 |
| 1994 | HEAVENLY PRIZE | SEEKING THE GOLD | NIJINSKY II | 10 - 3 - 17 - 4 - 0 | 1.72 | 0.56 | 34 |
| 1995 | PRETTY DISCREET | PRIVATE ACCOUNT | BELIEVE IT | 6 - 6 - 17 - 0 - 3 | 1.78 | 0.38 | 32 |
| 1996 | YANKS MUSIC | AIR FORBES WON | DARBY CREEK ROAD | 4 - 3 - 7 - 0 - 0 | 3.00 | 0.79 | 14 |
| 1997 | RUNUP THE COLORS | A.P. INDY | HOIST THE FLAG | 11 - 7 - 15 - 2 - 5 | 1.76 | 0.43 | 40 |
| 1998 | BANSHEE BREEZE | UNBRIDLED | KNOWN FACT | 8 - 9 - 9 - 0 - 6 | 2.05 | 0.41 | 32 |
| 1999 | SILVERBULLETDAY | SILVER DEPUTY | TOM ROLFE | 6 - 1 - 9 - 0 - 6 | 1.10 | 0.05 | 22 |

| | | | | DP | DI | CD | PTS |
|---|---|---|---|---|---|---|---|
| 2000 | JOSTLE | BROCCO | DRONE | 2 - 7 - 12 - 1 - 0 | 2.14 | 0.45 | 22 |
| 2001 | FLUTE | SEATTLE SLEW | BLUSHING GROOM | 15 - 1 - 14 - 2 - 2 | 2.09 | 0.74 | 34 |
| 2002 | FARDA AMIGA | BROAD BRUSH | PLEASANT COLONY | 4 - 16 - 18 - 0 - 2 | 2.64 | 0.50 | 40 |
| | | | MEDIAN = | | **2.09** | **0.54** | **32.0** |

## APPLE BLOSSOM H, FOUR-YEAR-OLDS & UP, FILLES & MARES, 8.50F, DIRT:

| YEAR | WINNER | SIRE | BROODMARE SIRE | DP | DI | CD | PTS |
|---|---|---|---|---|---|---|---|
| 1992 | PASEANA | AHMAD | FLINTHAM | 4 - 4 - 2 - 0 - 0 | 9.00 | 1.20 | 10 |
| 1993 | PASEANA | AHMAD | FLINTHAM | 4 - 4 - 2 - 0 - 0 | 9.00 | 1.20 | 10 |
| 1994 | NINE KEYS | FORTY NINER | KEY TO THE MINT | 15 - 6 - 18 - 3 - 4 | 1.88 | 0.54 | 46 |
| 1995 | HEAVENLY PRIZE | SEEKING THE GOLD | NIJINSKY II | 10 - 3 - 17 - 4 - 0 | 1.72 | 0.56 | 34 |
| 1996 | TWICE THE VICE | VICE REGENT | RESURGENT | 9 - 2 - 10 - 1 - 0 | 2.67 | 0.86 | 22 |
| 1997 | HALO AMERICA | WAQUOIT | HALO | 14 - 6 - 12 - 2 - 0 | 3.25 | 0.94 | 34 |
| 1998 | ESCENA | STRAWBERRY ROAD | SEATTLE SLEW | 11 - 1 - 8 - 2 - 0 | 2.67 | 0.95 | 22 |
| 1999 | BANSHEE BREEZE | UNBRIDLED | KNOWN FACT | 8 - 9 - 9 - 0 - 6 | 2.05 | 0.41 | 32 |
| 2000 | HERITAGE OF GOLD | GOLD LEGEND | LYPHARD | 13 - 1 - 18 - 0 - 0 | 2.56 | 0.84 | 32 |
| 2001 | GOURMET GIRL | CEE'S TIZZY | WELSH PAGEANT | 8 - 1 - 11 - 0 - 0 | 2.64 | 0.85 | 20 |
| 2002 | AZERI | JADE HUNTER | AHONOORA | 9 - 2 - 9 - 0 - 0 | 3.44 | 1.00 | 20 |
| | | | MEDIAN = | | **2.67** | **0.86** | **22.0** |

## ARLINGTON MILLION, THREE-YEAR-OLDS & UP, 10F, TURF:

| YEAR | WINNER | SIRE | BROODMARE SIRE | DP | DI | CD | PTS |
|---|---|---|---|---|---|---|---|
| 1990 | GOLDEN PHEASANT | CARO | ROUND TABLE | 8 - 14 - 10 - 10 - 4 | 1.42 | 0.26 | 46 |
| 1991 | TIGHT SPOT | HIS MAJESTY | LYPHARD | 9 - 2 - 35 - 0 - 4 | 1.33 | 0.24 | 50 |
| 1992 | DEAR DOCTOR | CRYSTAL GLITTERS | ZEDDAAN | 12 - 0 - 6 - 0 - 2 | 3.00 | 1.00 | 20 |
| 1993 | STAR OF COZZENE | COZZENE | PIA STAR | 10 - 7 - 10 - 9 - 0 | 1.57 | 0.50 | 36 |
| 1994 | PARADISE CREEK | IRISH RIVER | NORTHFIELDS | 6 - 6 - 10 - 0 - 0 | 3.40 | 0.82 | 22 |
| 1995 | AWAD | CAVEAT | NOBLE DANCER | 2 - 6 - 4 - 1 - 1 | 2.50 | 0.50 | 14 |
| 1996 | MECKE | MAUDLIN | BALDSKI | 11 - 10 - 5 - 2 - 0 | 5.22 | 1.07 | 28 |
| 1997 | MARLIN | SWORD DANCE | DAMASCUS | 5 - 7 - 14 - 4 - 0 | 1.73 | 0.43 | 30 |
| 1998 | NOT RUN | | | | | | |
| 1999 | NOT RUN | | | | | | |
| 2000 | CHESTER HOUSE | MR. PROSPECTOR | EL GRAN SENOR | 23 - 7 - 20 - 0 - 0 | 4.00 | 1.06 | 50 |
| 2001 | SILVANO | LOMITAS | BEAU'S EAGLE | 1 - 1 - 6 - 5 - 1 | 0.56 | -0.29 | 14 |
| 2002 | BEAT HOLLOW | SADLER'S WELLS | DANCING BRAVE | 7 - 5 - 25 - 12 - 0 | 1.00 | 0.14 | 49 |
| | | | MEDIAN = | | **1.73** | **0.50** | **30.0** |

## ASHLAND S, THREE-YEAR-OLD FILLIES, 8.50F, DIRT:

| YEAR | WINNER | SIRE | BROODMARE SIRE | DP | DI | CD | PTS |
|------|--------|------|----------------|-----|-----|-----|-----|
| 1990 | GO FOR WAND | DEPUTY MINISTER | CYANE | 6 - 2 - 4 - 0 - 0 | 5.00 | 1.17 | 12 |
| 1991 | DO IT WITH STYLE | PANCHO VILLA | FLIP SAL | 10 - 8 - 5 - 1 - 0 | 5.86 | 1.13 | 24 |
| 1992 | PROSPECTORS DELITE | MR. PROSPECTOR | HOIST THE FLAG | 24 - 10 - 21 - 2 - 5 | 2.54 | 0.74 | 62 |
| 1993 | LUNAR SPOOK | SILVER GHOST | IDLE MINDS | 12 - 2 - 10 - 0 - 0 | 3.80 | 1.08 | 24 |
| 1994 | INSIDE INFORMATION | PRIVATE ACCOUNT | KEY TO THE MINT | 10 - 9 - 17 - 3 - 1 | 2.20 | 0.60 | 40 |
| 1995 | URBANE | CITIDANCER | PLEASANT COLONY | 9 - 3 - 9 - 0 - 1 | 3.00 | 0.86 | 22 |
| 1996 | MY FLAG | EASY GOER | PRIVATE ACCOUNT | 6 - 6 - 19 - 0 - 1 | 2.05 | 0.50 | 32 |
| 1997 | GLITTER WOMAN | GLITTERMAN | TAYLOR'S FALLS | 10 - 4 - 4 - 0 - 0 | 8.00 | 1.33 | 18 |
| 1998 | WELL CHOSEN | DEPUTY MINISTER | SECRETARIAT | 10 - 7 - 8 - 1 - 0 | 4.20 | 1.00 | 26 |
| 1999 | SILVERBULLETDAY | SILVER DEPUTY | TOM ROLFE | 6 - 1 - 9 - 0 - 6 | 1.10 | 0.05 | 22 |
| 2000 | RINGS A CHIME | METFIELD | RED RYDER | 9 - 3 - 10 - 2 - 0 | 2.43 | 0.79 | 24 |
| 2001 | FLEET RENEE | SEATTLE SLEW | MR. LEADER | 10 - 3 - 15 - 2 - 0 | 2.16 | 0.70 | 30 |
| 2002 | TAKE CHARGE LADY | DEHERE | RUBIANO | 5 - 6 - 10 - 1 - 0 | 2.67 | 0.68 | 22 |
| | | | MEDIAN = | | 2.67 | 0.79 | 24.0 |

## BALLERINA H, THREE-YEAR-OLDS & UP, FILLIES & MARES, 7F, DIRT:

| YEAR | WINNER | SIRE | BROODMARE SIRE | DP | DI | CD | PTS |
|------|--------|------|----------------|-----|-----|-----|-----|
| 1990 | FEEL THE BEAT | SHIMATOREE | TULYAR | 10 - 2 - 6 - 2 - 0 | 3.00 | 1.00 | 20 |
| 1991 | QUEENA | MR. PROSPECTOR | BLUSHING GROOM | 25 - 10 - 19 - 0 - 2 | 3.87 | 1.00 | 56 |
| 1992 | SERAPE | FAPPIANO | IN REALITY | 16 - 18 - 25 - 1 - 0 | 3.44 | 0.82 | 60 |
| 1993 | SPINNING ROUND | DIXIELAND BAND | SECRETARIAT | 9 - 8 - 10 - 1 - 0 | 3.67 | 0.89 | 28 |
| 1994 | ROAMIN RACHEL | MINING | CLEVER TRICK | 13 - 4 - 13 - 4 - 0 | 2.24 | 0.76 | 34 |
| 1995 | CLASSY MIRAGE | STORM BIRD | RIVA RIDGE | 9 - 5 - 8 - 0 - 0 | 4.50 | 1.05 | 22 |
| 1996 | CHAPOSA SPRINGS | BALDSKI | UPS | 14 - 10 - 6 - 4 - 0 | 3.86 | 1.00 | 34 |
| 1997 | PEARL CITY | CARSON CITY | HAWAII | 10 - 3 - 10 - 1 - 0 | 3.00 | 0.92 | 24 |
| 1998 | STOP TRAFFIC | CURE THE BLUES | IMA HELL RAISER | 8 - 8 - 8 - 0 - 0 | 5.00 | 1.00 | 24 |
| 1999 | FURLOUGH | EASY GOER | RIVA RIDGE | 7 - 3 - 14 - 0 - 0 | 2.43 | 0.71 | 24 |
| 2000 | DREAM SUPREME | SEEKING THE GOLD | DIXIELAND BAND | 11 - 6 - 15 - 0 - 0 | 3.27 | 0.88 | 32 |
| 2001 | SHINE AGAIN | WILD AGAIN | TWO PUNCH | 13 - 6 - 10 - 0 - 1 | 4.00 | 1.00 | 30 |
| 2002 | SHINE AGAIN | WILD AGAIN | TWO PUNCH | 13 - 6 - 10 - 0 - 1 | 4.00 | 1.00 | 30 |
| | | | MEDIAN = | | 3.67 | 1.00 | 30.0 |

**BELDAME S, THREE-YEAR-OLDS & UP, FILLIES & MARES, 9F, DIRT:**

| YEAR | WINNER | SIRE | BROODMARE SIRE | DP | DI | CD | PTS |
|---|---|---|---|---|---|---|---|
| 1990 | GO FOR WAND | DEPUTY MINISTER | CYANE | 6 - 2 - 4 - 0 - 0 | 5.00 | 1.17 | 12 |
| 1991 | SHARP DANCE | DANCING CZAR | PIERCER | 3 - 2 - 11 - 6 - 0 | 0.91 | 0.09 | 22 |
| 1992 | SARATOGA DEW | CORMORANT | IN REALITY | 12 - 3 - 17 - 0 - 2 | 2.24 | 0.68 | 34 |
| 1993 | DISPUTE | DANZIG | REVIEWER | 13 - 16 - 18 - 1 - 0 | 3.80 | 0.85 | 48 |
| 1994 | HEAVENLY PRIZE | SEEKING THE GOLD | NIJINSKY II | 10 - 3 - 17 - 4 - 0 | 1.72 | 0.56 | 34 |
| 1995 | SERENA'S SONG | RAHY | NORTHFIELDS | 12 - 1 - 12 - 1 - 2 | 2.11 | 0.71 | 28 |
| 1996 | YANKS MUSIC | AIR FORBES WON | DARBY CREEK ROAD | 4 - 3 - 7 - 0 - 0 | 3.00 | 0.79 | 14 |
| 1997 | HIDDEN LAKE | QUIET AMERICAN | ROUND TABLE | 7 - 12 - 9 - 10 - 0 | 1.62 | 0.42 | 38 |
| 1998 | SHARP CAT | STORM CAT | ACK ACK | 5 - 9 - 8 - 0 - 0 | 4.50 | 0.86 | 22 |
| 1999 | BEAUTIFUL PLEASURE | MAUDLIN | BALDSKI | 11 - 10 - 5 - 2 - 0 | 5.22 | 1.07 | 28 |
| 2000 | RIBOLETTA | ROI NORMAND | GHADEER | 7 - 1 - 18 - 0 - 0 | 1.89 | 0.58 | 26 |
| 2001 | EXOGENOUS | UNBRIDLED | PHONE TRICK | 7 - 6 - 9 - 0 - 6 | 1.67 | 0.29 | 28 |
| 2002 | IMPERIAL GESTURE | LANGFUHR | HOIST THE FLAG | 6 - 8 - 11 - 0 - 3 | 2.29 | 0.50 | 28 |
| | | | MEDIAN = | | 2.24 | 0.68 | 28.0 |

**BELMONT S, THREE-YEAR-OLDS, 12F, DIRT:**

| YEAR | WINNER | SIRE | BROODMARE SIRE | DP | DI | CD | PTS |
|---|---|---|---|---|---|---|---|
| 1990 | GO AND GO | BE MY GUEST | ALLEGED | 11 - 3 - 10 - 1 - 1 | 2.71 | 0.85 | 26 |
| 1991 | HANSEL | WOODMAN | DANCING COUNT | 10 - 3 - 13 - 2 - 0 | 2.29 | 0.75 | 28 |
| 1992 | A.P. INDY | SEATTLE SLEW | SECRETARIAT | 13 - 10 - 20 - 3 - 0 | 2.54 | 0.72 | 46 |
| 1993 | COLONIAL AFFAIR | PLEASANT COLONY | NIJINSKY II | 8 - 1 - 19 - 4 - 2 | 1.19 | 0.26 | 34 |
| 1994 | TABASCO CAT | STORM CAT | SAUCE BOAT | 7 - 5 - 7 - 1 - 0 | 3.44 | 0.90 | 20 |
| 1995 | THUNDER GULCH | GULCH | STORM BIRD | 10 - 2 - 8 - 0 - 0 | 4.00 | 1.10 | 20 |
| 1996 | EDITOR'S NOTE | FORTY NINER | CAVEAT | 10 - 4 - 11 - 0 - 3 | 2.29 | 0.64 | 28 |
| 1997 | TOUCH GOLD | DEPUTY MINISTER | BUCKPASSER | 4 - 3 - 17 - 0 - 0 | 1.82 | 0.46 | 24 |
| 1998 | VICTORY GALLOP | CRYPTOCLEARANCE | VICE REGENT | 10 - 8 - 13 - 0 - 1 | 3.27 | 0.81 | 32 |
| 1999 | LEMON DROP KID | KINGMAMBO | SEATTLE SLEW | 13 - 4 - 21 - 0 - 0 | 2.62 | 0.79 | 38 |
| 2000 | COMMENDABLE | GONE WEST | IN REALITY | 17 - 11 - 14 - 0 - 0 | 5.00 | 1.07 | 42 |
| 2001 | POINT GIVEN | THUNDER GULCH | TURKOMAN | 8 - 0 - 8 - 0 - 0 | 3.00 | 1.00 | 16 |
| 2002 | SARAVA | WILD AGAIN | DEPUTY MINISTER | 8 - 6 - 8 - 0 - 0 | 4.50 | 1.00 | 22 |
| | | | MEDIAN = | | 2.71 | 0.81 | 28.0 |

**BEVERLY D S, THREE-YEAR-OLDS & UP, FILLIES & MARES, 9.5F, TURF:**

| YEAR | WINNER | SIRE | BROODMARE SIRE | DP | DI | CD | PTS |
|---|---|---|---|---|---|---|---|
| 1991 | FIRE THE GROOM | BLUSHING GROOM | MR. PROSPECTOR | 25 - 6 - 17 - 0 - 4 | 3.16 | 0.92 | 52 |
| 1992 | KOSTROMA | CAERLEON | BUSTED | 2 - 1 - 9 -17 - 7 | 0.26 | -0.72 | 36 |
| 1993 | FLAWLESSLY | AFFIRMED | NIJINSKY II | 6 - 2 - 15 - 9 - 0 | 0.94 | 0.16 | 32 |
| 1994 | HATOOF | IRISH RIVER | LYPHARD | 8 - 6 - 16 - 0 - 6 | 1.57 | 0.28 | 36 |
| 1995 | POSSIBLY PERFECT | NORTHERN BABY | AVATAR | 5 - 2 - 9 - 7 - 1 | 0.92 | 0.13 | 24 |
| 1996 | TIMARIDA | KALAGLOW | TRACK SPARE | 3 - 2 - 5 - 2 - 0 | 1.67 | 0.50 | 12 |
| 1997 | MEMORIES OF SILVER | SILVER HAWK | LITTLE CURRENT | 4 - 2 - 17 - 6 - 1 | 0.94 | 0.07 | 30 |
| 1998 | NOT RUN | | | | | | |
| 1999 | NOT RUN | | | | | | |
| 2000 | SNOW POLINA | TREMPOLINO | VACARME | 6 - 1 - 11 - 0 - 0 | 2.27 | 0.72 | 18 |
| 2001 | ENGLAND'S LEGEND | LURE | COMMANCHE RUN | 4 - 4 - 15 - 0 - 5 | 1.24 | 0.07 | 28 |
| 2002 | GOLDEN APPLES | PIVOTAL | KALDOUN | 1 - 3 - 8 - 0 - 0 | 2.00 | 0.42 | 12 |
| | | | MEDIAN = | | **1.41** | **0.22** | **29.0** |

**BEVERLY HILLS H, THREE-YEAR-OLDS & UP, FILLIES & MARES, 10F, TURF:**

| YEAR | WINNER | SIRE | BROODMARE SIRE | DP | DI | CD | PTS |
|---|---|---|---|---|---|---|---|
| 1990 | BEAUTIFUL MELODY | ALYDAR | BOLD BIDDER | 14 - 11 - 22 - 1 - 0 | 3.00 | 0.79 | 48 |
| 1990 | RELUCTANT GUEST | HOSTAGE | VAGUELY NOBLE | 7 - 3 - 17 - 5 - 4 | 1.06 | 0.11 | 36 |
| 1991 | ALCANDO | ALZAO | DARIUS II | 7 - 4 - 15 - 0 - 2 | 1.95 | 0.50 | 28 |
| 1992 | FLAWLESSLY | AFFIRMED | NIJINSKY II | 6 - 2 - 15 - 9 - 0 | 0.94 | 0.16 | 32 |
| 1993 | FLAWLESSLY | AFFIRMED | NIJINSKY II | 6 - 2 - 15 - 9 - 0 | 0.94 | 0.16 | 32 |
| 1994 | CORRAZONA | EL GRAN SENOR | STAGE DOOR JOHNNY | 5 - 5 - 17 - 7 - 4 | 0.95 | 0.00 | 38 |
| 1995 | ALPRIDE | ALZAO | ROBERTO | 6 - 6 - 27 - 1 - 0 | 1.76 | 0.43 | 40 |
| 1996 | DIFFERENT | CANDY STRIPES | PROPICIO | 7 - 0 - 9 - 0 - 2 | 1.77 | 0.56 | 18 |
| 1997 | WINDSHARP | LEAR FAN | SHARPEN UP | 6 - 6 - 22 - 0 - 0 | 2.09 | 0.53 | 34 |
| 1998 | SQUEAK | SELKIRK | SIR IVOR | 6 - 9 - 11 - 0 - 0 | 3.73 | 0.81 | 26 |
| 1999 | VIRGINIE | LEGAL CASE | BARONIUS | 2 - 3 - 4 - 2 - 1 | 1.40 | 0.25 | 12 |
| 2000 | HAPPYANUNOIT | YACHTIE | RAJAH | 0 - 2 - 2 - 0 - 0 | 3.00 | 0.50 | 4 |
| 2001 | ASTRA | THEATRICAL | SEATTLE SLEW | 6 - 0 - 20 - 0 - 0 | 1.60 | 0.46 | 26 |
| 2002 | ASTRA | THEATRICAL | SEATTLE SLEW | 6 - 0 - 20 - 0 - 0 | 1.60 | 0.46 | 26 |
| | | | MEDIAN = | | **1.68** | **0.46** | **30.0** |

**BLUE GRASS S, THREE-YEAR-OLDS, 9F, DIRT:**

| YEAR | WINNER | SIRE | BROODMARE SIRE | DP | DI | CD | PTS |
|---|---|---|---|---|---|---|---|
| 1990 | SUMMER SQUALL | STORM BIRD | SECRETARIAT | 9 - 6 - 12 - 1 - 0 | 3.00 | 0.82 | 28 |
| 1991 | STRIKE THE GOLD | ALYDAR | HATCHET MAN | 10 - 6 - 4 - 0 - 0 | 9.00 | 1.30 | 20 |
| 1992 | PISTOLS AND ROSES | DARN THAT ALARM | PRINCELY PLEASURE | 5 - 5 - 8 - 0 - 0 | 3.50 | 0.83 | 18 |
| 1993 | PRAIRIE BAYOU | LITTLE MISSOURI | WAVERING MONARCH | 6 - 4 - 6 - 0 - 0 | 4.33 | 1.00 | 16 |
| 1994 | HOLY BULL | GREAT ABOVE | AL HATTAB | 6 - 5 - 2 - 1 - 0 | 6.00 | 1.14 | 14 |
| 1995 | WILD SYN | WILD AGAIN | SOVEREIGN DANCER | 9 - 6 - 9 - 0 - 0 | 4.33 | 1.00 | 24 |
| 1996 | SKIP AWAY | SKIP TRIAL | DIPLOMAT WAY | 5 - 6 - 4 - 1 - 0 | 4.33 | 0.94 | 16 |
| 1997 | PULPIT | A.P. INDY | MR. PROSPECTOR | 15 - 3 - 13 - 1 - 0 | 3.27 | 1.00 | 32 |
| 1998 | HALORY HUNTER | JADE HUNTER | HALO | 15 - 3 - 18 - 0 - 0 | 3.00 | 0.92 | 36 |
| 1999 | MENIFEE | HARLAN | NEVER BEND | 12 - 6 - 8 - 0 - 0 | 5.50 | 1.15 | 26 |
| 2000 | HIGH YIELD | STORM CAT | FORTY NINER | 8 - 3 - 11 - 3 - 1 | 1.74 | 0.54 | 26 |
| 2001 | MILLENNIUM WIND | CRYPTOCLEARANCE | DRONE | 12 - 15 - 10 - 0 - 1 | 5.33 | 0.97 | 38 |
| 2002 | HARLAN'S HOLIDAY | HARLAN | AFFIRMED | 7 - 2 - 10 - 1 - 0 | 2.33 | 0.75 | 20 |
| | | | MEDIAN = | | 4.33 | 0.97 | 24.0 |

**BREEDERS' CUP CLASSIC, THREE-YEAR-OLDS & UP, 10F, DIRT:**

| YEAR | WINNER | SIRE | BROODMARE SIRE | DP | DI | CD | PTS |
|---|---|---|---|---|---|---|---|
| 1990 | UNBRIDLED | FAPPIANO | LE FABULEUX | 12 - 15 - 19 - 0 - 12 | 1.70 | 0.26 | 58 |
| 1991 | BLACK TIE AFFAIR | MISWAKI | AL HATTAB | 11 - 6 - 12 - 1 - 0 | 3.29 | 0.90 | 30 |
| 1992 | A.P. INDY | SEATTLE SLEW | SECRETARIAT | 13 - 10 - 20 - 3 - 0 | 2.54 | 0.72 | 46 |
| 1993 | ARCANGUES | SAGACE | IRISH RIVER | 1 - 3 - 10 - 0 - 6 | 0.82 | -0.35 | 20 |
| 1994 | CONCERN | BROAD BRUSH | TUNERUP | 6 - 16 - 14 - 1 - 1 | 3.22 | 0.66 | 38 |
| 1995 | CIGAR | PALACE MUSIC | SEATTLE SLEW | 7 - 2 - 10 - 1 - 0 | 2.33 | 0.75 | 20 |
| 1996 | ALPHABET SOUP | COZZENE | ARTS AND LETTERS | 2 - 6 - 11 - 1 - 2 | 1.59 | 0.23 | 22 |
| 1997 | SKIP AWAY | SKIP TRIAL | DIPLOMAT WAY | 5 - 6 - 8 - 1 - 0 | 3.00 | 0.75 | 20 |
| 1998 | AWESOME AGAIN | DEPUTY MINISTER | BLUSHING GROOM | 12 - 0 - 8 - 0 - 2 | 2.67 | 0.91 | 22 |
| 1999 | CAT THIEF | STORM CAT | ALYDAR | 7 - 4 - 13 - 0 - 0 | 2.69 | 0.75 | 24 |
| 2000 | TIZNOW | CEE'S TIZZY | SEATTLE SONG | 7 - 1 - 10 - 2 - 0 | 1.86 | 0.65 | 20 |
| 2001 | TIZNOW | CEE'S TIZZY | SEATTLE SONG | 7 - 1 - 10 - 2 - 0 | 1.86 | 0.65 | 20 |
| 2002 | VOLPONI | CRYPTOCLEARANCE | SIR HARRY LEWIS | 9 - 11 - 11 - 0 - 1 | 3.92 | 0.84 | 32 |
| | | | MEDIAN = | | 2.44 | 0.69 | 22.0 |

**BREEDERS' CUP DISTAFF, THREE-YEAR-OLDS & UP, FILLIES & MARES, 9F, DIRT:**

| YEAR | WINNER | SIRE | BROODMARE SIRE | DP | DI | CD | PTS |
|---|---|---|---|---|---|---|---|
| 1990 | BAYAKOA | CONSULTANT'S BID | GOOD MANNERS | 8 - 8 - 6 - 0 - 0 | 6.33 | 1.09 | 22 |
| 1991 | DANCE SMARTLY | DANZIG | SMARTEN | 7 - 12 - 15 - 0 - 0 | 3.53 | 0.76 | 34 |
| 1992 | PASEANA | AHMAD | FLINTHAM | 4 - 4 - 2 - 0 - 0 | 9.00 | 1.20 | 10 |
| 1993 | HOLLYWOOD WILDCAT | KRIS S. | MR. PROSPECTOR | 9 - 6 - 21 - 2 - 0 | 2.04 | 0.58 | 38 |
| 1994 | ONE DREAMER | RELAUNCH | PRETENSE | 12 - 3 - 15 - 0 - 0 | 3.00 | 0.90 | 30 |
| 1995 | INSIDE INFORMATION | PRIVATE ACCOUNT | KEY TO THE MINT | 10 - 9 - 17 - 3 - 1 | 2.20 | 0.60 | 40 |
| 1996 | JEWEL PRINCESS | KEY TO THE MINT | MALYNO | 8 - 3 - 23 - 6 - 2 | 1.15 | 0.21 | 42 |
| 1997 | AJINA | STRAWBERRY ROAD | ALYDAR | 8 - 4 - 14 - 2 - 0 | 2.11 | 0.64 | 28 |
| 1998 | ESCENA | STRAWBERRY ROAD | SEATTLE SLEW | 11 - 1 - 8 - 2 - 0 | 2.67 | 0.95 | 22 |
| 1999 | BEAUTIFUL PLEASURE | MAUDLIN | BALDSKI | 11 - 10 - 5 - 2 - 0 | 5.22 | 1.07 | 28 |
| 2000 | SPAIN | THUNDER GULCH | REGAL AND ROYAL | 5 - 2 - 8 - 1 - 2 | 1.57 | 0.39 | 18 |
| 2001 | UNBRIDLED ELAINE | UNBRIDLED'S SONG | TAYLOR'S FALLS | 4 - 5 - 7 - 0 - 2 | 2.27 | 0.50 | 18 |
| 2002 | AZERI | JADE HUNTER | AHONOORA | 9 - 2 - 9 - 0 - 0 | 3.44 | 1.00 | 20 |
| | | | MEDIAN = | | **2.67** | **0.76** | **28.0** |

**BREEDERS' CUP FILLY AND MARE TURF, THREE-YEAR-OLDS & UP, FILLIES & MARES, 10F, TURF:**

| YEAR | WINNER | SIRE | BROODMARE SIRE | DP | DI | CD | PTS |
|---|---|---|---|---|---|---|---|
| 1999 | SOARING SOFTLY | KRIS S. | KEY TO THE MINT | 6 - 5 - 25 - 7 - 1 | 1.15 | 0.18 | 44 |
| 2000 | PERFECT STING | RED RANSOM | VALID APPEAL | 5 - 9 - 18 - 0 - 0 | 2.56 | 0.59 | 32 |
| 2001 | BANKS HILL | DANEHILL | KAHYASI | 3 - 4 - 17 - 1 - 1 | 1.48 | 0.27 | 26 |
| 2002 | STARINE | MENDOCINO | KALDOUN | 2 - 7 - 11 - 2 - 0 | 1.93 | 0.41 | 22 |
| | | | MEDIAN = | | **1.70** | **0.34** | **29.0** |

**BREEDERS' CUP JUVENILE, TWO-YEAR-OLDS, 8.5F, DIRT (9F IN 2002):**

| YEAR | WINNER | SIRE | BROODMARE SIRE | DP | DI | CD | PTS |
|---|---|---|---|---|---|---|---|
| 1990 | FLY SO FREE | TIME FOR A CHANGE | STEWARD | 7 - 11 - 12 - 0 - 0 | 4.00 | 0.83 | 30 |
| 1991 | ARAZI | BLUSHING GROOM | NORTHERN DANCER | 22 - 1 - 15 - 0 - 10 | 1.74 | 0.52 | 48 |
| 1992 | GILDED TIME | TIMELESS MOMENT | WHAT A PLEASURE | 16 - 13 - 11 - 2 - 0 | 4.60 | 1.02 | 42 |
| 1993 | BROCCO | KRIS S. | AURELIUS II | 3 - 6 - 15 - 2 - 0 | 1.74 | 0.38 | 26 |
| 1994 | TIMBER COUNTRY | WOODMAN | PRETENSE | 11 - 5 - 22 - 0 - 0 | 2.45 | 0.71 | 38 |
| 1995 | UNBRIDLED'S SONG | UNBRIDLED | CARO | 9 - 10 - 11 - 0 - 6 | 2.13 | 0.44 | 36 |
| 1996 | BOSTON HARBOR | CAPOTE | VICE REGENT | 8 - 0 - 6 - 0 - 0 | 3.67 | 1.14 | 14 |
| 1997 | FAVORITE TRICK | PHONE TRICK | MEDIEVAL MAN | 7 - 2 - 5 - 0 - 0 | 4.60 | 1.14 | 14 |
| 1998 | ANSWER LIVELY | LIVELY ONE | TWO'S A PLENTY | 6 - 2 - 10 - 2 - 0 | 1.86 | 0.60 | 20 |

| | | | DP | DI | CD | PTS |
|---|---|---|---|---|---|---|
| 1999 | ANEES | UNBRIDLED | 9 - 10 - 19 - 0 - 6 | 1.84 | 0.36 | 44 |
| 2000 | MACHO UNO | HOLY BULL | 13 - 2 - 7 - 0 - 2 | 3.36 | 1.00 | 24 |
| 2001 | JOHANNESBURG | HENNESSY | 5 - 3 - 6 - 0 - 0 | 3.67 | 0.93 | 14 |
| 2002 | VINDICATION | SEATTLE SLEW | 10 - 2 - 15 - 3 - 0 | 1.86 | 0.63 | 30 |
| | | | MEDIAN = | 2.45 | 0.71 | 30.0 |

**BREEDERS' CUP JUVENILE FILLIES, TWO-YEAR-OLD FILLIES, 8.5F, DIRT (9F IN 2002):**

| YEAR | WINNER | SIRE | BROODMARE SIRE | DP | DI | CD | PTS |
|---|---|---|---|---|---|---|---|
| 1990 | MEADOW STAR | MEADOWLAKE | IN REALITY | 15 - 11 - 10 - 0 - 0 | 6.20 | 1.14 | 36 |
| 1991 | PLEASANT STAGE | PLEASANT COLONY | STAGE DOOR JOHNNY | 4 - 1 - 18 - 7 - 6 | 0.64 | -0.28 | 36 |
| 1992 | ELIZA | MT. LIVERMORE | BOLD BIDDER | 12 - 7 - 8 - 1 - 2 | 3.29 | 0.87 | 30 |
| 1993 | PHONE CHATTER | PHONE TRICK | PASS THE GLASS | 4 - 3 - 7 - 0 - 0 | 3.00 | 0.79 | 14 |
| 1994 | FLANDERS | SEEKING THE GOLD | STORM BIRD | 11 - 6 - 15 - 0 - 0 | 3.27 | 0.88 | 32 |
| 1995 | MY FLAG | EASY GOER | PRIVATE ACCOUNT | 6 - 6 - 19 - 0 - 1 | 2.05 | 0.50 | 32 |
| 1996 | STORM SONG | SUMMER SQUALL | FAPPIANO | 8 - 9 - 13 - 0 - 0 | 3.62 | 0.83 | 30 |
| 1997 | COUNTESS DIANA | DEERHOUND | T. V. COMMERCIAL | 3 - 10 - 15 - 0 - 0 | 2.73 | 0.57 | 28 |
| 1998 | SILVERBULLETDAY | SILVER DEPUTY | TOM ROLFE | 6 - 1 - 9 - 0 - 6 | 1.10 | 0.05 | 22 |
| 1999 | CASH RUN | SEEKING THE GOLD | PLEASANT COLONY | 10 - 8 - 17 - 0 - 1 | 2.79 | 0.72 | 36 |
| 2000 | CARESSING | HONOUR AND GLORY | MAJESTIC PRINCE | 11 - 2 - 5 - 0 - 0 | 6.20 | 1.33 | 18 |
| 2001 | TEMPERA | A.P. INDY | MR. PROSPECTOR | 15 - 5 - 18 - 1 - 1 | 2.64 | 0.80 | 40 |
| 2002 | STORM FLAG FLYING | STORM CAT | EASY GOER | 6 - 5 - 11 - 0 - 0 | 3.00 | 0.77 | 22 |
| | | | MEDIAN = | | 3.00 | 0.79 | 30.0 |

**BREEDERS' CUP MILE, THREE-YEAR-OLDS & UP, 8.5F, TURF:**

| YEAR | WINNER | SIRE | BROODMARE SIRE | DP | DI | CD | PTS |
|---|---|---|---|---|---|---|---|
| 1990 | ROYAL ACADEMY | NIJINSKY II | CRIMSON SATAN | 9 - 3 - 16 - 8 - 0 | 1.25 | 0.36 | 36 |
| 1991 | OPENING VERSE | THE MINSTREL | GREY DAWN II | 9 - 8 - 9 - 2 - 2 | 2.53 | 0.67 | 30 |
| 1992 | LURE | DANZIG | ALYDAR | 9 - 12 - 23 - 0 - 0 | 2.83 | 0.68 | 44 |
| 1993 | LURE | DANZIG | ALYDAR | 9 - 12 - 23 - 0 - 0 | 2.83 | 0.68 | 44 |
| 1994 | BARATHEA | SADLER'S WELLS | HABITAT | 14 - 6 - 20 - 8 - 0 | 1.67 | 0.54 | 48 |
| 1995 | RIDGEWOOD PEARL | INDIAN RIDGE | TAP ON WOOD | 0 - 0 - 0 - 0 - 0 | | | 0 |
| 1996 | DA HOSS | GONE WEST | WELSH SAINT | 11 - 3 - 8 - 0 - 2 | 3.00 | 0.88 | 24 |
| 1997 | SPINNING WORLD | NUREYEV | RIVERMAN | 10 - 8 - 34 - 0 - 0 | 2.06 | 0.54 | 52 |
| 1998 | DA HOSS | GONE WEST | WELSH SAINT | 11 - 5 - 10 - 0 - 2 | 3.00 | 0.82 | 28 |
| 1999 | SILIC | SILLERY | SADLER'S WELLS | 8 - 1 - 13 - 4 - 2 | 1.24 | 0.32 | 28 |
| 2000 | WAR CHANT | DANZIG | KRIS S. | 9 - 12 - 22 - 1 - 0 | 2.67 | 0.66 | 44 |

| YEAR | WINNER | SIRE | BROODMARE SIRE | DP | DI | CD | PTS |
|---|---|---|---|---|---|---|---|
| 2001 | VAL ROYAL | ROYAL ACADEMY | BIKALA | 6 - 0 - 11 - 7 - 0 | 0.92 | 0.21 | 24 |
| 2002 | DOMEDRIVER | INDIAN RIDGE | BAILLAMONT | 4 - 0 - 6 - 0 - 0 | 2.33 | 0.80 | 10 |
| | | | MEDIAN = | | 2.43 | 0.66 | **30.0** |

## BREEDERS' CUP SPRINT, THREE-YEAR-OLDS & UP, 6F, DIRT:

| YEAR | WINNER | SIRE | BROODMARE SIRE | DP | DI | CD | PTS |
|---|---|---|---|---|---|---|---|
| 1990 | SAFELY KEPT | HORATIUS | WINNING HIT | 9 - 6 - 1 - 0 - 0 | 31.00 | 1.50 | 16 |
| 1991 | SHEIKH ALBADOU | GREEN DESERT | WELSH PAGEANT | 7 - 8 - 11 - 0 - 0 | 3.73 | 0.85 | 26 |
| 1992 | THIRTY SLEWS | SLEWPY | HATCHET MAN | 4 - 5 - 12 - 1 - 0 | 2.14 | 0.55 | 22 |
| 1993 | CARDMANIA | COX'S RIDGE | J. O. TOBIN | 9 - 4 - 13 - 0 - 0 | 3.00 | 0.85 | 26 |
| 1994 | CHEROKEE RUN | RUNAWAY GROOM | SILVER SABER | 10 - 1 - 5 - 0 - 2 | 3.00 | 0.94 | 18 |
| 1995 | DESERT STORMER | STORM CAT | DAMASCUS | 5 - 7 - 8 - 0 - 0 | 4.00 | 0.85 | 20 |
| 1996 | LIT DE JUSTICE | EL GRAN SENOR | KENMARE | 5 - 2 - 11 - 0 - 0 | 2.27 | 0.67 | 18 |
| 1997 | ELMHURST | WILD AGAIN | RAISE A NATIVE | 14 - 9 - 11 - 2 - 2 | 3.00 | 0.82 | 38 |
| 1998 | RERAISE | DANZATORE | POLICEMAN | 10 - 5 - 12 - 2 - 1 | 2.33 | 0.70 | 30 |
| 1999 | ARTAX | MARQUETRY | APALACHEE | 15 - 6 - 4 - 5 - 0 | 3.29 | 1.03 | 30 |
| 2000 | KONA GOLD | JAVA GOLD | SLEW O' GOLD | 8 - 2 - 14 - 5 - 1 | 1.31 | 0.37 | 30 |
| 2001 | SQUIRTLE SQUIRT | MARQUETRY | LOST CODE | 6 - 2 - 4 - 0 - 0 | 5.00 | 1.17 | 12 |
| 2002 | ORIENTATE | MT. LIVERMORE | COX'S RIDGE | 10 - 3 - 9 - 0 - 2 | 2.69 | 0.79 | 24 |
| | | | MEDIAN = | | 3.00 | 0.85 | **24.0** |

## BREEDERS' CUP TURF, THREE-YEAR-OLDS & UP, 12F, TURF:

| YEAR | WINNER | SIRE | BROODMARE SIRE | DP | DI | CD | PTS |
|---|---|---|---|---|---|---|---|
| 1990 | IN THE WINGS | SADLER'S WELLS | SHIRLEY HEIGHTS | 6 - 2 - 25 - 11 - 4 | 0.75 | -0.10 | 48 |
| 1991 | MISS ALLEGED | ALLEGED | BOLDNESIAN | 8 - 11 - 9 - 1 - 3 | 2.76 | 0.63 | 32 |
| 1992 | FRAISE | STRAWBERRY ROAD | DICTUS | 1 - 0 - 3 - 4 - 2 | 0.33 | -0.60 | 10 |
| 1993 | KOTASHAAN | DARSHAAN | ELOCUTIONIST | 2 - 2 - 7 - 3 - 4 | 0.71 | -0.28 | 18 |
| 1994 | TIKKANEN | COZZENE | TARGOWICE | 3 - 8 - 10 - 6 - 1 | 1.33 | 0.21 | 28 |
| 1995 | NORTHERN SPUR | SADLER'S WELLS | RHEINGOLD | 5 - 1 - 18 - 8 - 2 | 0.79 | -0.03 | 34 |
| 1996 | PILSUDSKI | POLISH PRECEDENT | TROY | 3 - 9 - 14 - 2 - 0 | 2.11 | 0.46 | 2 |
| 1997 | CHIEF BEARHART | CHIEF'S CROWN | BOLD HOUR | 7 - 10 - 11 - 0 - 2 | 3.00 | 0.67 | 30 |
| 1998 | BUCK'S BOY | BUCKSPLASHER | VERBATIM | 4 - 4 - 18 - 0 - 0 | 1.89 | 0.46 | 26 |
| 1999 | DAYLAMI | DOYOUN | MISWAKI | 8 - 4 - 9 - 5 - 2 | 1.43 | 0.39 | 28 |
| 2000 | KALANISI | DOYOUN | GREEN DANCER | 6 - 6 - 9 - 7 - 0 | 1.43 | 0.39 | 28 |
| 2001 | FANTASTIC LIGHT | RAHY | NIJINSKY II | 12 - 0 - 18 - 6 - 2 | 1.24 | 0.37 | 38 |
| 2002 | HIGH CHAPARRAL | SADLER'S WELLS | DARSHAAN | 6 - 1 - 22 - 9 - 2 | 0.82 | 0.00 | 40 |
| | | | MEDIAN = | | 1.33 | 0.37 | **28.0** |

## CARTER H, THREE-YEAR-OLDS & UP, 7F, DIRT:

| YEAR | WINNER | SIRE | BROODMARE SIRE | DP | DI | CD | PTS |
|---|---|---|---|---|---|---|---|
| 1990 | DANCING SPREE | NIJINSKY II | RIVA RIDGE | 8 - 2 - 16 - 8 - 0 | 1.13 | 0.29 | 34 |
| 1991 | HOUSEBUSTER | MT. LIVERMORE | GREAT ABOVE | 11 - 2 - 5 - 0 - 2 | 3.44 | 1.00 | 20 |
| 1992 | RUBIANO | FAPPIANO | NIJINSKY II | 14 - 15 - 23 - 4 - 0 | 2.61 | 0.70 | 56 |
| 1993 | ALYDEED | SHADEED | ALYDAR | 6 - 3 - 19 - 4 - 0 | 1.37 | 0.34 | 32 |
| 1994 | VIRGINIA RAPIDS | RIVERMAN | SIR IVOR | 12 - 21 - 20 - 1 - 0 | 3.91 | 0.81 | 54 |
| 1995 | LITE THE FUSE | BUCKAROO | DROLL ROLE | 0 - 2 - 17 - 0 - 3 | 0.91 | -0.18 | 22 |
| 1996 | LITE THE FUSE | BUCKAROO | DROLL ROLE | 0 - 2 - 17 - 0 - 3 | 0.91 | -0.18 | 22 |
| 1997 | LANGFUHR | DANZIG | BRIARTIC | 6 - 11 - 15 - 2 - 0 | 2.58 | 0.62 | 34 |
| 1998 | WILD RUSH | WILD AGAIN | PLUGGED NICKLE | 8 - 6 - 13 - 1 - 0 | 2.73 | 0.75 | 28 |
| 1999 | ARTAX | MARQUETRY | APALACHEE | 15 - 6 - 4 - 5 - 0 | 3.29 | 1.03 | 30 |
| 2000 | BRUTALLY FRANK | GROOVY | RARE PERFORMER | 5 - 1 - 8 - 0 - 0 | 2.50 | 0.79 | 14 |
| 2001 | PEEPING TOM | EAGLE EYED | NASTY AND BOLD | 4 - 7 - 14 - 0 - 1 | 2.25 | 0.50 | 26 |
| 2002 | AFFIRMED SUCCESS | AFFIRMED | IRISH TOWER | 5 - 2 - 9 - 0 - 0 | 2.56 | 0.75 | 16 |
| | | | MEDIAN = | | 2.56 | 0.70 | 28.0 |

## CHAMPAGNE S, TWO-YEAR-OLDS, 8.5F, DIRT:

| YEAR | WINNER | SIRE | BROODMARE SIRE | DP | DI | CD | PTS |
|---|---|---|---|---|---|---|---|
| 1990 | FLY SO FREE | TIME FOR A CHANGE | STEVWARD | 7 - 11 - 12 - 0 - 0 | 4.00 | 0.83 | 30 |
| 1991 | TRI TO WATCH | TRI JET | MICKEY MCGUIRE | 6 - 8 - 5 - 1 - 0 | 4.71 | 0.95 | 20 |
| 1992 | SEA HERO | POLISH NAVY | GRAUSTARK | 3 - 5 - 22 - 4 - 2 | 1.12 | 0.08 | 36 |
| 1993 | DEHERE | DEPUTY MINISTER | SECRETARIAT | 6 - 9 - 8 - 1 - 0 | 3.80 | 0.83 | 24 |
| 1994 | TIMBER COUNTRY | WOODMAN | PRETENSE | 11 - 5 - 22 - 0 - 0 | 2.45 | 0.71 | 38 |
| 1995 | MARIA'S MON | WAVERING MONARCH | CARO | 4 - 5 - 10 - 0 - 1 | 2.33 | 0.55 | 20 |
| 1996 | ORDWAY | SALT LAKE | VAGUELY NOBLE | 3 - 1 - 14 - 0 - 4 | 1.00 | -0.05 | 22 |
| 1997 | GRAND SLAM | GONE WEST | EL GRAN SENOR | 14 - 6 - 15 - 1 - 0 | 3.24 | 0.92 | 36 |
| 1998 | THE GROOM IS RED | RUNAWAY GROOM | FAST GOLD | 12 - 1 - 7 - 0 - 4 | 2.20 | 0.71 | 24 |
| 1999 | GREENWOOD LAKE | MEADOWLAKE | DANCING CHAMP | 8 - 6 - 8 - 2 - 0 | 3.00 | 0.83 | 24 |
| 2000 | A P VALENTINE | A.P. INDY | ALYDAR | 10 - 4 - 20 - 2 - 2 | 1.71 | 0.47 | 38 |
| 2001 | OFFICER | BERTRANDO | SEPTIEME CIEL | 5 - 3 - 4 - 0 - 0 | 5.00 | 1.08 | 12 |
| 2002 | TOCCET | AWESOME AGAIN | COZZENE | 4 - 2 - 8 - 0 - 0 | 2.50 | 0.71 | 14 |
| | | | MEDIAN = | | 2.50 | 0.71 | 24.0 |

## CHARLES WHITTINGHAM MEMORIAL H, THREE-YEAR-OLDS&UP, 10F, TURF:

| YEAR | WINNER | SIRE | BROODMARE SIRE | DP | DI | CD | PTS |
|---|---|---|---|---|---|---|---|
| 1999 | RIVER BAY | IRISH RIVER | GOOD COUNSEL | 5 - 9 - 13 - 2 - 1 | 2.16 | 0.50 | 30 |
| 2000 | WHITE HEART | GREEN DESERT | BLUSHING GROOM | 11 - 8 - 17 - 1 - 3 | 2.20 | 0.58 | 40 |
| 2001 | BIENAMADO | BIEN BIEN | VITIGES | 1 - 1 - 12 - 3 - 3 | 0.67 | -0.30 | 20 |
| 2002 | DENON | PLEASANT COLONY | NORTHFIELDS | 4 - 3 - 17 - 0 - 2 | 1.48 | 0.27 | 26 |
| | | | MEDIAN = | | **1.82** | **0.38** | **28.0** |

## CIGAR MILE H, THREE-YEAR-OLDS & UP, 8F, DIRT:

| YEAR | WINNER | SIRE | BROODMARE SIRE | DP | DI | CD | PTS |
|---|---|---|---|---|---|---|---|
| 1990 | QUIET AMERICAN | FAPPIANO | DR. FAGER | 12 - 23 - 18 - 1 - 0 | 4.40 | 0.85 | 54 |
| 1991 | RUBIANO | FAPPIANO | NIJINSKY II | 14 - 15 - 23 - 4 - 0 | 2.61 | 0.70 | 56 |
| 1992 | IBERO | CINCO GRANDE | TREVIGLIO | 8 - 10 - 6 - 1 - 1 | 4.20 | 0.88 | 26 |
| 1994 | CIGAR | PALACE MUSIC | SEATTLE SLEW | 7 - 2 - 10 - 1 - 0 | 2.33 | 0.75 | 20 |
| 1995 | FLYING CHEVRON | CARSON CITY | HERBAGER | 10 - 2 - 13 - 5 - 4 | 1.19 | 0.26 | 34 |
| 1996 | GOLD FEVER | FORTY NINER | MAJESTIC LIGHT | 12 - 4 - 14 - 0 - 4 | 2.09 | 0.59 | 34 |
| 1997 | DEVIOUS COURSE | CRAFTY PROSPECTOR | MR. LEADER | 14 - 4 - 12 - 0 - 0 | 4.00 | 1.07 | 30 |
| 1998 | SIR BEAR | SIR LEON | BET BIG | 1 - 3 - 8 - 4 - 0 | 1.00 | 0.06 | 16 |
| 1999 | AFFIRMED SUCCESS | AFFIRMED | IRISH TOWER | 5 - 2 - 9 - 0 - 0 | 2.56 | 0.75 | 16 |
| 2000 | EL CORREDOR | MR. GREELEY | SILVER DEPUTY | 9 - 5 - 6 - 0 - 0 | 5.67 | 1.15 | 20 |
| 2001 | LEFT BANK | FRENCH DEPUTY | DR. BLUM | 4 - 7 - 6 - 1 - 0 | 3.50 | 0.78 | 18 |
| | | | MEDIAN = | | **2.61** | **0.75** | **26.0** |

## COACHING CLUB AMERICAN OAKS, THREE-YEAR-OLD FILLIES, 12F, DIRT:

| YEAR | WINNER | SIRE | BROODMARE SIRE | DP | DI | CD | PTS |
|---|---|---|---|---|---|---|---|
| 1990 | CHARON | MO EXCEPTION | SIR WIGGLE | 2 - 1 - 3 - 0 - 0 | 3.00 | 0.83 | 6 |
| 1991 | LITE LIGHT | MAJESTIC LIGHT | IN REALITY | 15 - 3 - 13 - 1 - 2 | 2.58 | 0.82 | 34 |
| 1992 | TURNBACK THE ALARM | DARN THAT ALARM | FIGONERO | 0 - 4 - 8 - 0 - 0 | 2.00 | 0.33 | 12 |
| 1993 | SKY BEAUTY | BLUSHING GROOM | NIJINSKY II | 21 - 0 - 17 - 4 - 4 | 1.79 | 0.65 | 46 |
| 1994 | TWO ALTAZANO | MANZOTTI | TOPSIDER | 8 - 1 - 12 - 6 - 3 | 1.00 | 0.17 | 30 |
| 1995 | GOLDEN BRI | GOLD ALERT | BRIARTIC | 11 - 2 - 8 - 2 - 1 | 2.43 | 0.83 | 24 |
| 1996 | MY FLAG | EASY GOER | PRIVATE ACCOUNT | 6 - 6 - 19 - 0 - 1 | 2.05 | 0.50 | 32 |
| 1997 | AJINA | STRAWBERRY ROAD | ALYDAR | 8 - 4 - 14 - 2 - 0 | 2.11 | 0.64 | 28 |
| 1998 | BANSHEE BREEZE | UNBRIDLED | KNOWN FACT | 8 - 9 - 9 - 0 - 6 | 2.05 | 0.41 | 32 |
| 1999 | ON A SOAPBOX | MI CIELO | STAGE DOOR JOHNNY | 6 - 3 - 12 - 7 - 4 | 0.88 | 0.00 | 32 |
| 2000 | JOSTLE | BROCCO | DRONE | 2 - 7 - 12 - 1 - 0 | 2.14 | 0.45 | 22 |

| YEAR | WINNER | SIRE | BROODMARE SIRE | DP | DI | CD | PTS |
|---|---|---|---|---|---|---|---|
| 2001 | TWEEDSIDE | THUNDER GULCH | ROBERTO | 9 - 3 - 18 - 0 - 0 | 2.33 | 0.70 | 30 |
| 2002 | JILBAB | A.P. INDY | MACHIAVELLIAN | 11 - 4 - 11 - 0 - 0 | 3.73 | 1.00 | 26 |
|  |  |  | MEDIAN = |  | **2.11** | **0.64** | **30.0** |

## DEL MAR OAKS, THREE-YEAR-OLD FILLIES, 9F, DIRT:

| YEAR | WINNER | SIRE | BROODMARE SIRE | DP | DI | CD | PTS |
|---|---|---|---|---|---|---|---|
| 1995 | BAIL OUT BECKY | RED RANSOM | NASKRA | 4 - 5 - 15 - 0 - 0 | 2.20 | 0.54 | 24 |
| 1996 | ANTESPEND | SPEND A BUCK | PRACTICANTE | 2 - 3 - 7 - 0 - 0 | 2.43 | 0.58 | 12 |
| 1997 | FAMOUS DIGGER | QUEST FOR FAME | MR. PROSPECTOR | 10 - 2 - 10 - 4 - 0 | 1.89 | 0.69 | 26 |
| 1998 | SICY D'ALSACE | SICYOS | RIVER RIVER | 9 - 4 - 13 - 0 - 0 | 3.00 | 0.85 | 26 |
| 1999 | TOUT CHARMANT | SLEWVESCENT | BATONNIER | 4 - 2 - 13 - 2 - 3 | 1.09 | 0.08 | 24 |
| 2000 | NO MATTER WHAT | NUREYEV | LORD AT WAR | 6 - 2 - 26 - 0 - 0 | 1.62 | 0.41 | 34 |
| 2001 | GOLDEN APPLES | PIVOTAL | KALDOUN | 1 - 3 - 8 - 0 - 0 | 2.00 | 0.42 | 12 |
|  |  |  | MEDIAN = |  | **2.00** | **0.54** | **24.0** |

## DONN H, THREE-YEAR-OLDS & UP, 9F, DIRT:

| YEAR | WINNER | SIRE | BROODMARE SIRE | DP | DI | CD | PTS |
|---|---|---|---|---|---|---|---|
| 1990 | PRIMAL | MAUDLIN | GRAUSTARK | 6 - 8 - 14 - 6 - 2 | 1.40 | 0.28 | 36 |
| 1991 | JOLIE'S HALO | HALO | SIR IVOR | 17 - 10 - 23 - 0 - 0 | 3.35 | 0.88 | 50 |
| 1992 | SEA CADET | BOLGER | AL HATTAB | 6 - 6 - 5 - 5 - 0 | 1.93 | 0.59 | 22 |
| 1993 | PISTOLS AND ROSES | DARN THAT ALARM | PRINCELY PLEASURE | 5 - 5 - 8 - 0 - 0 | 3.50 | 0.83 | 18 |
| 1994 | PISTOLS AND ROSES | DARN THAT ALARM | PRINCELY PLEASURE | 5 - 5 - 8 - 0 - 0 | 3.50 | 0.83 | 18 |
| 1995 | CIGAR | PALACE MUSIC | SEATTLE SLEW | 7 - 2 - 10 - 1 - 0 | 2.33 | 0.75 | 20 |
| 1996 | CIGAR | PALACE MUSIC | SEATTLE SLEW | 7 - 2 - 10 - 1 - 0 | 2.33 | 0.75 | 20 |
| 1997 | FORMAL GOLD | BLACK TIE AFFAIR | SCREEN KING | 5 - 2 - 7 - 0 - 0 | 3.00 | 0.86 | 14 |
| 1998 | SKIP AWAY | SKIP TRIAL | DIPLOMAT WAY | 5 - 6 - 8 - 1 - 0 | 3.00 | 0.75 | 20 |
| 1999 | PUERTO MADERO | GALLANTSKY | SARATOGA GAME | 6 - 2 - 12 - 6 - 0 | 1.17 | 0.31 | 26 |
| 2000 | STEPHEN GOT EVEN | A.P. INDY | COX'S RIDGE | 8 - 4 - 14 - 0 - 0 | 2.71 | 0.77 | 26 |
| 2001 | CAPTAIN STEVE | FLY SO FREE | VICE REGENT | 4 - 5 - 7 - 0 - 0 | 3.57 | 0.81 | 16 |
| 2002 | MONGOOSE | BROAD BRUSH | COX'S RIDGE | 5 - 17 - 18 - 0 - 2 | 2.82 | 0.55 | 42 |
|  |  |  | MEDIAN = |  | **2.82** | **0.75** | **20.0** |

## EDDIE READ H, THREE-YEAR-OLDS & UP, 9F, TURF:

| YEAR | WINNER | SIRE | BROODMARE SIRE | DP | DI | CD | PTS |
|---|---|---|---|---|---|---|---|
| 1990 | FLY TILL DAWN | SWING TILL DAWN | CARWHITE | 4 - 8 - 8 - 2 - 2 | 2.00 | 0.42 | 24 |
| 1991 | TIGHT SPOT | HIS MAJESTY | LYPHARD | 9 - 2 - 35 - 0 - 4 | 1.33 | 0.24 | 50 |

| YEAR | WINNER | SIRE | BROODMARE SIRE | DP | DI | CD | PTS |
|------|--------|------|----------------|-----|-----|-----|-----|
| 1992 | MARQUETRY | CONQUISTADOR CIELO | VICE REGENT | 18 - 6 - 8 - 0 - 0 | 7.00 | 1.31 | 32 |
| 1993 | KOTASHAAN | DARSHAAN | ELOCUTIONIST | 2 - 2 - 7 - 3 - 4 | 0.71 | -0.28 | 18 |
| 1994 | APPROACH THE BENCH | LAW SOCIETY | PHARLY | 4 - 3 - 8 - 0 - 3 | 1.57 | 0.28 | 18 |
| 1995 | FASTNESS | ROUSILLON | TROY | 8 - 8 - 8 - 0 - 0 | 5.00 | 1.00 | 24 |
| 1996 | FASTNESS | ROUSILLON | TROY | 8 - 8 - 8 - 0 - 0 | 5.00 | 1.00 | 24 |
| 1997 | EXPELLED | EXPLODENT | FORUM | 7 - 2 - 3 - 0 - 0 | 7.00 | 1.33 | 12 |
| 1998 | SUBORDINATION | MT. LIVERMORE | DESERT WINE | 11 - 4 - 7 - 0 - 2 | 3.36 | 0.92 | 24 |
| 1999 | JOE WHO | JOLLY QUICK | BIG LARK | 0 - 2 - 0 - 0 - 2 | 1.00 | -0.50 | 4 |
| 2000 | LADIES DIN | DIN'S DANCER | KRIS S. | 3 - 2 - 8 - 1 - 0 | 1.80 | 0.50 | 14 |
| 2001 | REDATTORE | ROI NORMAND | DEPUTY MINISTER | 5 - 2 - 19 - 0 - 0 | 1.74 | 0.46 | 26 |
| 2002 | SARAFAN | LEAR FAN | CARO | 4 - 9 - 21 - 0 - 0 | 2.24 | 0.50 | 34 |
| | | | MEDIAN = | | 2.00 | 0.50 | 24.0 |

**FLORIDA DERBY, THREE-YEAR-OLDS, 9F, DIRT:**

| YEAR | WINNER | SIRE | BROODMARE SIRE | DP | DI | CD | PTS |
|------|--------|------|----------------|-----|-----|-----|-----|
| 1990 | UNBRIDLED | FAPPIANO | LE FABULEUX | 12 - 15 - 19 - 0 - 12 | 1.70 | 0.26 | 58 |
| 1991 | FLY SO FREE | TIME FOR A CHANGE | STEVWARD | 7 - 11 - 12 - 0 - 0 | 4.00 | 0.83 | 30 |
| 1992 | TECHNOLOGY | TIME FOR A CHANGE | ONE FOR ALL | 7 - 6 - 10 - 1 - 0 | 3.00 | 0.79 | 24 |
| 1993 | BULL INTHE HEATHER | FERDINAND | THE AXE II | 6 - 3 - 10 - 5 - 0 | 1.40 | 0.42 | 24 |
| 1994 | HOLY BULL | GREAT ABOVE | AL HATTAB | 6 - 5 - 4 - 1 - 0 | 4.33 | 1.00 | 16 |
| 1995 | THUNDER GULCH | GULCH | STORM BIRD | 10 - 2 - 8 - 0 - 0 | 4.00 | 1.10 | 20 |
| 1996 | UNBRIDLED'S SONG | UNBRIDLED | CARO | 9 - 10 - 11 - 0 - 6 | 2.13 | 0.44 | 36 |
| 1997 | CAPTAIN BODGIT | SAINT BALLADO | GREEK ANSWER | 6 - 2 - 12 - 2 - 2 | 1.40 | 0.33 | 24 |
| 1998 | CAPE TOWN | SEEKING THE GOLD | SEATTLE SLEW | 14 - 3 - 18 - 1 - 0 | 2.60 | 0.83 | 36 |
| 1999 | VICAR | WILD AGAIN | EL GRAN SENOR | 9 - 8 - 13 - 0 - 0 | 3.62 | 0.87 | 30 |
| 2000 | HAL'S HOPE | JOLIE'S HALO | REXSON'S HOPE | 7 - 5 - 12 - 6 - 0 | 1.50 | 0.43 | 30 |
| 2001 | MONARCHOS | MARIA'S MON | DIXIELAND BAND | 2 - 2 - 13 - 1 - 0 | 1.40 | 0.28 | 18 |
| 2002 | HARLAN'S HOLIDAY | HARLAN | AFFIRMED | 7 - 2 - 10 - 1 - 0 | 2.33 | 0.75 | 20 |
| | | | MEDIAN = | | 2.33 | 0.75 | 24.0 |

**FLOWER BOWL INVITATIONAL S, THREE-YEAR-OLDS & UP, FILLIES & MARES, 10F, TURF:**

| YEAR | WINNER | SIRE | BROODMARE SIRE | DP | DI | CD | PTS |
|------|--------|------|----------------|-----|-----|-----|-----|
| 1990 | LAUGH AND BE MERRY | ERINS ISLE | REVIEWER | 11 - 2 - 7 - 8 - 6 | 0.94 | 0.12 | 34 |
| 1991 | LADY SHIRL | THAT'S A NICE | NATIVE HERITAGE | 8 - 3 - 5 - 0 - 0 | 5.40 | 1.19 | 16 |
| 1992 | CHRISTIECAT | MAJESTIC LIGHT | BUCKPASSER | 10 - 5 - 15 - 0 - 2 | 2.37 | 0.66 | 32 |
| 1993 | FAR OUT BEAST | FAR OUT EAST | FORMIDABLE | 8 - 2 - 4 - 2 - 0 | 3.00 | 1.00 | 16 |

| YEAR | WINNER | SIRE | BROODMARE SIRE | DP | DI | CD | PTS |
|------|--------|------|----------------|-----|----|----|-----|
| 1994 | DAHLIA'S DREAMER | THEATRICAL | VAGUELY NOBLE | 3 - 0 - 23 - 0 - 4 | 0.94 | -0.07 | 30 |
| 1995 | NORTHERN EMERALD | GREEN DANCER | NASKRA | 6 - 1 - 9 - 4 - 0 | 1.35 | 0.45 | 20 |
| 1996 | CHELSEY FLOWER | HIS MAJESTY | AFFIRMED | 4 - 0 - 30 - 0 - 4 | 1.00 | 0.00 | 38 |
| 1997 | YASHMAK | DANZIG | ROBERTO | 10 - 14 - 30 - 0 - 0 | 2.60 | 0.63 | 54 |
| 1998 | AUNTIE MAME | THEATRICAL | SIR IVOR | 3 - 11 - 20 - 0 - 0 | 2.40 | 0.50 | 34 |
| 1999 | SOARING SOFTLY | KRIS S. | KEY TO THE MINT | 6 - 5 - 25 - 7 - 1 | 1.15 | 0.18 | 44 |
| 2000 | COLSTAR | OPENING VERSE | RISEN STAR | 6 - 6 - 9 - 1 - 0 | 3.00 | 0.77 | 22 |
| 2001 | LAILANI | UNFUWAIN | MR. PROSPECTOR | 13 - 4 - 17 - 4 - 0 | 2.04 | 0.68 | 38 |
| 2002 | KAZZIA | ZINAAD | LAGUNAS | 1 - 1 - 8 - 3 - 5 | 0.50 | -0.56 | 18 |
| | | | MEDIAN = | | **2.04** | **0.50** | **32.0** |

## FOUNTAIN OF YOUTH S, THREE-YEAR-OLDS, 8.5F, DIRT:

| YEAR | WINNER | SIRE | BROODMARE SIRE | DP | DI | CD | PTS |
|------|--------|------|----------------|-----|----|----|-----|
| 1990 | SHOT GUN SCOTT | EXUBERANT | RAMBUNCTIOUS | 12 - 3 - 1 - 0 - 0 | 31.00 | 1.69 | 16 |
| 1991 | FLY SO FREE | TIME FOR A CHANGE | STEVWARD | 7 - 11 - 12 - 0 - 0 | 4.00 | 0.83 | 30 |
| 1992 | DANCE FLOOR | STAR DE NASKRA | NATIVE CHARGER | 8 - 6 - 2 - 0 - 0 | 15.00 | 1.38 | 16 |
| 1993 | STORM TOWER-dead heat | IRISH TOWER | STORM BIRD | 6 - 3 - 3 - 0 - 0 | 7.00 | 1.25 | 12 |
| 1993 | DUC D'SLIGOVIL-dead heat | SEZYOU | AL HATTAB | 8 - 3 - 4 - 0 - 1 | 4.33 | 1.06 | 16 |
| 1994 | DEHERE | DEPUTY MINISTER | SECRETARIAT | 6 - 5 - 4 - 1 - 0 | 4.33 | 1.00 | 16 |
| 1995 | THUNDER GULCH | GULCH | STORM BIRD | 10 - 2 - 8 - 0 - 0 | 4.00 | 1.10 | 20 |
| 1996 | BUILT FOR PLEASURE | HOMEBUILDER | I'MA HELL RAISER | 12 - 3 - 9 - 0 - 2 | 3.00 | 0.88 | 26 |
| 1997 | PULPIT | A.P. INDY | MR. PROSPECTOR | 15 - 3 - 13 - 1 - 0 | 3.27 | 1.00 | 32 |
| 1998 | LIL'S LAD | PINE BLUFF | VANLANDINGHAM | 5 - 5 - 14 - 0 - 0 | 2.43 | 0.63 | 24 |
| 1999 | VICAR | WILD AGAIN | EL GRAN SENOR | 9 - 8 - 13 - 0 - 0 | 3.62 | 0.87 | 30 |
| 2000 | HIGH YIELD | STORM CAT | FORTY NINER | 8 - 3 - 11 - 3 - 1 | 1.74 | 0.54 | 26 |
| 2001 | SONGANDAPRAYER | UNBRIDLED'S SONG | PREMIERSHIP | 4 - 5 - 9 - 0 - 2 | 2.08 | 0.45 | 20 |
| 2002 | BOOKLET | NOTEBOOK | BOB'S DUSTY | 3 - 4 - 6 - 0 - 3 | 1.67 | 0.25 | 16 |
| | | | MEDIAN = | | **3.81** | **0.94** | **20.0** |

## FRIZETTE S, TWO-YEAR-OLD FILLIES, 8.5F, DIRT:

| YEAR | WINNER | SIRE | BROODMARE SIRE | DP | DI | CD | PTS |
|------|--------|------|----------------|-----|----|----|-----|
| 1990 | MEADOW STAR | MEADOWLAKE | IN REALITY | 15 - 11 - 10 - 0 - 0 | 6.20 | 1.14 | 36 |
| 1991 | PREACH | MR. PROSPECTOR | HONEST PLEASURE | 24 - 8 - 17 - 3 - 0 | 3.52 | 1.02 | 52 |
| 1992 | EDUCATED RISK | MR. PROSPECTOR | KEY TO THE MINT | 26 - 10 - 22 - 3 - 1 | 3.13 | 0.92 | 62 |
| 1993 | HEAVENLY PRIZE | SEEKING THE GOLD | NIJINSKY II | 10 - 3 - 17 - 4 - 0 | 1.72 | 0.56 | 34 |
| 1994 | FLANDERS | SEEKING THE GOLD | STORM BIRD | 11 - 6 - 15 - 0 - 0 | 3.27 | 0.88 | 32 |

| YEAR | WINNER | SIRE | BROODMARE SIRE | DP | DI | CD | PTS |
|---|---|---|---|---|---|---|---|
| 1995 | GOLDEN ATTRACTION | MR. PROSPECTOR | SEATTLE SLEW | 24 - 6 - 21 - 1 - 0 | 3.52 | 1.02 | 52 |
| 1996 | STORM SONG | SUMMER SQUALL | FAPPIANO | 8 - 9 - 13 - 0 - 0 | 3.62 | 0.83 | 30 |
| 1997 | SILVER MAIDEN | SILVER BUCK | QUACK | 2 - 10 - 17 - 3 - 0 | 1.78 | 0.34 | 32 |
| 1998 | CONFESSIONAL | HOLY BULL | GREEN DANCER | 4 - 6 - 4 - 2 - 0 | 3.00 | 0.75 | 16 |
| 1999 | SURFSIDE | SEATTLE SLEW | SEEKING THE GOLD | 14 - 2 - 16 - 2 - 0 | 2.40 | 0.82 | 34 |
| 2000 | RAGING FEVER | STORM CAT | SEATTLE SLEW | 8 - 4 - 8 - 0 - 0 | 4.00 | 1.00 | 20 |
| 2001 | YOU | YOU AND I | HOMEBUILDER | 5 - 2 - 9 - 1 - 1 | 1.77 | 0.50 | 18 |
| 2002 | STORM FLAG FLYING | STORM CAT | EASY GOER | 6 - 5 - 11 - 0 - 0 | 3.00 | 0.77 | 22 |
| | | | MEDIAN = | | **3.13** | **0.83** | **32.0** |

## FUTURITY S, TWO-YEAR-OLDS, 8F, DIRT:

| YEAR | WINNER | SIRE | BROODMARE SIRE | DP | DI | CD | PTS |
|---|---|---|---|---|---|---|---|
| 1990 | EASTERN ECHO | DAMASCUS | NORTHERN DANCER | 9 - 11 - 19 - 2 - 1 | 2.36 | 0.60 | 42 |
| 1991 | AGINCOURT | CAPOTE | CONQUISTADOR CIELO | 12 - 2 - 8 - 0 - 0 | 4.50 | 1.18 | 22 |
| 1992 | STROLLING ALONG | DANZIG | ALYDAR | 9 - 13 - 28 - 0 - 0 | 2.57 | 0.62 | 50 |
| 1993 | HOLY BULL | GREAT ABOVE | AL HATTAB | 6 - 5 - 4 - 1 - 0 | 4.33 | 1.00 | 16 |
| 1994 | MONTREAL RED | D'ACCORD | GROTON | 8 - 9 - 12 - 1 - 0 | 3.29 | 0.80 | 30 |
| 1995 | MARIA'S MON | WAVERING MONARCH | CARO | 4 - 5 - 10 - 0 - 1 | 2.33 | 0.55 | 20 |
| 1996 | TRAITOR | CRYPTOCLEARANCE | CLEVER TRICK | 8 - 9 - 9 - 1 - 1 | 3.31 | 0.79 | 28 |
| 1997 | GRAND SLAM | GONE WEST | EL GRAN SENOR | 14 - 6 - 15 - 1 - 0 | 3.24 | 0.92 | 36 |
| 1998 | LEMON DROP KID | KINGMAMBO | SEATTLE SLEW | 13 - 4 - 21 - 0 - 0 | 2.62 | 0.79 | 38 |
| 1999 | BEVO | PROSPECTORS GAMBLE | WHEATLY HALL | 8 - 1 - 5 - 0 - 0 | 4.60 | 1.21 | 14 |
| 2000 | BURNING ROMA | RUBIANO | OVERSKATE | 10 - 8 - 13 - 3 - 0 | 2.58 | 0.74 | 34 |
| 2001 | NOT RUN | | | | | | |
| 2002 | WHYWHYWHY | MR. GREELEY | QUIET AMERICAN | 10 - 6 - 8 - 0 - 0 | 5.00 | 1.08 | 24 |
| | | | MEDIAN = | | **3.26** | **0.79** | **29.0** |

## GAMELY BREEDERS' CUP H, THREE-YEAR-OLDS & UP, FILLIES & MARES, 9F, TURF:

| YEAR | WINNER | SIRE | BROODMARE SIRE | DP | DI | CD | PTS |
|---|---|---|---|---|---|---|---|
| 1990 | DOUBLE WEDGE | NORTHERN BABY | SPRING DOUBLE | 10 - 2 - 7 - 5 - 0 | 1.82 | 0.71 | 24 |
| 1991 | MISS JOSH | NASTY AND BOLD | PIA STAR | 9 - 2 - 1 - 8 - 0 | 1.35 | 0.60 | 20 |
| 1992 | METAMORPHOSE | LORD AVIE | NORTHFIELDS | 5 - 7 - 6 - 4 - 0 | 2.14 | 0.59 | 22 |
| 1993 | TOUSSAUD | EL GRAN SENOR | IN REALITY | 13 - 5 - 16 - 0 - 0 | 3.25 | 0.91 | 34 |
| 1994 | HOLLYWOOD WILDCAT | KRIS S. | MR. PROSPECTOR | 9 - 6 - 21 - 2 - 0 | 2.04 | 0.58 | 38 |
| 1995 | POSSIBLY PERFECT | NORTHERN BABY | AVATAR | 5 - 2 - 9 - 7 - 1 | 0.92 | 0.13 | 24 |
| 1996 | AURIETTE | CAERLEON | CRYSTAL GLITTERS | 4 - 1 - 10 - 9 - 0 | 0.71 | 0.00 | 24 |

| YEAR | WINNER | SIRE | BROODMARE SIRE | DP | DI | CD | PTS |
|---|---|---|---|---|---|---|---|
| 1997 | DONNA VIOLA | BE MY CHIEF | PRINCE TENDERFOOT | 3 - 7 - 7 - 1 - 0 | 3.00 | 0.67 | 18 |
| 1998 | FIJI | RAINBOW QUEST | EXPLODENT | 9 - 0 - 7 - 2 - 4 | 1.32 | 0.36 | 22 |
| 1999 | TRANQUILITY LAKE | RAHY | DANZIG | 11 - 6 - 16 - 1 - 2 | 2.27 | 0.64 | 36 |
| 2000 | ASTRA | THEATRICAL | SEATTLE SLEW | 6 - 0 - 20 - 0 - 0 | 1.60 | 0.46 | 26 |
| 2001 | HAPPYANUNOIT | YACHTIE | RAJAH | 0 - 2 - 2 - 0 - 0 | 3.00 | 0.50 | 4 |
| 2002 | ASTRA | THEATRICAL | SEATTLE SLEW | 6 - 0 - 20 - 0 - 0 | 1.60 | 0.46 | 26 |
| | | | MEDIAN = | | 1.82 | 0.58 | 24.0 |

## GAZELLE H, THREE-YEAR-OLD FILLIES, 9F, DIRT:

| YEAR | WINNER | SIRE | BROODMARE SIRE | DP | DI | CD | PTS |
|---|---|---|---|---|---|---|---|
| 1990 | HIGHLAND TALK | HIGHLAND PARK | ELOCUTIONIST | 11 - 5 - 2 - 0 - 0 | 17.00 | 1.50 | 18 |
| 1991 | VERSAILLES TREATY | DANZIG | BUCKPASSER | 5 - 17 - 28 - 0 - 0 | 2.57 | 0.54 | 50 |
| 1992 | SARATOGA DEW | CORMORANT | IN REALITY | 12 - 3 - 17 - 0 - 2 | 2.24 | 0.68 | 34 |
| 1993 | DISPUTE | DANZIG | REVIEWER | 13 - 16 - 18 - 1 - 0 | 3.80 | 0.85 | 48 |
| 1994 | HEAVENLY PRIZE | SEEKING THE GOLD | NIJINSKY II | 10 - 3 - 17 - 4 - 0 | 1.72 | 0.56 | 34 |
| 1995 | SERENA'S SONG | RAHY | NORTHFIELDS | 12 - 1 - 12 - 1 - 2 | 2.11 | 0.71 | 28 |
| 1996 | MY FLAG | EASY GOER | PRIVATE ACCOUNT | 6 - 6 - 19 - 0 - 1 | 2.05 | 0.50 | 32 |
| 1997 | ROYAL INDY | A.P. INDY | ON TO GLORY | 7 - 6 - 9 - 0 - 0 | 3.89 | 0.91 | 22 |
| 1998 | TAP TO MUSIC | PLEASANT TAP | NUREYEV | 4 - 2 - 19 - 2 - 3 | 1.07 | 0.07 | 30 |
| 1999 | SILVERBULLETDAY | SILVER DEPUTY | TOM ROLFE | 6 - 1 - 9 - 0 - 6 | 1.10 | 0.05 | 22 |
| 2000 | CRITICAL EYE | DYNAFORMER | DR. BLUM | 4 - 7 - 22 - 0 - 1 | 1.83 | 0.38 | 34 |
| 2001 | EXOGENOUS | UNBRIDLED | PHONE TRICK | 7 - 6 - 9 - 0 - 6 | 1.67 | 0.29 | 28 |
| 2002 | IMPERIAL GESTURE | LANGFUHR | HOIST THE FLAG | 6 - 8 - 11 - 0 - 3 | 2.29 | 0.50 | 28 |
| | | | MEDIAN = | | 2.11 | 0.54 | 30.0 |

## GO FOR WAND H, THREE-YEAR-OLDS & UP, FILLIES & MARES, 9F, DIRT:

| YEAR | WINNER | SIRE | BROODMARE SIRE | DP | DI | CD | PTS |
|---|---|---|---|---|---|---|---|
| 1993 | TURNBACK THE ALARM | DARN THAT ALARM | FIGONERO | 0 - 4 - 8 - 0 - 0 | 2.00 | 0.33 | 12 |
| 1994 | SKY BEAUTY | BLUSHING GROOM | NIJINSKY II | 21 - 0 - 17 - 4 - 4 | 1.79 | 0.65 | 46 |
| 1995 | HEAVENLY PRIZE | SEEKING THE GOLD | NIJINSKY II | 10 - 3 - 17 - 4 - 0 | 1.72 | 0.56 | 34 |
| 1996 | EXOTIC WOOD | RAHY | DIXIELAND BAND | 11 - 3 - 14 - 1 - 3 | 1.91 | 0.56 | 32 |
| 1997 | HIDDEN LAKE | QUIET AMERICAN | ROUND TABLE | 7 - 12 - 9 - 10 - 0 | 1.62 | 0.42 | 38 |
| 1998 | ALDIZA | STORM CAT | ALYDAR | 11 - 6 - 15 - 0 - 0 | 3.27 | 0.88 | 32 |
| 1999 | BANSHEE BREEZE | UNBRIDLED | KNOWN FACT | 8 - 9 - 9 - 0 - 6 | 2.05 | 0.41 | 32 |
| 2000 | HERITAGE OF GOLD | GOLD LEGEND | LYPHARD | 13 - 1 - 18 - 0 - 0 | 2.56 | 0.84 | 32 |

| 2001 | SERRA LAKE | SEATTLE SLEW | LYPHARD | 18 - 1 - 23 - 2 - 0 | 2.26 | 0.80 | 44 |
| 2001 | DANCETHRUTHEDAWN | MR.PROSPECTOR | DANZIG | 20 - 10 - 20 - 0 - 0 | 4.00 | 1.00 | 50 |
| | | | MEDIAN = | | 2.02 | 0.61 | 33.0 |

## GULFSTREAM PARK H, THREE-YEAR-OLDS & UP, 10F, DIRT:

| YEAR | WINNER | SIRE | BROODMARE SIRE | DP | DI | CD | PTS |
|------|--------|------|----------------|----|----|----|-----|
| 1990 | MI SELECTO | EXPLODENT | RIBOT | 9 - 2 - 7 - 0 - 4 | 1.93 | 0.55 | 22 |
| 1991 | JOLIE'S HALO | HALO | SIR IVOR | 17 - 10 - 23 - 0 - 0 | 3.35 | 0.88 | 50 |
| 1992 | SEA CADET | BOLGER | AL HATTAB | 6 - 6 - 5 - 5 - 0 | 1.93 | 0.59 | 22 |
| 1993 | DEVIL HIS DUE | DEVIL'S BAG | RAISE A CUP | 13 - 3 - 12 - 2 - 2 | 2.20 | 0.72 | 32 |
| 1994 | SCUFFLEBURG | COX'S RIDGE | ROUND TABLE | 6 - 4 - 15 -10 - 3 | 0.85 | 0.00 | 38 |
| 1995 | CIGAR | PALACE MUSIC | SEATTLE SLEW | 7 - 2 - 10 - 1 - 0 | 2.33 | 0.75 | 20 |
| 1996 | WEKIVA SPRINGS | RUNAWAY GROOM | TRI JET | 10 - 2 - 6 - 0 - 2 | 3.00 | 0.90 | 20 |
| 1997 | MT. SASSAFRAS | MT. LIVERMORE | SASSAFRAS | 8 - 0 - 5 - 1 - 4 | 1.40 | 0.39 | 18 |
| 1998 | SKIP AWAY | SKIP TRIAL | DIPLOMAT WAY | 5 - 6 - 8 - 1 - 0 | 3.00 | 0.75 | 20 |
| 1999 | BEHRENS | PLEASANT COLONY | MARI'S BOOK | 5 - 0 - 15 - 0 - 2 | 1.32 | 0.27 | 22 |
| 2000 | BEHRENS | PLEASANT COLONY | MARI'S BOOK | 5 - 0 - 15 - 0 - 2 | 1.32 | 0.27 | 22 |
| 2001 | SIR BEAR | SIR LEON | BET BIG | 1 - 3 - 8 - 4 - 0 | 1.00 | 0.06 | 16 |
| 2002 | HAL'S HOPE | JOLIE'S HALO | REXSON'S HOPE | 7 - 5 - 12 - 6 - 0 | 1.50 | 0.43 | 30 |
| | | | MEDIAN = | | 1.93 | 0.55 | 22.0 |

## HASKELL INVITATIONAL H, THREE-YEAR-OLDS, 9F, DIRT:

| YEAR | WINNER | SIRE | BROODMARE SIRE | DP | DI | CD | PTS |
|------|--------|------|----------------|----|----|----|-----|
| 1990 | RESTLESS CON | RESTLESS NATIVE | WALLET LIFTER | 3 - 12 - 11 - 2 - 2 | 2.16 | 0.40 | 30 |
| 1991 | LOST MOUNTAIN | COX'S RIDGE | TO THE QUICK | 8 - 5 - 10 - 1 - 0 | 3.00 | 0.83 | 24 |
| 1992 | TECHNOLOGY | TIME FOR A CHANGE | ONE FOR ALL | 7 - 6 - 10 - 1 - 0 | 3.00 | 0.79 | 24 |
| 1993 | KISSIN KRIS | KRIS S. | YOUR ALIBHAI | 3 - 6 - 21 - 2 - 0 | 1.56 | 0.31 | 32 |
| 1994 | HOLY BULL | GREAT ABOVE | AL HATTAB | 6 - 5 - 4 - 1 - 0 | 4.33 | 1.00 | 16 |
| 1995 | SERENA'S SONG | RAHY | NORTHFIELDS | 12 - 1 - 12 - 1 - 2 | 2.11 | 0.71 | 28 |
| 1996 | SKIP AWAY | SKIP TRIAL | DIPLOMAT WAY | 5 - 6 - 8 - 1 - 0 | 3.00 | 0.75 | 20 |
| 1997 | TOUCH GOLD | DEPUTY MINISTER | BUCKPASSER | 4 - 3 - 17 - 0 - 0 | 1.82 | 0.46 | 24 |
| 1998 | CORONADO'S QUEST | FORTY NINER | DAMASCUS | 16 - 9 - 14 - 0 - 3 | 3.20 | 0.83 | 42 |
| 1999 | MENIFEE | HARLAN | NEVER BEND | 12 - 6 - 8 - 0 - 0 | 5.50 | 1.15 | 26 |
| 2000 | DIXIE UNION | DIXIELAND BAND | CAPOTE | 11 - 1 - 10 - 0 - 0 | 3.40 | 1.05 | 22 |
| 2001 | POINT GIVEN | THUNDER GULCH | TURKOMAN | 8 - 0 - 8 - 0 - 0 | 3.00 | 1.00 | 16 |
| 2001 | WAR EMBLEM | OUR EMBLEM | LORD AT WAR | 9 - 4 - 8 - 1 - 0 | 3.40 | 0.95 | 22 |
| | | | MEDIAN = | | 3.00 | 0.83 | 24.0 |

## HOLLYWOOD DERBY, THREE-YEAR-OLDS, 9F, TURF:

| YEAR | WINNER | SIRE | BROODMARE SIRE | DP | DI | CD | PTS |
|---|---|---|---|---|---|---|---|
| 1990 | ITSALLGREEKTOME | SOVEREIGN DANCER | GREY DAWN II | 15 - 9 - 10 - 6 - 2 | 2.23 | 0.69 | 42 |
| 1991 | ETERNITY STAR | MAJESTIC LIGHT | NORTHERN DANCER | 11 - 4 - 14 - 1 - 2 | 2.20 | 0.66 | 32 |
| 1991 | OLYMPIO | NASKRA | WHITESBURG | 8 - 1 - 5 - 0 - 0 | 4.60 | 1.21 | 14 |
| 1992 | PARADISE CREEK | IRISH RIVER | NORTHFIELDS | 6 - 6 - 10 - 0 - 0 | 3.40 | 0.82 | 22 |
| 1993 | EXPLOSIVE RED | EXPLODENT | BOLD HOUR | 7 - 5 - 6 - 0 - 2 | 3.00 | 0.75 | 20 |
| 1994 | RIVER FLYER | RIVERMAN | FLYING PASTER | 11 - 16 - 14 - 1 - 0 | 4.25 | 0.88 | 42 |
| 1995 | LABEEB | LEAR FAN | PRINCE TENDERFOOT | 4 - 4 - 17 - 1 - 0 | 1.74 | 0.42 | 26 |
| 1996 | MARLIN | SWORD DANCE | DAMASCUS | 5 - 7 - 14 - 4 - 0 | 1.73 | 0.43 | 30 |
| 1997 | SUBORDINATION | MT. LIVERMORE | DESERT WINE | 11 - 4 - 7 - 0 - 2 | 3.36 | 0.92 | 24 |
| 1998 | VERGENNES | DYNAFORMER | FABULEUX DANCER | 8 - 2 - 21 - 2 - 3 | 1.32 | 0.28 | 36 |
| 1999 | SUPER QUERCUS | HERO'S HONOR | HILAL | 5 - 1 - 12 - 2 - 2 | 1.20 | 0.23 | 22 |
| 2000 | BRAHMS | DANZIG | MR. PROSPECTOR | 15 - 15 - 22 - 0 - 0 | 3.73 | 0.87 | 52 |
| 2001 | DENON | PLEASANT COLONY | NORTHFIELDS | 4 - 3 - 17 - 0 - 2 | 1.48 | 0.27 | 26 |
| | | | MEDIAN = | | 2.23 | 0.69 | 26.0 |

## HOLLYWOOD FUTURITY, TWO-YEAR-OLDS, 8.5F, DIRT:

| YEAR | WINNER | SIRE | BROODMARE SIRE | DP | DI | CD | PTS |
|---|---|---|---|---|---|---|---|
| 1990 | BEST PAL | HABITONY | KING PELLINORE | 11 - 6 - 4 - 5 - 0 | 2.71 | 0.88 | 26 |
| 1991 | A.P. INDY | SEATTLE SLEW | SECRETARIAT | 13 - 10 - 20 - 3 - 0 | 2.54 | 0.72 | 46 |
| 1992 | RIVER SPECIAL | RIVERMAN | NIJINSKY II | 14 - 18 - 21 - 5 - 0 | 2.74 | 0.71 | 58 |
| 1993 | VALIANT NATURE | HIS MAJESTY | LYPHARD | 9 - 2 - 35 - 0 - 4 | 1.33 | 0.24 | 50 |
| 1994 | AFTERNOON DEELITES | PRIVATE TERMS | MEDAILLE D'OR | 7 - 11 - 10 - 0 - 0 | 4.60 | 0.89 | 28 |
| 1995 | MATTY G | CAPOTE | PIA STAR | 14 - 1 - 5 - 8 - 0 | 1.67 | 0.75 | 28 |
| 1996 | SWISS YODELER | EASTERN ECHO | RAJA BABA | 12 - 9 - 9 - 1 - 1 | 3.92 | 0.94 | 32 |
| 1997 | REAL QUIET | QUIET AMERICAN | BELIEVE IT | 14 - 12 - 12 - 0 - 0 | 5.33 | 1.05 | 38 |
| 1998 | TACTICAL CAT | STORM CAT | CARO | 7 - 7 - 10 - 0 - 0 | 3.80 | 0.88 | 24 |
| 1999 | CAPTAIN STEVE | FLY SO FREE | VICE REGENT | 4 - 5 - 7 - 0 - 0 | 3.57 | 0.81 | 16 |
| 2000 | POINT GIVEN | THUNDER GULCH | TURKOMAN | 8 - 0 - 8 - 0 - 0 | 3.00 | 1.00 | 16 |
| 2001 | SIPHONIC | SIPHON | CHEROKEE COLONY | 1 - 0 - 6 - 1 - 0 | 1.00 | 0.13 | 8 |
| | | | MEDIAN = | | 2.87 | 0.84 | 28.0 |

## HOLLYWOOD GOLD CUP S, THREE-YEAR-OLDS & UP, 10F, DIRT:

| YEAR | WINNER | SIRE | BROODMARE SIRE | DP | DI | CD | PTS |
|---|---|---|---|---|---|---|---|
| 1990 | CRIMINAL TYPE | ALYDAR | NO ROBBERY | 10 - 6 - 20 - 0 - 0 | 2.60 | 0.72 | 36 |
| 1991 | MARQUETRY | CONQUISTADOR CIELO | VICE REGENT | 18 - 6 - 8 - 0 - 0 | 7.00 | 1.31 | 32 |

| YEAR | WINNER | SIRE | BROODMARE SIRE | DP | DI | CD | PTS |
|---|---|---|---|---|---|---|---|
| 1992 | SULTRY SONG | COX'S RIDGE | BUCKFINDER | 4 - 7 - 16 - 1 - 0 | 2.11 | 0.50 | 28 |
| 1993 | BEST PAL | HABITONY | KING PELLINORE | 11 - 6 - 4 - 5 - 0 | 2.71 | 0.88 | 26 |
| 1994 | SLEW OF DAMASCUS | SLEWACIDE | ACCIPITER | 5 - 4 - 11 - 0 - 0 | 2.64 | 0.70 | 20 |
| 1995 | CIGAR | PALACE MUSIC | SEATTLE SLEW | 7 - 2 - 10 - 1 - 0 | 2.33 | 0.75 | 20 |
| 1996 | SIPHON | ITAJARA | KUBLAI KHAN | 0 - 0 - 6 - 2 - 0 | 0.60 | -0.25 | 8 |
| 1997 | GENTLEMEN | ROBIN DES BOIS | LOOSE CANNON | 5 - 0 - 19 - 4 - 0 | 1.07 | 0.21 | 28 |
| 1998 | SKIP AWAY | SKIP TRIAL | DIPLOMAT WAY | 5 - 6 - 8 - 1 - 0 | 3.00 | 0.75 | 20 |
| 1999 | REAL QUIET | QUIET AMERICAN | BELIEVE IT | 14 - 12 - 12 - 0 - 0 | 5.33 | 1.05 | 38 |
| 2000 | EARLY PIONEER | RAHY | SLEW O' GOLD | 10 - 1 - 14 - 1 - 2 | 1.80 | 0.57 | 28 |
| 2001 | APTITUDE | A.P. INDY | NORTHERN DANCER | 10 - 5 - 19 - 0 - 0 | 2.58 | 0.74 | 34 |
| 2002 | SKY JACK | JAKLIN KLUGMAN | SKYWALKER | 3 - 0 - 5 - 0 - 0 | 2.20 | 0.75 | 8 |
| | | | MEDIAN = | | 2.58 | 0.74 | 28.0 |

## HOLLYWOOD STARLET S, TWO-YEAR-OLD FILLIES, 8.5F, DIRT:

| YEAR | WINNER | SIRE | BROODMARE SIRE | DP | DI | CD | PTS |
|---|---|---|---|---|---|---|---|
| 1990 | CUDDLES | MR. PROSPECTOR | TENTAM | 20 - 8 - 14 - 0 - 0 | 5.00 | 1.14 | 42 |
| 1991 | MAGICAL MAIDEN | LORD AVIE | MAGESTERIAL | 6 - 7 - 5 - 0 - 0 | 6.20 | 1.06 | 18 |
| 1992 | CREAKING BOARD | NIGHT SHIFT | HOMING | 9 - 2 - 7 - 0 - 0 | 4.14 | 1.11 | 18 |
| 1993 | SARDULA | STORM CAT | HOIST THE FLAG | 7 - 5 - 7 - 0 - 3 | 2.38 | 0.59 | 22 |
| 1994 | SERENA'S SONG | RAHY | NORTHFIELDS | 12 - 1 - 12 - 1 - 2 | 2.11 | 0.71 | 28 |
| 1995 | CARA RAFAELA | QUIET AMERICAN | SPECTACULAR BID | 8 - 10 - 10 - 0 - 0 | 4.60 | 0.93 | 28 |
| 1996 | SHARP CAT | STORM CAT | ACK ACK | 5 - 9 - 8 - 0 - 0 | 4.50 | 0.86 | 22 |
| 1997 | LOVE LOCK | SILVER GHOST | SPEND A BUCK | 12 - 4 - 16 - 0 - 0 | 3.00 | 0.88 | 32 |
| 1998 | EXCELLENT MEETING | GENERAL MEETING | CHIEF'S CROWN | 7 - 4 - 14 - 1 - 0 | 2.25 | 0.65 | 26 |
| 1999 | SURFSIDE | SEATTLE SLEW | SEEKING THE GOLD | 14 - 2 - 16 - 2 - 0 | 2.40 | 0.82 | 34 |
| 2000 | I BELIEVE IN YOU | PLEASANT TAP | COPELAN | 6 - 2 - 7 - 4 - 3 | 1.10 | 0.18 | 22 |
| 2001 | HABIBTI | TABASCO CAT | TEMPERENCE HILL | 2 - 2 - 5 - 1 - 0 | 1.86 | 0.50 | 10 |
| | | | MEDIAN = | | 2.70 | 0.84 | 24.0 |

## HOLLYWOOD TURF CUP S, THREE-YEAR-OLDS & UP, 12F, TURF:

| YEAR | WINNER | SIRE | BROODMARE SIRE | DP | DI | CD | PTS |
|---|---|---|---|---|---|---|---|
| 1990 | ITSALLGREEKTOME | SOVEREIGN DANCER | GREY DAWN II | 15 - 9 - 10 - 6 - 2 | 2.23 | 0.69 | 42 |
| 1991 | MISS ALLEGED | ALLEGED | BOLDNESIAN | 8 - 11 - 9 - 1 - 3 | 2.76 | 0.63 | 32 |
| 1992 | BIEN BIEN | MANILA | GRAUSTARK | 5 - 3 - 22 - 6 - 8 | 0.76 | -0.20 | 44 |
| 1993 | FRAISE | STRAWBERRY ROAD | DICTUS | 1 - 0 - 3 - 4 - 2 | 0.33 | -0.60 | 10 |
| 1994 | FRENCHPARK | FOOLS HOLME | SHIRLEY HEIGHTS | 5 - 5 - 16 - 2 - 6 | 1.13 | 0.03 | 34 |
| 1995 | ROYAL CHARIOT | STRAWBERRY ROAD | KEY TO THE MINT | 5 - 1 - 10 - 9 - 1 | 0.73 | 0.00 | 26 |

| YEAR | WINNER | SIRE | BROODMARE SIRE | DP | DI | CD | PTS |
|---|---|---|---|---|---|---|---|
| 1996 | RUNNING FLAME | ASSERT | FANNING THE FLAME | 4- 0- 3- 4- 5 | 0.52 | -0.38 | 16 |
| 1997 | RIVER BAY | IRISH RIVER | GOOD COUNSEL | 5- 9-13- 2- 1 | 2.16 | 0.50 | 30 |
| 1998 | LAZY LODE | LODE | BABAS FABLES | 11- 6-11- 0- 6 | 1.96 | 0.47 | 34 |
| 1999 | LAZY LODE | LODE | BABAS FABLES | 11- 6-11- 0- 6 | 1.96 | 0.47 | 34 |
| 2000 | BIENAMADO | BIEN BIEN | VITIGES | 1- 1-12- 3- 3 | 0.67 | -0.30 | 20 |
| 2001 | SUPER QUERCUS | HERO'S HONOR | HILAL | 5- 1-12- 2- 2 | 1.20 | 0.23 | 22 |
| | | | | MEDIAN = | **1.16** | **0.13** | **31.0** |

## HOPEFUL S, TWO-YEAR-OLDS, 7F, DIRT:

| YEAR | WINNER | SIRE | BROODMARE SIRE | DP | DI | CD | PTS |
|---|---|---|---|---|---|---|---|
| 1990 | DEPOSIT TICKET | NORTHERN BABY | MR. PROSPECTOR | 13- 4-12- 5- 0 | 2.09 | 0.74 | 34 |
| 1991 | SALT LAKE | DEPUTY MINISTER | QUEEN CITY LAD | 2- 0- 2- 0- 0 | 3.00 | 1.00 | 4 |
| 1992 | GREAT NAVIGATOR | GULCH | NONOALCO | 9- 2- 9- 0- 0 | 3.44 | 1.00 | 20 |
| 1993 | DEHERE | DEPUTY MINISTER | SECRETARIAT | 6- 9- 8- 1- 0 | 3.80 | 0.83 | 24 |
| 1994 | WILD ESCAPADE | WILD AGAIN | RAMAHORN | 9- 7- 8- 0- 0 | 5.00 | 1.04 | 24 |
| 1995 | HENNESSY | STORM CAT | HAWAII | 3- 4- 5- 0- 0 | 3.80 | 0.83 | 12 |
| 1996 | SMOKE GLACKEN | TWO PUNCH | MAGESTERIAL | 13- 5- 9- 1- 0 | 4.09 | 1.07 | 28 |
| 1997 | FAVORITE TRICK | PHONE TRICK | MEDIEVAL MAN | 7- 2- 5- 0- 0 | 4.60 | 1.14 | 14 |
| 1998 | LUCKY ROBERTO | BELONG TO ME | ROBERTO | 5- 6-26- 1- 0 | 1.71 | 0.39 | 38 |
| 1999 | HIGH YIELD | STORM CAT | FORTY NINER | 8- 3-11- 3- 1 | 1.74 | 0.54 | 26 |
| 2000 | CITY ZIP | CARSON CITY | RELAUNCH | 13- 3-11- 1- 0 | 3.31 | 1.00 | 28 |
| 2000 | YONAGUSKA | CHEROKEE RUN | SILVER GHOST | 7- 0- 7- 0- 0 | 3.00 | 1.00 | 14 |
| 2001 | CAME HOME | GONE WEST | CLEVER TRICK | 12- 6-12- 0- 0 | 4.00 | 1.00 | 30 |
| 2002 | SKY MESA | PULPIT | STORM CAT | 7- 2- 9- 2- 0 | 2.08 | 0.70 | 20 |
| | | | | MEDIAN = | **3.38** | **1.00** | **24.0** |

## JOCKEY CUP GOLD CUP S, THREE-YEAR-OLDS & UP, 10F, DIRT:

| YEAR | WINNER | SIRE | BROODMARE SIRE | DP | DI | CD | PTS |
|---|---|---|---|---|---|---|---|
| 1990 | FLYING CONTINENTAL | FLYING PASTER | TRANSWORLD | 4- 3- 6- 1- 0 | 2.50 | 0.71 | 14 |
| 1991 | FESTIN | MAT-BOY | CON BRIO II | 0- 2- 2- 0- 2 | 1.00 | -0.33 | 6 |
| 1992 | PLEASANT TAP | PLEASANT COLONY | STAGE DOOR JOHNNY | 6- 5-16- 7- 6 | 0.90 | -0.05 | 40 |
| 1993 | MINER'S MARK | MR. PROSPECTOR | PRIVATE ACCOUNT | 20-10-19- 0- 1 | 3.76 | 0.96 | 50 |
| 1994 | COLONIAL AFFAIR | PLEASANT COLONY | NIJINSKY II | 8- 1-19- 4- 2 | 1.19 | 0.26 | 34 |
| 1995 | CIGAR | PALACE MUSIC | SEATTLE SLEW | 7- 2-10- 1- 0 | 2.33 | 0.75 | 20 |
| 1996 | SKIP AWAY | SKIP TRIAL | DIPLOMAT WAY | 5- 6- 8- 1- 0 | 3.00 | 0.75 | 20 |
| 1997 | SKIP AWAY | SKIP TRIAL | DIPLOMAT WAY | 5- 6- 8- 1- 0 | 3.00 | 0.75 | 20 |

| YEAR | WINNER | SIRE | BROODMARE SIRE | DP | DI | CD | PTS |
|---|---|---|---|---|---|---|---|
| 1998 | WAGON LIMIT | CONQUISTADOR CIELO | COX'S RIDGE | 13 - 5 - 14 - 0 - 0 | 3.57 | 0.97 | 32 |
| 1999 | RIVER KEEN | KEEN | CAERLEON | 11 - 3 - 8 - 6 - 2 | 1.50 | 0.50 | 30 |
| 2000 | ALBERT THE GREAT | GO FOR GIN | FAPPIANO | 8 - 7 - 16 - 2 - 3 | 1.77 | 0.42 | 36 |
| 2001 | APTITUDE | A.P. INDY | NORTHERN DANCER | 10 - 5 - 19 - 0 - 0 | 2.58 | 0.74 | 34 |
| 2002 | EVENING ATTIRE | BLACK TIE AFFAIR | OUR NATIVE | 7 - 0 - 9 - 0 - 0 | 2.56 | 0.88 | 16 |
| | | | MEDIAN = | | 2.50 | 0.74 | 30.0 |

## KENTUCKY DERBY, THREE-YEAR-OLDS, 10F, DIRT:

| YEAR | WINNER | SIRE | BROODMARE SIRE | DP | DI | CD | PTS |
|---|---|---|---|---|---|---|---|
| 1990 | UNBRIDLED | FAPPIANO | LE FABULEUX | 12 - 15 - 19 - 0 - 12 | 1.70 | 0.26 | 58 |
| 1991 | STRIKE THE GOLD | ALYDAR | HATCHET MAN | 10 - 6 - 20 - 0 - 0 | 2.60 | 0.72 | 36 |
| 1992 | LIL E. TEE | AT THE THRESHOLD | FOR THE MOMENT | 6 - 2 - 8 - 0 - 0 | 3.00 | 0.88 | 16 |
| 1993 | SEA HERO | POLISH NAVY | GRAUSTARK | 3 - 5 - 22 - 4 - 2 | 1.12 | 0.08 | 36 |
| 1994 | GO FOR GIN | CORMORANT | STAGE DOOR JOHNNY | 8 - 5 - 16 - 7 - 6 | 1.00 | 0.05 | 42 |
| 1995 | THUNDER GULCH | GULCH | STORM BIRD | 10 - 2 - 8 - 0 - 0 | 4.00 | 1.10 | 20 |
| 1996 | GRINDSTONE | UNBRIDLED | DRONE | 6 - 10 - 10 - 0 - 6 | 1.91 | 0.31 | 32 |
| 1997 | SILVER CHARM | SILVER BUCK | POKER | 3 - 5 - 17 - 5 - 0 | 1.22 | 0.20 | 30 |
| 1998 | REAL QUIET | QUIET AMERICAN | BELIEVE IT | 14 - 12 - 12 - 0 - 0 | 5.33 | 1.05 | 38 |
| 1999 | CHARISMATIC | SUMMER SQUALL | DRONE | 9 - 10 - 9 - 0 - 0 | 5.22 | 1.00 | 28 |
| 2000 | FUSAICHI PEGASUS | MR. PROSPECTOR | DANZIG | 22 - 10 - 24 - 0 - 0 | 3.67 | 0.96 | 56 |
| 2001 | MONARCHOS | MARIA'S MON | DIXIELAND BAND | 2 - 2 - 13 - 1 - 0 | 1.40 | 0.28 | 18 |
| 2002 | WAR EMBLEM | OUR EMBLEM | LORD AT WAR | 9 - 4 - 8 - 1 - 0 | 3.40 | 0.95 | 22 |
| | | | MEDIAN = | | 2.60 | 0.72 | 32.0 |

## KENTUCKY OAKS, THREE-YEAR-OLD FILLIES, 9F, DIRT:

| YEAR | WINNER | SIRE | BROODMARE SIRE | DP | DI | CD | PTS |
|---|---|---|---|---|---|---|---|
| 1990 | SEASIDE ATTRACTION | SEATTLE SLEW | KEY TO THE MINT | 13 - 2 - 17 - 5 - 1 | 1.62 | 0.55 | 38 |
| 1991 | LITE LIGHT | MAJESTIC LIGHT | IN REALITY | 15 - 3 - 13 - 1 - 2 | 2.58 | 0.82 | 34 |
| 1992 | LUV ME LUV ME NOT | IT'S FREEZING | BOLD REASON | 5 - 5 - 8 - 4 - 0 | 1.75 | 0.50 | 22 |
| 1993 | DISPUTE | DANZIG | REVIEWER | 13 - 16 - 18 - 1 - 0 | 3.80 | 0.85 | 48 |
| 1994 | SARDULA | STORM CAT | HOIST THE FLAG | 7 - 7 - 9 - 0 - 3 | 2.47 | 0.58 | 26 |
| 1995 | GAL IN A RUCKUS | BOLD RUCKUS | GUMMO | 12 - 9 - 3 - 2 - 0 | 6.43 | 1.19 | 26 |
| 1996 | PIKE PLACE DANCER | SEATTLE DANCER | WAVERING MONARCH | 3 - 1 - 8 - 6 - 0 | 0.80 | 0.06 | 18 |
| 1997 | BLUSHING K. D. | BLUSHING JOHN | ROBERTO | 8 - 3 - 25 - 4 - 2 | 1.27 | 0.26 | 42 |
| 1998 | KEEPER HILL | DEPUTY MINISTER | LYPHEOR | 8 - 1 - 7 - 0 - 0 | 3.57 | 1.06 | 16 |
| 1999 | SILVERBULLETDAY | SILVER DEPUTY | TOM ROLFE | 6 - 1 - 9 - 0 - 6 | 1.10 | 0.05 | 22 |

| YEAR | WINNER | SIRE | BROODMARE SIRE | DP | DI | CD | PTS |
|---|---|---|---|---|---|---|---|
| 2000 | SECRET STATUS | A.P. INDY | ALYDAR | 9 - 4 - 18 - 0 - 1 | 2.20 | 0.63 | 32 |
| 2001 | FLUTE | SEATTLE SLEW | BLUSHING GROOM | 15 - 1 - 14 - 2 - 2 | 2.09 | 0.74 | 34 |
| 2002 | FARDA AMIGA | BROAD BRUSH | PLEASANT COLONY | 4 - 16 - 18 - 0 - 2 | 2.64 | 0.50 | 40 |
| | | | MEDIAN = | | **2.20** | **0.58** | **32.0** |

## LA BREA S, THREE-YEAR-OLD FILLIES, 7F, DIRT:

| YEAR | WINNER | SIRE | BROODMARE SIRE | DP | DI | CD | PTS |
|---|---|---|---|---|---|---|---|
| 1998 | MAGICAL ALLURE | GENERAL MEETING | NEVER BEND | 19 - 4 - 10 - 3 - 0 | 3.50 | 1.08 | 36 |
| 1999 | HOOKEDONTHEFEELIN | CITIDANCER | ALLEN'S PROSPECT | 8 - 2 - 4 - 0 - 0 | 6.00 | 1.29 | 14 |
| 2000 | SPAIN | THUNDER GULCH | REGAL AND ROYAL | 5 - 2 - 8 - 1 - 2 | 1.57 | 0.39 | 18 |
| 2001 | AFFLUENT | AFFIRMED | STRAWBERRY ROAD | 4 - 2 - 11 - 1 - 0 | 1.77 | 0.50 | 18 |
| | | | MEDIAN = | | **2.63** | **0.79** | **18.0** |

## LAS VIRGENES S, THREE-YEAR-OLD FILLIES, 7F, DIRT:

| YEAR | WINNER | SIRE | BROODMARE SIRE | DP | DI | CD | PTS |
|---|---|---|---|---|---|---|---|
| 1990 | CHEVAL VOLANT | KRIS S. | BARACHOIS | 5 - 6 - 19 - 2 - 0 | 1.78 | 0.44 | 32 |
| 1991 | LITE LIGHT | MAJESTIC LIGHT | IN REALITY | 15 - 3 - 13 - 1 - 2 | 2.58 | 0.82 | 34 |
| 1992 | MAGICAL MAIDEN | LORD AVIE | MAGESTERIAL | 6 - 7 - 5 - 0 - 0 | 6.20 | 1.06 | 18 |
| 1993 | LIKEABLE STYLE | NIJINSKY II | NO ROBBERY | 7 - 5 - 16 - 8 - 0 | 1.25 | 0.31 | 36 |
| 1994 | LAKEWAY | SEATTLE SLEW | ALYDAR | 14 - 3 - 19 - 2 - 0 | 2.30 | 0.76 | 38 |
| 1995 | SERENA'S SONG | RAHY | NORTHFIELDS | 12 - 1 - 12 - 1 - 2 | 2.11 | 0.71 | 28 |
| 1996 | ANTESPEND | SPEND A BUCK | PRACTICANTE | 2 - 3 - 7 - 0 - 0 | 2.43 | 0.58 | 12 |
| 1997 | SHARP CAT | STORM CAT | ACK ACK | 5 - 9 - 8 - 0 - 0 | 4.50 | 0.86 | 22 |
| 1998 | KEEPER HILL | DEPUTY MINISTER | LYPHEOR | 8 - 1 - 7 - 0 - 0 | 3.57 | 1.06 | 16 |
| 1999 | EXCELLENT MEETING | GENERAL MEETING | CHIEF'S CROWN | 7 - 4 - 14 - 1 - 0 | 2.25 | 0.65 | 26 |
| 2000 | SURFSIDE | SEATTLE SLEW | SEEKING THE GOLD | 14 - 2 - 16 - 2 - 0 | 2.40 | 0.82 | 34 |
| 2001 | GOLDEN BALLET | MOSCOW BALLET | SLEW O' GOLD | 6 - 2 - 11 - 5 - 0 | 1.29 | 0.38 | 24 |
| 2002 | YOU | YOU AND I | HOMEBUILDER | 5 - 2 - 9 - 1 - 1 | 1.77 | 0.50 | 18 |
| | | | MEDIAN = | | **2.30** | **0.71** | **26.0** |

## MALIBU S, THREE-YEAR-OLDS, 7F, DIRT:

| YEAR | WINNER | SIRE | BROODMARE SIRE | DP | DI | CD | PTS |
|---|---|---|---|---|---|---|---|
| 1996 | KING OF THE HEAP | ALLEN'S PROSPECT | TOPSIDER | 11 - 5 - 10 - 2 - 0 | 3.00 | 0.89 | 28 |
| 1997 | LORD GRILLO | ENGRILLADO | MATCH THE HATCH | 0 - 1 - 3 - 0 - 0 | 1.67 | 0.25 | 4 |
| 1998 | RUN MAN RUN | THEATRICAL | MARSHUA'S DANCER | 6 - 2 - 17 - 0 - 1 | 1.74 | 0.46 | 26 |
| 1999 | LOVE THAT RED | HIGHLAND PARK | CIRCLE HOME | 11 - 8 - 9 - 1 - 1 | 3.62 | 0.90 | 30 |

| | | | | | | | |
|---|---|---|---|---|---|---|---|
| 2000 | DIXIE UNION | DIXIELAND BAND | CAPOTE | 11 - 1 - 10 - 0 - 0 | 3.40 | 1.05 | 22 |
| 2001 | MIZZEN MAST | COZZENE | GRAUSTARK | 2 - 8 - 19 - 5 - 2 | 1.18 | 0.08 | 36 |
| | | | MEDIAN = | | 2.37 | 0.68 | 27.0 |

## MAN O' WAR S, THREE-YEAR-OLDS & UP, 10F, TURF:

| YEAR | WINNER | SIRE | BROODMARE SIRE | DP | DI | CD | PTS |
|---|---|---|---|---|---|---|---|
| 1990 | DEFENSIVE PLAY | FAPPIANO | SHAM | 10 - 16 - 19 - 1 - 0 | 3.38 | 0.76 | 46 |
| 1991 | SOLAR SPLENDOR | MAJESTIC LIGHT | BUCKFINDER | 6 - 6 - 11 - 1 - 2 | 2.06 | 0.50 | 26 |
| 1992 | SOLAR SPLENDOR | MAJESTIC LIGHT | BUCKFINDER | 6 - 6 - 11 - 1 - 2 | 2.06 | 0.50 | 26 |
| 1993 | STAR OF COZZENE | COZZENE | PIA STAR | 10 - 7 - 10 - 9 - 0 | 1.57 | 0.50 | 36 |
| 1994 | ROYAL MOUNTAIN INN | VIGORS | PIA STAR | 10 - 6 - 4 - 10 - 2 | 1.29 | 0.38 | 32 |
| 1995 | MILLKOM | CYRANO DE BERGERAC | MUMMY'S GAME | 4 - 2 - 0 - 0 - 0 | 1.67 | | 6 |
| 1996 | DIPLOMATIC JET | ROMAN DIPLOMAT | TRI JET | 6 - 4 - 14 - 0 - 0 | 2.43 | 0.67 | 24 |
| 1997 | INFLUENT | ASCOT KNIGHT | KEY TO THE MINT | 6 - 5 - 13 - 3 - 1 | 1.67 | 0.43 | 28 |
| 1998 | DAYLAMI | DOYOUN | MISWAKI | 8 - 4 - 9 - 5 - 2 | 1.43 | 0.39 | 28 |
| 1999 | VAL'S PRINCE | ETERNAL PRINCE | VALID APPEAL | 13 - 3 - 6 - 0 - 0 | 6.33 | 1.32 | 22 |
| 2000 | FANTASTIC LIGHT | RAHY | NIJINSKY II | 12 - 0 - 18 - 6 - 2 | 1.24 | 0.37 | 38 |
| 2001 | WITH ANTICIPATION | RELAUNCH | SAROS | 7 - 3 - 6 - 2 - 0 | 2.60 | 0.83 | 18 |
| 2002 | WITH ANTICIPATION | RELAUNCH | SAROS | 7 - 3 - 6 - 2 - 0 | 2.60 | 0.83 | 18 |
| | | | MEDIAN = | | 2.06 | 0.50 | 26.0 |

## MANHATTAN H, THREE-YEAR-OLDS & UP, 10F, TURF:

| YEAR | WINNER | SIRE | BROODMARE SIRE | DP | DI | CD | PTS |
|---|---|---|---|---|---|---|---|
| 1995 | AWAD | CAVEAT | NOBLE DANCER | 2 - 6 - 4 - 1 - 1 | 2.50 | 0.50 | 14 |
| 1996 | DIPLOMATIC JET | ROMAN DIPLOMAT | TRI JET | 6 - 4 - 14 - 0 - 0 | 2.43 | 0.67 | 24 |
| 1997 | OPS SMILE | CAVEAT | NORTHERN JOVE | 6 - 5 - 6 - 0 - 1 | 3.50 | 0.83 | 18 |
| 1998 | CHIEF BEARHART | CHIEF'S CROWN | BOLD HOUR | 7 - 10 - 11 - 0 - 2 | 3.00 | 0.67 | 30 |
| 1999 | YAGLI | JADE HUNTER | NIJINSKY II | 10 - 2 - 16 - 4 - 0 | 1.67 | 0.56 | 32 |
| 2000 | MANNDAR | DOYOUN | DIESIS | 6 - 3 - 6 - 5 - 0 | 1.50 | 0.50 | 20 |
| 2001 | FORBIDDEN APPLE | PLEASANT COLONY | NORTHFIELDS | 4 - 0 - 16 - 0 - 2 | 1.20 | 0.18 | 22 |
| 2002 | BEAT HOLLOW | SADLER'S WELLS | DANCING BRAVE | 7 - 2 - 25 - 12 - 0 | 0.88 | 0.09 | 46 |
| | | | MEDIAN = | | 2.05 | 0.53 | 23.0 |

**MATRIARCH S, THREE-YEAR-OLDS & UP, FILLIES & MARES, 9F, TURF:**

| YEAR | WINNER | SIRE | BROODMARE SIRE | DP | DI | CD | PTS |
|---|---|---|---|---|---|---|---|
| 1990 | COUNTUS IN | DANCING COUNT | CLOUDY DAWN | 11 - 3 - 7 - 1 - 0 | 3.89 | 1.09 | 22 |
| 1991 | FLAWLESSLY | AFFIRMED | NIJINSKY II | 6 - 2 - 15 - 9 - 0 | 0.94 | 0.16 | 32 |
| 1992 | FLAWLESSLY | AFFIRMED | NIJINSKY II | 6 - 2 - 15 - 9 - 0 | 0.94 | 0.16 | 32 |
| 1993 | FLAWLESSLY | AFFIRMED | NIJINSKY II | 6 - 2 - 15 - 9 - 0 | 0.94 | 0.16 | 32 |
| 1994 | EXCHANGE | EXPLODENT | IRISH STRONGHOLD | 7 - 4 - 3 - 0 - 6 | 1.67 | 0.30 | 20 |
| 1995 | DUDA | THEATRICAL | DRUMS OF TIME | 2 - 0 - 15 - 2 - 1 | 0.90 | 0.00 | 20 |
| 1996 | WANDESTA | NASHWAN | NIJINSKY II | 8 - 0 - 12 - 6 - 2 | 1.00 | 0.21 | 28 |
| 1997 | RYAFAN | LEAR FAN | NORTHERN DANCER | 6 - 3 - 24 - 2 - 1 | 1.40 | 0.31 | 36 |
| 1998 | SQUEAK | SELKIRK | SIR IVOR | 6 - 9 - 11 - 0 - 0 | 3.73 | 0.81 | 26 |
| 1999 | HAPPYANUNOIT | YACHTIE | RAJAH | 0 - 2 - 2 - 0 - 0 | 3.00 | 0.50 | 4 |
| 2000 | TOUT CHARMANT | SLEWVESCENT | BATONNIER | 4 - 2 - 13 - 2 - 3 | 1.09 | 0.08 | 24 |
| 2001 | STARINE | MENDOCINO | KALDOUN | 2 - 7 - 11 - 2 - 0 | 1.93 | 0.41 | 22 |
| | | | MEDIAN = | | **1.24** | **0.26** | **25.0** |

**MATRON S, TWO-YEAR-OLD FILLIES, 8F, DIRT:**

| YEAR | WINNER | SIRE | BROODMARE SIRE | DP | DI | CD | PTS |
|---|---|---|---|---|---|---|---|
| 1990 | MEADOW STAR | MEADOWLAKE | IN REALITY | 15 - 11 - 10 - 0 - 0 | 6.20 | 1.14 | 36 |
| 1991 | ANH DUONG | MOGAMBO | BOLD COMMANDER | 16 - 4 - 6 - 0 - 0 | 7.67 | 1.38 | 26 |
| 1992 | SKY BEAUTY | BLUSHING GROOM | NIJINSKY II | 21 - 0 - 17 - 4 - 4 | 1.79 | 0.65 | 46 |
| 1993 | STRATEGIC MANEUVER | CRYPTOCLEARANCE | CONQUISTADOR CIELO | 13 - 8 - 14 - 0 - 1 | 3.50 | 0.89 | 36 |
| 1994 | FLANDERS | SEEKING THE GOLD | STORM BIRD | 11 - 6 - 15 - 0 - 0 | 3.27 | 0.88 | 32 |
| 1995 | GOLDEN ATTRACTION | MR. PROSPECTOR | SEATTLE SLEW | 24 - 6 - 21 - 1 - 0 | 3.52 | 1.02 | 52 |
| 1996 | SHARP CAT | STORM CAT | ACK ACK | 5 - 9 - 8 - 0 - 0 | 4.50 | 0.86 | 22 |
| 1997 | BEAUTIFUL PLEASURE | MAUDLIN | BALDSKI | 11 - 10 - 5 - 2 - 0 | 5.22 | 1.07 | 28 |
| 1998 | OH WHAT A WINDFALL | SEEKING THE GOLD | NIJINSKY II | 10 - 3 - 17 - 4 - 0 | 1.72 | 0.56 | 34 |
| 1999 | FINDER'S FEE | STORM CAT | MR. PROSPECTOR | 11 - 5 - 10 - 0 - 0 | 4.20 | 1.04 | 26 |
| 2000 | RAGING FEVER | STORM CAT | SEATTLE SLEW | 8 - 4 - 8 - 0 - 0 | 4.00 | 1.00 | 20 |
| 2001 | NOT RUN | | | | | | |
| 2002 | STORM FLAG FLYING | STORM CAT | EASY GOER | 6 - 5 - 11 - 0 - 0 | 3.00 | 0.77 | 22 |
| | | | MEDIAN = | | **3.76** | **0.94** | **30.0** |

**METROPOLITAN H, THREE-YEAR-OLDS & UP, 8F, DIRT:**

| YEAR | WINNER | SIRE | BROODMARE SIRE | DP | DI | CD | PTS |
|---|---|---|---|---|---|---|---|
| 1990 | CRIMINAL TYPE | ALYDAR | NO ROBBERY | 10 - 6 - 20 - 0 - 0 | 2.60 | 0.72 | 36 |
| 1991 | IN EXCESS | SIBERIAN EXPRESS | SAULINGO | 4 - 4 - 4 - 0 - 0 | 5.00 | 1.00 | 12 |

| YEAR | WINNER | SIRE | BROODMARE SIRE | DP | DI | CD | PTS |
|---|---|---|---|---|---|---|---|
| 1992 | DIXIE BRASS | DIXIELAND BAND | SHAM | 6- 3- 10- 1- 0 | 2.33 | 0.70 | 20 |
| 1993 | IBERO | CINCO GRANDE | TREVIGLIO | 8- 10- 6- 1- 1 | 4.20 | 0.88 | 26 |
| 1994 | HOLY BULL | GREAT ABOVE | AL HATTAB | 6- 5- 4- 1- 0 | 4.33 | 1.00 | 16 |
| 1995 | YOU AND I | KRIS S. | UPS | 3- 6- 15- 2- 0 | 1.74 | 0.38 | 26 |
| 1996 | HONOUR AND GLORY | RELAUNCH | AL NASR | 10- 4- 12- 0- 0 | 3.33 | 0.92 | 26 |
| 1997 | LANGFUHR | DANZIG | BRIARTIC | 6- 11- 15- 2- 0 | 2.58 | 0.62 | 34 |
| 1998 | WILD RUSH | WILD AGAIN | PLUGGED NICKLE | 8- 6- 13- 1- 0 | 2.73 | 0.75 | 28 |
| 1999 | SIR BEAR | SIR LEON | BET BIG | 1- 3- 8- 4- 0 | 1.00 | 0.06 | 16 |
| 2000 | YANKEE VICTOR | SAINT BALLADO | CARO | 8- 6- 14- 2- 2 | 1.91 | 0.50 | 32 |
| 2001 | EXCITING STORY | DIABLO | VALID APPEAL | 9- 3- 11- 1- 0 | 2.69 | 0.83 | 24 |
| 2002 | SWEPT OVERBOARD | END SWEEP | CUTLASS | 5- 2- 6- 0- 1 | 2.50 | 0.71 | 14 |
|  |  |  | MEDIAN = | | 2.60 | 0.72 | 26.0 |

## MILADY BREEDERS' CUP H, THREE-YEAR-OLDS & UP, FILLIES & MARES, 8.5F, DIRT:

| YEAR | WINNER | SIRE | BROODMARE SIRE | DP | DI | CD | PTS |
|---|---|---|---|---|---|---|---|
| 1990 | BAYAKOA | CONSULTANT'S BID | GOOD MANNERS | 8- 8- 6- 0- 0 | 6.33 | 1.09 | 22 |
| 1991 | BROUGHT TO MIND | RUTHIE'S NATIVE | ICECAPADE | 11- 2- 16- 1- 0 | 2.33 | 0.77 | 30 |
| 1992 | PASEANA | AHMAD | FLINTHAM | 4- 4- 2- 0- 0 | 9.00 | 1.20 | 10 |
| 1993 | PASEANA | AHMAD | FLINTHAM | 4- 4- 2- 0- 0 | 9.00 | 1.20 | 10 |
| 1994 | ANDESTINE | NATIVE PROSPECTOR | DON B. | 10- 2- 10- 0- 0 | 3.40 | 1.00 | 22 |
| 1995 | PIRATE'S REVENGE | PIRATE'S BOUNTY | FLYING PASTER | 6- 5- 6- 0- 3 | 2.33 | 0.55 | 20 |
| 1996 | TWICE THE VICE | VICE REGENT | RESURGENT | 9- 2- 10- 1- 0 | 2.67 | 0.86 | 22 |
| 1997 | LISTENING | NIGHT SHIFT | SECRETARIAT | 9- 9- 11- 1- 0 | 3.62 | 0.87 | 30 |
| 1998 | I AIN'T BLUFFING | PINE BLUFF | RAISE A CUP | 8- 6- 14- 2- 2 | 1.91 | 0.50 | 32 |
| 1999 | GOURMET GIRL | CEE'S TIZZY | WELSH PAGEANT | 8- 1- 11- 0- 0 | 2.64 | 0.85 | 20 |
| 2000 | RIBOLETTA | ROI NORMAND | GHADEER | 7- 1- 18- 0- 0 | 1.89 | 0.58 | 26 |
| 2001 | LAZY SLUSAN | SLEWVESCENT | TOPSIDER | 7- 1- 8- 4- 2 | 1.20 | 0.32 | 22 |
| 2002 | AZERI | JADE HUNTER | AHONOORA | 9- 2- 9- 0- 0 | 3.44 | 1.00 | 20 |
|  |  |  | MEDIAN = | | 2.67 | 0.86 | 22.0 |

## MOTHER GOOSE S, THREE-YEAR-OLD FILLIES, 8F, DIRT:

| YEAR | WINNER | SIRE | BROODMARE SIRE | DP | DI | CD | PTS |
|---|---|---|---|---|---|---|---|
| 1990 | GO FOR WAND | DEPUTY MINISTER | CYANE | 6- 2- 4- 0- 0 | 5.00 | 1.17 | 12 |
| 1991 | MEADOW STAR | MEADOWLAKE | IN REALITY | 15- 11- 10- 0- 0 | 6.20 | 1.14 | 36 |
| 1992 | TURNBACK THE ALARM | DARN THAT ALARM | FIGONERO | 0- 4- 8- 0- 0 | 2.00 | 0.33 | 12 |
| 1993 | SKY BEAUTY | BLUSHING GROOM | NIJINSKY II | 21- 0- 17- 4- 4 | 1.79 | 0.65 | 46 |

| YEAR | WINNER | SIRE | BROODMARE SIRE | | | DP | | | DI | CD | PTS |
|------|--------|------|----------------|---|---|----|---|---|----|----|-----|
| 1994 | LAKEWAY | SEATTLE SLEW | ALYDAR | 14 - | 3 - | 19 - | 2 - | 0 | 2.30 | 0.76 | 38 |
| 1995 | SERENA'S SONG | RAHY | NORTHFIELDS | 12 - | 1 - | 12 - | 1 - | 2 | 2.11 | 0.71 | 28 |
| 1997 | AJINA | STRAWBERRY ROAD | ALYDAR | 8 - | 4 - | 14 - | 2 - | 0 | 2.11 | 0.64 | 28 |
| 1998 | JERSEY GIRL | BELONG TO ME | VALID APPEAL | 8 - | 8 - | 16 - | 0 - | 0 | 3.00 | 0.75 | 32 |
| 1999 | DREAMS GALLORE | SILVER GHOST | FIT TO FIGHT | 14 - | 2 - | 12 - | 0 - | 0 | 3.67 | 1.07 | 28 |
| 2000 | SECRET STATUS | A.P. INDY | ALYDAR | 9 - | 4 - | 18 - | 0 - | 1 | 2.20 | 0.63 | 32 |
| 2001 | FLEET RENEE | SEATTLE SLEW | MR. LEADER | 10 - | 3 - | 15 - | 2 - | 0 | 2.16 | 0.70 | 30 |
| 2002 | NONSUCH BAY | MR. GREELEY | LIGHT IDEA | 7 - | 2 - | 7 - | 0 - | 0 | 3.57 | 1.00 | 16 |
| | | | | | | MEDIAN = | | | 2.25 | 0.73 | 29.0 |

## OAK LEAF S, TWO-YEAR-OLD FILLIES, 8F, DIRT:

| YEAR | WINNER | SIRE | BROODMARE SIRE | | | DP | | | DI | CD | PTS |
|------|--------|------|----------------|---|---|----|---|---|----|----|-----|
| 1993 | PHONE CHATTER | PHONE TRICK | PASS THE GLASS | 4 - | 3 - | 7 - | 0 - | 0 | 3.00 | 0.79 | 14 |
| 1994 | SERENA'S SONG | RAHY | NORTHFIELDS | 12 - | 1 - | 12 - | 1 - | 2 | 2.11 | 0.71 | 28 |
| 1995 | TIPICALLY IRISH | METFIELD | FULL OUT | 10 - | 4 - | 8 - | 2 - | 0 | 3.00 | 0.92 | 24 |
| 1996 | CITY BAND | CARSON CITY | MIGHTY APPEALING | 11 - | 2 - | 12 - | 1 - | 0 | 2.71 | 0.88 | 26 |
| 1997 | VIVID ANGEL | SEPTIEME CIEL | EXCLUSIVE NATIVE | 8 - | 2 - | 14 - | 6 - | 0 | 1.31 | 0.40 | 30 |
| 1998 | EXCELLENT MEETING | GENERAL MEETING | CHIEF'S CROWN | 7 - | 4 - | 14 - | 1 - | 0 | 2.25 | 0.65 | 26 |
| 1999 | CHILUKKI | CHEROKEE RUN | DAMASCUS | 7 - | 8 - | 7 - | 0 - | 0 | 5.29 | 1.00 | 22 |
| 2000 | NOTABLE CAREER | AVENUE OF FLAGS | SMARTEN | 7 - | 2 - | 9 - | 2 - | 0 | 2.08 | 0.70 | 20 |
| 2001 | TALI'SLUCKYBUSRIDE | DELINEATOR | LORD AT WAR | 4 - | 4 - | 3 - | 1 - | 0 | 3.80 | 0.92 | 12 |
| | | | | | | MEDIAN = | | | 2.71 | 0.79 | 24.0 |

## OAKLAWN H, FOUR-YEAR-OLDS & UP, 9F, DIRT:

| YEAR | WINNER | SIRE | BROODMARE SIRE | | | DP | | | DI | CD | PTS |
|------|--------|------|----------------|---|---|----|---|---|----|----|-----|
| 1990 | OPENING VERSE | THE MINSTREL | GREY DAWN II | 9 - | 8 - | 9 - | 2 - | 2 | 2.53 | 0.67 | 30 |
| 1991 | FESTIN | MAT-BOY | CON BRIO II | 0 - | 2 - | 2 - | 0 - | 2 | 1.00 | -0.33 | 6 |
| 1992 | BEST PAL | HABITONY | KING PELLINORE | 11 - | 6 - | 4 - | 5 - | 0 | 2.71 | 0.88 | 26 |
| 1993 | JOVIAL | NORTHERN JOVE | STOP THE MUSIC | 7 - | 4 - | 11 - | 0 - | 0 | 3.00 | 0.82 | 22 |
| 1994 | THE WICKED NORTH | FAR NORTH | GOOD BEHAVING | 5 - | 1 - | 8 - | 0 - | 0 | 2.50 | 0.79 | 14 |
| 1995 | CIGAR | PALACE MUSIC | SEATTLE SLEW | 7 - | 2 - | 10 - | 1 - | 0 | 2.33 | 0.75 | 20 |
| 1996 | GERI | THEATRICAL | MR. PROSPECTOR | 12 - | 3 - | 21 - | 0 - | 0 | 2.43 | 0.75 | 36 |
| 1997 | ATTICUS | NUREYEV | SECRETARIAT | 9 - | 4 - | 30 - | 1 - | 0 | 1.75 | 0.48 | 44 |
| 1998 | PRECOCITY | AFERD | SUPER CONCORDE | 10 - | 4 - | 7 - | 0 - | 3 | 2.69 | 0.75 | 24 |
| 1999 | BEHRENS | PLEASANT COLONY | MARI'S BOOK | 5 - | 0 - | 15 - | 0 - | 2 | 1.32 | 0.27 | 22 |
| 2000 | K ONE KING | APALACHEE | NATIVE CHARGER | 22 - | 6 - | 4 - | 10 - | 0 | 2.50 | 0.95 | 42 |

| | | | | DP | DI | CD | PTS |
|---|---|---|---|---|---|---|---|
| 2001 | TRADITIONALLY | MR. PROSPECTOR | PRIVATE ACCOUNT | 20 - 10 - 19 - 0 - 1 | 3.76 | 0.96 | 50 |
| 2002 | KUDOS | KRIS S. | DAMASCUS | 7 - 10 - 19 - 2 - 0 | 2.30 | 0.58 | 38 |
| | | | | MEDIAN = | 2.50 | 0.75 | 26.0 |

## OGDEN PHIPPS H*, THREE-YEAR-OLDS & UP, FILLIES & MARES, 8.5F, DIRT:

| YEAR | WINNER | SIRE | BROODMARE SIRE | DP | DI | CD | PTS |
|---|---|---|---|---|---|---|---|
| 1990 | FANTASTIC FIND | MR. PROSPECTOR | RIVA RIDGE | 21 - 7 - 14 - 0 - 0 | 5.00 | 1.17 | 42 |
| 1991 | A WILD RIDE | WILD AGAIN | INVERNESS DRIVE | 10 - 6 - 8 - 1 - 1 | 3.33 | 0.88 | 26 |
| 1992 | MISSY'S MIRAGE | STOP THE MUSIC | RIVA RIDGE | 8 - 8 - 14 - 0 - 0 | 3.29 | 0.80 | 30 |
| 1993 | TURNBACK THE ALARM | DARN THAT ALARM | FIGONERO | 0 - 4 - 8 - 0 - 0 | 2.00 | 0.33 | 12 |
| 1994 | SKY BEAUTY | BLUSHING GROOM | NIJINSKY II | 21 - 0 - 17 - 4 - 4 | 1.79 | 0.65 | 46 |
| 1995 | HEAVENLY PRIZE | SEEKING THE GOLD | NIJINSKY II | 10 - 3 - 17 - 4 - 0 | 1.72 | 0.56 | 34 |
| 1996 | SERENA'S SONG | RAHY | NORTHFIELDS | 12 - 1 - 12 - 1 - 2 | 2.11 | 0.71 | 28 |
| 1997 | HIDDEN LAKE | QUIET AMERICAN | ROUND TABLE | 7 - 12 - 9 - 10 - 0 | 1.62 | 0.42 | 38 |
| 1998 | MOSSFLOWER | AFFIRMED | GREEN DANCER | 5 - 1 - 12 - 4 - 0 | 1.20 | 0.32 | 22 |
| 1999 | SISTER ACT | SAINT BALLADO | ICECAPADE | 10 - 3 - 19 - 2 - 2 | 1.67 | 0.47 | 36 |
| 2000 | BEAUTIFUL PLEASURE | MAUDLIN | BALDSKI | 11 - 10 - 5 - 2 - 0 | 5.22 | 1.07 | 28 |
| 2001 | CRITICAL EYE | DYNAFORMER | DR. BLUM | 4 - 7 - 22 - 0 - 1 | 1.83 | 0.38 | 34 |
| 2002 | RAGING FEVER | STORM CAT | SEATTLE SLEW | 8 - 4 - 8 - 0 - 0 | 4.00 | 1.00 | 20 |
| | | | | MEDIAN = | 2.00 | 0.65 | 30.0 |

* RUN AS THE HEMPSTEAD H AT 9F PRIOR TO 2002

## PACIFIC CLASSIC S, THREE-YEAR-OLDS & UP, 10F, DIRT:

| YEAR | WINNER | SIRE | BROODMARE SIRE | DP | DI | CD | PTS |
|---|---|---|---|---|---|---|---|
| 1994 | TINNERS WAY | SECRETARIAT | THE MINSTREL | 11 - 14 - 13 - 4 - 0 | 3.00 | 0.76 | 42 |
| 1995 | TINNERS WAY | SECRETARIAT | THE MINSTREL | 11 - 14 - 13 - 4 - 0 | 3.00 | 0.76 | 42 |
| 1996 | DARE AND GO | ALYDAR | SECRETARIAT | 15 - 12 - 23 - 2 - 0 | 2.85 | 0.77 | 52 |
| 1997 | GENTLEMEN | ROBIN DES BOIS | LOOSE CANNON | 5 - 0 - 19 - 4 - 0 | 1.07 | 0.21 | 28 |
| 1998 | FREE HOUSE | SMOKESTER | VIGORS | 8 - 4 - 5 - 3 - 0 | 2.64 | 0.85 | 20 |
| 1999 | GENERAL CHALLENGE | GENERAL MEETING | SMARTEN | 9 - 1 - 11 - 3 - 0 | 1.82 | 0.67 | 24 |
| 2000 | SKIMMING | NUREYEV | LYPHARD | 10 - 2 - 36 - 0 - 0 | 1.67 | 0.46 | 48 |
| 2001 | SKIMMING | NUREYEV | LYPHARD | 10 - 2 - 36 - 0 - 0 | 1.67 | 0.46 | 48 |
| 2002 | CAME HOME | GONE WEST | CLEVER TRICK | 12 - 6 - 12 - 0 - 0 | 4.00 | 1.00 | 30 |
| | | | | MEDIAN = | 2.64 | 0.76 | 42.0 |

**PIMLICO SPECIAL H, THREE-YEAR-OLDS & UP, 9.5F, DIRT:**

| YEAR | WINNER | SIRE | BROODMARE SIRE | DP | DI | CD | PTS |
|---|---|---|---|---|---|---|---|
| 1990 | CRIMINAL TYPE | ALYDAR | NO ROBBERY | 10 - 6 - 20 - 0 - 0 | 2.60 | 0.72 | 36 |
| 1991 | FARMA WAY | MARFA | DIPLOMAT WAY | 7 - 5 - 3 - 1 - 0 | 5.40 | 1.13 | 16 |
| 1992 | STRIKE THE GOLD | ALYDAR | HATCHET MAN | 10 - 6 - 20 - 0 - 0 | 2.60 | 0.72 | 36 |
| 1993 | DEVIL HIS DUE | DEVIL'S BAG | RAISE A CUP | 13 - 3 - 12 - 2 - 2 | 2.20 | 0.72 | 32 |
| 1994 | AS INDICATED | CZARAVICH | OUR MICHAEL | 2 - 2 - 6 - 4 - 0 | 1.00 | 0.14 | 14 |
| 1995 | CIGAR | PALACE MUSIC | SEATTLE SLEW | 7 - 2 - 10 - 1 - 0 | 2.33 | 0.75 | 20 |
| 1996 | STAR STANDARD | RISEN STAR | HOIST THE FLAG | 8 - 11 - 16 - 1 - 4 | 2.08 | 0.45 | 40 |
| 1997 | GENTLEMEN | ROBIN DES BOIS | LOOSE CANNON | 5 - 0 - 19 - 4 - 0 | 1.07 | 0.21 | 28 |
| 1998 | SKIP AWAY | SKIP TRIAL | DIPLOMAT WAY | 5 - 6 - 8 - 1 - 0 | 3.00 | 0.75 | 20 |
| 1999 | REAL QUIET | QUIET AMERICAN | BELIEVE IT | 14 - 12 - 12 - 0 - 0 | 5.33 | 1.05 | 38 |
| 2000 | GOLDEN MISSILE | A.P. INDY | CURE THE BLUES | 5 - 5 - 12 - 0 - 0 | 2.67 | 0.68 | 22 |
| 2001 | INCLUDE | BROAD BRUSH | STOP THE MUSIC | 7 - 20 - 19 - 1 - 1 | 3.17 | 0.65 | 48 |
| | | | MEDIAN = | | 2.60 | 0.72 | 30.0 |

**PREAKNESS S, THREE-YEAR-OLDS, 9.5F, DIRT:**

| YEAR | WINNER | SIRE | BROODMARE SIRE | DP | DI | CD | PTS |
|---|---|---|---|---|---|---|---|
| 1990 | SUMMER SQUALL | STORM BIRD | SECRETARIAT | 9 - 10 - 16 - 1 - 0 | 3.00 | 0.75 | 36 |
| 1991 | HANSEL | WOODMAN | DANCING COUNT | 10 - 3 - 13 - 2 - 0 | 2.29 | 0.75 | 28 |
| 1992 | PINE BLUFF | DANZIG | HALO | 10 - 12 - 22 - 0 - 0 | 3.00 | 0.73 | 44 |
| 1993 | PRAIRIE BAYOU | LITTLE MISSOURI | WAVERING MONARCH | 6 - 4 - 6 - 0 - 0 | 4.33 | 1.00 | 16 |
| 1994 | TABASCO CAT | STORM CAT | SAUCE BOAT | 7 - 5 - 7 - 1 - 0 | 3.44 | 0.90 | 20 |
| 1995 | TIMBER COUNTRY | WOODMAN | PRETENSE | 11 - 5 - 22 - 0 - 0 | 2.45 | 0.71 | 38 |
| 1996 | LOUIS QUATORZE | SOVEREIGN DANCER | ON TO GLORY | 11 - 7 - 8 - 0 - 0 | 5.50 | 1.12 | 26 |
| 1997 | SILVER CHARM | SILVER BUCK | POKER | 3 - 5 - 17 - 5 - 0 | 1.22 | 0.20 | 30 |
| 1998 | REAL QUIET | QUIET AMERICAN | BELIEVE IT | 14 - 12 - 12 - 0 - 0 | 5.33 | 1.05 | 38 |
| 1999 | CHARISMATIC | SUMMER SQUALL | DRONE | 9 - 10 - 9 - 0 - 0 | 5.22 | 1.00 | 28 |
| 2000 | RED BULLET | UNBRIDLED | CARO | 7 - 10 - 11 - 0 - 6 | 1.96 | 0.35 | 34 |
| 2001 | POINT GIVEN | THUNDER GULCH | TURKOMAN | 8 - 0 - 8 - 0 - 0 | 3.00 | 1.00 | 16 |
| 2002 | WAR EMBLEM | OUR EMBLEM | LORD AT WAR | 9 - 4 - 8 - 1 - 0 | 3.40 | 0.95 | 22 |
| | | | MEDIAN = | | 3.00 | 0.90 | 28.0 |

## QUEEN ELIZABETH II CHALLENGE CUP S, THREE-YEAR-OLD FILLIES, 9F, TURF:

| YEAR | WINNER | SIRE | BROODMARE SIRE | DP | DI | CD | PTS |
|---|---|---|---|---|---|---|---|
| 1990 | PLENTY OF GRACE | ROBERTO | KEY TO THE MINT | 11 - 5 - 38 - 5 - 1 | 1.40 | 0.33 | 60 |
| 1991 | LA GUERIERE | LORD AT WAR | SECRETARIAT | 5 - 8 - 11 - 1 - 1 | 2.47 | 0.58 | 26 |
| 1992 | CAPTIVE MISS | ACAROID | SECRETARIAT | 7 - 10 - 11 - 4 - 4 | 1.67 | 0.33 | 36 |
| 1993 | TRIBULATION | DANZIG | HIS MAJESTY | 9 - 12 - 27 - 0 - 2 | 2.23 | 0.52 | 50 |
| 1994 | DANISH | DANEHILL | SASSAFRAS | 2 - 4 - 13 - 0 - 3 | 1.32 | 0.09 | 22 |
| 1995 | PERFECT ARC | BROWN ARC | PETRONISI | 2 - 5 - 4 - 0 - 3 | 1.80 | 0.21 | 14 |
| 1996 | MEMORIES OF SILVER | SILVER HAWK | LITTLE CURRENT | 4 - 2 - 17 - 6 - 1 | 0.94 | 0.07 | 30 |
| 1997 | RYAFAN | LEAR FAN | NORTHERN DANCER | 6 - 3 - 24 - 2 - 1 | 1.40 | 0.31 | 36 |
| 1998 | TENSKI | POLISH NUMBERS | LORD GAYLORD | 3 - 8 - 13 - 0 - 0 | 2.69 | 0.58 | 24 |
| 1999 | PERFECT STING | RED RANSOM | VALID APPEAL | 5 - 9 - 18 - 0 - 0 | 2.56 | 0.59 | 32 |
| 2000 | COLLECT THE CASH | DYNAFORMER | VALID APPEAL | 7 - 7 - 21 - 0 - 1 | 2.13 | 0.53 | 36 |
| 2001 | AFFLUENT | AFFIRMED | STRAWBERRY ROAD | 4 - 2 - 11 - 1 - 0 | 1.77 | 0.50 | 18 |
| 2002 | RISKAVERSE | DYNAFORMER | SEEKING THE GOLD | 8 - 2 - 25 - 0 - 1 | 1.67 | 0.44 | 36 |
| | | | | MEDIAN = | 1.77 | 0.44 | 32.0 |

## RAMONA H, THREE-YEAR-OLDS & UP, FILLIES & MARES, 9F, TURF:

| YEAR | WINNER | SIRE | BROODMARE SIRE | DP | DI | CD | PTS |
|---|---|---|---|---|---|---|---|
| 1990 | DOUBLE WEDGE | NORTHERN BABY | SPRING DOUBLE | 10 - 2 - 7 - 5 - 0 | 1.82 | 0.71 | 24 |
| 1991 | CAMPAGNARDE | OAK DANCER | LEFTY | 1 - 1 - 9 - 5 - 2 | 0.57 | -0.33 | 18 |
| 1992 | FLAWLESSLY | AFFIRMED | NIJINSKY II | 6 - 2 - 15 - 9 - 0 | 0.94 | 0.16 | 32 |
| 1993 | FLAWLESSLY | AFFIRMED | NIJINSKY II | 6 - 2 - 15 - 9 - 0 | 0.94 | 0.16 | 32 |
| 1994 | FLAWLESSLY | AFFIRMED | NIJINSKY II | 6 - 2 - 15 - 9 - 0 | 0.94 | 0.16 | 32 |
| 1995 | POSSIBLY PERFECT | NORTHERN BABY | AVATAR | 5 - 2 - 9 - 7 - 1 | 0.92 | 0.13 | 24 |
| 1996 | MATIARA | BERING | NUREYEV | 3 - 0 - 21 - 4 - 2 | 0.82 | -0.07 | 30 |
| 1997 | ESCENA | STRAWBERRY ROAD | SEATTLE SLEW | 11 - 1 - 8 - 2 - 0 | 2.67 | 0.95 | 22 |
| 1998 | SEE YOU SOON | KALDOUN | AKARAD | 2 - 4 - 6 - 2 - 0 | 1.80 | 0.43 | 14 |
| 1999 | TUZLA | PANORAMIC | KAUTOKEINO | 2 - 0 - 11 - 7 - 0 | 0.60 | -0.15 | 20 |
| 2000 | CAFFE LATTE | SEATTLE DANCER | ARCTIC TERN | 7 - 1 - 8 -10 - 0 | 0.86 | 0.19 | 26 |
| 2001 | JANET | EMPEROR JONES | SPECTACULAR BID | 7 - 7 - 10 - 0 - 0 | 3.80 | 0.88 | 24 |
| 2002 | AFFLUENT | AFFIRMED | STRAWBERRY ROAD | 4 - 2 - 11 - 1 - 0 | 1.77 | 0.50 | 18 |
| | | | | MEDIAN = | 0.94 | 0.16 | 24.0 |

**RUFFIAN H, THREE-YEAR-OLDS & UP, FILLIES & MARES, 8.5F, DIRT:**

| YEAR | WINNER | SIRE | BROODMARE SIRE | DP | DI | CD | PTS |
|---|---|---|---|---|---|---|---|
| 1990 | QUICK MISCHIEF | DISTINCTIVE PRO | PRONTO | 10 - 4 - 7 - 0 - 1 | 3.89 | 1.00 | 22 |
| 1991 | QUEENA | MR. PROSPECTOR | BLUSHING GROOM | 25 - 10 - 19 - 0 - 2 | 3.87 | 1.00 | 56 |
| 1992 | VERSAILLES TREATY | DANZIG | BUCKPASSER | 5 - 17 - 28 - 0 - 0 | 2.57 | 0.54 | 50 |
| 1993 | SHARED INTEREST | PLEASANT COLONY | DR. FAGER | 8 - 10 - 16 - 0 - 2 | 2.60 | 0.61 | 36 |
| 1994 | SKY BEAUTY | BLUSHING GROOM | NIJINSKY II | 21 - 0 - 17 - 4 - 4 | 1.79 | 0.65 | 46 |
| 1995 | INSIDE INFORMATION | PRIVATE ACCOUNT | KEY TO THE MINT | 10 - 9 - 17 - 3 - 1 | 2.20 | 0.60 | 40 |
| 1996 | YANKS MUSIC | AIR FORBES WON | DARBY CREEK ROAD | 4 - 3 - 7 - 0 - 0 | 3.00 | 0.79 | 14 |
| 1997 | TOMISUE'S DELIGHT | A.P. INDY | MR. PROSPECTOR | 15 - 7 - 16 - 1 - 1 | 3.00 | 0.85 | 40 |
| 1998 | SHARP CAT | STORM CAT | ACK ACK | 5 - 9 - 8 - 0 - 0 | 4.50 | 0.86 | 22 |
| 1999 | CATINCA | STORM CAT | SARATOGA SIX | 6 - 4 - 12 - 0 - 0 | 2.67 | 0.73 | 22 |
| 2000 | RIBOLETTA | ROI NORMAND | GHADEER | 7 - 1 - 18 - 0 - 0 | 1.89 | 0.58 | 26 |
| 2001 | NOT RUN | | | | | | |
| 2002 | MANDY'S GOLD | GILDED TIME | ALOMA'S RULER | 7 - 7 - 3 - 1 - 0 | 6.20 | 1.11 | 18 |
| | | | MEDIAN = | | 2.83 | 0.76 | 31.0 |

**SAN JUAN CAPISTRANO INVITATIONAL H, FOUR-YEAR-OLDS & UP, 14F, TURF:**

| YEAR | WINNER | SIRE | BROODMARE SIRE | DP | DI | CD | PTS |
|---|---|---|---|---|---|---|---|
| 1990 | DELEGANT | GREY DAWN II | VAGUELY NOBLE | 9 - 10 - 16 - 5 - 8 | 1.29 | 0.15 | 48 |
| 1991 | MASHKOUR | IRISH RIVER | KARABAS | 4 - 6 - 6 - 6 - 2 | 1.18 | 0.17 | 24 |
| 1992 | FLY TILL DAWN | SWING TILL DAWN | CARWHITE | 4 - 8 - 8 - 2 - 2 | 2.00 | 0.42 | 24 |
| 1993 | KOTASHAAN | DARSHAAN | ELOCUTIONIST | 2 - 2 - 7 - 3 - 4 | 0.71 | -0.28 | 18 |
| 1994 | BIEN BIEN | MANILA | GRAUSTARK | 5 - 3 - 22 - 6 - 8 | 0.76 | -0.20 | 44 |
| 1995 | RED BISHOP | SILVER HAWK | SILLY SEASON | 4 - 4 - 16 - 0 - 0 | 2.00 | 0.50 | 24 |
| 1996 | RAINTRAP | RAINBOW QUEST | ROBERTO | 10 - 2 - 20 - 2 - 4 | 1.38 | 0.32 | 38 |
| 1997 | MARLIN | SWORD DANCE | DAMASCUS | 5 - 7 - 14 - 4 - 0 | 1.73 | 0.43 | 30 |
| 1998 | AMERIQUE | ST. JOVITE | ROBERTO | 6 - 3 - 20 - 2 - 1 | 1.46 | 0.34 | 32 |
| 1999 | SINGLE EMPIRE | KRIS | NORTHFIELDS | 6 - 1 - 7 - 2 - 2 | 1.40 | 0.39 | 18 |
| 2000 | SUNSHINE STREET | SUNSHINE FOREVER | CHIEF'S CROWN | 2 - 5 - 23 - 4 - 2 | 1.06 | 0.03 | 36 |
| 2001 | BIENAMADO | BIEN BIEN | VITIGES | 1 - 1 - 12 - 3 - 3 | 0.67 | -0.30 | 20 |
| 2002 | RINGASKIDDY | SLEWVESCENT | HALO | 9 - 2 - 15 - 2 - 2 | 1.61 | 0.47 | 30 |
| | | | MEDIAN = | | 1.38 | 0.32 | 30.0 |

## SANTA ANITA DERBY, THREE-YEAR-OLDS, 9F, DIRT:

| YEAR | WINNER | SIRE | BROODMARE SIRE | DP | DI | CD | PTS |
|---|---|---|---|---|---|---|---|
| 1990 | MISTER FRISKY | MARSAYAS | HIGHEST TIDE | 2 - 5 - 4 - 5 - 0 | 1.29 | 0.25 | 16 |
| 1991 | DINARD | STRAWBERRY ROAD | BOLD BIDDER | 5 - 7 - 7 - 3 - 0 | 2.38 | 0.64 | 22 |
| 1992 | A.P. INDY | SEATTLE SLEW | SECRETARIAT | 13 - 10 - 20 - 3 - 0 | 2.54 | 0.72 | 46 |
| 1993 | PERSONAL HOPE | STORM BIRD | ALYDAR | 10 - 3 - 15 - 0 - 0 | 2.73 | 0.82 | 28 |
| 1994 | BROCCO | KRIS S. | AURELIUS II | 3 - 6 - 15 - 2 - 0 | 1.74 | 0.38 | 26 |
| 1995 | LARRY THE LEGEND | LOCAL TALENT | SAILS PRIDE | 5 - 1 - 12 - 2 - 2 | 1.20 | 0.23 | 22 |
| 1996 | CAVONNIER | BATONNIER | CAVEAT | 2 - 1 - 17 - 0 - 2 | 1.10 | 0.05 | 22 |
| 1997 | FREE HOUSE | SMOKESTER | VIGORS | 8 - 4 - 5 - 3 - 0 | 2.64 | 0.85 | 20 |
| 1998 | INDIAN CHARLIE | IN EXCESS | LEO CASTELLI | 3 - 3 - 5 - 1 - 0 | 2.43 | 0.67 | 12 |
| 1999 | GENERAL CHALLENGE | GENERAL MEETING | SMARTEN | 9 - 1 - 11 - 3 - 0 | 1.82 | 0.67 | 24 |
| 2000 | THE DEPUTY | PETARDIA | LAST TYCOON | 1 - 0 - 2 - 1 - 0 | 1.00 | 0.25 | 4 |
| 2001 | POINT GIVEN | THUNDER GULCH | TURKOMAN | 8 - 0 - 8 - 0 - 0 | 3.00 | 1.00 | 16 |
| 2002 | CAME HOME | GONE WEST | CLEVER TRICK | 12 - 6 - 12 - 0 - 0 | 4.00 | 1.00 | 30 |
| | | | MEDIAN = | | **2.38** | **0.67** | **22.0** |

## SANTA ANITA H, FOUR-YEAR-OLDS & UP, 10F, DIRT:

| YEAR | WINNER | SIRE | BROODMARE SIRE | DP | DI | CD | PTS |
|---|---|---|---|---|---|---|---|
| 1990 | RUHLMANN | MR. LEADER | CHIEFTAIN | 11 - 7 - 8 - 0 - 0 | 5.50 | 1.12 | 26 |
| 1991 | FARMA WAY | MARFA | DIPLOMAT WAY | 7 - 5 - 3 - 1 - 0 | 5.40 | 1.13 | 16 |
| 1992 | BEST PAL | HABITONY | KING PELLINORE | 11 - 6 - 4 - 5 - 0 | 2.71 | 0.88 | 26 |
| 1993 | SIR BEAUFORT | PLEASANT COLONY | CARO | 6 - 4 - 19 - 3 - 2 | 1.34 | 0.26 | 34 |
| 1994 | STUKA | JADE HUNTER | CAERLEON | 12 - 3 - 11 - 4 - 0 | 2.16 | 0.77 | 30 |
| 1995 | URGENT REQUEST | RAINBOW QUEST | CARO | 10 - 4 - 10 - 2 - 4 | 1.73 | 0.47 | 30 |
| 1996 | MR PURPLE | DEPUTY MINISTER | STOP THE MUSIC | 3 - 2 - 7 - 0 - 0 | 2.43 | 0.67 | 12 |
| 1997 | SIPHON | ITAJARA | KUBLAI KHAN | 0 - 0 - 6 - 2 - 0 | 0.60 | -0.25 | 8 |
| 1998 | MALEK | MOCITO GUAPO | CHAIRMAN WALKER | 3 - 4 - 7 - 0 - 0 | 3.00 | 0.71 | 14 |
| 1999 | FREE HOUSE | SMOKESTER | VIGORS | 8 - 4 - 5 - 3 - 0 | 2.64 | 0.85 | 20 |
| 2000 | GENERAL CHALLENGE | GENERAL MEETING | SMARTEN | 9 - 1 - 11 - 3 - 0 | 1.82 | 0.67 | 24 |
| 2001 | TIZNOW | CEE'S TIZZY | SEATTLE SONG | 7 - 1 - 10 - 2 - 0 | 1.86 | 0.65 | 20 |
| 2002 | MILWAUKEE BREW | WILD AGAIN | WOLF POWER | 6 - 5 - 7 - 2 - 0 | 2.64 | 0.75 | 20 |
| | | | MEDIAN = | | **2.43** | **0.71** | **20.0** |

**SANTA ANITA OAKS, THREE-YEAR-OLD FILLIES, 8.5F, DIRT:**

| YEAR | WINNER | SIRE | BROODMARE SIRE | DP | DI | CD | PTS |
|------|--------|------|----------------|-----|-----|-----|-----|
| 1990 | HAIL ATLANTIS | SEATTLE SLEW | COASTAL | 13 - 1 - 12 - 2 - 0 | 2.50 | 0.89 | 28 |
| 1991 | LITE LIGHT | MAJESTIC LIGHT | IN REALITY | 15 - 3 - 13 - 1 - 2 | 2.58 | 0.82 | 34 |
| 1992 | GOLDEN TREAT | THEATRICAL | DUSTY CANYON | 8 - 2 - 14 - 0 - 0 | 2.43 | 0.75 | 24 |
| 1993 | ELIZA | MT. LIVERMORE | BOLD BIDDER | 12 - 7 - 8 - 1 - 2 | 3.29 | 0.87 | 30 |
| 1994 | LAKEWAY | SEATTLE SLEW | ALYDAR | 14 - 3 - 19 - 2 - 0 | 2.30 | 0.76 | 38 |
| 1995 | SERENA'S SONG | RAHY | NORTHFIELDS | 12 - 1 - 12 - 1 - 2 | 2.11 | 0.71 | 28 |
| 1996 | ANTESPEND | SPEND A BUCK | PRACTICANTE | 2 - 3 - 7 - 0 - 0 | 2.43 | 0.58 | 12 |
| 1997 | SHARP CAT | STORM CAT | ACK ACK | 5 - 9 - 8 - 0 - 0 | 4.50 | 0.86 | 22 |
| 1998 | HEDONIST | ALYDEED | STEADY GROWTH | 4 - 2 - 8 - 2 - 2 | 1.25 | 0.22 | 18 |
| 1999 | EXCELLENT MEETING | GENERAL MEETING | CHIEF'S CROWN | 7 - 4 - 14 - 1 - 0 | 2.25 | 0.65 | 26 |
| 2000 | SURFSIDE | SEATTLE SLEW | SEEKING THE GOLD | 14 - 2 - 16 - 2 - 0 | 2.40 | 0.82 | 34 |
| 2001 | GOLDEN BALLET | MOSCOW BALLET | SLEW O' GOLD | 6 - 2 - 11 - 5 - 0 | 1.29 | 0.38 | 24 |
| 2002 | YOU | YOU AND I | HOMEBUILDER | 5 - 2 - 9 - 1 - 1 | 1.77 | 0.50 | 18 |
| | | | MEDIAN = | | **2.40** | **0.75** | **26.0** |

**SANTA MARGARITA INVITATIONAL H, FOUR-YEAR-OLDS & UP, FILLIES & MARES, 9F, DIRT:**

| YEAR | WINNER | SIRE | BROODMARE SIRE | DP | DI | CD | PTS |
|------|--------|------|----------------|-----|-----|-----|-----|
| 1990 | BAYAKOA | CONSULTANT'S BID | GOOD MANNERS | 8 - 8 - 6 - 0 - 0 | 6.33 | 1.09 | 22 |
| 1991 | LITTLE BRIANNE | COASTAL | CORNISH PRINCE | 13 - 8 - 7 - 0 - 0 | 7.00 | 1.21 | 28 |
| 1992 | PASEANA | AHMAD | FLINTHAM | 4 - 4 - 2 - 0 - 0 | 9.00 | 1.20 | 10 |
| 1993 | SOUTHERN TRUCE | TRUCE MAKER | CHIEFTAIN | 10 - 10 - 6 - 0 - 0 | 7.67 | 1.15 | 26 |
| 1994 | PASEANNA | AHMAD | FLINTHAM | 4 - 4 - 2 - 0 - 0 | 9.00 | 1.20 | 10 |
| 1995 | QUEENS COURT QUEEN | LYPHARD | STOP THE MUSIC | 12 - 3 - 27 - 0 - 0 | 2.11 | 0.64 | 42 |
| 1996 | TWICE THE VICE | VICE REGENT | RESURGENT | 9 - 2 - 10 - 1 - 0 | 2.67 | 0.86 | 22 |
| 1997 | JEWEL PRINCESS | KEY TO THE MINT | MELYNO | 8 - 3 - 23 - 6 - 2 | 1.15 | 0.21 | 42 |
| 1998 | TODA UNA DAMA | CIPAYO | STALLWOOD | 0 - 0 - 4 - 0 - 6 | 0.25 | -1.20 | 10 |
| 1999 | MANISTIQUE | UNBRIDLED | NUREYEV | 8 - 9 - 21 - 0 - 6 | 1.67 | 0.30 | 44 |
| 2000 | RIBOLETTA | ROI NORMAND | GHADEER | 7 - 1 - 18 - 0 - 0 | 1.89 | 0.58 | 26 |
| 2001 | LAZY SLUSAN | SLEWVESCENT | TOPSIDER | 7 - 1 - 8 - 4 - 2 | 1.20 | 0.32 | 22 |
| 2002 | AZERI | JADE HUNTER | AHONOORA | 9 - 2 - 9 - 0 - 0 | 3.44 | 1.00 | 20 |
| | | | MEDIAN = | | **2.67** | **0.86** | **22.0** |

## SANTA MARIA H, FOUR-YEAR-OLDS & UP, FILLIES & MARES, 8.5F, DIRT:

| YEAR | WINNER | SIRE | BROODMARE SIRE | DP | DI | CD | PTS |
|------|--------|------|----------------|-----|-----|-----|-----|
| 1990 | BAYAKOA | CONSULTANT'S BID | GOOD MANNERS | 8 - 8 - 6 - 0 - 0 | 6.33 | 1.09 | 22 |
| 1991 | LITTLE BRIANNE | COASTAL | CORNISH PRINCE | 13 - 8 - 7 - 0 - 0 | 7.00 | 1.21 | 28 |
| 1992 | PASEANA | AHMAD | FLINTHAM | 4 - 4 - 2 - 0 - 0 | 9.00 | 1.20 | 10 |
| 1993 | RACE THE WILD WIND | SUNNY'S HALO | INDIAN CHIEF II | 7 - 3 - 9 - 1 - 0 | 2.64 | 0.80 | 20 |
| 1994 | SUPAH GEM | GOLD MERIDIAN | GREAT ABOVE | 8 - 1 - 5 - 0 - 0 | 4.60 | 1.21 | 14 |
| 1995 | QUEENS COURT QUEEN | LYPHARD | STOP THE MUSIC | 12 - 3 - 27 - 0 - 0 | 2.11 | 0.64 | 42 |
| 1996 | SERENA'S SONG | RAHY | NORTHFIELDS | 12 - 1 - 12 - 1 - 2 | 2.11 | 0.71 | 28 |
| 1997 | JEWELL PRINCESS | KEY TO THE MINT | MELYNO | 8 - 3 - 23 - 6 - 2 | 1.15 | 0.21 | 42 |
| 1998 | EXOTIC WOOD | RAHY | DIXIELAND BAND | 11 - 3 - 14 - 1 - 3 | 1.91 | 0.56 | 32 |
| 1999 | INDIA DIVINA | ROY | CARRAL | 8 - 8 - 8 - 10 - 0 | 1.43 | 0.41 | 34 |
| 2000 | MANISTIQUE | UNBRIDLED | NUREYEV | 8 - 9 - 21 - 0 - 6 | 1.67 | 0.30 | 44 |
| 2001 | LOVELLON | POTRILLON | SHAM | 2 - 2 - 9 - 1 - 0 | 1.55 | 0.36 | 14 |
| 2002 | FAVORITE FUNTIME | SEEKING THE GOLD | YOUTH | 8 - 5 - 14 - 0 - 1 | 2.50 | 0.68 | 28 |
| | | | MEDIAN = | | **2.11** | **0.68** | **28.0** |

## SANTA MONICA H, FOUR-YEAR-OLDS & UP, FILLIES & MARES, 7F, DIRT:

| YEAR | WINNER | SIRE | BROODMARE SIRE | DP | DI | CD | PTS |
|------|--------|------|----------------|-----|-----|-----|-----|
| 1990 | STORMY BUT VALID | VALID APPEAL | TROPICAL BREEZE | 7 - 3 - 13 - 1 - 0 | 2.20 | 0.67 | 24 |
| 1991 | DEVIL'S ORCHID | DEVIL'S BAG | OLDEN TIMES | 5 - 3 - 10 - 2 - 2 | 1.44 | 0.32 | 22 |
| 1992 | LARAMIE MOON | LARAMIE TRAIL | RIGOLO | 2 - 7 - 7 - 0 - 0 | 3.57 | 0.69 | 16 |
| 1993 | FREEDOM CRY | WOLF POWER | VALID APPEAL | 4 - 3 - 4 - 5 - 0 | 1.29 | 0.38 | 16 |
| 1994 | SOUTHERN TRUCE | TRUCE MAKER | CHIEFTAIN | 10 - 10 - 6 - 0 - 0 | 7.67 | 1.15 | 26 |
| 1995 | KEY PHRASE | FLYING PASTER | GRENFALL | 4 - 1 - 4 - 2 - 1 | 1.40 | 0.42 | 12 |
| 1996 | SERENA'S SONG | RAHY | NORTHFIELDS | 12 - 1 - 12 - 1 - 2 | 2.11 | 0.71 | 28 |
| 1997 | TOGA TOGA TOGA | SARATOGA SIX | NORTHERN BABY | 7 - 3 - 16 - 2 - 0 | 1.80 | 0.54 | 28 |
| 1998 | EXOTIC WOOD | RAHY | DIXIELAND BAND | 11 - 3 - 14 - 1 - 3 | 1.91 | 0.56 | 32 |
| 1999 | STOP TRAFFIC | CURE THE BLUES | IMA HELL RAISER | 8 - 8 - 8 - 0 - 0 | 5.00 | 1.00 | 24 |
| 2000 | HONEST LADY | SEATTLE SLEW | EL GRAN SENOR | 14 - 2 - 16 - 2 - 0 | 2.40 | 0.82 | 34 |
| 2001 | NANY'S SWEEP | END SWEEP | VALID APPEAL | 8 - 1 - 6 - 0 - 1 | 3.00 | 0.94 | 16 |
| 2002 | KALOOKAN QUEEN | LOST CODE | MAJESTIC PRINCE | 8 - 3 - 4 - 0 - 1 | 4.33 | 1.06 | 16 |
| | | | MEDIAN = | | **2.20** | **0.69** | **24.0** |

## SECRETARIAT S, THREE-YEAR-OLDS, 10F, TURF:

| YEAR | WINNER | SIRE | BROODMARE SIRE | DP | DI | CD | PTS |
|---|---|---|---|---|---|---|---|
| 1990 | SUPER ABOUND | SUPERBITY | DAMASCUS | 4 - 4 - 10 - 2 - 2 | 1.44 | 0.27 | 22 |
| 1991 | JACKIE WACKIE | HOSTAGE | TILT UP | 2 - 0 - 10 - 4 - 0 | 0.78 | 0.00 | 16 |
| 1992 | GHAZI | POLISH NAVY | DAMASCUS | 6 - 8 - 12 - 0 - 0 | 3.33 | 0.77 | 26 |
| 1993 | AWAD | CAVEAT | NOBLE DANCER | 2 - 6 - 4 - 1 - 1 | 2.50 | 0.50 | 14 |
| 1994 | VAUDEVILLE | THEATRICAL | RIVERMAN | 6 - 6 - 20 - 0 - 0 | 2.20 | 0.56 | 32 |
| 1995 | HAWK ATTACK | SILVER HAWK | ELOCUTIONIST | 3 - 3 - 14 - 0 - 0 | 1.86 | 0.45 | 20 |
| 1996 | MARLIN | SWORD DANCE | DAMASCUS | 5 - 7 - 14 - 4 - 0 | 1.73 | 0.43 | 30 |
| 1997 | HONOR GLIDE | HONOR GRADES | RUN THE GANTLET | 3 - 7 - 13 - 0 - 11 | 0.94 | -0.26 | 34 |
| 1998 | NOT RUN | | | | | | |
| 1999 | NOT RUN | | | | | | |
| 2000 | CIRO | WOODMAN | NIJINSKY II | 11 - 7 - 20 - 4 - 0 | 2.00 | 0.60 | 42 |
| 2001 | STARTAC | THEATRICAL | MR. PROSPECTOR | 12 - 3 - 23 - 0 - 0 | 2.30 | 0.71 | 38 |
| 2002 | CHISELLING | WOODMAN | EL GRAN SENOR | 13 - 4 - 23 - 0 - 0 | 2.48 | 0.75 | 40 |
| | | | MEDIAN = | | **2.00** | **0.50** | **30.0** |

## SPINAWAY S, TWO-YEAR-OLD FILLIES, 7F, DIRT:

| YEAR | WINNER | SIRE | BROODMARE SIRE | DP | DI | CD | PTS |
|---|---|---|---|---|---|---|---|
| 1990 | MEADOW STAR | MEADOWLAKE | IN REALITY | 15 - 11 - 10 - 0 - 0 | 6.20 | 1.14 | 36 |
| 1991 | MISS IRON SMOKE | IRON CONSTITUTION | GALLANT ROMEO | 9 - 6 - 7 - 0 - 0 | 5.29 | 1.09 | 22 |
| 1992 | FAMILY ENTERPRIZE | TRI JET | HIS MAJESTY | 7 - 6 - 20 - 1 - 2 | 1.77 | 0.42 | 36 |
| 1993 | STRATEGIC MANEUVER | CRYPTOCLEARANCE | CONQUISTADOR CIELO | 13 - 8 - 14 - 0 - 1 | 3.50 | 0.89 | 36 |
| 1994 | FLANDERS | SEEKING THE GOLD | STORM BIRD | 11 - 6 - 15 - 0 - 0 | 3.27 | 0.88 | 32 |
| 1995 | GOLDEN ATTRACTION | MR. PROSPECTOR | SEATTLE SLEW | 24 - 6 - 21 - 1 - 0 | 3.52 | 1.02 | 52 |
| 1996 | OATH | KNOWN FACT | MR. PROSPECTOR | 20 - 8 - 13 - 0 - 1 | 4.60 | 1.10 | 42 |
| 1997 | COUNTESS DIANA | DEERHOUND | T. V. COMMERCIAL | 3 - 10 - 15 - 0 - 0 | 2.73 | 0.57 | 28 |
| 1998 | THINGS CHANGE | STALWART | GATO DEL SOL | 7 - 5 - 11 - 0 - 3 | 2.06 | 0.50 | 26 |
| 1999 | CIRCLE OF LIFE | BELONG TO ME | SHADEED | 7 - 5 - 20 - 4 - 0 | 1.57 | 0.42 | 36 |
| 2000 | STORMY PICK | STORM CREEK | PETERHOF | 6 - 2 - 6 - 0 - 0 | 3.67 | 1.00 | 14 |
| 2001 | CASHIER'S DREAM | SERVICE STRIPE | MONETARY GIFT | 4 - 2 - 4 - 0 - 0 | 4.00 | 1.00 | 10 |
| 2002 | AWESOME HUMOR | DISTORTED HUMOR | PASS THE TAB | 5 - 2 - 8 - 0 - 1 | 2.20 | 0.63 | 16 |
| | | | MEDIAN = | | **3.50** | **0.89** | **32.0** |

## SPINSTER S, THREE-YEAR-OLDS & UP, FILLIES & MARES, 9F, DIRT:

| YEAR | WINNER | SIRE | BROODMARE SIRE | DP | DI | CD | PTS |
|------|--------|------|----------------|-----|------|------|-----|
| 1990 | BAYAKOA | CONSULTANT'S BID | GOOD MANNERS | 8 - 8 - 6 - 0 - 0 | 6.33 | 1.09 | 22 |
| 1991 | WILDERNESS SONG | WILD AGAIN | NALEES MAN | 8 - 8 - 8 - 0 - 0 | 5.00 | 1.00 | 24 |
| 1992 | FOWDA | STRAWBERRY ROAD | RARE PERFORMER | 7 - 0 - 5 - 2 - 0 | 2.11 | 0.86 | 14 |
| 1993 | PASEANA | AHMAD | FLINTHAM | 4 - 4 - 2 - 0 - 0 | 9.00 | 1.20 | 10 |
| 1994 | DISPUTE | DANZIG | REVIEWER | 13 - 16 - 18 - 1 - 0 | 3.80 | 0.85 | 48 |
| 1995 | INSIDE INFORMATION | PRIVATE ACCOUNT | KEY TO THE MINT | 10 - 9 - 17 - 3 - 1 | 2.20 | 0.60 | 40 |
| 1996 | DIFFERENT | CANDY STRIPES | PROPICIO | 7 - 0 - 9 - 0 - 2 | 1.77 | 0.56 | 18 |
| 1997 | CLEAR MANDATE | DEPUTY MINISTER | SHARPEN UP | 6 - 1 - 7 - 0 - 0 | 3.00 | 0.93 | 14 |
| 1998 | BANSHEE BREEZE | UNBRIDLED | KNOWN FACT | 8 - 9 - 9 - 0 - 6 | 2.05 | 0.41 | 32 |
| 1999 | KEEPER HILL | DEPUTY MINISTER | LYPHEOR | 8 - 3 - 7 - 0 - 0 | 4.14 | 1.06 | 18 |
| 2000 | PLENTY OF LIGHT | COLONY LIGHT | NORTHROP | 6 - 1 - 8 - 0 - 1 | 2.20 | 0.69 | 16 |
| 2001 | MISS LINDA | SOUTHERN HALO | FITZCARRALDO | 7 - 1 - 10 - 2 - 0 | 1.86 | 0.65 | 20 |
| | | | MEDIAN = | | **2.60** | **0.86** | **19.0** |

## SUPER DERBY, THREE-YEAR-OLDS, 10F, DIRT:

| YEAR | WINNER | SIRE | BROODMARE SIRE | DP | DI | CD | PTS |
|------|--------|------|----------------|-----|------|------|-----|
| 1990 | HOME AT LAST | QUADRATIC | ACK ACK | 3 - 6 - 7 - 0 - 0 | 3.57 | 0.75 | 16 |
| 1991 | FREE SPIRIT'S JOY | JOEY BOB | STAUNCH AVENGER | 5 - 1 - 2 - 0 - 0 | 7.00 | 1.38 | 8 |
| 1992 | SENOR TOMAS | EL GRAN SENOR | LAOMEDONTE | 11 - 6 - 13 - 2 - 0 | 2.76 | 0.81 | 32 |
| 1993 | WALLENDA | GULCH | LILOY | 11 - 5 - 10 - 0 - 0 | 4.20 | 1.04 | 26 |
| 1994 | SOUL OF THE MATTER | PRIVATE TERMS | T. V. COMMERCIAL | 5 - 10 - 7 - 2 - 0 | 3.36 | 0.75 | 24 |
| 1995 | MECKE | MAUDLIN | BALDSKI | 11 - 10 - 5 - 2 - 0 | 5.22 | 1.07 | 28 |
| 1996 | EDITOR'S NOTE | FORTY NINER | CAVEAT | 10 - 4 - 11 - 0 - 3 | 2.29 | 0.64 | 28 |
| 1997 | DEPUTY COMMANDER | DEPUTY MINISTER | MALINOWSKI | 2 - 3 - 5 - 0 - 0 | 3.00 | 0.70 | 10 |
| 1998 | ARCH | KRIS S. | DANZIG | 6 - 9 - 25 - 2 - 0 | 1.90 | 0.45 | 42 |
| 1999 | ECTON PARK | FORTY NINER | DANZIG | 12 - 6 - 15 - 0 - 3 | 2.43 | 0.67 | 36 |
| 2000 | TIZNOW | CEE'S TIZZY | SEATTLE SONG | 7 - 1 - 10 - 2 - 0 | 1.86 | 0.65 | 20 |
| 2001 | OUTOFTHEBOX | MONTBROOK | NOTEBOOK | 0 - 1 - 8 - 0 - 1 | 1.00 | -0.10 | 10 |
| | | | MEDIAN = | | **2.88** | **0.73** | **25.0** |

## SWORD DANCER INVITATIONAL H, THREE-YEAR-OLDS & UP, 12F, TURF:

| YEAR | WINNER | SIRE | BROODMARE SIRE | DP | | | | | DI | CD | PTS |
|---|---|---|---|---|---|---|---|---|---|---|---|
| 1990 | EL SENOR | VALDEZ | GREY DAWN II | 9 - | 8 - | 15 - | 5 - | 3 | 1.58 | 0.38 | 40 |
| 1991 | DR. ROOT | SLEW O' GOLD | KNIGHTLY MANNER | 6 - | 4 - | 9 - | 5 - | 0 | 1.53 | 0.46 | 24 |
| 1992 | FRAISE | STRAWBERRY ROAD | DICTUS | 1 - | 0 - | 3 - | 4 - | 2 | 0.33 | -0.60 | 10 |
| 1993 | SPECTACULAR TIDE | TSUNAMI SLEW | SPECTACULAR BID | 6 - | 6 - | 9 - | 0 - | 1 | 3.00 | 0.73 | 22 |
| 1994 | ALEX THE GREAT | BAIRN | WELSH PAGEANT | 6 - | 3 - | 5 - | 2 - | 6 | 1.10 | 0.05 | 22 |
| 1995 | KIRI'S CLOWN | FOOLISH PLEASURE | KRIS | 15 - | 8 - | 8 - | 0 - | 1 | 5.40 | 1.13 | 32 |
| 1996 | BROADWAY FLYER | THEATRICAL | JAN EKELS | 2 - | 0 - | 16 - | 0 - | 2 | 1.00 | 0.00 | 20 |
| 1997 | AWAD | CAVEAT | NOBLE DANCER | 2 - | 6 - | 4 - | 1 - | 1 | 2.50 | 0.50 | 14 |
| 1998 | CETEWAYO | HIS MAJESTY | DIESIS | 3 - | 0 - | 29 - | 0 - | 6 | 0.85 | -0.16 | 38 |
| 1999 | HONOR GLIDE | HONOR GRADES | RUN THE GANTLET | 3 - | 7 - | 13 - | 0 - | 11 | 0.94 | -0.26 | 34 |
| 2000 | JOHN'S CALL | LORD AT WAR | BE MY GUEST | 6 - | 0 - | 3 - | 0 - | 3 | 1.67 | 0.50 | 12 |
| 2001 | WITH ANTICIPATION | RELAUNCH | SAROS | 7 - | 3 - | 6 - | 2 - | 0 | 2.60 | 0.83 | 18 |
| 2002 | WITH ANTICIPATION | RELAUNCH | SAROS | 7 - | 3 - | 6 - | 2 - | 0 | 2.60 | 0.83 | 18 |
| | | | | | | | MEDIAN = | | 1.58 | 0.46 | 22.0 |

## TEST S, THREE-YEAR-OLD FILLIES, 7F, DIRT:

| YEAR | WINNER | SIRE | BROODMARE SIRE | DP | | | | | DI | CD | PTS |
|---|---|---|---|---|---|---|---|---|---|---|---|
| 1990 | GO FOR WAND | DEPUTY MINISTER | CYANE | 6 - | 2 - | 4 - | 0 - | 0 | 5.00 | 1.17 | 12 |
| 1991 | VERSAILLES TREATY | DANZIG | BUCKPASSER | 5 - | 17 - | 28 - | 0 - | 0 | 2.57 | 0.54 | 50 |
| 1992 | NOVEMBER SNOW | STORM CAT | ALYDAR | 7 - | 4 - | 13 - | 0 - | 0 | 2.69 | 0.75 | 24 |
| 1993 | MISSED THE STORM | STORM CAT | BLUSHING GROOM | 9 - | 7 - | 8 - | 0 - | 2 | 3.33 | 0.81 | 26 |
| 1994 | TWIST AFLEET | AFLEET | NATIVO | 14 - | 5 - | 11 - | 0 - | 0 | 4.45 | 1.10 | 30 |
| 1995 | CHAPOSA SPRINGS | BALDSKI | UPS | 14 - | 10 - | 6 - | 4 - | 0 | 3.86 | 1.00 | 34 |
| 1996 | CAPOTE BELLE | CAPOTE | FAPPIANO | 12 - | 6 - | 13 - | 1 - | 0 | 3.27 | 0.91 | 32 |
| 1997 | FABULOUSLY FAST | DEPUTY MINISTER | SOMETHINGFABULOUS | 6 - | 2 - | 5 - | 1 - | 0 | 3.00 | 0.93 | 14 |
| 1998 | JERSEY GIRL | BELONG TO ME | VALID APPEAL | 8 - | 8 - | 16 - | 0 - | 0 | 3.00 | 0.75 | 32 |
| 1999 | MARLEY VALE | FORTY NINER | HAGLEY | 10 - | 2 - | 9 - | 0 - | 3 | 2.20 | 0.67 | 24 |
| 2000 | DREAM SUPREME | SEEKING THE GOLD | DIXIELAND BAND | 11 - | 6 - | 15 - | 0 - | 0 | 3.27 | 0.88 | 32 |
| 2001 | VICTORY RIDE | SEEKING THE GOLD | FLYING PASTER | 9 - | 5 - | 12 - | 0 - | 0 | 3.33 | 0.88 | 26 |
| 2002 | YOU | YOU AND I | HOMEBUILDER | 5 - | 2 - | 9 - | 1 - | 0 | 2.09 | 0.65 | 17 |
| | | | | | | | MEDIAN = | | 3.27 | 0.88 | 26.0 |

**TRAVERS S, THREE-YEAR-OLDS, 10F, DIRT:**

| YEAR | WINNER | SIRE | BROODMARE SIRE | DP | DI | CD | PTS |
|---|---|---|---|---|---|---|---|
| 1990 | RHYTHM | MR. PROSPECTOR | NORTHERN DANCER | 23 - 8 - 25 - 0 - 0 | 3.48 | 0.96 | 56 |
| 1991 | CORPORATE REPORT | PRIVATE ACCOUNT | KEY TO THE MINT | 8 - 6 - 16 - 3 - 1 | 1.83 | 0.50 | 34 |
| 1992 | THUNDER RUMBLE | THUNDER PUDDLES | LYPHARD | 12 - 5 - 14 - 1 - 0 | 3.00 | 0.88 | 32 |
| 1993 | SEA HERO | POLISH NAVY | GRAUSTARK | 3 - 5 - 22 - 4 - 2 | 1.12 | 0.08 | 36 |
| 1994 | HOLY BULL | GREAT ABOVE | AL HATTAB | 6 - 5 - 4 - 1 - 0 | 4.33 | 1.00 | 16 |
| 1995 | THUNDER GULCH | GULCH | STORM BIRD | 10 - 2 - 8 - 0 - 0 | 4.00 | 1.10 | 20 |
| 1996 | WILL'S WAY | EASY GOER | TENTAM | 9 - 6 - 16 - 0 - 1 | 2.56 | 0.69 | 32 |
| 1997 | DEPUTY COMMANDER | DEPUTY MINISTER | MALINOWSKI | 2 - 3 - 5 - 0 - 0 | 3.00 | 0.70 | 10 |
| 1998 | CORONADO'S QUEST | FORTY NINER | DAMASCUS | 16 - 9 - 14 - 0 - 3 | 3.20 | 0.83 | 42 |
| 1999 | LEMON DROP KID | KINGMAMBO | SEATTLE SLEW | 13 - 4 - 21 - 0 - 0 | 2.62 | 0.79 | 38 |
| 2000 | UNSHADED | UNBRIDLED | CAUCASUS | 8 - 7 - 10 - 3 - 6 | 1.43 | 0.24 | 34 |
| 2001 | POINT GIVEN | THUNDER GULCH | TURKOMAN | 8 - 0 - 8 - 0 - 0 | 3.00 | 1.00 | 16 |
| 2002 | MEDAGLIA D'ORO | EL PRADO | BAILJUMPER | 2 - 6 - 14 - 4 - 0 | 1.36 | 0.23 | 26 |
| | | | MEDIAN = | | **3.00** | **0.79** | **32.0** |

**TURF CLASSIC INVITATIONAL S, THREE-YEAR-OLDS & UP, 12F, TURF:**

| YEAR | WINNER | SIRE | BROODMARE SIRE | DP | DI | CD | PTS |
|---|---|---|---|---|---|---|---|
| 1990 | CACOETHES | ALYDAR | JESTER | 15 - 8 - 5 - 0 - 0 | 10.20 | 1.36 | 28 |
| 1991 | SOLAR SPLENDOR | MAJESTIC LIGHT | BUCKFINDER | 6 - 6 - 11 - 1 - 2 | 2.06 | 0.50 | 26 |
| 1992 | SKY CLASSIC | NIJINSKY II | NODOUBLE | 11 - 3 - 19 - 9 - 0 | 1.27 | 0.38 | 42 |
| 1993 | APPLE TREE | BIKALA | CARVIN II | 2 - 0 - 2 - 6 - 0 | 0.43 | -0.20 | 10 |
| 1994 | TIKKANEN | COZZENE | TARGOWICE | 3 - 8 - 10 - 6 - 1 | 1.33 | 0.21 | 28 |
| 1995 | TURK PASSER | TURKOMAN | BUCKPASSER | 4 - 3 - 22 - 3 - 0 | 1.29 | 0.25 | 32 |
| 1996 | DIPLOMATIC JET | ROMAN DIPLOMAT | TRI JET | 6 - 4 - 14 - 0 - 0 | 2.43 | 0.67 | 24 |
| 1997 | VAL'S PRINCE | ETERNAL PRINCE | VALID APPEAL | 13 - 3 - 6 - 0 - 0 | 6.33 | 1.32 | 22 |
| 1998 | BUCK'S BOY | BUCKSPLASHER | VERBATIM | 4 - 4 - 18 - 0 - 0 | 1.89 | 0.46 | 26 |
| 1999 | VAL'S PRINCE | ETERNAL PRINCE | VALID APPEAL | 13 - 3 - 6 - 0 - 0 | 6.33 | 1.32 | 22 |
| 2000 | JOHN'S CALL | LORD AT WAR | BE MY GUEST | 6 - 0 - 3 - 0 - 3 | 1.67 | 0.50 | 12 |
| 2001 | TIMBOROA | SALSE | DAMISTER | 6 - 1 - 12 - 3 - 0 | 1.44 | 0.45 | 22 |
| 2002 | DENON | PLEASANT COLONY | NORTHFIELDS | 4 - 3 - 17 - 0 - 2 | 1.48 | 0.27 | 26 |
| | | | MEDIAN = | | **1.67** | **0.46** | **26.0** |

## UNITED NATIONS H*, THREE-YEAR-OLDS & UP, 11F, TURF:

| YEAR | WINNER | SIRE | BROODMARE SIRE | DP | DI | CD | PTS |
|------|--------|------|----------------|----|----|----|-----|
| 1990 | STEINLEN | HABITAT | JIM FRENCH | 22 - 8 - 9 - 4 - 1 | 3.63 | 1.05 | 44 |
| 1991 | EXBOURNE | EXPLODENT | FORUM | 7 - 2 - 3 - 0 - 0 | 7.00 | 1.33 | 12 |
| 1992 | SKY CLASSIC | NIJINSKY II | NODOUBLE | 11 - 3 - 19 - 9 - 0 | 1.27 | 0.38 | 42 |
| 1993 | STAR OF COZZENE | COZZENE | PIA STAR | 10 - 7 - 10 - 9 - 0 | 1.57 | 0.50 | 36 |
| 1994 | LURE | DANZIG | ALYDAR | 9 - 12 - 23 - 0 - 0 | 2.83 | 0.68 | 44 |
| 1995 | SANDPIT | BAYNOUN | GREEN DANCER | 2 - 0 - 8 - 6 - 4 | 0.43 | -0.50 | 20 |
| 1996 | SANDPIT | BAYNOUN | GREEN DANCER | 2 - 0 - 8 - 6 - 4 | 0.43 | -0.50 | 20 |
| 1997 | INFLUENT | ASCOT KNIGHT | KEY TO THE MINT | 6 - 5 - 13 - 3 - 1 | 1.67 | 0.43 | 28 |
| 1998 | NOT RUN | | | | | | |
| 1999 | YAGLI | JADE HUNTER | NIJINSKY II | 10 - 2 - 16 - 4 - 0 | 1.67 | 0.56 | 32 |
| 2000 | DOWN THE AISLE | RUNAWAY GROOM | L'ENJOLEUR | 7 - 2 - 14 - 1 - 2 | 1.60 | 0.42 | 26 |
| 2001 | WITH ANTICIPATION | RELAUNCH | SAROS | 7 - 3 - 6 - 2 - 0 | 2.60 | 0.83 | 18 |
| 2002 | WITH ANTICIPATION | RELAUNCH | SAROS | 7 - 3 - 6 - 2 - 0 | 2.60 | 0.83 | 18 |
| | | | | MEDIAN = | 1.67 | 0.53 | 27.0 |

* RUN AS CAESARS INTERNATIONAL FROM 1991-1997

## VANITY H, THREE-YEAR-OLDS & UP, FILLIES & MARES, 9F, DIRT:

| YEAR | WINNER | SIRE | BROODMARE SIRE | DP | DI | CD | PTS |
|------|--------|------|----------------|----|----|----|-----|
| 1990 | GORGEOUS | SLEW O' GOLD | KEY TO THE MINT | 8 - 2 - 16 - 3 - 1 | 1.50 | 0.43 | 30 |
| 1991 | BROUGHT TO MIND | RUTHIE'S NATIVE | ICECAPADE | 11 - 2 - 16 - 1 - 0 | 2.33 | 0.77 | 30 |
| 1992 | PASEANA | AHMAD | FLINTHAM | 4 - 4 - 2 - 0 - 0 | 9.00 | 1.20 | 10 |
| 1993 | RE TOSS | EGG TOSS | PRACTICANTE | 2 - 2 - 12 - 0 - 0 | 1.67 | 0.38 | 16 |
| 1994 | POTRIDEE | POTRILLAZO | BANNER SPORT | 4 - 3 - 2 - 1 - 0 | 4.00 | 1.00 | 10 |
| 1995 | PRIVATE PERSUASION | PIRATE'S BOUNTY | SALEM | 5 - 6 - 6 - 0 - 3 | 2.33 | 0.50 | 20 |
| 1996 | JEWELL PRINCESS | KEY TO THE MINT | MELYNO | 8 - 3 - 23 - 6 - 2 | 1.15 | 0.21 | 42 |
| 1997 | TWICE THE VICE | VICE REGENT | RESURGENT | 9 - 2 - 10 - 1 - 0 | 2.67 | 0.86 | 22 |
| 1998 | ESCENA | STRAWBERRY ROAD | SEATTLE SLEW | 11 - 1 - 8 - 2 - 0 | 2.67 | 0.95 | 22 |
| 1999 | MANISTIQUE | UNBRIDLED | NUREYEV | 8 - 9 - 21 - 0 - 6 | 1.67 | 0.30 | 44 |
| 2000 | RIBOLETTA | ROI NORMAND | GHADEER | 7 - 1 - 18 - 0 - 0 | 1.89 | 0.58 | 26 |
| 2001 | GOURMET GIRL | CEE'S TIZZY | WELSH PAGEANT | 8 - 1 - 11 - 0 - 0 | 2.64 | 0.85 | 20 |
| 2002 | AZERI | JADE HUNTER | AHONOORA | 9 - 2 - 9 - 0 - 0 | 3.44 | 1.00 | 20 |
| | | | | MEDIAN = | 2.33 | 0.77 | 22.0 |

## VOSBURGH H, THREE-YEAR-OLDS & UP, 7F, DIRT:

| YEAR | WINNER | SIRE | BROODMARE SIRE | DP | DI | CD | PTS |
|---|---|---|---|---|---|---|---|
| 1990 | SEWICKLEY | STAR DE NASKRA | DR. FAGER | 12 - 10 - 4 - 0 - 0 | 12.00 | 1.31 | 26 |
| 1991 | HOUSEBUSTER | MT. LIVERMORE | GREAT ABOVE | 11 - 2 - 5 - 0 - 2 | 3.44 | 1.00 | 20 |
| 1992 | RUBIANO | FAPPIANO | NIJINSKY II | 14 - 15 - 23 - 4 - 0 | 2.61 | 0.70 | 56 |
| 1993 | BRIDONTHEWIRE | PROUD BIRDIE | JONTILLA | 3 - 7 - 6 - 0 - 0 | 4.33 | 0.81 | 16 |
| 1994 | HARLAN | STORM CAT | HALO | 8 - 4 - 12 - 0 - 0 | 3.00 | 0.83 | 24 |
| 1995 | NOT SURPRISING | MEDIEVAL MAN | ALWAYS GALLANT | 5 - 6 - 7 - 0 - 0 | 4.14 | 0.89 | 18 |
| 1996 | LANGFUHR | DANZIG | BRIARTIC | 6 - 11 - 15 - 2 - 0 | 2.58 | 0.62 | 34 |
| 1997 | VICTOR COOLEY | COOL VICTOR | LEND LEASE | 3 - 3 - 6 - 0 - 0 | 3.00 | 0.75 | 12 |
| 1998 | AFFIRMED SUCCESS | AFFIRMED | IRISH TOWER | 5 - 2 - 9 - 0 - 0 | 2.56 | 0.75 | 16 |
| 1999 | ARTAX | MARQUETRY | APALACHEE | 15 - 6 - 4 - 5 - 0 | 3.29 | 1.03 | 30 |
| 2000 | TRIPPI | END SWEEP | VALID APPEAL | 9 - 2 - 6 - 0 - 1 | 3.50 | 1.00 | 18 |
| 2001 | LEFT BANK | FRENCH DEPUTY | DR. BLUM | 4 - 7 - 6 - 1 - 0 | 3.50 | 0.78 | 18 |
| 2002 | BONAPAW | SANONA | NIJINSKY II | 7 - 2 - 19 - 4 - 0 | 1.37 | 0.38 | 32 |
| | | | MEDIAN = | | 3.29 | 0.81 | 20.0 |

## WHITNEY H, THREE-YEAR-OLDS & UP, 9F, DIRT:

| YEAR | WINNER | SIRE | BROODMARE SIRE | DP | DI | CD | PTS |
|---|---|---|---|---|---|---|---|
| 1990 | CRIMINAL TYPE | ALYDAR | NO ROBBERY | 10 - 6 - 20 - 0 - 0 | 2.60 | 0.72 | 36 |
| 1991 | IN EXCESS | SIBERIAN EXPRESS | SAULINGO | 4 - 4 - 4 - 0 - 0 | 5.00 | 1.00 | 12 |
| 1992 | SULTRY SONG | COX'S RIDGE | BUCKFINDER | 4 - 7 - 16 - 1 - 0 | 2.11 | 0.50 | 28 |
| 1993 | BRUNSWICK | PRIVATE ACCOUNT | MR. PROSPECTOR | 14 - 9 - 16 - 0 - 1 | 3.44 | 0.88 | 40 |
| 1994 | COLONIAL AFFAIR | PLEASANT COLONY | NIJINSKY II | 8 - 1 - 19 - 4 - 2 | 1.19 | 0.26 | 34 |
| 1995 | UNACCOUNTED FOR | PRIVATE ACCOUNT | THE MINSTREL | 4 - 5 - 11 - 0 - 2 | 1.93 | 0.41 | 22 |
| 1996 | MAHOGANY HALL | WOODMAN | MAJESTIC LIGHT | 10 - 3 - 12 - 0 - 1 | 2.71 | 0.81 | 26 |
| 1997 | WILL'S WAY | EASY GOER | TENTAM | 9 - 6 - 16 - 0 - 1 | 2.56 | 0.69 | 32 |
| 1998 | AWESOME AGAIN | DEPUTY MINISTER | BLUSHING GROOM | 12 - 0 - 8 - 0 - 2 | 2.67 | 0.91 | 22 |
| 1999 | VICTORY GALLOP | CRYPTOCLEARANCE | VICE REGENT | 10 - 8 - 13 - 0 - 1 | 3.27 | 0.81 | 32 |
| 2000 | LEMON DROP KID | KINGMAMBO | SEATTLE SLEW | 13 - 4 - 21 - 0 - 0 | 2.62 | 0.79 | 38 |
| 2001 | LIDO PALACE | RICH MAN'S GOLD | QUICK DECISION | 6 - 1 - 4 - 0 - 1 | 3.00 | 0.92 | 12 |
| 2002 | LEFT BANK | FRENCH DEPUTY | DR. BLUM | 4 - 7 - 6 - 1 - 0 | 3.50 | 0.78 | 18 |
| | | | MEDIAN = | | 2.67 | 0.79 | 28.0 |

## WOODFORD RESERVE TURF CLASSIC S, THREE-YEAR-OLDS & UP, 9F, TURF:

| YEAR | WINNER | SIRE | BROODMARE SIRE | DP | DI | CD | PTS |
|---|---|---|---|---|---|---|---|
| 1996 | MECKE | MAUDLIN | BALDSKI | 10 - 6 - 4 - 2 - 0 | 4.50 | 1.09 | 22 |
| 1997 | ALWAYS A CLASSIC | DEPUTY MINISTER | NODOUBLE | 8 - 2 - 5 - 1 - 0 | 3.57 | 1.06 | 16 |
| 1998 | JOYEUX DANSEUR | NUREYEV | LE FABULEUX | 9 - 3 - 28 - 0 -12 | 1.00 | -0.06 | 52 |
| 1999 | WILD EVENT | WILD AGAIN | NORTHFIELDS | 8 - 5 - 11 - 0 - 0 | 3.36 | 0.88 | 24 |
| 2000 | MANNDAR | DOYOUN | DIESIS | 6 - 3 - 6 - 5 - 0 | 1.50 | 0.50 | 20 |
| 2001 | WHITE HEART | GREEN DESERT | BLUSHING GROOM | 11 - 8 - 17 - 1 - 3 | 2.20 | 0.58 | 40 |
| 2002 | BEAT HOLLOW | SADLER'S WELLS | DANCING BRAVE | 7 - 2 - 25 -12 - 0 | 0.88 | 0.09 | 46 |
| | | | MEDIAN = | | 2.20 | 0.58 | 24.0 |

## WOODWARD S, THREE-YEAR-OLDS & UP, 9F, DIRT:

| YEAR | WINNER | SIRE | BROODMARE SIRE | DP | DI | CD | PTS |
|---|---|---|---|---|---|---|---|
| 1990 | DISPERSAL | SUNNY'S HALO | JOHNNY APPLESEED | 5 - 4 - 12 - 3 - 2 | 1.36 | 0.27 | 26 |
| 1991 | IN EXCESS | SIBERIAN EXPRESS | SAULINGO | 4 - 4 - 4 - 0 - 0 | 5.00 | 1.00 | 12 |
| 1992 | SULTRY SONG | COX'S RIDGE | BUCKFINDER | 4 - 7 - 16 - 1 - 0 | 2.11 | 0.50 | 28 |
| 1993 | BERTRANDO | SKYWALKER | BUFFALO LARK | 4 - 7 - 3 - 0 - 0 | 8.33 | 1.07 | 14 |
| 1994 | HOLY BULL | GREAT ABOVE | AL HATTAB | 6 - 5 - 4 - 1 - 0 | 4.33 | 1.00 | 16 |
| 1995 | CIGAR | PALACE MUSIC | SEATTLE SLEW | 7 - 2 - 10 - 1 - 0 | 2.33 | 0.75 | 20 |
| 1996 | CIGAR | PALACE MUSIC | SEATTLE SLEW | 7 - 2 - 10 - 1 - 0 | 2.33 | 0.75 | 20 |
| 1997 | FORMAL GOLD | BLACK TIE AFFAIR | SCREEN KING | 5 - 2 - 7 - 0 - 0 | 3.00 | 0.86 | 14 |
| 1998 | SKIP AWAY | SKIP TRIAL | DIPLOMAT WAY | 5 - 6 - 8 - 1 - 0 | 3.00 | 0.75 | 20 |
| 1999 | RIVER KEEN | KEEN | CAERLEON | 11 - 3 - 8 - 6 - 2 | 1.50 | 0.50 | 30 |
| 2000 | LEMON DROP KID | KINGMAMBO | SEATTLE SLEW | 13 - 4 - 21 - 0 - 0 | 2.62 | 0.79 | 38 |
| 2001 | LIDO PALACE | RICH MAN'S GOLD | QUICK DECISION | 6 - 1 - 4 - 0 - 1 | 3.00 | 0.92 | 12 |
| | | | MEDIAN = | | 2.81 | 0.77 | 20.0 |

## YELLOW RIBBON S, THREE-YEAR-OLDS & UP, FILLIES & MARES, 10F, TURF:

| YEAR | WINNER | SIRE | BROODMARE SIRE | DP | DI | CD | PTS |
|---|---|---|---|---|---|---|---|
| 1990 | PLENTY OF GRACE | ROBERTO | KEY TO THE MINT | 11 - 5 - 38 - 5 - 1 | 1.40 | 0.33 | 60 |
| 1991 | KOSTROMA | CAERLEON | BUSTED | 2 - 1 - 9 -17 - 7 | 0.26 | -0.72 | 36 |
| 1992 | SUPER STAFF | SECRETARIAT | PHARLY | 10 -15 - 19 - 4 - 0 | 2.56 | 0.65 | 48 |
| 1993 | POSSIBLY PERFECT | NORTHERN BABY | AVATAR | 5 - 2 - 9 - 7 - 1 | 0.92 | 0.13 | 24 |
| 1994 | AUBE INDIENNE | BLUEBIRD | SPECTACULAR BID | 4 - 9 - 13 - 0 - 0 | 3.00 | 0.65 | 26 |
| 1995 | ALPRIDE | ALZAO | ROBERTO | 6 - 6 - 27 - 1 - 0 | 1.76 | 0.43 | 40 |
| 1996 | DONNA VIOLA | BE MY CHIEF | PRINCE TENDERFOOT | 3 - 7 - 7 - 1 - 0 | 3.00 | 0.67 | 18 |

| Year | | | | | | | |
|------|------|------|------|------|------|------|------|
| 1997 | RYAFAN | LEAR FAN | NORTHERN DANCER | 6 - 3 - 24 - 2 - 1 | 1.40 | 0.31 | 36 |
| 1998 | FIJI | RAINBOW QUEST | EXPLODENT | 9 - 0 - 7 - 2 - 4 | 1.32 | 0.36 | 22 |
| 1999 | SPANISH FERN | EL GRAN SENOR | BLUSHING GROOM | 12 - 2 - 16 - 0 - 2 | 2.20 | 0.69 | 32 |
| 2000 | TRANQUILITY LAKE | RAHY | DANZIG | 11 - 6 - 16 - 1 - 2 | 2.27 | 0.64 | 36 |
| 2001 | JANET | EMPEROR JONES | SPECTACULAR BID | 7 - 7 - 10 - 0 - 0 | 3.80 | 0.88 | 24 |
| 2002 | GOLDEN APPLES | PIVOTAL | KALDOUN | 1 - 3 - 6 - 0 - 0 | 2.33 | 0.50 | 10 |
| | | | | **MEDIAN =** | **2.20** | **0.50** | **32.0** |

# APPENDIX II

## DP CONTRIBUTIONS OF THE 150 LEADING SIRES OF 2001

| | DP CONTRIBUTION: | | | | | EQUIVALENT TO: | | |
|---|---|---|---|---|---|---|---|---|
| **SIRE** | **B** | **I** | **C** | **S** | **P** | **DI** | **CD** | **PTS** |
| A.P. Indy | 5 - | 3 - | 8 - | 0 - | 0 | 3.00 | 0.81 | 16 |
| Affirmed | 4 - | 1 - | 9 - | 0 - | 0 | 2.11 | 0.64 | 14 |
| Allen's Prospect | 8 - | 4 - | 8 - | 0 - | 0 | 4.00 | 1.00 | 20 |
| Alydeed | 3 - | 1 - | 8 - | 2 - | 0 | 1.33 | 0.36 | 14 |
| Ascot Knight | 2 - | 4 - | 6 - | 0 - | 0 | 3.00 | 0.67 | 12 |
| Bahri | 5 - | 7 - | 10 - | 2 - | 0 | 2.43 | 0.63 | 24 |
| Beau Genius | 4 - | 1 - | 1 - | 0 - | 0 | 11.00 | 1.50 | 6 |
| Belong to Me | 4 - | 4 - | 12 - | 0 - | 0 | 2.33 | 0.60 | 20 |
| Bertrando | 1 - | 2 - | 1 - | 0 - | 0 | 7.00 | 1.00 | 4 |
| Bold Executive | 3 - | 1 - | 0 - | 0 - | 0 | | 1.75 | 4 |
| Bold Ruckus | 10 - | 5 - | 1 - | 0 - | 0 | 31.00 | 1.56 | 16 |
| Boundary | 2 - | 6 - | 8 - | 2 - | 0 | 2.00 | 0.44 | 18 |
| Broad Brush | 4 - | 16 - | 13 - | 0 - | 1 | 3.53 | 0.65 | 34 |
| Capote | 6 - | 0 - | 4 - | 0 - | 0 | 4.00 | 1.20 | 10 |
| Carnivalay | 6 - | 2 - | 6 - | 0 - | 0 | 3.67 | 1.00 | 14 |
| Carson City | 10 - | 2 - | 9 - | 1 - | 0 | 3.00 | 0.95 | 22 |
| Cee's Tizzy | 4 - | 1 - | 7 - | 0 - | 0 | 2.43 | 0.75 | 12 |
| Cherokee Run | 2 - | 0 - | 2 - | 0 - | 0 | 3.00 | 1.00 | 4 |
| Chimes Band | 6 - | 0 - | 6 - | 0 - | 0 | 3.00 | 1.00 | 12 |
| Citidancer | 4 - | 2 - | 2 - | 0 - | 0 | 7.00 | 1.25 | 8 |
| Clever Trick | 5 - | 1 - | 6 - | 0 - | 0 | 3.00 | 0.92 | 12 |
| Colonial Affair | 3 - | 0 - | 8 - | 2 - | 1 | 1.00 | 0.14 | 14 |
| Concorde's Tune | 0 - | 0 - | 0 - | 0 - | 0 | | | 0 |
| Conquistador Cielo | 10 - | 4 - | 6 - | 0 - | 0 | 5.67 | 1.20 | 20 |
| Cozzene | 2 - | 6 - | 9 - | 1 - | 0 | 2.27 | 0.50 | 18 |
| Crafty Prospector | 11 - | 3 - | 8 - | 0 - | 0 | 4.50 | 1.14 | 22 |
| Cryptoclearance | 6 - | 8 - | 7 - | 0 - | 1 | 3.89 | 0.82 | 22 |
| Cure the Blues | 3 - | 7 - | 6 - | 0 - | 0 | 4.33 | 0.81 | 16 |
| Danzig | 5 - | 11 - | 14 - | 0 - | 0 | 3.29 | 0.70 | 30 |
| Dehere | 2 - | 4 - | 4 - | 0 - | 0 | 4.00 | 0.80 | 10 |
| Deposit Ticket | 6 - | 0 - | 4 - | 2 - | 0 | 2.00 | 0.83 | 12 |
| Deputy Minister | 2 - | 0 - | 2 - | 0 - | 0 | 3.00 | 1.00 | 4 |
| Devil His Due | 4 - | 0 - | 5 - | 1 - | 0 | 1.86 | 0.70 | 10 |
| Diablo | 5 - | 1 - | 5 - | 1 - | 0 | 2.43 | 0.83 | 12 |
| Distinctive Pro | 9 - | 3 - | 6 - | 0 - | 0 | 5.00 | 1.17 | 18 |
| Dixie Brass | 2 - | 0 - | 4 - | 0 - | 0 | 2.00 | 0.67 | 6 |
| Dixieland Band | 5 - | 1 - | 6 - | 0 - | 0 | 3.00 | 0.92 | 12 |

| | | | | |
|---|---|---|---|---|
| Dynaformer | 3 - 2 - 18 - 0 - 1 | 1.40 | 0.25 | 24 |
| El Gran Senor | 5 - 2 - 11 - 0 - 0 | 2.27 | 0.67 | 18 |
| El Prado | 2 - 4 - 10 - 4 - 0 | 1.22 | 0.20 | 20 |
| End Sweep | 5 - 0 - 4 - 0 - 1 | 2.33 | 0.80 | 10 |
| Fit to Fight | 6 - 4 - 2 - 0 - 0 | 11.00 | 1.33 | 12 |
| Fly So Free | 1 - 4 - 5 - 0 - 0 | 3.00 | 0.60 | 10 |
| Flying Continental | 0 - 0 - 2 - 0 - 0 | 1.00 | 0.00 | 2 |
| Forest Wildcat | 3 - 1 - 2 - 0 - 0 | 5.00 | 1.17 | 6 |
| Formal Dinner | 4 - 4 - 1 - 0 - 1 | 5.67 | 1.00 | 10 |
| Fortunate Prospect | 5 - 0 - 3 - 0 - 0 | 4.33 | 1.25 | 8 |
| French Deputy | 3 - 2 - 1 - 0 - 0 | 11.00 | 1.33 | 6 |
| Friendly Lover | 3 - 0 - 3 - 0 - 0 | 3.00 | 1.00 | 6 |
| Future Storm | 1 - 1 - 2 - 4 - 0 | 0.60 | -0.13 | 8 |
| General Meeting | 6 - 0 - 9 - 1 - 0 | 1.91 | 0.69 | 16 |
| Gilded Time | 5 - 5 - 3 - 1 - 0 | 4.60 | 1.00 | 14 |
| Glitterman | 7 - 3 - 2 - 0 - 0 | 11.00 | 1.42 | 12 |
| Go for Gin | 3 - 1 - 7 - 2 - 3 | 0.88 | -0.06 | 16 |
| Gone West | 9 - 5 - 8 - 0 - 0 | 4.50 | 1.05 | 22 |
| Gulch | 8 - 2 - 6 - 0 - 0 | 4.33 | 1.13 | 16 |
| Hansel | 5 - 0 - 5 - 0 - 0 | 3.00 | 1.00 | 10 |
| Hennessy | 1 - 1 - 2 - 0 - 0 | 3.00 | 0.75 | 4 |
| High Brite | 4 - 3 - 12 - 1 - 0 | 1.86 | 0.50 | 20 |
| Holy Bull | 3 - 2 - 1 - 0 - 0 | 11.00 | 1.33 | 6 |
| Honor Grades | 3 - 7 - 10 - 0 - 0 | 3.00 | 0.65 | 20 |
| Honour and Glory | 3 - 1 - 4 - 0 - 0 | 3.00 | 0.88 | 8 |
| Housebuster | 2 - 0 - 2 - 0 - 0 | 3.00 | 1.00 | 4 |
| In Excess | 0 - 1 - 1 - 0 - 0 | 3.00 | 0.50 | 2 |
| Irish River | 4 - 6 - 6 - 0 - 0 | 4.33 | 0.88 | 16 |
| Jeblar | 6 - 1 - 9 - 0 - 0 | 2.56 | 0.81 | 16 |
| JudgeT C | 4 - 4 - 6 - 0 - 0 | 3.67 | 0.86 | 14 |
| Kingmambo | 9 - 2 - 11 - 0 - 0 | 3.00 | 0.91 | 22 |
| Kissin Kris | 0 - 1 - 8 - 1 - 0 | 1.00 | 0.00 | 10 |
| Known Fact | 9 - 3 - 6 - 0 - 0 | 5.00 | 1.17 | 18 |
| Kris S. | 1 - 4 - 15 - 2 - 0 | 1.32 | 0.18 | 22 |
| Line in the Sand | 10 - 3 - 9 - 0 - 0 | 3.89 | 1.05 | 22 |
| Lord at War | 0 - 0 - 1 - 0 - 1 | 0.33 | -1.00 | 2 |
| Lord Avie | 3 - 6 - 3 - 0 - 0 | 7.00 | 1.00 | 12 |
| Lost Code | 0 - 2 - 3 - 0 - 1 | 1.40 | 0.00 | 6 |
| Maria's Mon | 0 - 2 - 4 - 0 - 0 | 2.00 | 0.33 | 6 |
| Marquetry | 6 - 1 - 3 - 0 - 0 | 5.67 | 1.30 | 10 |
| Meadowlake | 6 - 5 - 3 - 0 - 0 | 8.33 | 1.21 | 14 |
| Miner's Mark | 9 - 4 - 7 - 0 - 0 | 4.71 | 1.10 | 20 |
| Miswaki | 8 - 4 - 11 - 1 - 0 | 2.69 | 0.79 | 24 |
| Montbrook | 0 - 1 - 5 - 0 - 0 | 1.40 | 0.17 | 6 |
| Mountain Cat | 4 - 2 - 5 - 1 - 0 | 2.43 | 0.75 | 12 |

| Mr. Greeley | 7 - 2 - 5 - 0 - 0 | 4.60 | 1.14 | 14 |
|---|---|---|---|---|
| Mr. Prospector | 18 - 6 - 14 - 0 - 0 | 4.43 | 1.11 | 38 |
| Mt. Livermore | 8 - 0 - 4 - 0 - 2 | 2.50 | 0.86 | 14 |
| Mutakddim | 7 - 0 - 7 - 0 - 0 | 3.00 | 1.00 | 14 |
| Norquestor | 6 - 0 - 4 - 2 - 0 | 2.00 | 0.83 | 12 |
| Not for Love | 10 - 2 - 10 - 0 - 0 | 3.40 | 1.00 | 22 |
| Notebook | 1 - 2 - 4 - 0 - 3 | 1.00 | -0.20 | 10 |
| Numerous | 9 - 2 - 11 - 2 - 0 | 2.20 | 0.75 | 24 |
| Nureyev | 5 - 1 - 26 - 0 - 0 | 1.46 | 0.34 | 32 |
| Olympio | 2 - 0 - 0 - 0 - 0 | | 2.00 | 2 |
| Out Of Place | 1 - 3 - 8 - 0 - 0 | 2.00 | 0.42 | 12 |
| Pentelicus | 7 - 7 - 10 - 0 - 0 | 3.80 | 0.88 | 24 |
| Personal Flag | 2 - 4 - 5 - 0 - 1 | 2.43 | 0.50 | 12 |
| Phone Trick | 4 - 0 - 2 - 0 - 0 | 5.00 | 1.33 | 6 |
| Pine Bluff | 4 - 4 - 10 - 0 - 0 | 2.60 | 0.67 | 18 |
| Pleasant Colony | 2 - 0 - 12 - 0 - 2 | 1.00 | 0.00 | 16 |
| Pleasant Tap | 1 - 1 - 7 - 2 - 3 | 0.65 | -0.36 | 14 |
| Polish Numbers | 2 - 5 - 11 - 0 - 0 | 2.27 | 0.50 | 18 |
| Press Card | 8 - 8 - 8 - 0 - 0 | 5.00 | 1.00 | 24 |
| Private Terms | 4 - 5 - 5 - 0 - 0 | 4.60 | 0.93 | 14 |
| Prized | 0 - 1 - 6 - 1 - 0 | 1.00 | 0.00 | 8 |
| Prospectors Gamble | 5 - 0 - 3 - 0 - 0 | 4.33 | 1.25 | 8 |
| Quiet American | 5 - 10 - 7 - 0 - 0 | 5.29 | 0.91 | 22 |
| Rahy | 8 - 0 - 9 - 1 - 2 | 1.67 | 0.55 | 20 |
| Red Ransom | 1 - 4 - 15 - 0 - 0 | 1.67 | 0.30 | 20 |
| Regal Classic | 3 - 0 - 3 - 0 - 0 | 3.00 | 1.00 | 6 |
| Relaunch | 7 - 3 - 6 - 0 - 0 | 4.33 | 1.06 | 16 |
| Rizzi | 5 - 1 - 4 - 0 - 0 | 4.00 | 1.10 | 10 |
| Robyn Dancer | 5 - 1 - 4 - 0 - 0 | 4.00 | 1.10 | 10 |
| Royal Academy | 4 - 0 - 6 - 4 - 0 | 1.00 | 0.29 | 14 |
| Rubiano | 6 - 6 - 10 - 2 - 0 | 2.43 | 0.67 | 24 |
| Runaway Groom | 6 - 0 - 4 - 0 - 2 | 2.00 | 0.67 | 12 |
| Saint Ballado | 5 - 1 - 10 - 2 - 2 | 1.22 | 0.25 | 20 |
| Salt Lake | 1 - 0 - 1 - 0 - 0 | 3.00 | 1.00 | 2 |
| Sea Hero | 1 - 2 - 8 - 2 - 1 | 1.00 | 0.00 | 14 |
| SeattleSlew | 9 - 1 - 10 - 2 - 0 | 2.14 | 0.77 | 22 |
| Seeking the Gold | 8 - 3 - 11 - 0 - 0 | 3.00 | 0.86 | 22 |
| Silver Deputy | 5 - 0 - 3 - 0 - 0 | 4.33 | 1.25 | 8 |
| Silver Ghost | 10 - 2 - 10 - 0 - 0 | 3.40 | 1.00 | 22 |
| Skip Trial | 2 - 2 - 6 - 0 - 0 | 2.33 | 0.60 | 10 |
| Sky Classic | 3 - 0 - 7 - 4 - 0 | 0.87 | 0.14 | 14 |
| Skywalker | 4 - 3 - 3 - 0 - 0 | 5.67 | 1.10 | 10 |
| Slew City Slew | 4 - 0 - 4 - 0 - 0 | 3.00 | 1.00 | 8 |
| Smart Strike | 8 - 2 - 6 - 0 - 0 | 4.33 | 1.13 | 16 |
| Southern Halo | 7 - 1 - 10 - 2 - 0 | 1.86 | 0.65 | 20 |

| | | | | |
|---|---|---|---|---|
| Star de Naskra | 6 - 0 - 0 - 0 -0 | | 2.00 | 6 |
| Storm Boot | 5 - 1 - 4 - 2 -0 | 2.00 | 0.75 | 12 |
| Storm Cat | 3 - 3 - 4 - 0 -0 | 4.00 | 0.90 | 10 |
| Storm Creek | 5 - 2 - 5 - 0 -0 | 3.80 | 1.00 | 12 |
| Strike the Gold | 4 - 1 - 9 - 0 -0 | 2.11 | 0.64 | 14 |
| Summer Squall | 3 - 3 - 6 - 0 -0 | 3.00 | 0.75 | 12 |
| Sword Dance | 3 - 3 - 10 - 4 -0 | 1.22 | 0.25 | 20 |
| Tabasco Cat | 2 - 1 - 3 - 0 -0 | 3.00 | 0.83 | 6 |
| Tactical Advantage | 5 - 0 - 10 - 0 -1 | 1.67 | 0.50 | 16 |
| Theatrical | 2 - 0 - 14 - 0 -0 | 1.29 | 0.25 | 16 |
| Thunder Gulch | 5 - 0 - 3 - 0 -0 | 4.33 | 1.25 | 8 |
| Tour D'or | 3 - 4 - 3 - 0 -0 | 5.67 | 1.00 | 10 |
| Twining | 8 - 2 - 5 - 0 -1 | 3.57 | 1.00 | 16 |
| Two Punch | 10 - 4 - 7 - 1 -0 | 3.89 | 1.05 | 22 |
| Unaccounted For | 1 - 2 - 5 - 0 -0 | 2.20 | 0.50 | 8 |
| Unbridled | 5 - 6 - 7 - 0 -6 | 1.53 | 0.17 | 24 |
| Unbridled's Song | 1 - 4 - 5 - 0 -2 | 1.67 | 0.17 | 12 |
| Valid Wager | 4 - 4 - 4 - 0 -0 | 5.00 | 1.00 | 12 |
| West by West | 4 - 1 - 5 - 0 -0 | 3.00 | 0.90 | 10 |
| Wild Again | 6 - 5 - 7 - 0 -0 | 4.14 | 0.94 | 18 |
| With Approval | 3 - 5 - 10 - 0 -0 | 2.60 | 0.61 | 18 |
| Woodman | 8 - 3 - 11 - 0 -0 | 3.00 | 0.86 | 22 |
| You and I | 0 - 1 - 6 - 1 -0 | 1.00 | 0.00 | 8 |

# APPENDIX III

## DOSAGE FIGURES FOR PROMINENT THOROUGHBRED RUNNERS

Since almost all *chefs-de-race* were born since 1900, and assuming an average of ten years per generation, the Dosage figures below for prominent runners born much before 1940 may not reflect all sources of aptitudinal prepotence within four generations.

| HORSE | DP | DI | CD |
|---|---|---|---|
| A.P. Indy, 1989 | 13 - 10 - 20 - 3 - 0 | 2.54 | 0.72 |
| Ack Ack, 1966 | 9 - 6 - 7 - 2 - 2 | 2.47 | 0.69 |
| Affectionately, 1960 | 6 - 12 - 14 - 7 - 3 | 1.47 | 0.26 |
| Affirmed, 1975 | 8 - 6 - 26 - 0 - 0 | 2.08 | 0.55 |
| All Along, 1979 | 7 - 4 - 21 - 10 - 0 | 1.05 | 0.19 |
| Alsab, 1939 | 2 - 6 - 0 - 2 - 2 | 2.00 | 0.33 |
| Alydar, 1975 | 21 - 8 - 9 - 4 - 0 | 3.94 | 1.10 |
| Alysheba, 1984 | 12 - 4 - 22 - 2 - 0 | 2.08 | 0.65 |
| Armed, 1941 | 10 - 0 - 16 - 6 - 4 | 1.00 | 0.17 |
| Arts and Letters, 1966 | 5 - 2 - 11 - 2 - 8 | 0.81 | -0.21 |
| Assault, 1943 | 6 - 6 - 8 - 1 - 3 | 2.00 | 0.46 |
| Bald Eagle, 1955 | 26 - 10 - 8 - 5 - 1 | 4.00 | 1.10 |
| Bayakoa, 1984 | 8 - 8 - 6 - 0 - 0 | 6.33 | 1.09 |
| Bed o' Roses, 1947 | 0 - 8 - 4 - 9 - 1 | 0.83 | -0.14 |
| Bewitch, 1945 | 12 - 6 - 16 - 4 - 2 | 1.86 | 0.55 |
| Bimelech, 1937 | 16 - 12 - 0 - 8 - 0 | 3.50 | 1.00 |
| Black Helen, 1932 | 16 - 12 - 0 - 8 - 0 | 3.50 | 1.00 |
| Black Tie Affair, 1986 | 11 - 6 - 12 - 1 - 0 | 3.29 | 0.90 |
| Bold 'n Determined, 1977 | 10 - 5 - 10 - 2 - 1 | 2.50 | 0.75 |
| Bold Ruler, 1954 | 26 - 8 - 8 - 11 - 1 | 2.38 | 0.87 |
| Bon Nouvel, 1960 | 9 - 3 - 0 - 4 - 0 | 3.00 | 1.06 |
| Buckpasser, 1963 | 6 - 11 - 21 - 9 - 1 | 1.34 | 0.25 |
| Busher, 1942 | 0 - 8 - 17 - 17 - 2 | 0.60 | -0.30 |
| Café Prince, 1970 | 2 - 2 - 14 - 10 - 0 | 1.71 | 0.70 |
| Carry Back, 1958 | 4 - 2 - 12 - 6 - 0 | 1.00 | 0.17 |
| Cavalcade, 1931 | 0 - 0 - 8 - 0 - 14 | 0.22 | -1.27 |
| Challedon, 1936 | 0 - 0 - 16 - 4 - 2 | 0.57 | -0.36 |
| Charismatic, 1996 | 9 - 10 - 9 - 0 - 0 | 5.22 | 1.00 |
| Chris Evert, 1971 | 6 - 10 - 2 - 2 - 0 | 5.67 | 1.00 |
| Cicada, 1959 | 6 - 0 - 10 - 4 - 0 | 1.22 | 0.40 |
| Cigar, 1990 | 7 - 2 - 10 - 1 - 0 | 2.33 | 0.75 |
| Citation, 1945 | 12 - 0 - 24 - 6 - 8 | 0.92 | 0.04 |
| Coaltown, 1945 | 8 - 0 - 26 - 8 - 2 | 0.91 | 0.09 |
| Conquistador Cielo, 1979 | 26 - 10 - 14 - 0 - 0 | 6.14 | 1.24 |
| Count Fleet, 1940 | 0 - 2 - 1 - 1 - 0 | 1.67 | 0.25 |
| Criminal Type, 1985 | 10 - 6 - 20 - 0 - 0 | 2.60 | 0.72 |

185

| | | | | | | | | | |
|---|---|---|---|---|---|---|---|---|---|
| Dahlia, 1970 | 4 - | 4 - | 20 - | 0 - | 8 | 1.00 | -0.11 |
| Damascus, 1964 | 10 - | 4 - | 3 - | 0 - | 1 | 6.20 | 1.22 |
| Dark Mirage, 1965 | 3 - | 6 - | 19 - | 4 - | 0 | 1.37 | 0.25 |
| Davona Dale, 1976 | 9 - | 8 - | 25 - | 0 - | 2 | 2.03 | 0.50 |
| Desert Vixen, 1970 | 15 - | 4 - | 15 - | 2 - | 0 | 2.79 | 0.89 |
| Devil Diver, 1939 | 0 - | 2 - | 8 - | 0 - | 0 | 1.50 | 0.20 |
| Discovery, 1931 | 0 - | 0 - | 0 - | 4 - | 6 | 0.00 | -1.60 |
| Dr. Fager, 1971 | 15 - | 1 - | 10 - | 2 - | 0 | 3.00 | 1.04 |
| Easy Goer, 1986 | 10 - | 6 - | 30 - | 0 - | 0 | 2.07 | 0.57 |
| Eight Thirty, 1936 | 4 - | 4 - | 18 - | 7 - | 3 | 0.89 | -0.03 |
| Elkridge, 1938 | 8 - | 6 - | 0 - | 0 - | 2 | 7.00 | 1.13 |
| Equipoise, 1928 | 8 - | 12 - | 0 - | 0 - | 0 | | 1.40 |
| Exceller, 1973 | 10 - | 4 - | 1 - | 0 - | 8 | 1.38 | 0.21 |
| Favorite Trick, 1995 | 7 - | 2 - | 5 - | 0 - | 0 | 4.60 | 1.14 |
| Ferdinand, 1983 | 14 - | 2 - | 16 - | 8 - | 0 | 1.50 | 0.55 |
| Flatterer, 1979 | 9 - | 2 - | 3 - | 0 - | 0 | 8.33 | 1.43 |
| Foolish Pleasure, 1972 | 28 - | 10 - | 11 - | 4 - | 2 | 3.70 | 1.04 |
| Forego, 1970 | 8 - | 2 - | 26 - | 2 - | 2 | 1.35 | 0.30 |
| Fort Marcy, 1964 | 7 - | 10 - | 15 - | 6 - | 6 | 1.26 | 0.14 |
| Gallant Bloom, 1966 | 10 - | 11 - | 12 - | 7 - | 2 | 1.80 | 0.48 |
| Gallant Man, 1954 | 0 - | 4 - | 18 - | 16 - | 2 | 0.48 | -0.40 |
| Gallorette, 1942 | 0 - | 0 - | 16 - | 4 - | 4 | 0.50 | -0.50 |
| Gamely, 1964 | 28 - | 14 - | 6 - | 5 - | 1 | 5.00 | 1.17 |
| Genuine Risk, 1977 | 14 - | 10 - | 24 - | 2 - | 0 | 2.57 | 0.72 |
| Go For Wand, 1987 | 6 - | 2 - | 4 - | 0 - | 0 | 5.00 | 1.17 |
| Granville, 1933 | 0 - | 0 - | 9 - | 5 - | 6 | 0.29 | -0.85 |
| Gun Bow, 1960 | 6 - | 2 - | 20 - | 9 - | 5 | 0.75 | -0.12 |
| Hill Prince, 1947 | 2 - | 10 - | 10 - | 10 - | 0 | 1.13 | 0.13 |
| Holy Bull, 1991 | 8 - | 5 - | 4 - | 1 - | 0 | 5.00 | 1.11 |
| Jay Trump, 1957 | 0 - | 10 - | 4 - | 2 - | 0 | 3.00 | 0.50 |
| John Henry, 1975 | 13 - | 4 - | 9 - | 2 - | 0 | 3.31 | 1.00 |
| Johnstown, 1936 | 0 - | 0 - | 9 - | 7 - | 8 | 0.23 | -0.96 |
| Kelso, 1957 | 2 - | 2 - | 27 - | 6 - | 1 | 0.85 | -0.05 |
| Kotashaan, 1988 | 2 - | 2 - | 7 - | 3 - | 4 | 0.71 | -0.28 |
| La Prevoyante, 1970 | 5 - | 11 - | 32 - | 2 - | 0 | 1.78 | 0.38 |
| Lady's Secret, 1982 | 18 - | 15 - | 17 - | 4 - | 0 | 3.32 | 0.87 |
| L'Escargot, 1963 | 0 - | 0 - | 2 - | 0 - | 2 | 0.33 | -1.00 |
| Lure, 1989 | 9 - | 12 - | 23 - | 0 - | 0 | 2.83 | 0.68 |
| Majestic Prince, 1966 | 27 - | 11 - | 12 - | 4 - | 2 | 3.67 | 1.02 |
| Man o' War, 1917 | 0 - | 0 - | 4 - | 12 - | 8 | 0.09 | -1.17 |
| Miesque, 1984 | 5 - | 2 - | 29 - | 3 - | 1 | 1.16 | 0.17 |
| Myrtlewood, 1932 | 4 - | 8 - | 16 - | 2 - | 0 | 2.00 | 0.47 |
| Nashua, 1952 | 22 - | 8 - | 10 - | 2 - | 4 | 3.18 | 0.91 |
| Native Dancer, 1950 | 4 - | 18 - | 0 - | 9 - | 1 | 2.20 | 0.47 |
| Needles, 1953 | 4 - | 2 - | 10 - | 2 - | 2 | 1.22 | 0.20 |

| | | | | | | | | |
|---|---|---|---|---|---|---|---|---|
| Neji, 1950 | 2 - | 2 - | 0 - | 6 - | 8 | 0.29 | -0.89 |
| Noor, 1945 | 22 - | 8 - | 22 - | 2 - | 2 | 2.73 | 0.82 |
| Northern Dancer, 1961 | 8 - | 16 - | 15 - | 3 - | 0 | 3.00 | 0.69 |
| Oedipus, 1946 | 12 - | 4 - | 16 - | 6 - | 0 | 1.71 | 0.58 |
| Omaha, 1932 | 0 - | 0 - | 8 - | 4 - | 4 | 0.33 | -0.75 |
| Paseana, 1987 | 4 - | 4 - | 2 - | 0 - | 0 | 9.00 | 1.20 |
| Personal Ensign, 1984 | 7 - | 9 - | 15 - | 0 - | 3 | 2.24 | 0.50 |
| Phar Lap, 1926 | 0 - | 0 - | 0 - | 0 - | 4 | 0.00 | -2.00 |
| Point Given, 1998 | 8 - | 0 - | 8 - | 0 - | 0 | 3.00 | -2.00 |
| Princess Rooney, 1980 | 9 - | 9 - | 11 - | 1 - | 0 | 3.62 | 0.87 |
| Real Delight, 1949 | 9 - | 1 - | 24 - | 4 - | 4 | 1.10 | 0.17 |
| Riva Ridge, 1969 | 19 - | 4 - | 7 - | 2 - | 2 | 3.53 | 1.06 |
| Roman Brother, 1961 | 4 - | 8 - | 8 - | 11 - | 3 | 0.89 | -0.03 |
| Round Table, 1954 | 12 - | 8 - | 10 - | 8 - | 2 | 1.67 | 0.50 |
| Ruffian, 1972 | 18 - | 13 - | 15 - | 4 - | 0 | 3.35 | 0.90 |
| Seabiscuit, 1933 | 0 - | 6 - | 3 - | 13 - | 6 | 0.37 | -0.68 |
| Searching, 1952 | 8 - | 12 - | 17 - | 15 - | 2 | 1.12 | 0.17 |
| Seattle Slew, 1974 | 7 - | 6 - | 4 - | 5 - | 0 | 2.14 | 0.68 |
| Secretariat, 1970 | 20 - | 14 - | 7 - | 9 - | 0 | 3.00 | 0.90 |
| Shuvee, 1966 | 12 - | 12 - | 15 - | 3 - | 2 | 2.52 | 0.66 |
| Silver Charm, 1994 | 3 - | 5 - | 17 - | 5 - | 0 | 1.22 | 0.20 |
| Silver Spoon, 1956 | 6 - | 6 - | 24 - | 6 - | 2 | 1.20 | 0.18 |
| Skip Away, 1993 | 5 - | 6 - | 8 - | 1 - | 0 | 3.00 | 0.75 |
| Slew o' Gold, 1980 | 9 - | 4 - | 22 - | 3 - | 0 | 1.71 | 0.50 |
| Spectacular Bid, 1976 | 9 - | 14 - | 18 - | 3 - | 0 | 2.67 | 0.66 |
| Spend a Buck, 1982 | 6 - | 7 - | 18 - | 1 - | 0 | 2.20 | 0.56 |
| Stymie, 1941 | 2 - | 8 - | 14 - | 10 - | 2 | 0.86 | -0.08 |
| Sunday Silence, 1986 | 12 - | 3 - | 21 - | 0 - | 0 | 2.43 | 0.75 |
| Susan's Girl, 1969 | 10 - | 2 - | 9 - | 1 - | 0 | 3.00 | 0.95 |
| Swaps, 1952 | 4 - | 18 - | 14 - | 4 - | 8 | 1.53 | 0.13 |
| Sword Dancer, 1956 | 2 - | 0 - | 2 - | 5 - | 1 | 0.43 | -0.30 |
| Ta Wee, 1966 | 11 - | 9 - | 2 - | 6 - | 0 | 3.00 | 0.89 |
| Tim Tam, 1955 | 10 - | 11 - | 17 - | 4 - | 0 | 2.36 | 0.64 |
| Tiznow, 1997 | 7 - | 1 - | 10 - | 2 - | 0 | 1.86 | 0.65 |
| Tom Fool, 1949 | 14 - | 2 - | 2 - | 6 - | 2 | 1.89 | 0.77 |
| Top Flight, 1929 | 8 - | 2 - | 0 - | 0 - | 8 | 1.25 | 0.11 |
| Tosmah, 1961 | 6 - | 6 - | 13 - | 1 - | 0 | 2.47 | 0.65 |
| Twenty Grand, 1928 | 0 - | 6 - | 8 - | 0 - | 0 | 2.50 | 0.43 |
| Twilight Tear, 1941 | 9 - | 1 - | 24 - | 4 - | 2 | 1.22 | 0.28 |
| Two Lea, 1946 | 8 - | 6 - | 16 - | 4 - | 4 | 1.38 | 0.26 |
| War Admiral, 1934 | 0 - | 12 - | 2 - | 22 - | 6 | 0.45 | -0.52 |
| Whirlaway, 1938 | 0 - | 12 - | 20 - | 8 - | 0 | 1.22 | 0.10 |
| Winning Colors, 1985 | 10 - | 14 - | 8 - | 0 - | 4 | 3.50 | 0.72 |
| Zaccio, 1976 | 2 - | 1 - | 2 - | 0 - | 2 | 5.00 | 0.67 |

# APPENDIX IV

## APTITUDINAL GUIDELINES
## FOR *NON-CHEF-DE-RACE* SIRES AND BROODMARE SIRES

### SIRES:

| Dominant Speed | Intermediate Speed | Balanced Speed | Intermediate Stamina | Dominant Stamina |
|---|---|---|---|---|
| Allen's Prospect | Afleet | Affirmed | A.P. Indy | Alleged |
| Baederwood | Air Forbes Won | Al Hattab | Ascot Knight | Assert |
| Bet Big | Buckaroo | Bates Motel | Avatar | Big Spruce |
| Bold Ruckus | Buckfinder | Believe It | Coastal | Bucksplasher |
| Capote | Conquistador Cielo | Black Tie Affair | Codex | Caerleon |
| Carson City | Copelan | Bold Forbes | Cox's Ridge | Caucasus |
| Citidancer | Cure the Blues | Carnivalay | Darby Creek Road | Caveat |
| Clever Trick | Dixieland Band | Cee's Tizzy | Dynaformer | Chief's Crown |
| Crafty Prospector | El Prado | Chieftain | El Gran Senor | Cozzene |
| Cutlass | Fire Dancer | Cormorant | Exceller | Green Dancer |
| Distinctive Pro | Foolish Pleasure | Cryptoclearance | Forceten | Irish River |
| Drone | Forty Niner | Deputy Minister | Hold Your Tricks | Kingmambo |
| End Sweep | Gone West | Devil's Bag | Jade Hunter | Lear Fan |
| Exuberant | Gulch | Explodent | Kris S. | Lyphard's Wish |
| Full Out | Hero's Honor | Farma Way | Lord at War | Manila |
| Full Pocket | Hold Your Peace | Fit to Fight | Majestic Light | Persian Bold |
| Geiger Counter | Honest Pleasure | Flying Paster | Maudlin | Petrone |
| Gilded Time | Lypheor | Fortunate Prospect | Mr. Leader | Rainbow Quest |
| Glitterman | Marfa | General Meeting | Naskra | Rich Cream |
| Great Above | Mari's Book | Golden Act | Nodouble | Sky Classic |
| Hawkin's Special | Miswaki | Habitony | Northern Baby | Son of Briartic |
| High Brite | Norcliffe | John Alden | On the Sly | Steady Growth |
| Horatius | Northern Jove | L'Enjoleur | Our Native | Theatrical |
| Housebuster | Notebook | Lord Avie | Pleasant Colony | Trempolino |
| Irish Tower | On To Glory | Lt. Stevens | Private Account | Val de l'Orne |
| Island Whirl | Personal Flag | Magesterial | Proud Truth | |
| It's Freezing | Pirate's Bounty | Mt. Livermore | Quiet American | |
| Java Gold | Polish Numbers | Nasty and Bold | Red Ransom | |
| Kennedy Road | Rahy | Overskate | Seattle Dancer | |
| Known Fact | Raja Baba | Pine Bluff | Silver Buck | |
| Lost Code | Regal Classic | Pleasant Tap | Silver Hawk | |
| Marquetry | Relaunch | Private Terms | Skip Trial | |
| Meadowlake | Runaway Groom | Saros | Staff Writer | |
| Medieval Man | Saint Ballado | Sauce Boat | Strawberry Road | |
| Mining | Seeking The Gold | Skywalker | Summer Squall | |
| Northern Prospect | Silver Deputy | Slew City Slew | Sunny's Halo | |
| Ogygian | Silver Ghost | Slew o' Gold | The Minstrel | |
| Phone Trick | Slewacide | Sovereign Dancer | Thunder Gulch | |

| Dominant Speed | Intermediate Speed | Balanced Speed | Intermediate Stamina | Dominant Stamina |
|---|---|---|---|---|
| Premiership | Stalwart | Spectacular Bid | Unbridled | |
| Proud Birdie | Star De Naskra | Spend a Buck | Verbatim | |
| Salt Lake | Stop The Music | Temperence Hill | Waquoit | |
| Saratoga Six | Storm Bird | Time for a Change | | |
| Slewpy | Storm Cat | Topsider | | |
| Smarten | Tentam | Vigors | | |
| Storm Boot | Top Command | Wild Again | | |
| Timeless Moment | Tri Jet | With Approval | | |
| Two Punch | Vice Regent | Woodman | | |
| Valid Appeal | | | | |
| Wavering Monarch | | | | |
| Well Decorated | | | | |
| What Luck | | | | |

## BROODMARE SIRES:

| Dominant Speed | Intermediate Speed | Balanced Speed | Intermediate Stamina | Dominant Stamina |
|---|---|---|---|---|
| Bold Ruckus | Barbizon | Affirmed | Arts and Letters | Caerleon |
| Buckaroo | Believe It | Al Hattab | Bold Hour | Diesis |
| Clever Trick | Blade | Alleged | Buckfinder | Minnesota Mac |
| Crimson Satan | Bolinas Boy | Barachois | Dewan | Sassafras |
| Cutlass | Briartic | Big Spruce | Diplomat Way | Verbatim |
| Distinctive | Conquistador Cielo | Bold Ambition | Elocutionist | |
| Fast Hilarious | Cornish Prince | Boldnesian | Exceller | |
| Foolish Pleasure | Cox's Ridge | Chief's Crown | Far North | |
| Full Pocket | Crozier | Chieftain | Gleaming | |
| Great Above | Dancing Count | Copelan | Green Dancer | |
| Green Ticket | Deputy Minister | Cure the Blues | Inverness Drive | |
| Hold Your Peace | Dixieland Band | Cyane | King Pellinore | |
| I'ma Hell Raiser | Drone | Dancing Champ | L'Enjoleur | |
| Iron Constitution | Explodent | Delta Judge | Naskra | |
| Lucky Debonair | Fit to Fight | Dr. Blum | Northfields | |
| Magesterial | Fleet Nasrullah | First Landing | One for All | |
| Medieval Man | Francis S. | Flying Paster | Our Native | |
| Proudest Roman | Gallant Romeo | Great Nephew | Pleasant Colony | |
| Raja Baba | Gummo | Groton | Search for Gold | |
| Relaunch | Hagley | Hawaii | Seattle Song | |
| Sadair | Hard Work | Irish River | Super Concorde | |
| Shecky Greene | Hatchet Man | Jacinto | The Axe II | |
| Slew o' Gold | Impressive | King Emperor | Transworld | |
| Storm Cat | Irish Tower | Knightly Dawn | Upper Nile | |
| What Luck | Iron Ruler | Little Current | | |
| Whitesburg | Kris S. | Lt. Stevens | | |
| Winning Hit | Lord Gaylord | Majestic Light | | |

| Dominant Speed | Intermediate Speed | Balanced Speed | Intermediate Stamina | Dominant Stamina |
|---|---|---|---|---|
| | Mr. Leader | Majestic Prince | | |
| | Native Royalty | Nantallah | | |
| | New Policy | Native Charger | | |
| | Northern Jove | No Robbery | | |
| | Olden Times | Nodouble | | |
| | Our Michael | Private Account | | |
| | Personality | Raise A Cup | | |
| | Quack | Rising Market | | |
| | Quadrangle | Saratoga Six | | |
| | Restless Native | Seeking The Gold | | |
| | Restless Wind | Sham | | |
| | Riva Ridge | Smarten | | |
| | Ruritania | Spectacular Bid | | |
| | Sauce Boat | Stevward | | |
| | Silent Screen | Stop the Music | | |
| | Tentam | Storm Bird | | |
| | Timeless Moment | T. V. Commercial | | |
| | Topsider | The Minstrel | | |
| | Tsunami Slew | Tri Jet | | |
| | Valid Appeal | Turn To Reason | | |
| | | Vice Regent | | |
| | | Viceregal | | |
| | | Vigors | | |
| | | Wavering Monarch | | |

# APPENDIX V

## BRUCE LOWE FAMILIES OF U.S. CLASSIC, ENGLISH DERBY
## AND PRIX DE L'ARC DE TRIOMPHE WINNERS SINCE 1940

The following table groups Kentucky Derby, Preakness Stakes, Belmont Stakes, Breeders' Cup Classic, English Derby and Prix de l'Arc de Triomphe winners since 1940 according to their Bruce Lowe female family. The name of the foundation mare is shown next to the family number. If a family number is missing it means there are no examples among the classic winners over the historical timeframe.

| A1 (Ella Crump) | A5 (Election Bet) | 1 (Tregonwell's Natural Barb mare) | 2 (Burton's Barb mare) | 3 (Dam of Two True Blues |
|---|---|---|---|---|
| Gato del Sol | Concern | All Along | Alleged | A.P. Indy |
| Counterpoint | | Allez France | Ballymoss | Caveat |
| | | Alphabet Soup | Candy Spots | Citation |
| | | Ardan | Cannonade | Dancing Brave |
| | | Arts and Letters | Cavan | Dante |
| | | Awesome Again | Charlottown | Dark Star |
| | | Bimelech | Cigar | Dust Commander |
| | | Bold | Elocutionist | Fabius |
| | | Bon Mot | Empery | Gate Dancer |
| | | Bounding Home | Exbury | Hasty Road |
| | | Celtic Ash | Hansel | Henbit |
| | | Dr Devious | High Echelon | Lemon Drop Kid |
| | | Erhaab | Nashwan | Louis Quatorze |
| | | Genuine Risk | Northern Dancer | Lucky Debonair |
| | | Go For Gin | Parthia | Nashua |
| | | Greek Money | Point Given | Pinza |
| | | Grindstone | Quadrangle | Pont l'Eveque |
| | | Hail to All | Sea-Bird | Prince Royal |
| | | High Chapparal | Secretariat | Santa Claus |
| | | High Gun | Skywalker | Shahrastani |
| | | Larkspur | Spectacular Bid | Sherluck |
| | | Levmoss | Touch Gold | Silver Charm |
| | | Master Derby | | Summer Squall |
| | | Montjeu | | Sunday Silence |
| | | Never Say Die | | Teenoso |
| | | Oath | | Verso |
| | | Ocean Swell | | Wild Again |
| | | Pass Catcher | | |
| | | Pensive | | |
| | | Personality | | |
| | | Prairie Bayou | | |
| | | Proud Clarion | | |
| | | Riva Ridge | | |
| | | Royal Palace | | |
| | | Sea Hero | | |
| | | Shaamit | | |

**1 (continued)**

Shirley Heights
Spend a Buck
Stage Door Johnny
Straight Deal
Summing
Swale
Sword Dancer
Three Troikas
Tomy Lee
Troy
Unbridled
Vaguely Noble

**4 (Layton Barb mare)**

Assault
Canonero II
Faultless
Gallahadion
Generous
Lavandin
Majestic Prince
Middleground
Monarchos
Nikellora
Nuccio
Quest for Fame
Real Quiet
Ribot
Secreto
Suave Dancer
Subotica
Sunny's Halo
Temperence hill
Timber Country
Venetian Wa

**5 (Dtr. of Massy's Black barb)**

Avatar
Capot
Determine
Djebel
Gallant Man
Kahyasi
Native Dancer
Needles
Pleasant Colony
Star Appeal

**6 (Old Bald Peg)**

Count Fleet
Nimbus
Snow Knight

**7 (Darcy's Black-Legged Royal mare)**

La Sorellina
My Love
Royal Orbit
San San
Topyo
Watling Street

**8 (Bustler mare)**

Amberoid
Arcangues
Bold Ruler
Conquistador Cielo
Damascus
Editor's Note
Fusaichi Pegasus
Grundy
Jaipur
Nijinsky II
Phil Drake
Pine Bluff
Proud Truth
Sassafras
Sir Ivor
The Minstrel
Whirlaway

**9 (Old Vintner mare)**

Aloma's Ruler
Bee Bee Bee
Benny the Dip
Bet Twice
Black Tie Affair
Bold Forbes
Caracalla
Coastal
Codex
Creme Fraiche

**10 (Dtr. of Gower's Stallion)**

Airborne
Arctic Prince
Charismatic
Go and Go
Helissio
Owen Tudor
Pavot
Reference Point
Rheingold
Sarava

**11 (Sedbury Royal mare)**

Hill Gail
Sagamix
Soltikoff
Thunder Gulch

**12 (Montagu mare)**

Bally Ache
Ivanjica
Marienbard
Oroso
Puissant Chef
Roberto
Tabasco Cat
Victory Gallop

**13 (Darcy's Royal mare)**

Akiyda
Blue Man
Cat Thief
Colonial Affair
Ferdinand
Jet Pilot
Seattle Slew
Sinndar

**9 (continued)**
Forward Pass
Galcador
Galileo
High-Rise
Hill Prince
Hoop Jr.
Migoli
Peintre Celebre
Risen Star
Shergar
Snow Chief
Tom Rolfe
Urban Sea

**14 (Oldfield mare)**
Carroll House
Commander in Chief
Coronation
Foolish Pleasure
Le Paillon
Polynesian
Psidium
Rainbow Quest
Skip Away
St. Paddy

**16 (Sis. To Stripling Hutton's Spot**
Carnegie
Chateaugay
Commendable
Crepello
Detroit
Hard Ridden
Le Pacha
Little Current
Molvedo
Pearl Diver
Red Bullet
Relko
Sagace
Saumarez
Shut Out
Slip Anchor
Strike the Gold
Volponi

**17 (Byerly Turk mare)**
Danzig Connection
Decidedly
Phalanx

**19 (Dtr. Of Davill's Old Woodcock**
Sica Boy
Tony Bin

**20 (Dtr. Of Gascoigne's Foreign horse)**
Alysheba
Blakeney
Morston
Tantieme
War Emblem

**21 (Moona Barb mare)**
Deputed Testamony
Sakhee
Tank's Prospect

**22 (Belgrade Turk mare)**
Count Turf
Gold River
Lammtarra
Mill Reef
Saint Crespin
Tulyar

**23 (Piping Peg)**
Affirmed
Lil E. Tee
Ponder
Tim Tam
Winning Colors

**24 (Helmsley Turk mare)**
Carry Back

**25 (Brimmer mare)**
One Count

**26 (Dtr. of Merlin)**
Tiznow
Trempolino

# APPENDIX VI

## SIRE INFLUENCES FOR TURF ABILITY

The following table categorizes 247 contemporary and recent sires according to their success as sires of turf stakes winners in North America. The assignments are based on the percentage of their progeny wins in open stakes on grass.

| Superior | Above Average | Average | Below Average | Poor |
|----------|---------------|---------|---------------|------|
| Alleged | Affirmed | Ack Ack | A.P. Indy | Afleet |
| Assert | Air Forbes Won | Apalachee | Alydar | Allen's Prospect |
| Avatar | Al Hattab | Bates Motel | Capote | Baederwood |
| Caerleon | Ascot Knight | Black Tie Affair | Citidancer | Best Turn |
| Caro | Baldski | Bold Forbes | Codex | Bet Big |
| Caucasus | Believe It | Bold Ruckus | Copelan | Buckaroo |
| Caveat | Big Spruce | Broad Brush | Cox's Ridge | Carson City |
| Cozzene | Blushing Groom | Buckfinder | Crafty Prospector | Cee's Tizzy |
| Darby Creek Road | Bucksplasher | Carnivalay | End Sweep | Chieftain |
| Dynaformer | Chief's Crown | Conquistador Cielo | Fappiano | Cutlass |
| El Gran Senor | Clever Trick | Cormorant | Fire Dancer | D'Accord |
| Green Dancer | Coastal | Cryptoclearance | General Meeting | Dehere |
| Hero's Honor | Danzig | Cure the Blues | Glitterman | Distinctive Pro |
| His Majesty | El Prado | Damascus | Great Above | Drone |
| Hold Your Tricks | Exceller | Deputy Minister | Honest Pleasure | Exuberant |
| Irish River | Exclusive Native | Devil's Bag | In Reality | Fit to Fight |
| Kingmambo | Explodent | Dixieland Band | Island Whirl | Flying Paster |
| King's Bishop | Farma Way | Full Out | It's Freezing | Forceten |
| Lear Fan | Foolish Pleasure | Geiger Counter | Kennedy Road | Fortunate Prospect |
| Lord at War | Golden Act | Grey Dawn II | Lost Code | Forty Niner |
| Lyphard | Gone West | Hold Your Peace | Marfa | Full Pocket |
| Lyphard's Wish | Halo | Java Gold | Medieval Man | Gilded Time |
| Lypheor | Housebuster | John Alden | Mining | Gulch |
| Majestic Light | Icecapade | Key To The Mint | Mr. Leader | Habitony |
| Manila | Jade Hunter | Known Fact | Mr. Prospector | Hawkin's Special |
| Nijinsky II | Kris S. | L'Enjoleur | Norcliffe | High Brite |
| Northern Baby | Lord Avie | Maudlin | Notebook | Honor Grades |
| Northern Dancer | Lt. Stevens | Mt. Livermore | Ogygian | Horatius |
| Nureyev | Magesterial | Naskra | On to Glory | Irish Tower |
| Overskate | Mari's Book | Pleasant Colony | Personal Flag | Jolie's Halo |
| Persian Bold | Miswaki | Private Terms | Premiership | Marquetry |
| Petrone | Nasty and Bold | Proud Truth | Proud Birdie | Meadowlake |
| Polish Numbers | Nodouble | Raja Baba | Salt Lake | Northern Prospect |
| Rainbow Quest | Northern Jove | Regal Classic | Silver Buck | On the Sly |
| Red Ransom | Our Native | Relaunch | Silver Ghost | Phone Trick |

# SIRE INFLUENCES FOR TURF ABILITY (continued)

| Superior | Above Average | Average | Below Average | Poor |
|---|---|---|---|---|
| Riverman | Pine Bluff | Saratoga Six | Slew o' Gold | Pirate's Bounty |
| Roberto | Pleasant Tap | Saros | Slewacide | Private Account |
| Sadler's Wells | Rahy | Seattle Slew | Smarten | Quiet American |
| Seattle Dancer | Rich Cream | Secretariat | Stalwart | Saint Ballado |
| Silver Hawk | Runaway Groom | Silver Deputy | Steady Growth | Sauce Boat |
| Sky Classic | Sir Ivor | Skywalker | Stop The Music | Seeking the Gold |
| Spectacular Bid | Slew City Slew | Slewpy | Sunny's Halo | Skip Trial |
| Stage Door Johnny | Sovereign Dancer | Spend a Buck | Thunder Gulch | Son of Briartic |
| The Minstrel | Staff Writer | Storm Bird | Timeless Moment | Star de Naskra |
| Theatrical | Strawberry Road | Storm Cat | Top Command | Storm Boot |
| Trempolino | Topsider | Summer Squall | Unbridled | Temperence Hill |
| Vaguely Noble | Tri Jet | Time for a Change | Valid Appeal | Tentam |
| Val de L'orne | Vigors | Verbatim | Wavering Monarch | Two Punch |
| With Approval | Woodman | Vice Regent | | Well Decorated |
| | | Waquoit | | |
| | | What Luck | | |
| | | Wild Again | | |

# APPENDIX VII

## SIRE INFLUENCES FOR EARLY MATURITY

The following table categorizes 247 contemporary and recent sires according to their success as sires of early maturing stakes winners in North America. The assignments are based on the percentage of their progeny wins in open juvenile stakes races.

| Superior | Above Average | Average | Below Average | Poor |
|----------|---------------|---------|---------------|------|
| Air Forbes Won | A.P. Indy | Apalachee | Ack Ack | Al Hattab |
| Bet Big | Affirmed | Bold Ruckus | Afleet | Allen's Prospect |
| Capote | Alydar | Chief's Crown | Alleged | Ascot Knight |
| Carson City | Believe It | Citidancer | Assert | Avatar |
| Chieftain | Buckaroo | Clever Trick | Baederwood | Bates Motel |
| Cox's Ridge | Caro | Conquistador Cielo | Baldski | Best Turn |
| Cryptoclearance | Coastal | Cormorant | Big Spruce | Buckfinder |
| D'Accord | Cure the Blues | Cutlass | Black Tie Affair | Carnivalay |
| Darby Creek Road | Danzig | Damascus | Blushing Groom | Cee's Tizzy |
| Dehere | Drone | Devil's Bag | Bold Forbes | Cozzene |
| Deputy Minister | Dynaformer | Dixieland Band | Broad Brush | El Gran Senor |
| Distinctive Pro | End Sweep | Full Out | Bucksplasher | Exceller |
| Exuberant | Exclusive Native | Glitterman | Caerleon | Explodent |
| Farma Way | Fappiano | Grey Dawn II | Caucasus | Forceten |
| Flying Paster | Fit to Fight | Hawkin's Special | Caveat | His Majesty |
| Forty Niner | Fortunate Prospect | Honor Grades | Codex | Horatius |
| Full Pocket | Golden Act | Irish Tower | Copelan | Java Gold |
| General Meeting | Gone West | Island Whirl | Crafty Prospector | John Alden |
| Gilded Time | Great Above | Lord Avie | El Prado | Kennedy Road |
| High Brite | Gulch | Lyphard's Wish | Fire Dancer | King's Bishop |
| Hold Your Peace | Habitony | Mari's Book | Foolish Pleasure | L'Enjoleur |
| Housebuster | In Reality | Mining | Geiger Counter | Lyphard |
| Icecapade | Jolie's Halo | Mr. Leader | Green Dancer | Manila |
| It's Freezing | Known Fact | Mt. Livermore | Halo | Marfa |
| Magesterial | Kris S. | Norcliffe | Hero's Honor | Maudlin |
| Marquetry | Majestic Light | Northern Baby | Hold Your Tricks | Naskra |
| Meadowlake | Medieval Man | Overskate | Honest Pleasure | Nasty and Bold |
| Mr. Prospector | Notebook | Pine Bluff | Irish River | Northern Jove |
| Northern Prospect | Our Native | Premiership | Jade Hunter | Nureyev |
| Ogygian | Polish Numbers | Proud Birdie | Key To The Mint | On the Sly |
| Phone Trick | Private Terms | Regal Classic | Kingmambo | On to Glory |
| Pirate's Bounty | Rahy | Sauce Boat | Lear Fan | Persian Bold |
| Quiet American | Raja Baba | Skywalker | Lord at War | Personal Flag |
| Riverman | Red Ransom | Slew City Slew | Lost Code | Petrone |
| Saint Ballado | Relaunch | Slew o' Gold | Lt. Stevens | Pleasant Tap |

# SIRE INFLUENCES FOR EARLY MATURITY (continued)

| Superior | Above Average | Average | Below Average | Poor |
|---|---|---|---|---|
| Salt Lake | Roberto | Slewacide | Lypheor | Private Account |
| Saratoga Six | Runaway Groom | Son of Briartic | Miswaki | Proud Truth |
| Seattle Dancer | Seattle Slew | Sovereign Dancer | Nijinsky II | Rainbow Quest |
| Seeking The Gold | Silver Buck | Steady Growth | Nodouble | Sadler's Wells |
| Silver Deputy | Silver Hawk | Stop the Music | Northern Dancer | Secretariat |
| Silver Ghost | Smarten | Storm Boot | Pleasant Colony | Slewpy |
| Spend a Buck | Spectacular Bid | Temperence Hill | Rich Cream | Stage Door Johnny |
| Star de Naskra | Staff Writer | Tentam | Saros | Strawberry Road |
| Storm Cat | Stalwart | Top Command | Sir Ivor | Theatrical |
| Time for a Change | Storm Bird | Topsider | Skip Trial | Vaguely Noble |
| Valid Appeal | Summer Squall | Trempolino | Sky Classic | Val de L'orne |
| Wavering Monarch | Thunder Gulch | Wild Again | Sunny's Halo | Verbatim |
| Well Decorated | Timeless Moment | | The Minstrel | Vigors |
| Woodman | Tri Jet | | Unbridled | What Luck |
| | Two Punch | | Waquoit | |
| | Vice Regent | | | |
| | With Approval | | | |

# INDEX

# TABLES

# CHARTS